Coming over

Migration and communication between
England and New England in
the seventeenth century

Coming over

Migration and communication between
England and New England in
the seventeenth century

David Cressy

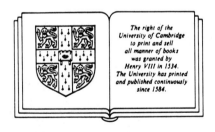

The right of the
University of Cambridge
to print and sell
all manner of books
was granted by
Henry VIII in 1534.
The University has printed
and published continuously
since 1584.

CAMBRIDGE UNIVERSITY PRESS

Cambridge
New York   New Rochelle   Melbourne   Sydney

Published by the Press Syndicate of the University of Cambridge
The Pitt Building, Trumpington Street, Cambridge CB2 1RP
32 East 57th Street, New York, NY 10022, USA
10 Stamford Road, Oakleigh, Melbourne 3166, Australia

First published 1987

Printed in the United States of America

Library of Congress Cataloging-in-Publication Data
Cressy, David.
Coming over.
Bibliography: p.
Includes index.
1. New England – History – Colonial period, ca. 1600–
1775. 2. Immigrants – New England – History – 17th
century. 3. New England – Emigration and immigration –
History – 17th century. 4. England – Emigration and
immigration – History – 17th century. 5. British –
New England – History – 17th century. I. Title.
F7.C93 1987 974'.02 87–6420

British Library Cataloging-in-Publication Data
Cressy, David.
Coming over: migration and communication
between England and New England in the
seventeenth century.
1. England – Emigration and immigration
– History. 2. New England – Emigration
and immigration – History.
I. Title.
304.8'74'042 JV6618.N/

ISBN 0 521 32951 5 hard covers
ISBN 0 521 33850 6 paperback

Contents

Preface

The movement of people across the Atlantic has naturally commanded more attention in American than in English history. The thousands who sailed to New England in the 1630s, forming what Americans know as the 'great migration', represented less than half of one per cent of the population of England. Even among transatlantic migrants they were outnumbered by those who went to the Caribbean and to the Chesapeake. Their departure mattered little and went mostly unnoticed. Even the episcopal authorities and government of Charles I, who are said to have cared about such things, paid only intermittent attention to those who went to the colonies. From the English point of view, colonial New England was a sideshow, an epiphenomenon on the outer margins, overshadowed by much more pressing events at home.

This indifference to American affairs has, to a large extent, been transferred to modern British historians. It is rare that one finds references to America, New England or Massachusetts in the indexes of modern texts and monographs about Stuart England. The English migrants, having disappeared from the shores of their homeland, seem also to have dropped out of English history. Their homeward-leaning thoughts, their contacts with other Englishmen and their involvement in the major developments of the period 1630 to 1700 have largely been ignored.

Yet from an American perspective the history of New England is of signal importance. The early colonists transformed the landscape and shaped a new society. They brought with them English notions of political order, religious seriousness, moral righteousness, literature, commerce and 'civilization', and adapted them to local conditions. Their families increased and multiplied; their institutions survived and prospered. Notwithstanding the claims and contributions of other colonial areas, the society, culture and religion of New

England have been seen as the foundation for many American values, and even as the source of the American 'identity'.

Although American historians customarily look to English history for the 'background' to colonization, they rarely follow English developments once the migrants have settled in the New World. Only the most recent generation of colonial historians has concerned itself with transatlantic connections. Their British colleagues pay even less attention to colonial America. The British and the American scholarly communities bring separate historiographical traditions to the study of the early modern period, use different academic styles and vocabularies, and are often unfamiliar with each other's work. The word 'Puritan', for example, appears to have completely different connotations in the hands of English and American historians. English historians use the word with increasing reluctance and self-consciousness, and rarely employ it to refer to religion after 1660; American colonialists continue to embrace the term, and use it even into the eighteenth century. One concession I have made here to the usage of American colonial historians has been to capitalize the word 'Puritan'. I believe I am in good company by choosing not to define it.

This book aims to span the Atlantic, making use of primary evidence and recent secondary studies from both sides. It is addressed to several communities of readers, including those interested in the topics of migration, communication and kinship, as well as the specific settings of England and New England. A more subversive purpose, mounted only partly as mischief, is to begin the repatriation of early American history. The colonists referred to themselves as 'the English', as distinct from the Dutch or the native Americans. It was to England that they looked for their history, their cultural lifeline, and for many of their future expectations. It seems to me more appropriate to consider seventeenth-century New England as an outlier of the old country, as a detached English province, than as the seed-bed of a new nation.

My principal concern is with the origins, the inhabitants and the social relations of English New England, and the continuing connections that linked the colony and the homeland. The early colonists were never as severely cut off as some have feared, nor did they fully turn their backs on old England. Migration, return migration, trade, kinship, inheritance, money and messages tied London to Boston, and sustained a community of interest between provincial Massachusetts and provincial England. Although New England developed a distinctive political, religious and intellectual history, its leaders were never utterly estranged from developments in England. Indeed, men like John Winthrop and John Davenport in the first generation, and

Preface

Samuel Sewall and Increase Mather in the second generation, depended on a flow of English books and correspondence, and sustained a ravenous appetite for English news. New England culture blossomed not in wilderness isolation but in an informed counterpoint to its English roots.

Although my title, *Coming Over*, may depend for its effectiveness on one's position in relation to the Atlantic, it will be apparent that I am concerned here with both coming and going, and also with staying and returning. My subject is the linkage between English and New England society in the seventeenth century. Rather than telling the story of the founders of a colony whose exceptional characteristics inexorably gave shape to America, my emphasis falls on their continuing attachments to the homeland.

Chapter 1 considers what English people knew about New England at the beginning of the colonial period, and how that pool of information changed over the course of the seventeenth century. Opinions favourable and hostile to New England affected the ability of the colonial sponsors to attract migrants. Chapter 2 examines the labour needs of the colonial planners, and describes the numbers and types of people who actually went to New England. Servants, who are more commonly thought of in connection with the southern colonies, formed a substantial and troublesome minority in the Massachusetts migration. Chapter 3 deals with migrants' motives, and traces the variety of considerations that fed into their decisions. Although religion was central to the enterprise, at least in the minds of the Puritan leaders, a host of personal and secular reasons may have motivated the bulk of those moving to New England. Chapter 4 examines the cost of emigration, and reviews the preparations an English family would have to undertake before crossing the ocean. Chapter 5 considers the administrative hurdles erected by Stuart governments, and traces the migrants' conformity to, and avoidance of, the departure regulations. In Chapter 6 the emigrants finally leave England. The voyage itself, which took six to ten weeks, formed a significant part of the migrant experience. It was a testing experience that set the travellers apart from their landbound contemporaries and successors.

Having set the migrants ashore in the New World, I am interested in their homeward leanings, contacts and dealings, and the overseas family connections and affections of these early New England settlers. The range and warmth of these contacts may come as a surprise to those who only know one side of the transatlantic story. Chapter 7 considers the continuing attachment of old England, and explores ways in which debts, obligations and inheritances linked colonial set-

tlers with their kinsfolk and contemporaries back home. Chapter 8
deals with return migration, and points out that early Americans were
not exempt from homesickness, and that a sizeable proportion of them
sought to retrace their path across the ocean. The Atlantic, as others
have pointed out, was a bridge as well as a barrier. Chapter 9 studies
the traffic of letters, news and personal contact across the ocean, and
adds to the discussion of opinion and information begun in Chapter
1. Chapter 10 examines the flow of English news to New England and
its circulation in the colonies. It focusses especially on the political
crisis of the 1640s and 1650s, as relayed through transatlantic correspondence. Chapter 11 discusses the claims of kinship and the extent of transatlantic extended family ties. Despite the difficulties of
distance, some families found emotional and material benefits in the
maintenance of kin connections, even into the third generation. Kinship in this context was more versatile and more durable than is often
suspected. The epilogue serves as a summary and attempts to set the
history of migration and communication between England and New
England into a broader perspective.

It will be obvious at once that this is not a numerical study. There
are few tables and no statistical tests. This should not be taken to
signify a loss of confidence in quantitative social history, a return to
narrative, or any such fashionable despair. Rather, it reflects the nature
of the evidence and the questions one can ask of it. For the most part
I have tried to allow the seventeenth-century sources to tell their own
story with the minimum of historiographical intervention. The result
is a series of stories, vignettes and episodes illustrating the lives of
people in the past. I have taken much delight in the research and
writing, not least because of the intriguing parallels between my own
experience and that of some of the people in this book.

Many colleagues have encouraged me, advised me, warned me, crit-
icized me and in various ways helped make the book better than it
might have been. I especially want to acknowledge James Axtell,
Charles Carlton, Esther Cope, Robert Dawidoff, David Galenson, Derek Hirst, Stephanie Livingston, Karen Kupperman, Kevin Sharpe,
Daniel Scott Smith and William Weber, each of whom read different
sections at different stages of their composition. The remaining errors
and perversities are mine alone.

I am grateful, too, to the John Simon Guggenheim Memorial Foundation for a fellowship that started my thinking on this topic, to the

Preface

American Antiquarian Society for a Daniels Fellowship that allowed me to get my teeth into it and to the National Endowment for the Humanities for a fellowship that enabled me to complete several early chapters. I have tried the patience of librarians and archivists on two continents, and wish to acknowledge their professional assistance. The Huntington Library in San Marino was especially hospitable. California State University at Long Beach indulged me with a lightened teaching load and summer stipend, while wondering why their English historian was so interested in early America. I hope it is now clear.

Throughout the book, spelling and punctuation in quotations have been modernized. Dates in the text follow the 'old style', except that the year is regarded as beginning on 1 January. Although written in California and edited in New York, this book adheres to British conventions in punctuation and spelling.

Figures and tables

Abbreviations

A.A.S.: American Antiquarian Society, Worcester, Mass.

Andrews, *Colonial Period*: Charles M. Andrews, *The Colonial Period in American History*, 4 vols. (New Haven, Conn., 1934–8).

Arber, *Smith*: Edward Arber and A. G. Bradley (eds.), *Travels and Works of Captain John Smith*, 2 vols. (Edinburgh, 1910).

Chronicles: Alexander Young (ed.), *Chronicles of the First Planters of the Colony of Massachusetts Bay, from 1623 to 1636* (Boston, 1846; reprinted, Williamstown, Mass., 1978).

D.N.B.: *Dictionary of National Biography*.

Essex Courts: *Records and Files of the Quarterly Courts of Essex County, Massachusetts, 1636–1686*, 9 vols. (Salem, Mass., 1911–75).

H.M.C.: Historical Manuscripts Commission, London.

Mass. Recs.: Nathaniel B. Shurtleff (ed.), *Records of the Governor and Company of the Massachusetts Bay*, 5 vols. (Boston, 1853–4).

M.H.S.: Massachusetts Historical Society, Boston.

N.E.H.G.R.: *New England Historical and Genealogical Register*, Boston.

P.R.O.: Public Record Office, London.

Savage, *Genealogical Dictionary*: James Savage, *A Genealogical Dictionary of the First Settlers of New England*, 4 vols. (Boston, 1853–4).

Winthrop's Journal: James Kendall Hosmer (ed.), *Winthrop's Journal, 'History of New England', 1630–1649*, 2 vols. (New York, 1908).

Winthrop Papers: *The Winthrop Papers*, vols. 2–5, 1623–49 (Boston, 1931–47).

Wonder-Working Providence: J. Franklin Jameson (ed.), *Johnson's Wonder-Working Providence* (New York, 1910).

'The excellency of the place': English impressions of New England

English impressions of New England on the eve of the 'great migration' were often muddled and unfocussed. Whereas most Englishmen of the seventeenth century probably gave no thought at all to North America, those who did take an interest in the New World drew on incomplete, confusing and sometimes erroneous information. Ordinary Englishmen could not be expected to locate New England in terms of latitude and longitude, nor could they give an accurate account of its climate and resources. Even prospective migrants and colonial investors struggled with information that was patchy and conflicting. Reports of the land north from Maine to Newfoundland mixed with accounts of the very different country south from Cape Cod to the Chesapeake. New England was a blur of contradictory images, of barren rock and beckoning pasture, crippling cold and balmy sunshine. The list went on to mention limitless forest and open meadows, gentle natives and treacherous savages, and by the 1630s, godly saints and cruel schismatics.

Communication was the seed as well as the spore of migration. Intending emigrants needed as much information as possible to prepare them for their endeavour; the news they sent back conditioned the expectations of their successors. This chapter sets out to trace the kinds of information about New England circulating in England in the periods before, during and after the great migration of the 1630s. Printed pamphlets, manuscript letters and oral reports produced a welter of impressions, images and news, of varying degrees of trustworthiness.

English familiarity with New England began in the sixteenth century and grew spasmodically in the early Stuart period. English fishermen had long made use of New England landfalls, and towards the end of Elizabeth's reign they were joined by mariners bent on a different purpose. Influenced by the promotional writings of the Richard Hakluyts (uncle and nephew), and building on the experience of the Roanoke settlement of the 1580s, a sequence of sea captains explored the coastline between Virginia and Newfoundland looking for a place to establish a colony. The reports of their voyages, often written to gain funding for future expeditions, presented America as a land of plenty and of immeasurable promise. The stony reality was often obscured in these first flickerings of the American dream. A series of publications early in the seventeenth century reinforced the rosy impressions of an earlier generation of voyagers and publicists by depicting the territory as ideal for English exploitation.[1]

Bartholemew Gosnold and John Brereton spent the early summer of 1602 on the island of Martha's Vineyard where they found a lush and fruitful country. Brereton described the attractions of the region, identified as 'the north part of Virginia', in his *Briefe and True Relation*, which was published soon after he returned to England. Besides fruits and berries, 'an incredible store of vines', and farmland 'in comparison whereof the most fertile part of all England is but barren', Brereton reported all manner of 'commodities' that English settlers could work, and from which English investors could profit. The land was 'full of high timbered oaks ... cedars straight and tall, beech, elm, holly, walnut trees in abundance'. The island teemed with wildlife, the sea with fish, the air with fowls, and the ground gave promise of a store of useful minerals. Coming to the mainland, almost in raptures, 'We stood a while like men ravished at the beauty and delicacy of this sweet soil.' To bolster these heady impressions Brereton saw fit to reprint Richard Hakluyt's 1585 arguments for colonizing Virginia, and to copy Thomas Harriot's account of the 'merchantable commodities' found there at the time of the Roanoke expeditions. Descriptions of what is now North Carolina became conflated with descriptions of the very different natural ecology of New England.[2]

---

[1] Richard Hakluyt, *The Principall Navigations, Voiages and Discoveries of the English Nation* (London, 1589); Thomas Harriot, *A Briefe and True Report of the New Found Land of Virginia* (London, 1588). The Elizabethan background is discussed in David Beers Quinn, *England and the Discovery of America, 1481–1620* (New York, 1974); David Beers Quinn (ed.), *The Roanoke Voyages 1584–1590* (London, 1955); and David Beers Quinn, *Set Fair for Roanoke: Voyages and Colonies, 1584–1606* (Chapel Hill, N.C., 1985). See also Howard Mumford Jones, 'The colonial impulse: an analysis of the "promotion" literature of colonization', *Proceedings of the American Philosophical Society*, 90 (1946), pp. 131–61.

[2] John Brereton, *A Briefe and True Relation of the Discouerie of the North Part of Virginia; Being a most Pleasant, Fruitful and Commodious Soile* (London, 1602), pp. 5–8, 25–36, 41–5. The text of the second impression, with added materials, is in George Parker Winship (ed.), *Sailors' Narratives of Voyages along the New England Coast 1524–1624* (Boston, 1905), pp. 33–50.

Inspired by Brereton's *Relation*, Martin Pring travelled from Bristol to New England the following year and sailed down from Maine to Cape Cod. Pring's report confirmed Brereton's impressions, and published again the useful observation that this part of America had good store of sassafras, 'a plant of sovereign virtue for the French pox'.[3] In 1605 Captain George Waymouth coasted New England and explored up the Kennebec River. James Rosier published an account of his findings in *A True Relation of the Most Prosperous Voyage*, which included yet another glowing account of New England. Like Brereton and his Elizabethan predecessors, Rosier appended a catalogue of 'what profits we saw the country yield', including lists of trees, fowls, beasts, fishes, fruits, plants and herbs.[4] James Davies likewise praised the abundance of fruits and extraordinary lobsters encountered along the northern coastline of New England in a voyage of 1607.[5]

The cumulative effect of these reports was to give New England (or northern Virginia, as it was still called) a highly favourable press. In the years after 1607, while the Virginia Company struggled to breathe life into its difficult southern outpost at Jamestown, New England beckoned as a superior alternative, a virgin land of untapped promise.[6] Wishful thinking, ecological conjecture and the balmy experience of summer coasting produced an image that was seriously at variance with reality.

Competing with this rosy picture, however, was a much bleaker set of impressions. Sir Ferdinando Gorges and Sir John Popham attempted to establish a colony in New England in 1607, but their pioneer outpost was an embarrassing failure. Ill-manned and badly organized, the settlement at Sagadahoc (Maine) was abandoned within a year of its foundation. The colonists found none of the precious metals they expected, and were disappointed with the natural commodities of the region. Moreover, the 'extreme unseasonable and frosty' winter took them by surprise, a sharp contrast to the fine weather of their arrival in August. Against all expectations they found New England to be 'a cold, barren, mountainous, rocky desert', and

---

[3] Pring's account is in Winship (ed.), *Sailors' Narratives of Voyages*, pp. 52–63. The quotation is from p. 59.

[4] James Rosier, *A True Relation of the Most Prosperous Voyage Made This Present Yeere 1605 by Captaine George Waymouth* (London, 1605), sigs. B2–B2v, E3v–E4.

[5] James Davies, 'Relation of a voyage unto New England . . . 1607', ed., B. F. De Costa and Charles Deane, M.H.S. *Proceedings*, 18 (1880), pp. 82–117.

[6] For the early history of Virgina see Charles M. Andrews, *The Colonial Period of American History* (New Haven, 1934), vol. 1, pp. 98–140; and Edmund S. Morgan, 'The labor problem at Jamestown, 1607–1618', *American Historical Review*, 76 (1971), pp. 595–611.

their experience set back the development of northern colonization for more than a decade. Those who survived the Sagadahoc fiasco spread the view that New England was worthless, cold and untenable, a view that found some favour with the champions of Jamestown. As one apologist put it, 'To justify the suddenness of their return they did coin many excuses, burdening the bounds where they had been with all aspersions that possibly they could devise, seeking by that means to discourage all others.'[7]

Fortunately for the promoters of New England the grievances of the Sagadahoc settlers did not appear in print, but reports about the failure of the northern colony circulated among courtiers and promoters, and found currency in the maritime community and beyond. Colonial investors directed their energies elsewhere. The negative impressions created by the abandonment of the first New England colony remained as an undercurrent, still discernible in the 1630s, while promotional books and pamphlets continued to present a much more positive image.

Captain John Smith, who travelled to the region in 1614, published a characteristically enthusiastic *Description of New England* in 1616. Smith actually coined the name 'New England' and did everything in his power to promote 'this unregarded country'. Although the English had made several probing voyages, 'The coast is yet still even as a coast unknown and undiscovered.... As for the goodness and true substance of the land, we are for the most part yet altogether ignorant of them.'[8] The potential of New England lay as much in its mystery as in its proven resources.

English 'Virginia' stretched from thirty-four degrees to forty-four degrees north, from modern South Carolina to Maine, and technically extended laterally from sea to sea, as far to the west as Drake's 'Nova Albion'. New England, in Smith's depiction, overlapped this territory in the region of forty-one to forty-five degrees, but most properly 'from Penobscot to Cape Cod'. Even for residents the region was something of a blur, while from the perspective of England the area lacked all geographical precision.[9]

---

[7] William Alexander, *The Mapp and Description of New-England* (London, 1630), p. 30; Karen Ordahl Kupperman, 'Climate and mastery of the wilderness in seventeenth-century New England', in David D. Hall and David Grayson Allen (eds.), *Seventeenth-Century New England* (Boston, 1984), p. 5. For the Sagadahoc experiment see Andrews, *Colonial Period*, vol. 1, pp. 78–97.

[8] John Smith, 'A description of New England', in Arber, *Smith*, pp. 175–231; John Smith, 'The generall historie of Virginia, New England and the Summer Isles', in Arber, *Smith*, pp. 699, 700, 703, 704.

[9] Smith, 'Description', pp. 188, 192; Smith, 'Generall Historie', pp. 695, 702, 706. For

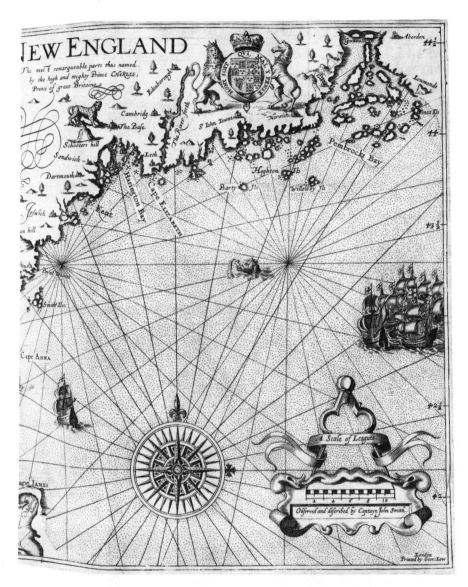

Figure 1. 'Approaching New England'. Detail from Captain John Smith, *A Description of New England* (London, 1616). By permission of The Huntington Library, San Marino, California (RB 3409 STC 22788).

According to a correspondent of 1645 the boundaries of New England stretched 'from Virginia southward to the French northward'. But 'New England' was as often equated with the limits of the patent of Massachusetts Bay, an area rendered in an Admiralty deposition of 1636 as 'Mathew Tewses Bay'.[10] Later in the seventeenth century people talked of 'New England' when they might have meant any part of Massachusetts, Maine, New Hampshire, New Haven, New Plymouth, Connecticut or Rhode Island, or wherever there were English settlers east of the Hudson River. The settlers themselves commonly referred to New England, often abbreviated as 'N.E.', without regard to particular political jurisdictions. The label differentiated their area of settlement from the French to the north, the Dutch to the south, and the other English plantations in the Chesapeake and the Caribbean. 'New England' appeared on the maps long before anyone imagined it as a place of spiritual regeneration.

New England, in Smith's opinion, was 'a most excellent place, both for health and fertility', and blessed with 'an excellent climate'. During the next few years Captain Smith criss-crossed England on a promotional tour, talking with gentlemen, visiting towns and giving away copies of his books and maps. Smith proselytized most vigorously in the West Country, which already had a tradition of interest in America, and he distributed thirty copies of his New England book to the London livery companies. Besides promoting himself, Smith was concerned to persuade people that a northern colony was both feasible and desirable. As an eyewitness, an expert, and a persuasive talker, Smith introduced a diverse audience to his views. He even distributed maps showing the rugged New England coastline comfortingly adorned with familiar English place-names.[11] Little was said of the disappointments of Sagadahoc, as Hakluyt's old arguments in praise of western planting were revived and revised. Pockets of people became aware of New England as a fruitful and potentially profitable territory within the English sphere of influence.

It was not until the 1620s, however, when an English settlement

Nova Albion see W. S. W. Vaux (ed.), *The World Encompassed by Sir Francis Drake* (London, 1854), pp. 115–33, 221–6; and *Calendar of State Papers, Domestic, 1635*, p. 410.

[10] Beinecke Library, Yale University, Osborne Files, 'Newsletter describing English settlements in New England', 24 December 1645 (Robert Child to Samuel Hartlib?); Peter Wilson Coldham (ed.), *English Adventurers and Emigrants, 1609–1660* (Baltimore, 1984), p. 65.

[11] Smith, 'Generall historie', pp. 708, 745, 748. Smith's map, with English place-names substituted for Indian names, first appeared in 1616. Subsequent editions included heraldic elaborations and the locations of actual English settlements to 1635.

actually took root in New England, that information about the land and its qualities became more common. With the establishment of Plymouth Plantation (1620), the projects of the Council for New England (from 1620), the Dorchester New England Company (1623), and the work of the New England Company (1628) which became the Massachusetts Bay Company (1629), news about New England circulated much more readily in old England.[12] Oral reports, letters and manuscript and printed accounts built up a pool of information that was mostly of an enthusiastic, apologetic or promotional nature.

Early accounts of Plymouth Plantation reported success and satisfaction, despite the accidental circumstances of the Pilgims' arrival. (The *Mayflower* was lost, several hundred miles north of its course, when it reached Cape Cod in 1620.) William Hilton, a London fishmonger, wrote home to his cousin in 1621 in praise of Plymouth's natural abundance.[13] The first published account, *A Relation or Iournall of the Beginning and Proceedings of the English Plantation Setled at Plimoth in New England*, waxed joyful about 'one of the most pleasant, most healthful, and most fruitful parts of the world'.[14]

In 1622 John Pory, secretary to the Virginia Company, travelled to New England to inspect the territory around Plymouth Plantation. Pory reported on 'the excellency of the place', although he also found some points to criticize. The ground, he found, was 'rocky, rough and uneven', quite unlike the soft tidewater lands of Virginia. The soil was 'passing good...yet culturable with hoe and spade rather than with the plough'. An agricultural living could be made in New England, as the Pilgrims had already proved, but Pory recognized that it would take a fearsome amount of work to turn Plymouth Colony into an English Goshen. The land certainly had its charms, including raspberries, cherries, gooseberries, strawberries, 'delicate plums', and 'five several sorts of grapes', enough sweet things to induce salivation. Wildlife, especially deer and turkeys, abounded in a parklike setting

[12] The complex history of the organization of New England colonial enterprise is traced in Andrews, *Colonial Period*, vol. 1, pp. 262–4, 320-2, 354-68; Frances Rose-Troup, *The Massachusetts Bay Company and Its Predecessors* (New York, 1930); and William G. Robbins, 'The Massachusetts Bay Company: an analysis of motives', *The Historian*, 32 (1969), pp. 84–5.

[13] Hilton's letter is in Smith, 'New-England's trials', in Arber, *Smith*, pp. 260–1.

[14] *A Relation or Iournall of the Beginning and Proceedings of the English Plantation Setled at Plimoth in New England* (London, 1622), sig. A3. This collection of reports was advertised as 'writ by the several actors themselves after their plain and rude manner, therefore doubt nothing of the truth thereof'; sig. A3v. For the history of Plymouth see William Bradford, *Of Plymouth Plantation 1620–1647*, ed. Samuel Eliot Morison (New York, 1963), and George D. Langdon, Jr., *Pilgrim Colony: A History of New Plymouth 1620–1691* (New Haven, Conn., 1966).

of fine woods and plentiful grazing. Most striking, however, was the wholesomeness of New England's water and air, a feature that impressed nearly every English visitor to the region. Pory had come from a Virginia racked with disease, a colony tormented by dysentery and malaria, to this more northerly land where people seemed to thrive. The robust settlers of Plymouth made a powerful impression. 'This healthfulness,' wrote Pory, 'is accompanied with much plenty both of fish and foul every day in the year, as I know no place in the world that can match it.'[15]

Pory shared his findings with the governor of Virginia and with the Earl of Southampton in London, and the news spread among English merchants and investors. Though not printed, Pory's report soon passed into the public domain to join other accounts of pristine New England. During the 1620s the mercantile and maritime communities in Stuart London gathered increasingly detailed information about New England, and anyone interested in America could dip into this pool of knowledge and impressions. Town libraries, like that at Dorchester, were increasingly likely to have books about American travel and exploration.[16]

Other early visitors to Plymouth brought home enthusiastic accounts that could only whet the appetite of prospective settlers. Emmanuel Altham, captain of the *Little James*, spent a festive summer in New England in 1623 and wrote home to his brother about the vitality and good cheer of Plymouth Plantation. Everyone was 'in good health, and neither man, woman or child sick'. Altham had attended William Bradford's wedding in August 1623, a celebration that conjures visions of the merry men in Sherwood Forest rather than dour pioneers in a hostile wilderness. 'We had about twelve pasty venisons besides others, pieces of roasted venison and other good cheer in such quantity that I could wish you some of our share.'[17]

[15] Sydney V. James, Jr. (ed.), *Three Visitors to Early Plymouth . . . John Pory, Emmanuel Altham, and Isaak d Rasieres* (Plymouth, Mass., 1963), pp. 6–17; William S. Powell, *John Pory, 1572–1636: The Life and Letters of a Man of Many Parts* (Chapel Hill, N.C., 1977), pp. 83, 93, 96, 98.

[16] Dorset Record Office, B2/28/1, 'A catalogue of the bookes in the library of Dorchester, with the givers, taken in the yeare 1631'. Another glimpse of the circulation of print concerning New England appears in the diary of the Suffolk minister John Rous, who recorded in June 1630, 'I saw a book at Bury at a bookseller's containing a declaration of their intent who be gone to New England, set out by themselves, and purposed for satisfaction to the king and state (as I conceive) because of some scandalous misconceivings that run abroad'; Mary Ann Everett Green (ed.), *Diary of John Rous . . . 1625 to 1642* (London, 1856), p. 54. Rous had evidently come across Winthrop's *Humble Request*.

[17] James (ed.), *Three Visitors to Early Plymouth*, pp. 23, 29.

8

Like others of a commercial bent, Altham had his eyes peeled for 'what profit is to be raised here'. He found no shortage of prospects. The fishing, he reported, 'is beyond belief', with cod, turbot, sturgeon, salmon, bass, trout and eels for the taking. The land sprouted cedar, beech, pine, oak, 'as good timber as ever I saw'. Sarsparilla, sassafras and berries abounded, 'all which are worth good store of money in England'. Sarsparilla, he noted, 'was of two shillings a pound, at the least' in London, 'and we have here enough to load a ship'. Altham warned, sensibly enough, that 'none of these commodities can be got without a little pains, and the most pains and cost is to be stowed at the beginning'. But he had no doubt at all that 'a better country was never seen nor heard of, for here are a multitude of God's blessings'.[18]

Altham wanted to spread the word. He instructed his brother in England to share the news with family and friends. 'I pray, sir, let them read this letter, either the same or a copy of the same.'[19] Altham's enthusiasm would find a widening audience of readers and listeners, to join with different ripples of information emanating from other encouraging accounts of the New World. It had to compete, however, with more pessimistic accounts of New England. 'Some say you are starved in body and soul; others, that you eat pigs and dogs that die alone; others, that the things here spoken of, the goodness of the country, are gross and palpable lies.'[20] Supporters of Plymouth Plantation on both sides of the Atlantic did their utmost to suppress such hostile opinions.

According to the favoured interpretation, New England promised wholesome air and brimming larders for the settlers, and enormous profits for the merchants and investors. Doubts about the barrenness of the soil or the harshness of the winters were overshadowed by the general confidence and enthusiasm. One writer of the 1620s praised the land as 'gorgeously garnished with all wherewith pregnant nature ravishing the sight with variety can grace a fertile field'.[21]

Captain John Smith went into print again in 1620 with *New England's Trials*, and followed it with a greatly expanded new edition in 1622. Here he celebrated the voyagers to New England – eighty ships within these last eight years – and praised the success of the colonists at Plymouth. In 1624 Smith published his great work, *The Generall Historie of Virginia, New-England and the Summer Isles*, which went through half a dozen printings by 1632. This was both a history of American

---

[18] *Ibid.*, pp. 24–8, 37.
[19] *Ibid.*, p. 34.
[20] Bradford, *Of Plymouth Plantation*, p. 374.
[21] Alexander, *The Mapp and Description of New-England*, pp. 30–1.

colonization and a prospectus for its further development. Smith was prolific, enthusiastic and authoritative, and his writings became, alongside those of Hakluyt, the standard work on America for English readers.[22]

Adjectives like 'excellent' and 'abundant' flowed freely across John Smith's pages. New England, according to Smith, boasted abundant resources, excellent harbours, bountiful woods and a health-giving climate. Furthermore, he advised, 'The ground is so fertile that questionless it is capable of producing any grain, fruit or seeds.' After more than a generation of attention for its raw materials, the land of New England was now being trumpeted for its agricultural possibilities. New England could be considered a suitable, nay, desirable, place for English settlement, and not just for long-distance commercial exploitation. Such claims would rouse the interest of land-hungry migrants as well as commercial investors.[23]

The pace of publication quickened as New England changed from a land of distant discovery to a place of active investment and colonization. Sir William Alexander published *An Encouragement to Colonies* in 1624, which was reissued in 1630 as *The Mapp and Description of New-England*. This supported a northern settlement, New Scotland, and promoted the aristocratic schemes of Sir Ferdinando Gorges. Gorges, Captain Smith's erstwhile employer, envisaged a feudal New England focussing profit and honour on himself.[24]

In 1625 an extravagant piece of puffery came off the London presses, entitled *New-England, or a Briefe Enarration of the Ayre, Earth, Water, Fish and Fowles of that Country . . . in Latine and English Verse*. The author, or perpetrator, was William Morrell, who had travelled to the New World as chaplain with Robert Gorges in 1623. New England, he wrote, was 'grand-child to earth's paradise', a land of 'sweet air' endowed with 'nature's bounties' and 'peace and plenty'.[25] Morrell's verse celebrated a naïve and idyllic image of America. It is not certain whether anyone was swayed by this poetic encomium, but it added to the climate of hyperbole and expectation.

---

[22] Smith, 'New England's trials', in Arber, *Smith*, pp. 233–72; 'Generall historie' in Arber, *Smith*, pp. 273–784.
[23] Smith, 'New England's trials', p. 237; Smith, 'Generall historie', pp. 708, 712. Virginia too, at this time, was being transformed from a garrison outpost to an agricultural settlement.
[24] William Alexander, *An Encouragement to Colonies* (London, 1624); Alexander, *The Mapp and Description of New-England*; Sir Ferdinando Gorges, *America Painted to the Life* (London, 1659).
[25] William Morrell, *New-England, or a Briefe Enarration of the Ayre, Earth, Water, Fish and Fowles of that Country . . . in Latine and English Verse* (London, 1625), pp. 13–17.

More persuasive, perhaps, was Christopher Levett's account, *A Voyage into New England begun in 1623 and ended in 1624*, published in London in 1628. An associate of Sir Ferdinando Gorges and a member of the Council for New England, Levett was a seaman, not a poet, and he promised his readers a straightforward account.

I will not tell you that you may smell the corn fields before you see the land, neither must men think that corn doth grow naturally (or on trees), nor will the deer come when they are called or stand still and look on a man until he shoot... nor will the fish leap into the kettle nor on the dry land, neither are they so plentiful that you may dip them up in baskets, nor take cod in nets to make a voyage, which is no truer than that the fowls will present themselves to you with spits through them. But certainly there is fowl, deer and fish enough for the taking if men be diligent.[26]

Levett's New England sported timber, vines, berries, nuts and herbs, and enjoyed a climate 'full as good if not better than England'. Although by no means an earthly paradise – Levett was among the first of New England's apologists to acknowledge problems with mosquitoes in summer and snow in winter – this America still promised an appealing alternative to an England that seemed tired, old, overpopulated, and fenced with manorial, parochial and guild restrictions. All it would take to exploit 'so good a country' would be hard work from the settlers and financial support from their friends at home.[27]

Levett set out to develop both categories, prospective planters and financial adventurers. In 1628 he helped secure letters patent authorizing widespread fund-raising for the colonial enterprise in New England. Local churchwardens were responsible for collecting the money. The publication of Levett's *Voyage* was clearly planned to coincide with this quickening colonial activity. The royal order invited people in every parish in England to turn their thoughts (and their purses) towards America. Even if little cash was actually forthcoming, the propaganda effect was potentially formidable. How many of the thousands who subsequently migrated to New England had the germ of the idea planted during this promotional flurry of 1628?[28]

The year 1628 also saw the granting of a patent to the New England Company and the start of planning for the company's first organized expedition to Massachusetts Bay. John Endecott went over with a pioneer party to prepare the ground. Information, organization and

[26] Christopher Levett, 'A voyage into New England begun in 1623 and ended in 1624', in James Phinney Baxter, *Christopher Levett, of York, the Pioneer Colonist in Casco Bay* (Portland, Maine, 1893), pp. 119–20.
[27] *Ibid.*, pp. 120, 123, 124, 128, 137.
[28] *Ibid.*, pp. 68–71. Records of this effort have yet to be found in any churchwarden's accounts.

money were coming together to make the Massachusetts settlement a possibility. With the addition of new patentees, many of them Puritans, the New England Company was reorganized in 1629 and granted its charter as the Massachusetts Bay Company. The Council for New England, fitfully active throughout the 1620s, became increasingly preoccupied with extinguishing the interests of its rivals. Competing groups of promoters and investors were interested in New England, and their political lobbying, fund-raising and propaganda heightened awareness about the region. The principals understood that political support, financial backing and the crucial commitment of prospective settlers depended on the continued circulation of favourable news, so long as it did not advance the interests of their enemies.[29]

In 1629 the Massachusetts Bay Company sent over Francis Higginson as minister to the new plantation at Naumkeag (later named Salem). Higginson's letters and reports had a potent effect on recruitment of settlers for New England. In July 1629 and again in September Higginson wrote enthusiastic letters to his friends at home in Leicestershire. 'I will... truly endeavour by God's help to report nothing but the naked truth,' he promised. 'I have been careful to report nothing of New England but what I have partly seen with my own eyes and partly heard and inquired from the mouths of very honest and religious persons.' Insisting on his credibility, the clergyman went on to extoll the virtues of the land. Higginson's account was rushed into print in 1630 under the title of *New-Englands Plantation*. The pamphlet was an immediate success and went through three editions within the year.[30]

In language more reminiscent of Richard Hakluyt than of Christopher Levett, Higginson reported his joyful appreciation of a land overflowing with milk and corn. Indeed, there are hints that Higginson, like some other early visitors to New England, allowed his report to be coloured by his literary expectations rather than the testimony of his own eyes. In every direction lay limitless timber, vegetables galore, marvellous wildlife, enormous fish. 'Both land and sea abound with store of blessings for the comfortable sustenance of man's life in New England.' Like others before him, Higginson drew particular attention to the air, which he rated 'of a most healing nature... for a sup of New England's air is better than a whole draught of old England's

---

[29] See note 12, this chapter.
[30] Francis Higginson, 'New-Englands plantation', in M.H.S., *The Founding of Massachusetts* (Boston, 1930), p. 81.

ale'. Agricultural returns, too, were staggeringly successful; 'Yea, Joseph's increase in Egypt is out-stripped here with us.'[31]

Printed as an appendix to the second and third editions of *New England's Plantation* was a letter from Thomas Graves, another company employee, who corroborated Higginson's testimony: 'I never came in a more goodly country in all my life...Everything that is here either sown or planted prospereth far better than in old England.'[32] The message was strong and appealing, and made New England seem a most attractive destination. These claims about natural plenty and agricultural productivity were seriously to mislead the next wave of settlers as the spectre of Sagadahoc retreated to the periphery of the colonial vision.

John White echoed Higginson's account in *The Planters Plea*, also published in 1630. Although he had never actually been to America, White depicted a country with 'a propitious air...so that rheums are very rare among our English there'. By this time it was no longer necessary to be an eyewitness to write authoritatively about New England. There were plenty of corroborative accounts in circulation. White wrote that the colonists would find excellent water, diet, fish, fowl and venison, and could expect to profit by the export of timber, 'planks, masts, oars, pitch, tar and iron'. To be honest, he confessed, New England did have minor 'discommodities' in the form of snow, snakes and mosquitoes, but these were nothing that an Englishmen could not bear. As for the natives, they 'invite us to sit down by them, and offer us what ground we will'. Good neighbours rather than savage enemies, the peaceable Indians would soon learn providence, industry and religion in the English manner.[33]

Cynics refused to believe in the American cornucopia, and satirists found enthusiasm for New England an easy target. *A Proper Newe Ballett Called the Summons to Newe England* took aim at such claims that 'there milk from springs like rivers flow, and honey upon hawthornes grow', and 'you never need to sow nor plough, there's plenty of all things enow'.[34] Some people remembered the debacle at Sagadahoc; others had heard the derogatory tales of disappointed returners from Plymouth and Salem.

None of these early promotional accounts characterizes the New

---

[31] *Ibid.*, pp. 85–9.

[32] *Ibid.*, p. 94.

[33] John White, 'The planters plea' (London, 1630), in M.H.S., *The Founding of Massachusetts*, pp. 160–5.

[34] The ballad is printed in Samuel Eliot Morison, *Builders of the Bay Colony*, rev. ed. (Boston, 1964), pp. 384–6.

England environment as a 'wilderness'. Rather, the prevailing image is of a garden or a park, a generous land inviting easy cultivation. Imagining America as 'a howling desert wilderness' was a Puritan conceit which became current for self-serving polemical purposes *after* the successful settlement of New England. Puritan preachers and historians used the term in order to depict the first comers as heroes, made of sterner stuff, and also to associate the English migrants with the Israelites under Moses. The first comers were more inclined to see Canaan or Goshen than the Sinai desert. A wilderness would be much too forbidding, and would not meet the promotional needs of the Massachusetts Bay Company.[35]

Many of the glowing accounts of New England had been composed in the first flush of enthusiasm after coming ashore or in the lulling warmth of a first New England summer. Winter, hardship, hunger and hard work forced a modification to the theme. Although many migrants were satisfied with what they found, others quickly became disappointed. Letters reaching England soon told contradictory stories. Disgruntled returners contributed to the pool of information, misinformation, wishful thinking and mixed impressions, and hostile reports circulated alongside promotional propaganda. Hostile and pessimistic undercurrents, never entirely subdued, swirled to the surface. The news from New England fanned out from London and the seaports to the inland villages and market towns, following informal lines of communication. Correspondents and kinsmen of colonists made copies and digests of letters for wider circulation. With no shortage of material to go on, the prospective settler would have to choose what to believe. Seventeenth-century migrants, like migrants of any age, had to match their experience to their expectations.

Arriving in Massachusetts early in the summer of 1630, as governor of a young plantation, John Winthrop was evidently delighted by what he saw. 'The country is exceeding good, and the climate very like our own,' he reported in a July letter to his son. 'Here is as good land as I have seen.'[36] Good news from a goodly land would inspire confidence among the colony's friends. Despite a desperate season of high mortality and food shortage, the misery of which may never be calculated, the governor continued to send back enthusiastic accounts of New England. References to scurvy and dearth, homesickness and disaffection, were deliberately muted. In any case, the disasters could be

---

[35] Kupperman, 'Climate and mastery of the wilderness', p. 24; Peter N. Carroll, *Puritanism and the Wilderness: The Intellectual Significance of the New England Frontier 1629–1700* (New York, 1969).
[36] *Winthrop Papers*, vol. 2, pp. 306, 307.

attributed to divine providence or human mismanagement so as not to lay blame on the land. 'We are here in a paradise,' Winthrop assured his wife in a letter of November 1630.[37] Having made such a huge investment, of emotion and reputation as well as money, it would be difficult for him to think otherwise. The Winthrop circle in England ensured that these optimistic letters from America enjoyed a wide circulation.

As winter approached, however, some of the early settlers were telling a different story. Official and unofficial accounts of the colony circulated alongside each other in England, and some of the unofficial news was alarming. 'One John Page, late of Dedham, that hath his wife and two children there', sent home from New England 'so lamentable a letter' to the effect that 'unless God stirring some friends to send him some provision he is like to starve'. John Rogers, vicar of Dedham, Essex, charitably dispatched twenty shillings towards a barrel of meal, noting, 'It cuts me to the heart to hear that any of our neighbours should be like to famish.' How could a land of plenty also appear as a land of famine? And how would these troubling reports affect the colonizing of New England?[38]

Crouched and crowded around a fire, balancing his writing paper on his knee for lack of a table, Thomas Dudley wrote candidly of the inconveniences he and his companions had suffered during 'this sharp winter' of 1630–1. Dudley was writing in March, a month when crocuses bloomed in England while New England was still frostbound. Death had visited Massachusetts in the wake of weakness, illness and lack of preparation. The colonists of the Winthrop fleet, Dudley suggested, had been misled by the 'too large commendations' of their predecessors. For the sake of those yet to come, Dudley set out to draw a more realistic picture. Yes, newcomers would find 'materials

---

[37] *Ibid.*, p. 320. The more seasoned observers of Plymouth saw the Bay Colony arrivals in a much less hopeful light. 'Many people arrive sick of the scurvy, which increases for want of houses, and by reason of wet lodging in their cottages, having no fresh food to cherish them. And though the people are very pitiful and loving, yet the sickness with other distempers so prevails, that the well are not able to tend them. Upon which many die, and are buried about the hill. Yet it was admirable to see with what Christian courage many carry it amidst these calamities'; William Bradford, *History of Plymouth Plantation 1620–1647* (Boston, 1912), vol. 2, p. 113n. Winthrop acknowledged that the settlers had 'met with many sad and discomfortable things', including 'much mortality, sickness and trouble', but declared, 'I would not have altered my course, though I had foreseen all these afflictions; I never fared better in my life'; *Winthrop Papers*, vol. 2, pp. 302, 312, 313.

[38] *Winthrop Papers*, vol. 2, p. 316. Page endured to become a successful colonist, a freeman of Massachusetts, and a constable of Watertown, and lived to the age of ninety. Savage, *Genealogical Dictionary*, vol. 3, p. 330.

to build, fuel to burn, ground to plant, seas and rivers to fish in, a pure air to breathe in, good water to drink', but little more. Here was no earthly paradise, neither Canaan nor Goshen. 'In a word, we yet enjoy little to be envied but endure much to be pitied in the sickness and mortality of our people.' Dudley went on,

I do the more willingly use this open and plain dealing lest other men should fall short of their expectations when they come hither, as we to our great prejudice did, by means of letters sent us from hence into England, wherein honest men, out of a desire to draw over others to them, wrote somewhat hyperbolically of many things here.

This was a rebuke to Higginson and the promotional tradition of which he was part. Hyperbole was not just a cheat, it could be lethal. Dudley's letter, addressed to the Countess of Lincoln but intended also 'for the use of such as shall hereafter intend to increase our plantation', was an attempt to set the record straight.[39]

John Pond also wrote home in March 1631, after his first winter in New England, complaining to his father about high prices and scarcity, burning fevers, diseases and deaths. 'I think that in the end if I live it must be by my leaving, for we do not know how long this plantation will stand.' Instead of profit and fortune, New England was likely to produce impoverishment, immiseration and death. According to Pond, many of the early settlers who came over 'worth two hundred pounds before they came out of old England' would 'be hardly worth thirty pounds' by the end of the year. This was a devastating charge that took a long time for the colony to live down.[40] As late as 1660, after a generation of settlement, growth and consolidation, and long after the starving time of 1630–1, the view persisted that newcomers to New England would go hungry. John Winthrop, Jr., had to reassure prospective English migrants at the time of the Restoration, 'It is not now as in our beginnings, when we were necessitated to bring with us provisions sufficient for a long time.' New migrants 'need not be put to any hardships as some of the first beginners might meet with'.[41]

Though of a higher rank than most, the Saltonstall family had mixed reactions to early New England that were not unusual. Sir Richard Saltonstall had been an enthusiastic projector for New England, a councillor of the Massachusetts Bay Company, who moved his family across the ocean. But he quit the colony in 1631 because he could not abide the scarcity of provisions or the meanness of the

---

[39] (Dudley), 'Dudley's letter to the Countess of Lincoln', in *Chronicles*, pp. 305, 310–6, 324–5.
[40] *Winthrop Papers*, vol. 3, pp. 17–19.
[41] M.H.S. *Collections*, ser. 5, vol. 8 (1882), pp. 65–6.

diet. His son, Richard, Jr., still had high hopes for New England, writing in 1632, 'The country abounds with good creatures needful for the sustentation of the life of man ... I doubt not but we shall raise good profit not only by our fishing trade, but by hemp, flax, pitch, tar, potashes, soap ashes, masts, pipe staves, clapboard and iron.'[42] Present disgruntlement often mixed with optimism about the future.

Thomas Weld reported more favourably about New England. He arrived in Massachusetts in the summer of 1632 and was therefore not a witness to the earlier destitution and despair. His letter, written for circulation among his former Essex parishioners, was eloquent testimony to the colony's resilience, and served to offset the more pessimistic reports. But Weld, like Winthrop, deliberately downplayed the shortcomings of the land and the continuing social and economic difficulties of the plantation.

Here we are come into as goodly a land as ever mine eyes beheld. Such groves, such trees, such an air ... Here I find three great blessings, peace, plenty and health ... Blessed be God, here is plenty of corn that the poorest have enough ... I know no other place on the whole globe of the earth where I would be rather than here. We say to our friends that doubt this, come and see and taste.[43]

By this time some three or four thousand English settlers had already crossed over to New England, and there were flourishing colonies in Virginia, Maryland, Barbados and elsewhere in the Caribbean. The number of eyewitnesses to America was greatly expanded, and with it the number of opinions.[44]

William Wood's *New England's Prospect* was published in London in 1634 with the intention of dispelling all misconceptions. The author promised an impartial description by one who had lived there four years and who intended to return. 'Because there hath been many scandalous and false reports passed upon the country, even from the sulphurous breath of every base ballad-monger', a clear and compre-

[42] Robert E. Moody (ed.), *The Saltonstall Papers, 1607–1815*, vol. 1, *1607–1789* (Boston, 1972), pp. 10–11; H.M.C., *Twelfth Report*, pt. 1 (London, 1888), p. 449.
[43] British Library, Sloan 922, ff. 90–3; Everett Emerson (ed.), *Letters from New England: The Massachusetts Bay Colony, 1629–1638* (Amherst, Mass., 1976), pp. 94–8.
[44] For estimates of the colonial population see John J. McCusker and Russell R. Menard, *The Economy of British America, 1607–1789* (Chapel Hill, N.C., 1985), pp. 102–3, 214–27; Henry A. Gemery, 'Emigration from the British Isles to the New World, 1630–1700: Inferences from colonial populations', *Research in Economic History*, 5 (1980), pp. 211–12; Richard S. Dunn, *Sugar and Slaves: The Rise of the Planter Class in the English West Indies, 1624–1713* (New York, 1973), pp. 87, 312; and R. C. Simmons, *The American Colonies: From Settlement to Independence* (New York, 1976), p. 24. See also chapter 2, this volume.

hensive treatment was necessary.[45] With new editions in 1635 and 1639, *New England's Prospect* became a standard reference work for prospective migrants, to set alongside the works of Hakluyt and Smith. Writing judiciously and without special pleading, Wood tackled such lies and misapprehensions as that the climate was intolerable, that women could not bear children, that the soil was barren, and that the country was plagued with rattlesnakes and flies.

> To wipe away all groundless calumniations, and to answer to every too, too curious objections and frivolous questions (some so simple as not ashamed to ask whether the sun shines there or no) were to run in *infinitum*. But I hope that the several manuscripts and letters and informations by word of mouth from some of our honest countrymen, which daily have recourse unto us, have given full satisfaction to such as are well-wishers to the plantations.

Those doubting the text could find corroboration in face-to-face communication from true witnesses.[46] What they learned, however, would depend on the experience and disposition of the informant.

Wood told his readers that the winters, though hard, were short, and that 'I saw not so much rain, raw colds, and misty fogs in four years in those parts as was in England in the space of four months the last winter'; that New England was healthful for all and that mothers and babies thrived; that the soil needed labour, but was not inferior in its natural state to the market-garden land around London; that there were 'strawberries in abundance . . . no better water in the world . . . good store of woods', and plentiful deer, fowl and fish. The list would be familiar to those who had read John Brereton's account of 1602 or even Thomas Harriot's Roanoke report of 1588. Flies, indeed, were 'troublesome' in New England, but no worse than in some parts of East Anglia, while the terror of the rattlesnake was 'nothing so bad as the report goes of him in England'. Critics, argued Wood, should not blame the country, but rather consider the mistakes and failings of unprepared settlers.[47]

One such settler, John Pratt, had been drawn to Massachusetts by 'larger reports into England of the country than I found to be true'. The truth, as Pratt experienced it, included barren land with 'rocks, sand and salt marshes'. To unburden himself of his disappointment, and to warn others what to expect, Pratt wrote home in 1634 or 1635 'of the improbability or impossibility of subsistence for ourselves or

---

[45] William Wood, *New England's Prospect*, ed. Alden T. Vaughan (Amherst, Mass., 1977), p. 20. For examples of ballads mocking New England see Morison, *Builders of the Bay Colony*, pp. 45–6, 62–3, 384–6.
[46] Wood, *New England's Prospect*, pp. 73–4.
[47] *Ibid.*, pp. 27–68.

our posterity without tempting God, or without extraordinary means'. Somehow this letter fell into the hands of the Massachusetts authorities, who interpreted it as a threat to their entire enterprise. Nervously, they forced Pratt to recant. As part of his submission Pratt wrote another letter, probably following dictation, repudiating his damaging statements. 'Whereas I am thought generally to charge all that have written into England by way of commendation of this land as if what they had written were generally false, I meant it only of such excessive commendations as I see did exceed and are contrary to that which I have here expressed.'[48] The case is interesting for what it reveals about the sensitivity of Massachusetts to criticism and concern with its image in England. The colony had multiple constituencies to cultivate, and several sets of enemies to deter.

Pratt was not alone in his disappointment, nor was he the only disgruntled settler to express his grievances in letters to family or friends in England. One correspondent of 1637 wrote that the land did not 'answer expectation'. 'For the present, we make a shift to live, but hereafter, when our numbers increase and the fertility of the soil doth decrease, if God discover not means to enrich the land, what shall become of us I will not determine.'[49] Another writer complained that 'the air of the country is sharp, the rocks many, the trees innumerable, the grass little, the winter cold, the summer hot, the gnats in summer biting, the wolves at midnight howling'.[50] Experience proved that New England was for the hardy and the determined, not for the soft or the slack. The unrealistic praise of the early explorers soon gave way to more modest expectations. If not a land of fat abundance, New England would at least reward the industrious and succour the devout. The land would yield a 'sufficiency' with hard work, not super riches with ease, and for some Puritans this became part of its attraction.

Gradually people learned that New England was not one landscape but several, with different properties and prospects across the region.

[48] Pratt's apology is printed in M.H.S. *Collections*, ser. 2, vol. 7 (1818), pp. 126–9. 255–77.

[49] Emerson, *Letters from New England*, p. 214.

[50] *Ibid.*, p. 215. *Cf.* Richard Mather's remarks in a letter of 1636: 'The land looks not pleasant to the eye in many places, being a rude and unsubdued wilderness yet with labour yields sufficient sustenance for men of moderate minds. The dearth and hardship which some sustained last winter was not through barrenness of the ground but by means of the many thousands that came in with slender provision after that foul weather near harvest had hurt the corn on the ground. This year there is more corn planted that looketh fair on the ground and promiseth by God's blessing a plentiful harvest'; in *ibid.*, p. 205.

Rocks and barren wasteland were interspersed with fertile fields and pastures. While New Haven Colony was said in 1645 to 'flourish indifferently well in corn and cattle', the neighbouring Connecticut settlements were 'exceedingly abounding in corn', and were rated 'the fruitfullest places in all New England'. At Plymouth Colony, the same observer continued, 'The land is barren and the people very poor,' whereas the best that could be said of Massachusetts was that it was 'indifferently fruitful'. The north-east territory, along the Saco and Kennebec rivers, 'abounds in fish and timber'.[51]

≈≈≈≈≈≈≈≈≈

As the settlements took root, and particularly as Massachusetts took on its Puritan political and religious coloration, the colonists and their friends and enemies back home encountered a variety of contradictory impressions about conditions in New England. Both supporters and opponents of the Bay Colony fed reports about the natural environment into their religious and political disputes. All sorts of opinions jostled for acceptance, in print, in manuscript and by word of mouth. Glowing reports of the land were in tension with criticisms of Puritan bigotry. Deficiencies in the natural environment offset commendations of the godly commonwealth. By the middle of the seventeenth century the English could draw on four main sets of opinion about New England: first, that the land was marvellous and that the saints were planting there a model of godliness and good government; second, that the land was indeed wonderful, but the Puritan experiment was gravely in error; third, that the environment was difficult and disappointing but worth enduring because of the righteousness of God's cause; and fourth, that both cause and environment were worthless and ought to be abandoned. Reporters faced the difficulty of separating their descriptions of the natural history of New England from their feelings about its government and people.

The standard view, set forth by John Winthrop and the ministers of New England, embraced the concept of 'a city upon a hill' and a model of Christian charity. Puritan New England was a Protestant showcase, a light to the world, a place of godly discipline and spiritual cleansing.[52] There was no shortage of adherents to this position, and

---

[51] Beinecke Library, 'Newsletter', 1645. See also William Cronon, *Changes in the Land: Indians, Colonists, and the Ecology of New England* (New York, 1983), pp. 19–33.
[52] John Cotton, *God's Promise to His Plantation* (London, 1630); [Winthrop], 'The humble request of His Maiesties loyall subjects, the governour and the company late gone

many Puritan advocates were articulate and persuasive. The fish merchant Robert Trelawny, for example, found Winthrop's Boston exactly to his liking. Writing to his brother in 1636, Trelawny enthused,

What a most heavenly and comfortable sight is it to see with what power and purity the Ordinances are administered, so that no one place in the world comes near it; I mean in the Bay, where there is such holy walking, such a sweet communion and fellowship on all sides, that I am persuaded unless a man were past all grace it would convince the weariest reprobate alive.[53]

But though prominent in the records and dominant in the historiography, such views did not go unchallenged.

Grievances and frustration had beset New England colonization from its beginnings. Plymouth Colony faced backbiting and 'objections' throughout the 1620s from unhappy immigrants and thwarted interlopers. Some objected to the primitive conditions of the settlement, and others to its innovations in religion. 'Malcontented persons and turbulent spirits' spread rumours of the colony's impending disintegration.[54] Complaints that 'the water is not wholesome...the ground is barren...the fish will not take salt to keep sweet...and... the people are much annoyed with mosquitoes', paled beside the fundamental charge against Plymouth: its separatist religion. Writing again to his brother in 1624 Emmanuel Altham allowed that Plymouth Plantation had problems, although, he was quick to point out, 'the fault is not in the country'.[55]

Similar complaints dogged early Massachusetts. The Browne brothers, John and Samuel, had been expelled from the colony in 1629 as 'factious and evil conditioned', though mostly because they stood for Church of England orthodoxy. The Brownes lost no time in avenging themselves by spreading slanderous reports about the religious irregularities and administrative high-handedness of the Salem regime. The company warned Governor Endecott in October 1629, 'The Brownes are likely to make the worst of anything they have observed in New England, by reason of your sending them back against their will for their offensive behaviour.' Although the brothers evidently liked New England enough to want to stay, they had no sympathy for

for New-England', in *Chronicles*, pp. 294–8; 'A Modell of Christian Charity', in *Winthrop Papers*, vol. 2, pp. 282–95.

[53] James Phinney Baxter, *Documentary History of the State of Maine*, Vol. 3, 'The Trelawny Papers' (Portland, Maine, 1884), p. 79.

[54] Bradford, *Of Plymouth Plantation*, pp. 372, 380.

[55] Bradford, *History of Plymouth Plantation*, pp. 362–7; James (ed.), *Three Visitors to Early Plymouth*, p. 38.

the new Puritan regime that was emerging.[56] Given the multiplicity of interests in America and the broad range of options for colonization, it was by no means a foregone conclusion that Massachusetts would become a Puritan experiment.

Hostile reports from America quickly found their way into English popular opinion. In November 1630 one Thomas Jarvis of Lyme, Dorset, asserted 'that all the projectors for New England business are rebels, and those sort that are gone over are idolators, captivates and separatists'.[57] Jarvis was no doubt in his cups, but he and his listeners probably knew people involved with the Winthrop fleet and had neighbours who were contemplating emigration to America. Though rarely the principal topic of the day, New England had become a subject of conversation in settings as far apart as the London wharfs and a Dorset alehouse. Ballad-mongers picked up the mockery, rhyming the migrants as 'all that putrifidean sect, I mean the counterfeit elect, all zealous bankrupts, punks devout, preachers suspended, rabble rout'.[58] Material abounded with which to form opinions, even if those opinions were inaccurate and malicious.

More complaints were raised against New England in the years that followed. The early colonists learned that 'they who went discontentedly from us the last year [1630], out of their evil affections towards us, have raised many false and scandalous reports against us, affirming us to be Brownists [separatists, no relation to the Browne brothers] in religion and ill-affected to our state at home, and that these vile reports have won credit with some who formerly wished us well'.[59] The Massachusetts government attempted to control the flow of opinion back across the Atlantic, but its censorious actions often made matters worse. Henry Linne suffered a whipping and banishment from Boston in 1631 'for writing into England falsely and maliciously against the government and execution of justice here'.[60] Such overbearing action cost Massachusetts friends and played into the hands of its enemies.

Even supporters of the Massachusetts enterprise were alarmed by some of the things they heard. News reached Edward Howes in Lon-

---

[56] *Chronicles*, pp. 287–90; *Mass. Recs.*, vol. 1, pp. 34–5, 37, 51–2, 69, 407–9. John Browne was a lawyer, and both brothers were sufficiently well connected to damage the colony's prospects.

[57] Jarvis further said that the magistrates of Lyme 'were a company of hypocrites and dissemblers'; Dorset Record Office, B2/8/1, 'Dorchester borough records, court book'.

[58] Morison, *Builders of the Bay Colony*, p. 384.

[59] *Chronicles*, p. 331.

[60] John Noble (ed.), *Records of the Court of Assistants of the Massachusetts Bay 1630–1692* (Boston, 1901–28), vol. 2, p. 19; *Winthrop's Journal*, vol. 1, p. 67.

don in 1632 that the New England government cut off the ears of miscreants. Howes cautioned his friend, John Winthrop, Jr., 'There are a thousand eyes watching over you to pick a hole in your coats, yet fear not, there are more with you than against you.'[61] Sadly, the story was true, even if the numbers were wrong. In 1631 the General Court of Massachusetts had sentenced Philip Ratcliffe to have his ears cut off, to be whipped, fined and banished, 'for uttering malicious and scandalous speeches against the government and church of Salem'. The news took less than a couple of months to reach England, where it spread to the further detriment of New England's moral credit.[62] The government of Massachusetts could be more vindictive than Charles I's Star Chamber and High Commission.

News and hearsay flourished in England, much of it hostile to New England. Rumours circulated throughout 1632 about the impending collapse of the Massachusetts Colony. Edward Howes had heard that 'you are all coming home' or that 'you are all gone or going for Virginia', because New England had proved untenable.[63] Some of the Winthrops' English neighbours even made plans to receive the failed colonists back into their home community. Thomas Ashley wrote to John Winthrop from Suffolk in March 1633, 'I am as sorry to hear many reports blemish the hopes of your plantation as I am pleased to be witness of several desires to place you at Groton.'[64] Of course, the rumours were false, but they must have had a depressing effect on recruiting and migration. Nobody gladly boards a sinking ship, or commits to a colony that is about to be abandoned.

Although the colony endured, and scored some remarkable successes, English opinion still wavered, fed as it was from a variety of different springs. The libertine Thomas Morton and the bigamist Christopher Gardiner, both of whom locked horns with the Puritan power group, spread malicious gossip about New England in the mid-1630s. Besides further muddying the streams of opinion, their charges provided more ammunition for attacks on the Massachusetts charter.[65] The clumsiness and arrogance of some of the Puritan leaders did little to improve understanding. Friends of Massachusetts were gravely embarrassed in 1635 when John Endecott defaced the royal ensign, claiming that its emblem of a cross (St. George's cross) was idolatrous. Such behaviour played into the hands of enemies who

[61] *Winthrop Papers*, vol. 3, p. 76.
[62] *Mass. Recs.*, vol. 1, p. 88; *Winthrop's Journal*, vol. 1, p. 64.
[63] *Winthrop Papers*, vol. 3, pp. 94, 114.
[64] *Ibid.*, p. 107.
[65] Young, *Chronicles of the First Planters*, pp. 334–5.

argued that the New England colonists were ill-affected to the king.[66] Muriel Gurdon of Assington, Suffolk, a staunch but troubled well-wisher, wrote to Margaret Winthrop in the spring of 1636, asking for reliable news of New England. 'We hear but very little, but what we hear from those which come over from you, and they for the most part differ so much either in their speech or in judgement.'[67]

Massachusetts's expulsion of Roger Williams in 1636 and the traumatic collision with Anne Hutchinson in 1637 further disturbed home opinion. By 1637 the news was mostly bad, tainted by reports of 'error and faction' and the long-distance echoes of the Antinomian controversy.[68] The leaders of the Bay Colony still attempted to limit the export of unfavourable news, to soften the impact of criticism, and to ensure that their spokesmen in London could control the damage, but contradictory and unflattering stories continued to leak out. In the aftermath of the Anne Hutchinson affair, John Wilson and John Cotton, who had taken different sides in the dispute, both appealed to a party of returning migrants to put a good face on the matter when they reached England.[69]

English Puritans regretted the bad image created by the Hutchinson affair as much as they were troubled by the issues in the controversy itself. Robert Stansby wrote from London to John Wilson in 1637, 'there is now so much talk of it, and such certain truth of it, as I know many of worth, for outward estate and ability for wisdom and grace, are much daunted from coming.'[70] Another correspondent warned the colonists that crisis and scandal 'hath caused a wonderful disaffection in very many towards you', even among the godly, and that some prospective migrants now 'are resolved to undergo much misery here rather than ever to remove hence'.[71] Such matters as the healthfulness of the air or the fruitfulness of the soil paled beside the crucial and divisive issues of godly discipline and Christian charity.

Thomas Morton, master of Merry-Mount and the bane of the Plymouth Pilgrims, loved New England but hated the separatists and zealots who had won control. Pristine New England, in his view, had been 'a

---

[66] Thomas Hutchinson, *The History of the Colony and Province of Massachusetts-Bay*, ed. Lawrence Shaw Mayo (Cambridge, Mass., 1936), vol. 1, pp. 35–6; *Winthrop's Journal*, vol. 1, pp. 147, 149–50.

[67] Moody (ed.), *Saltonstall Papers*, vol. 1, p. 128; *Winthrop Papers*, vol. 3, p. 243. *Cf.* Lucy Downing to John Winthrop, July 1636, *Winthrop Papers*, vol. 3, p. 279.

[68] *Winthrop Papers*, vol. 3, p. 398. See David D. Hall, *The Antinomian Controversy, 1636–1638* (Middletown, Conn., 1968).

[69] *Winthrop's Journal*, vol. 1, p. 209.

[70] *Winthrop Papers*, vol. 3, p. 390.

[71] *Ibid.*, p. 398.

rich, hopeful and very beautiful country, worthy the title of Nature's masterpiece'. But the current regime was despoiling it. Morton amassed his charges in a lively volume, *The New English Canaan*, published in 1637, crying, 'Repent, you cruel schismatics, repent.' Framed by Morton's invective was the best ethnographic report on New England yet written and a catalogue of the country's natural offerings.[72] Readers would have to weigh the value of brotherly love and sound religion (present or absent in New England according to different opinions) against the other attractions of the American strand.

More publications appeared in 1638 describing the colonists' bloody triumphs in the Pequot war. The Pequot Indians, a 'barbarous nation' to the south of Massachusetts, had been virtually exterminated 'by the sword of the Lord' and his English helpers. John Underhill told the story in *Newes from America, or a New and Experimentall Discoverie of New England*. Philip Vincent elaborated it in *A True Relation of the Late Battell Fought in New England between the English and the Pequet Salvages*.[73] Interspersed with stirring tales of English heroics in their search-and-destroy operation against the Pequots were remarks on the beauty and natural resources of the land, and inducements to prospective settlers. New England, according to Underhill, possessed 'a very good soil, good meadow, divers sorts of good wood . . . fowl in abundance . . . deer', much as Captain Smith had seen it but now safely cleared of hostile natives.[74] Peaceable or treacherous, the Indians were no longer a threat. Vincent saw New England no longer as a land awaiting development but a country replete with the marks of European civilization. The English in New England 'have built fair towns . . . and fair ships too . . . they have overcome cold and hunger . . . corn and cattle are wonderfully increased'. Logistically at least, New En-

---

[72] Thomas Morton, *The New English Canaan . . . or an Abstract of New England*, ed. Charles Francis Adams, Jr. (Boston, 1883), pp. 109, 345. William Bradford castigated *New English Canaan* as 'an infamous and scurrilous book against many godly and chief men of the country, full of lies and slanders, and freight with profane calumnies against their names and persons, and the ways of God'; Bradford, *History of Plymouth Plantation*, vol. 2, p. 76. A critic of the Puritans praised Morton's *New English Canaan* as 'the truest description of New England as then it was that ever I saw'; Samuel Maverick, 'Briefe description of New England', M.H.S. *Proceedings*, ser. 2, vol. 1 (1884–5), p. 238. For a fresh appraisal of Morton see Michael Zuckerman, 'Pilgrims in the wilderness: community, modernity and the maypole at Merry Mount', *New England Quarterly*, 50 (1971), pp. 255–77.

[73] John Underhill, 'Newes from America, or a new and experimentall discoverie of New England', in Charles Orr (ed.), *History of the Pequot War* (Cleveland, 1897), p. 49; Philip Vincent, 'A true relation of the late battell fought in New England between the English and the Pequet salvages', in Orr (ed.), *History of the Pequot War*, pp. 97–108.

[74] Underhill, 'News from America', pp. 63–4.

gland was a success, where migrants could settle without fear of privation.[75]

Rumour circulated in England again in 1640 to the effect that the Massachusetts Colony was about to fold. Migration faltered, even before the rapidly-evolving religious and political crisis in England transformed the situation. Sudden economic ruin and a crisis of spiritual confidence beset the holy commonwealth, leading to a further evolution of its image in England.[76] Some New England settlers, cold, depressed and disappointed, toyed with the idea of further migration to a more favoured place. Hundreds went back to England. Some returners gave out 'that they could not subsist here', although others came back for political and religious reasons.[77]

John Winthrop recorded in his journal for 1640, 'Many men began to inquire after the southern parts, and the greater advantages supposed to be had in Virginia and the West Indies.'[78] Lord Saye and Sele, a long-time friend of the colony, withdrew his support and counselled prospective migrants to look southward or to the islands. Saye and Sele came to view New England as a country where 'rich men grow poor and poor men, if they come over, are a burden', a far cry from the optimism of 1630.[79] The colony's leaders felt compelled to tackle this disturbing impression, 'the report of our poverty having been already a manifest cause of debarring most from us'.[80] Rumours of restlessness persisted through the 1640s. A Boston writer of 1645 advised his friends in England that the Delaware River to the south would be a better place to settle than Massachusetts Bay. 'If any leave the kingdom, pray counsel them to this place [Delaware], and many here [Massachusetts] will join with them'.[81]

If English people thought of New England at all in the 1640s and 1650s, it was as a distant curiosity or a subject for charity, rather than a magnet for migration. Massachusetts came to be viewed as an unhappy laboratory, safely isolated, whence came cautionary accounts of the pathology of religious experimentation. Those who were interested could turn to a series of publications, as several shades of Puritans and their enemies of many stripes aired their quarrels or

[75] Vincent, 'True relation of the late battell', pp. 108–10.
[76] Marion H. Gottfried, 'The first depression in Massachusetts', *New England Quarterly*, 9 (1936), pp. 655–75.
[77] *Winthrop Papers*, vol. 4, pp. 263, 283, 314. For the return of migrants to England see chapter 8, this volume.
[78] *Winthrop's Journal*, vol. 1, p. 333.
[79] *Ibid.*, pp. 334–5; *Winthrop Papers*, vol. 4, pp. 263–7.
[80] *Winthrop Papers*, vol. 4, p. 314.
[81] Beinecke Library, 'Newsletter', 1645.

expounded their disparate views. Alternative, and perhaps superior, sources of information lay with the hundreds of New Englanders who returned to their mother country to take part in the great events of the civil war and revolution. Discussion no longer turned on the commodities of the American landscape or the wholesomeness of its climate but focussed, rather, on the virtues or failings of New England's experiments in government and religion and the lessons that might be applied at home.

William Hooke led off in 1641 with *New Englands Teares, for Old Englands Feares.* This recapitulated a sermon, delivered in Massachusetts, expressing a somewhat smug 'brotherly compassion'during England's political crisis.[82] Thomas Lechford offered *Plain Dealing, or News from New England* in 1642, attacking the ecclesiastical polity of Massachusetts, where 'all is out of joint both in church and commonwealth', and by implication warning of what might result from dismantling the Church of England. The fracas at Northam, just inside New Hampshire, in which disputing religious factions faced each other brandishing a Bible on an halbert, could be seen as symptomatic of the failure of Christian fellowship in New England and a foretaste of the disorder and division that might be expected at home.[83] Lechford published an expanded text in 1644, retitled *New Englands Advice to Old England*, in which he repeated his attack on the cruel exclusiveness and arbitrariness of Massachusetts church government.[84]

The Antinominan dispute of the 1630s was rehashed in English pamphlet battles of the 1640s, through such publications as *A Short Story of the Rise, Reign and Ruin of the Antinomians, Familists, and Libertines, that Infected the Churches of New-England* and *Mercuricus Americanus, Mr. Welds his Antitype, or, Massachusetts Great Apologie Examined.*[85] These essays were marked by vituperation, recrimination and special pleading, and they were unlikely to attract a wide audience. Rather, they were aimed at the inner circle of divines, politicians and army

---

[82] William Hooke, *New Englands Teares, for Old Englands Feares* (London, 1641), p. 16.
[83] Thomas Lechford, *Plain Dealing, or News from New England*, ed. Darrett B. Rutman (New York, 1969), pp. 143–7.
[84] Thomas Lechford, *New-Englands Advice to Old England* (London, 1644), p. 44; David Cressy, 'Books as totems in seventeenth-century England and New England', *Journal of Library History*, 21 (1986), pp. 94–7.
[85] Thomas Weld, *A Short Story of the Rise, Reign and Ruin of the Antinomians, Familists, and Libertines, That Infected the Churches of New-England* (London, 1644); John Wheelwright, *Mercurius Americanus, Mr. Welds his Antitype, or, Massachusetts Great Apologie Examined* (London, 1645). For more in this vein see Thomas Weld, *An Answer to W. R. his Narration of the Opinions and Practices of the Churches Lately Erected in New-England, Vindicating those Churches from an Hundred Imputations Fathered on Them* (London, 1644).

grandees who were themselves striving for godly order in the chaos of the English revolution.

In 1647 John Child published *New-Englands Jonas Cast up at London*, demanding 'civil liberty and freedom' for all in Massachusetts. Child's brother Robert had been an author of the Massachusetts Remonstrance, a petition of grievances similar to some of those circulating in revolutionary England, and he charged that the colony, like the mother country, had succumbed to arbitrariness and ill-government.[86] Edward Winslow, former governor of Plymouth and now the agent for Massachusetts in England, replied at once with *New-Englands Salamander*, a systematic rebuttal containing 'a satisfactory answer to many aspersions cast upon New-England'.[87] Each publication appealed to a different faction and presented opposing views of political and religious organization. Later in the year London was treated to the spectacle of a public quarrel when two New England men, Dr. Robert Child and Mr. Francis Willoughby of Charleston, met 'upon the Exchange'. An audience gathered as the former colonists berated each other on behalf of their respective points of view. Witnesses spread their own versions of the confrontation on both sides of the Atlantic.[88]

Good News from New-England appeared anonymously in 1648, touting, in excruciating verse, the achievements of the godly commonwealth.[89] John Clarke followed in 1652 with *Ill Newes from New-England*, a 'tragical story' of intolerance by the Massachusetts authorities and their persecution of dissident Christians from Rhode Island.[90] And so it went on. The meanness and bitterness of most of these pamphlets lost New England friends and engendered isolation at a time when the colonies could ill-afford further estrangement. Instead of a model 'city upon a hill,' New England was in danger of becoming a forlorn and distant side-show. Sir Richard Saltonstall, a powerful backer of the Massachusetts Bay Colony since its inception, wrote to the Massachusetts ministers John Cotton and John Wilson

---

[86] John Child, *New-Englands Jonas Cast up at London*, ed. W. T. R. Marvin (Boston, 1869), pp. 8–15. For the Remonstrance see George Lyman Kittredge, 'Robert Child the Remonstrant', *Publications of the Colonial Society of Massachusetts*, 21 (1920), pp. 1–146; and Robert Emmet Wall, Jr., *Massachusetts Bay: The Crucial Decade, 1640–1650* (New Haven, Conn., 1972), pp. 157–224.

[87] Edward Winslow, *New-Englands Salamander*, in M.H.S. *Collections*, ser. 3, vol. 2 (1830), pp. 110–45; *Winthrop's Journal*, vol. 2, p. 339.

[88] *Winthrop's Journal*, vol. 2, p. 340.

[89] *Good News from New-England: With an Exact Relation of the First Planting of that Countrey* (London, 1648), reprinted in M.H.S. *Collections*, ser. 4, vol. 1 (1852), pp. 195–218.

[90] John Clarke, *Ill Newes from New-England, or, a Narrative of New-Englands Persecution*, in M.H.S. *Collections*, ser. 4, vol. 2 (1854), pp. 3–64.

in 1652, 'It doth not a little grieve my spirit to hear what sad things are reported daily of your tyranny and persecutions in New England ... These rigid ways have laid you very low in the hearts of the saints,' while the enemies of the lord were gloating.[91] More publications concerned themselves with New England than ever before, but they did little to win the colonies friends or inspire a new wave of migration.

This aspect of sadness and embattled partisanship continued to affect New England's image in England throughout the Interregnum, a sadness that contrasts with the joy and promise of the founding years. Quaker pamphlets such as *New England a Degenerate Plant* (1659) and *New-Englands Ensigne* (1659) added to the bleak picture. The former was 'published for the information of all sober people who desire to know how the state of New England now stands', the latter 'being the account of cruelty, the professors pride, and the articles of their faith, signified in characters written in blood, wickedly begun, barbarously continued, and inhumanely finished ... by the present power of darkness possessed in the priests and rulers in New England'.[92] Even if these pamphlets were strident, biased and wrong, their message no longer held any surprise. Pre-Restoration London was inured to such reports, and took a jaded view of the Puritan colonies. The promise of the 1630s had turned sour; few people in England looked to New England either for the advantages of its natural environment or for its superior social and religious organization.

Of course, the territory continued to hold certain strategic advantages, as a staging point in the Dutch and Spanish wars, for example, and as a source of masts, timber, naval stores and other raw materials. Thousands of English families had kinsmen in New England who were industriously working their farms and attending to daily affairs. But apart from its economic and military aspects, the principal attraction of New England in those troubled times was its remoteness from the distress of public affairs in old England. New England had become a refuge rather than a beacon.[93] John Winthrop, Jr., described

[91] Moody (ed.), *Saltonstall Papers*, vol. 1, pp. 148–9.

[92] John Rous, *New England a Degenerate Plant* (London, 1659); Humphrey Norton, *New-Englands Ensigne* (London, 1659). See also Francis Howgill, *The Popish Inquisition Newly Erected in New-England* (London, 1659); and George Bishop, *New England Judged, Not by Man but by the Lord: And the Summe Sealed up of New-Englands Persecutions* (London, 1661).

[93] This was not a new theme, but the outbreak of war in England gave it new poignancy. James Sherley in the 1620s and Richard Mather in the 1630s were among those who had earlier referred to New England as a place of refuge, Bradford, *Of Plymouth Plantation*, p. 382; Increase Mather, *The Life and Death of that Reverend Man of God, Mr. Richard Mather* (Cambridge, Mass., 1670), p. 17.

the colonies as 'an hiding place . . . when their precious brethren have been so long under the hurries, hazards and sufferings by civil wars'. New England could at least offer 'settled peace and prosperity' in contrast to the confusions in 'our dear native country', although Quakers, Baptists, Antinomians and Indians knew better.[94]

The missionary activities of the New England Puritans have been subjected to intense scrutiny in recent years. Their attempts to spread the gospel probably did as much harm to the native inhabitants as their territorial encroachment and periodic warfare.[95] Contemporaries, however, were proud of these efforts, and confidently drew attention to them when other aspects of the colonial enterprise were in shadow. *New-Englands First Fruits* (by Henry Dunster and/or Thomas Weld) defended New England by reference to 'the sprinklings of God's spirit' upon the Indians. Although the colonists had taken care of the necessaries for their own livelihood, had erected convenient places for God's worship, and had settled the civil government, their proudest boast, from this perspective, was of their college – Harvard College – and their work of Christianizing the native inhabitants.[96] Collections were held in English parishes to raise money for 'the godly poor in New England' and for the propagation of the gospel to the Indians. Thomas Weld, resettled in England after less than a decade in America, took charge of this activity in 1647 and collected over eight hundred pounds. Fund-raising was most successful in areas that had previously supplied colonists. Although the response was often disappointing, the missionary project at least kept New England in view. Contributions included £17 17s. 6d. from the parishioners of Dedham, Essex, and £8 5s. from Sudbury, Suffolk. The Corporation for the Propagation of the Gospel in New England followed up in the

---

[94] M.H.S. *Collections*, ser. 5, vol. 8 (1882), p. 65. See chapter 10, this volume.

[95] Puritan missionary activity is described in Francis Jennings, *The Invasion of America: Indians, Colonialism, and the Cant of Conquest* (New York, 1976); Karen Ordahl Kupperman, *Settling with the Indians: The Meeting of English and Indian Cultures in America, 1580–1640* (New York, 1980); Neal Salisbury, *Manitou and Providence: Indians, Europeans, and the Making of New England, 1500–1643* (New York, 1982); James P. Ronda, ' "We are well as we are": An Indian critique of seventeenth-century Christian missions', *William and Mary Quarterly*, ser. 3, vol. 34 (1977), pp. 66–82; and James P. Ronda, 'Generations of faith: The Christian Indians of Martha's Vineyard', *William and Mary Quarterly*, ser. 3, vol. 38 (1981), pp. 369–94.

[96] *New-Englands First Fruits* (1643, reprint, New York, 1865), pp. 14, 23. Other accounts of the mission to the Indians are *The Day-Breaking if not the Sun-Rising of the Gospel with the Indians in New-England* (London, 1647); Thomas Shepard, *The Clear Sunshine of the Gospel Breaking Forth upon the Indians in New-England* (London, 1648); and Henry Whitfield, *The Light Appearing More and More Towards the Perfect Day, or a Farther Discovery of the Present State of the Indians in New England* (London, 1651).

1650s with similar efforts, raising, for example, £68 1s. 1/2d. from 'the several parishes in the hundred of Blithing', Suffolk.[97]

At a prayer meeting in Essex in 1651 Ralph Josselin 'heard of the hopeful progress of the Gospel among the Indians of New England'. He pledged £5 to the Lord's work in New England in 1651 and 1652, and in 1653 collected £54 11s. 10d. from the parishioners of Earls Colne for missionary work among the New England Indians.[98] Josselin had kinsmen in New England, as did some of his congregation, but their philanthropy had little more passion than if they were subscribing for the victims of Turkish pirates or any other charitable collection. God's work in America warranted the support of English Puritans, but they had much more pressing problems of their own at home.[99]

New England faded from view for most Englishmen in the later seventeenth century. The great migration had reduced to a trickle. Massachusetts ceased to be interesting. Thomas Bailey may have captured a common view when he wrote in 1683, 'I have often heard of New England, and long ago, but never took no great heed to it, only as persons do often discourse of things remote and at random.' And this from a correspondent of Cotton Mather![100]

It is ironic that the time when preachers of Massachusetts were most agitated about the health and direction of God's cause in New England was one when very few people elsewhere were watching.[101] Only co-religionists, kinsmen and former settlers among the English population continued to monitor New England's internal affairs. Merchants, of course, attended to matters of commercial significance, and

---

[97] Guildhall Library, MS. 7938, 'Papers relating to the proceedings of the Corporation for Propagating the Gospel in New England', (transcript of Bodleian Library, Rawlinson MS. C.934), ff. 5, 19, 52; Guildhall Library, MS. 7936, 'Original correspondence of the New England Company 1657–1714'; Boston Public Library, MS. Am. 1502/1/12. Norfolk Record Office, PD 209/167, 'A noot of collection gathered by the collectors of North Elmeham ... for the promoting and propagating the gospel of Jesus Christ in Newe England and the perticular sum by everyone of them given', names thirty-one contributors who raised a total of 15s. 4d in January 1654.

[98] Alan Macfarlane (ed.), *The Diary of Ralph Josselin 1616–1683* (London, 1976), pp. 238, 263, 291, 299.

[99] For some Englishmen in the 1640s and 1650s the conversion of the Indians was a matter of eschatological urgency. Since Christ would not come to reign until the conversion of the Jews, and since, it was argued, the Indians were descended from the lost tribe of Israel, the missionary work in America was doubly important. See Philip F. Gura, *A Glimpse of Sion's Glory: Puritan Radicalism in New England, 1620–1660* (Middletown, Conn., 1984), pp. 133–5.

[100] 'Mather papers', M.H.S. *Collections*, ser. 4, vol. 8 (1868), pp. 488–9.

[101] See, for example, Michael Wigglesworth, 'God's controversy with New England', M.H.S. *Proceedings*, 12 (1871), pp. 84–92; John Oxenbridge, *New-England Freemen Warned and Warmed* (Cambridge, Mass., 1673); and Perry Miller, *Errand into the Wilderness* (1956; reprinted, New York, 1964), pp. 2–15.

the Privy Council paid periodic attention to New England's role in the imperial scheme. From most perspectives, however, New England had the air of a distant backwater, out of sight and out of mind. For Samuel Pepys, preoccupied with the navy but alert to many other things, New England was simply a source of supply for masts and mast ships, not a community of any intrinsic interest.[102]

In the 1660s Samuel Maverick, a long-time settler styling himself 'a faithful intelligencer as to the New England affairs', dispatched a series of reports that helped shape the attitude of the government of Charles II. Harping constantly on the refractory, factious, disloyal and seditious nature of the Puritan colonists, Maverick contributed to the view at Whitehall that New England was more trouble for England than it was worth.[103] Colonel George Cartwright reported on the state of affairs in Massachusetts in 1665 and found little to inspire him. Leaving aside his polite Anglican distaste for the local Puritan religion, Cartwright found New England to be backward, distant, out of touch, irreparably provincial and wholly unfashionable. The colonists, he announced, were hypocrites and probably rebels, and their towns were miserable and squalid. Even in Boston, 'their houses are generally wooden, their streets crooked and unpaved, with little decency and no uniformity'.[104] Massachusetts was evidently no place for a gentleman, or for any Englishman of taste. This was to be the view of most later Stuart courtiers and administrators. Massachusetts, in the eyes of one royal agent of the 1670s, 'is one of the smallest and poorest tracts of land and produces least of any of the other colonies for exportation'.[105]

This was a view some New Englanders were happy to encourage, if it meant they would be left alone. Complaining about the 'misinformations' that continually reached London, the General Court of Massachusetts told Charles II in 1664 that theirs was 'not a country where men can subsist without hard labour and great frugality'. Rather than living with profit, the most that ordinary people could expect was subsistence, 'such is the poverty and meanness of the peo-

---

[102] Robert Latham and William Mathews (eds.), *The Diary of Samuel Pepys*, vol. 5 (London, 1971), pp. 123, 127, 239, 321.

[103] 'The Clarendon papers', *Collections of the New York Historical Society* (New York, 1870), pp. 30–33, 45–6. John Josselyn, who was equally unsympathetic to the New England Puritans, called Maverick 'the only hospitable man in the country'; John Josselyn, *An Account of Two Voyages to New England* (Boston, 1865), p. 13.

[104] 'Clarendon papers', pp. 83–7.

[105] Quoted in Richard R. Johnson, *Adjustment to Empire: the New England Colonies, 1675–1715* (New Brunswick, N.J., 1981), p. 13.

ple of this country, by reason of the length and coldness of the winters, the difficulty of subduing a wilderness, defect of a staple commodity, the want of money, etc.'. A generation earlier the court would have censured anyone who dared make such an imputation. But in the new circumstances of the 1660s, when Massachusetts was trying to ward off unwelcome imperial attentions, it was shrewd to make the country appear inhospitable. The very harshness of the environment, which apologists had tried to soften in their writings of the 1630s, had become a cultural and political asset.[106]

The eclipse of New England can be gauged from the amount of space devoted to the region in George Gardyner's *Description of the New World,* published in 1651 and dedicated to the former governor of the Bay Colony, Sir Henry Vane. Only 3 of the 187 pages deal with New England. After cursory mention of the timber trade, fishing, shipbuilding and commerce, the author turns briefly to the inhabitants: 'The English people are well coloured and have many children, which thrive well in that country. They punish sin as severely as the Jews did in old time, but not with so good a warrant. And they have brought the Indians into great awe but not any gospel knowledge.' And there he stops, as if there was nothing more worth adding.[107]

John Ogilby had little more to say about New England in his voluminous work (674 pages) of 1671, *America: Being the Latest and Most Accurate Description of the New World.* Ogilby recounts the history of discovery and settlement, rehearses the history of the Indian wars, provides a standard list of natural commodities, and notes the existence of forty-five New England towns. But the author's tone is bored and distant, and his material is based almost entirely on books published in the 1630s. Massachusetts, he sniffs, was 'founded by the confluence of dissenting zealots', and 'the church government and discipline is Congregational and Independent, yet in some places more rigid than others'.[108]

The *London Gazette* occasionally printed snippets of news about New England, but never anything to spark much interest. In November 1667, for example, the *Gazette* reported, 'By a ship not long since put in from Boston in New England, we are informed of the quiet and

---

[106] Quoted in Jack P. Greene (ed.), *Great Britain and the American Colonies, 1606–1763* (Columbia, S.C., 1970), pp. 65–6.

[107] George Gardyner, *A Description of the New World. Or, America Islands and Continent* (London, 1651), pp. 90–2.

[108] John Ogilby, *America: Being the Latest and Most Accurate Description of the New World* (London, 1671), pp. 140–64.

thriving condition of that place, and their ready zeal for his majesty's service.'[109] This was a complacent filler, guaranteed to inspire neither curiosity nor the adventure of emigration. It did, at least, demur from the Cavalier characterization of the New Englanders as rebels.

John Josselyn, who had first seen Massachusetts in 1638, visited his brother in New England again between 1663 and 1671. On his return to London he published *New Englands Rareties Discovered* (a natural history) and *An Account of Two Voyages to New England*. Josselyn dedicated his account to the President and Fellows of the Royal Society and sprinkled it with observations of an astronomical, meteorological, medical, botanical and zoological nature. Like earlier travellers Josselyn took note of 'stately mountains...ample, rich and pregnant valleys...goodly trees...excellent waters'. On top of this he now found a bucolic English landscape. Dorchester, Massachusetts, for example, was 'a frontier town pleasantly seated and of large extent into the main land, well watered with two small rivers, her body and wings filled somewhat thick with houses to the number of two hundred and more, beautified with fair orchards and gardens, having also plenty of corn land and store of cattle'. Boston, once no more than a village, had become a handsome town, 'rich and very populous'.[110] Josselyn, however, was not writing to promote New England to potential migrants or investors but simply to describe it for the virtuoso community at home. Stories of New England's healthfulness he discounted, reporting (wrongly) that the morbidity was just as bad as England's. Agriculture had been afflicted with 'mildews and blasting of corn'. Earthquakes in 1658, 1662 and 1663 could be interpreted as geological phenomena or as prognosticators of divine retribution. Finally, Josselyn, like most English visitors, found fault with the cruelty, hypocrisy and intolerance of the Massachusetts Puritan administration.[111]

Following Josselyn's account came news of another crisis in New England's distant affairs. In 1675 the Wampanoag Indians attacked the outlying community of Swansea, precipitating three years of racial conflict that became known as King Philip's War. News of these attacks reached England and further troubled the minds of New England's remaining well-wishers. John Westgate, once a resident of Massachusetts but long resettled in East Anglia, noted in 1677,

---

[109] *The London Gazette*, 208, 11–14 November 1667.
[110] John Josselyn, *New Englands Rareties Discovered* (London, 1672); Josselyn, *An Account of Two Voyages to New England*, pp. 37–9, 123–5.
[111] Josselyn, *An Account of Two Voyages to New England*, pp. 138–41, 203–8.

The sad condition of N.E. [New England]...have been much upon our hearts. We have had many solemn days of humiliation, and the 25 of January last we had a solemn day of thanksgiving for the great deliverance the Lord had given you. This was very general among all the Congregational churches in city and country round about, we sending one to another and agreeing of the day beforehand, which was also kept by many of the Baptist congregations.[112]

The godly remnant, on both sides of the Atlantic, came to see New England as a land of troubles and vicissitudes, suffering and sadness, rather than the heroic city upon a hill.[113]

Jeremiads printed in America, memorializing the founders of New England, cataloguing the sins and sadness of the present, and chastising the rising generation, found a limited circulation among English Nonconformists. They did little to encourage enthusiasm for the Massachusetts Bay Colony. New England's difficulties, internal disputes, spiritual declension, Indian wars, earthquakes, fires and storms produced some sympathy among the dissenting congregations at home. But few English Nonconformists expressed a desire to join their American brethren.

The situation of the 1640s, when Boston churches held days of prayer 'for our dear native country', was now reversed. Thomas Bailey reported 'serious discourses' in England and Ireland about New England's troubles,

For during your disturbances were there frequent and fervent remembrances of you, I suppose the kingdom throughout, in country places as well as others, and many solemn particular occasions and opportunities set apart to seek God for you, God's interest in general, and N.E. especially being dear to all his, and a great measure of sympathy and spirit of prayer I well remember was seen that time among his people here.[114]

The religious crises of the 1680s produced a brief renewal of interest in emigration among some sectors of the dissenting community, but not much action. Bailey and his brother, both Nonconformist preachers, *did* migrate to New England; others, like Lancashire mercer Daniel Hemingway, sought information about New England but quickly lost

---

[112] The body count was recorded in *News from New-England, Being a True and Last Account of the Present Bloody Wars* (London, 1676). For Westgate see 'Mather papers', pp. 577–8. Westgate had moved to Massachusetts by 1640 but returned to Norfolk in 1647; Savage, *Genealogical Dictionary*, vol. 4, p. 489.

[113] In May 1684 William Stoughton wrote to his friend, Richard Streton, in London, about 'sorrows and troubles' in Boston. 'Our matters here are not in so good a frame as I could wish, by reason of many distempered spirits and actings'; British Library, Stowe MSS. 746, f. 89. See also the almost luxuriant despair of Cotton Mather, *Things for a Distress'd People to Think Upon* (Boston, 1696), pp. 9–24, which concludes with the chorus, 'God is much offended at New-England.'

[114] 'Mather papers', p. 489.

interest when the promise of toleration in old England removed the incentive.[115]

Less sympathetic commentators were content to view New England as 'a hodgepodge of all heresies and errors mixed together, the only cement being hypocrisy and dissimulation'.[116] Anglican visitors treated Massachusetts as a curiosity, still the source of potential commercial profit but hopelessly preoccupied with its censorious religious concerns. Who could match Ned Ward's insightful facetiousness in his description of Boston in 1699? 'The buildings, like their women, being neat and handsome, and their streets, like the hearts of the male inhabitants, are paved with pebble.'[117]

By 1700 Boston had grown to become a city of some 6,000 persons, and the united colonies of New England had a population of more than 90,000.[118] Most of the growth since the 1640s resulted from favourable demographic conditions, relatively high fertility and lower mortality. In the last decade of the seventeenth century New England may actually have lost population through further migration, either to other American colonies or back to England.[119] Small numbers of English, Irish and Scots migrants continued to add to the New England population, but expectations of religious purity or visions of the lushness, abundance and the excellency of the place no longer drew them over.

[115] *Ibid.*, pp. 486–93, 657–9.
[116] J. W., 'A letter from New-England in 1682', in George P. Winship (ed.), *Boston in 1682 and 1699* (Providence, R.I., 1905), p. 3.
[117] Ned Ward, 'A Trip to New-England', in Winship (ed.), *Boston in 1682 and 1699*, p. 38.
[118] 'A list of inhabitants in Boston, 1695', A.A.S. MSS., Boston papers, 1634–1893, Box 1, Folder 1, lists 1,363 householders in alphabetical order. For colonial population estimates see J. Potter, 'The growth of population in America, 1700–1860', in D. V. Glass and D. E. C. Eversley (eds.), *Population in History* (Chicago, 1965), p. 638, and sources in note 44, this chapter.
[119] David Galenson, *White Servitude in Colonial America: An Economic Analysis* (Cambridge, 1981), p. 216. Losses in the Indian wars may also have depleted the later seventeenth-century population.

2

'A mixed multitude': the peopling of early New England

This chapter is concerned with the social history of migration to New England. It sets out to describe the kinds of people thought most suitable to populate an American colony, examines how prospective migrants of various sorts were recruited, includes a brief study of servants (who are often neglected in accounts of New England) and concludes with a review of the social composition and population history of those who actually took part in the settlement of the Bay Colony and its neighbours. The matter of motivation is reserved for discussion in Chapter 3.

Early promoters of an English presence in the New World pitched America as a development opportunity for speculators and strategic planners, rather than a haven for Englishmen on the move. Hardly any Elizabethan considered America a suitable place for family settlement, a potential New England. Instead, the English in America would be company agents, engaged for particular tasks. The first planters and colonists would serve as front-line operatives for their masters who remained comfortably at home in London or Bristol. When they had completed their contracts the employees would, if they survived, return home.

One of the first to consider manpower requirements in any detail was Richard Hakluyt, in his 'Discourse of western planting' of 1585. Hakluyt enumerated seventy-six separate occupations, from archers to whittawyers, who would be needed in an American plantation. In Hakluyt's scheme, which endured as a model for colonial management well into the seventeenth century, an English American plantation would need to employ the following:

1. 'Men ... incident ... to the continue of victual', such as 'grafters for fruit trees' and 'freshwater fishers', who would be responsible for feeding the rest of the task force. They would also establish cash crops for export.
2. 'Men ... tending to force', including 'gunpowder makers' and 'harquebus-

iers of skill', responsible for fortification and defence, who would secure the colony against Indian or Spanish attack.

3. 'Men...incident to the first traffic and trade of merchandize', like black-smiths, 'grubbers and rooters up' of trees, millwrights and sawyers, whose labour would transform the wilderness into an industrial and commercial complex.

4. 'Artisans serving our first planters not in traffic but for buildings', including brickmakers and thatchers, who would construct shelters from local materials.

5. A miscellaneous group including laundry workers and tailors, shoemakers and makers of leather bottles.

This was an ideal compendium of talents, needing only governors and chaplains to make it complete. But no mention was made of women and children. The pioneer colony would be exclusively male, to be replenished by fresh shipments of manpower as required.[1]

The prototypical colony looked more like a garrison or a fortified trading factory than any of the communities that eventually developed in seventeenth-century America. Its closest realization was at James-town and at Sagadahoc in 1607.[2] The model, however, was persuasive and long-lasting. Emmanuel Altham, writing in 1623, still thought of America as a store of raw materials, rather than a location for family settlement. As a mariner rather than a planter, Altham saw himself in the Elizabethan tradition, and treasured his copy of Hakluyt's *Navigations*. Captain Altham imagined the future of New England in terms of its fishing and timber. In his view the young Plymouth colony of the 1620s could best be developed by sending over able-bodied workers, especially fishermen.[3]

William Morrell, writing in 1625, also thought in traditional terms when it came to peopling 'this bounteous land' of New England. 'Fishermen, manual artificers, engineers, and good fowlers are excellent servants, and only fit for plantations.' Gentlemen and 'citizens', who might support the colony financially, could not, of course, be expected to take part except in positions of command. Planting a colony would demand hard physical work, and gentlemen were 'too high' for such

[1] Richard Hakluyt, 'Discourse of western planting', in E. G. R. Taylor (ed.), *The Original Writings and Correspondence of the Two Richard Hakluyts* (London, 1935), vol. 2, pp. 320–4. For similar lists of 'sorts of men' most suitable for colonization see Hakluyt's 'Pamphlet for the Virginia enterprise' in *ibid.*, pp. 336–8; and John Brereton, *A Briefe and True Relation* (London, 1602), pp. 34–7.

[2] Andrews, *Colonial Period*, vol. 1, p. 93; Edmund S. Morgan, 'The labor problem at Jamestown, 1607–1618', *American Historical Review*, 76 (1971), pp. 595–611. For the Roanoke colonists see David Beers Quinn (ed.), *The Roanoke Voyages 1584–1590* (London, 1955), vol. 1, pp. 194–7; vol. 2, pp. 539–43.

[3] Sydney V. James, Jr. (ed.), *Three Visitors to Early Plymouth ... John Pory, Emmanuel Altham and Isaac de Rasieres* (Plymouth, Mass., 1963), pp. 25, 26, 28, 33, 38.

demanding (and demeaning) labour.[4] Morrell was associated with Sir Ferdinando Gorges and the Council for New England, a group whose plans for America were entirely material, imperial and secular. Writers like Morrell emphasized the economic advantages of New England, with little concern for its spiritual or cultural development.

By this time, however, the New England projectors were forced to give serious thought to the practical matter of selecting real emigrants. Plymouth Plantation was putting down roots, and several other groups had immediate plans to settle New England. The organizers were guided partly by Hakluyt, partly by the experimental work of colonization in Virginia and Ireland, and partly by the Holy Spirit.[5]

At the beginning of Plymouth Colony the leaders looked to commercial fishing and trading, rather than subsistence agriculture, for their primary economic foundation. The holy brethren from Scrooby and Leyden sought fellow-colonists who could attend to those profitable activities, rather than simple saints who might be a drag on resources. John Robinson advised John Carver in 1620, 'And let this specially be borne in mind, that the greatest part of the colony is like to be employed constantly, not upon dressing their particular land and building houses, but upon fishing, trading, etc.'[6] The immediate need, therefore, was for fishermen and tradesmen rather than subsistence farmers, whether or not they were sympathetic to the Plymouth religion.

Plymouth Plantation's managers in London, more concerned with the economic manpower requirements of the plantation than with its spiritual or social well-being, sent out servants and recruits who inevitably grated against the separatist saints of New Plymouth. William Bradford wrote in 1621, 'It is our calamity that we are, beyond expectation, yoked with some ill-conditioned people, who will never do good, but corrupt and abuse others.'[7] 'From the first', the Pilgrims

---

[4] William Morrell, *New-England, or a Briefe Enarration* (London, 1625), postscript. *Cf.* the social prospectus in 'Good news from New England', which calls for 'merchants ... seamen ... husbandmen ... and ... all manual occupations ... only printers of cards and dice-makers I could wish to forebear'; M.H.S. *Collections*, ser. 4, vol. 1 (1852), p. 218.

[5] Nicholas Canny, 'The permissive frontier: the problem of social control in English settlements in Ireland and Virginia 1550–1650', in K. R. Andrews, N. P. Canny and P. E. H. Hair (eds.), *The Westward Enterprise: English Activities in Ireland, the Atlantic, and America 1480–1650* (Liverpool, 1978), pp. 17–44. The Irish model is described in more detail in Philip S. Robinson, *The Plantation of Ulster: British Settlement in an Irish Landscape, 1600–1670* (Dublin, 1984).

[6] William Bradford, *History of Plymouth Plantation 1620–1647* (Boston, 1912), vol. 1, p. 109.

[7] *Ibid.*, vol. 1, p. 239.

regretted, 'they had some untoward persons mixed amongst them', but they could not manage alone. Their combined efforts succeeded in turning a place of mere promise into a place of permanent English habitation.[8]

Some advocates of colonization in the 1620s wrote as if the settlement at New Plymouth was an eccentric exception with little chance of success, rather than a model for the effective exploitation of New England. A proper colony, of the sort that Altham, Gorges and the Council for New England advocated, would be arranged on more traditional lines, with fewer allowances for separatist saints and their families. The ideas of the promoters and recruiters in England, who rounded up prospective emigrants for the settlements in New England, were completely at variance with the wishes of the hard-pressed religious leaders of New Plymouth. The Council for New England, in particular, had firm ideas about who should go to America.

At an important meeting in January 1623 the Council for New England sketched out its design for the 'three sorts of men' who would populate its American colony: 'One, gentlemen to bear arms and to attend upon the governor. Two, handicraftsmen of all sorts. Three, husbandmen for tillage and manuring of the lands; these to be employed by the public, and accounts to be taken of them every week.' Altogether the Council estimated that two hundred men (no women) would be necessary to establish an effective plantation in New England.[9] Since the major profit was expected to come from fish the council counted fishermen among its most important employees. To them they quickly added the useful occupations of a distiller and tailor, having found two men of those trades who 'offer themselves to go for New England'.[10]

Meeting several times in the 1620s to consider the peopling of New England, the council's deliberations touched on the skills, social position, morality, availability and cost of prospective migrants. Naturally the plantation would have both employers and employees, masters and servants, governors and subjects, and would replicate, to some degree, the power-and-dependency relationships of the English social order. The masters might emerge from the London merchant class or gentry. Servants could be found among the poor. Both in London and in rural England there were thought to be reserves of poor children, easy to recruit and ideal for service in plantations overseas. As

---

[8] *Ibid.*, vol. 2, p. 7; George D. Langdon, Jr., *Pilgrim Colony: A History of New Plymouth 1620–1691* (New Haven, Conn., 1966). pp. 14–25.
[9] A.A.S. MSS. 'Records of the Council for New England 1622–23', p. 28.
[10] *Ibid.*, pp. 12, 23.

Hakluyt had argued in the Elizabethan period, recruiting the poor for work in America tackled several problems at once. The home community would be relieved, the poor themselves would find honest work, and the new plantation (and its English backers) would reap the benefits of their labour.[11]

The Council for New England pressed the king and Privy Council for permission to recruit in London and throughout England. Council members used their connections in parliament and at court to advance the work. Sir Henry Spelman suggested that they could use the Elizabethan Statute of Apprentices to obtain children for service in New England. But only the respectable poor would do. The council specified, 'It is thought convenient to admit young youths from parishes, that have not been tainted with any villainies or misdemeanors, to be sent out to New England, and there to be placed out and bound apprentices to such as shall have occasion and means to employ them.'[12]

Early in 1623 the council obtained 'the letter...from his majesty to the Lieutenants of every shire for the setting forth of their poorer sort of people to New England'.[13] This document listed eleven 'reasons showing the benefit of planting in New England'. It is worth quoting at length for what it tells about the officially-approved approach to colonization in the decade before the great migration.

First, it enlargeth the bounds of his Majesty's dominions, and annexeth unto his crown one of the goodliest territories for soil, havens, harbours and habitable islands that hath ever been discovered by our nation.

Secondly, it will afford a world of employment to many thousands of our nation, of all sorts of people, who are we know at this present ready to starve for want of it.

Thirdly, it will thereby disburden the commonwealth of a multitude of poor that are likely daily to increase to the infinite trouble and prejudice of the public state.

Fourth, it will be a marvellous increase to our navigation and a most excellent opportunity for the breeding of mariners...

Fifthly, the clime being so temperate and healthful as it is, it will doubtless afford in short time a notable vent for our cloth...

Sixthly, we shall be able to furnish ourselves out of our own territories with many of those commodities that now we are beholding to our neighbours for, as namely: pitch, tar, rosin, flax, hemp, masts, deals, spruce and other

[11] Charles Deane, 'Records of the Council for New England', A.A.S. *Proceedings* (1867), pp. 51–131; A.A.S. *Proceedings* (1876), pp. 49–63; Clarence S. Brigham, 'The records of the Council for New England', A.A.S. *Proceedings*, n.s. 22 (1912), pp. 237–47. The classic statement of Hakluyt's position is his 'Discourse of western planting', in Taylor (ed.), *Original Writings and Correspondence*, vol. 2, pp. 233–9.
[12] A.A.S. MSS. 'Records of the Council for New England 1622–23', pp. 2, 37–8.
[13] *Ibid.*, p. 27.

timber of all sorts, salt and wine...besides madder, woad and many other dyeing roots, stuffs and grains, as also several rich furs, together with one of the best fishings in the known parts of the world, and sundry sorts of apothecary drugs not yet spoken of.

Seventhly...the difficulty of the enterprise...is in a manner already past...

Eighthly, the soil being so fertile and the clime so healthful, with what content shall the particular person employ himself there when he shall find that for £12 10s. adventure he shall be made lord of 200 acres of land, to him and his heirs forever...

Ninthly, if he be a gentleman...who hath no great stock to continue his reputation here at home, how happy shall he be if he can make but a matter of one or two hundred pounds providently employed...wherewith he shall not only be able to live without scorn of his maligners but in a plentiful and worthy manner, with assurance to leave good fortunes to his posterity...

Tenthly...so may the county not only frame themselves to relieve the state of their poorer sort of people but find worthy employment for many younger brothers that now are ruined for want thereof.

Lastly and above all the rest...a special occasion and means...to settle the Christian faith in those heathenish and desert parts of the world...[14]

These were traditional arguments that drew heavily on the Elizabethan writings of Richard Hakluyt and the more recent work of Captain John Smith. They were inspired by the view that colonization was a public project, conducted for the benefit of king and commonwealth, and requiring the co-operation of central and local government to make it work. Recruitment for New England, according to this philosophy, would be co-ordinated by the county Lieutenants and magistrates, rather than by private networks or local congregations.[15] When the Council for New England was revived in the 1630s it again proposed turning the county Lieutenants into recruiters, 'setting forth their poorer sort of people to New England'.[16]

Christopher Levett's plans of 1628 similarly involved royal letters patent and the machinery of ecclesiastical government to promote New England. Writing almost on the eve of the 'great migration', Levett argued that New England was no place for a man with a wife and small children. Rather, he envisaged a company-controlled settlement, a factory rather than a town, manned by indentured workmen on short-term contracts. These company employees or servants would send back the fruits of their labour to the homeland to which they themselves would ultimately return. Based on commercial fishing, shipping and timber, such a colony

[14] H.M.C., *Report on the Records of the City of Exeter* (London, 1916), pp. 166–9.
[15] *Calendar of State Papers, Colonial Series, 1574–1660*, pp. 54–5. Richard Eburne similarly expected the government to take the initiative; see *A Plain Pathway to Plantations (1624)*, ed. Louis B. Wright (Ithaca, N.Y., 1962), pp. 74–6.
[16] Deane, 'Records of the Council for New England', p. 111.

would provide employment, generate wealth and add to the power and prestige of the king of England. Invoking one of the classic Elizabethan justifications for activity in America, Levett had also claimed in 1625, at a time of renewed hostilities, that a naval base in New England would 'do more hurt to the king of Spain and his West Indies than all England besides'.[17]

The leaders of the Massachusetts Bay Company shared some of these ideas when they developed their outpost at Salem between 1628 and 1630. Establishing order, securing supplies and developing a source of revenue naturally took precedence over ideological or religious considerations. Seeking the Lord was a luxury to be afforded only after safety and sustenance were secured. Company officers circulated a plan in 1629 to raise £10,000 by subscription, 'wherewith might be transported two hundred carpenters, masons, smiths, coopers, turners, brickburners, potters, husbandmen, fowlers, vignerons, saltmakers, fishermen, and other labourers, one hundred kine and bulls, twenty-five horse and mares, by whose labours in three years space may be provided at least for a thousand persons dwellings and means of livelihood beside'.[18] These workmen would go over, under company supervision, to establish the infrastructure for subsequent migrants. As an all-male outpost, strictly controlled from London, the first plantation recalled earlier pioneer settlements at Roanoke, Sagadahoc and Jamestown, and was strongly infused with the ideas of the Council for New England. Early Salem was a company town in a potentially hostile environment, subject to company discipline and dedicated to the dream of profit as well as the work of the Lord. While hoping for settlers of good character, the organizers knew that they might be dealing with a rough lot of mariners, fishermen and adventurers. They understood, too, that such men were vital to the initial success of the enterprise.[19] In this lay the seed of future problems.

During the spring of 1629 the Massachusetts Bay Company set about selecting the workmen it needed to establish its new American outpost. The company's official correspondence dealt with projects for making salt and planting vines, collecting furs, setting up iron

[17] James Phinney Baxter, *Christopher Levett of York, the Pioneer Colonist in Casco Bay* (Portland, Maine, 1893), pp. 128–39, 52. Hostility to Spain also drew Puritan aristocrats like the Earl of Warwick in favour of American colonization, though not necessarily in New England; William Hunt, *The Puritan Moment: The Coming of Revolution in an English County* (Cambridge, Mass., 1983), pp. 172, 265.

[18] *Winthrop Papers*, vol. 2, p. 147.

[19] 'The Company's first general letter of instructions to Endecott and his Council', April 1629, in *Chronicles*, pp. 157–8.

mines, and exploiting New England's vast timber reserves.[20] The leaders needed specialist craftsmen, and set out to recruit them through their various contacts. John Endecott had the idea that Frenchmen would be especially useful for certain technical tasks, but the company was unable to find any. 'We have inquired diligently for such, but cannot meet with any of that nation. Nevertheless, God hath not left us altogether unprovided of a man able to undertake that work; for that we have entertained Mr. Thomas Graves, a man commended to us as well for his honesty as skill in many things very useful.'[21] This was the Thomas Graves whose letter in praise of the territory was appended to Higginson's *New-Englands Plantation*. Other specialists recruited to perform particular tasks included the huntsman 'Richard Waterman, whose chief employment will be to get you good venison ... six shipwrights, of whom Robert Molton is chief ... William Ryall and Thomas Brude [or Brand], coopers and cleavers of timber', and various carpenters, gardeners, husbandmen, a surgeon and three clergymen, including Francis Higginson.[22] Higginson advised his friends in England, 'Of all trades carpenters are most needful, therefore bring as many as you can.'[23]

The first settlers would be men, wholesome in body and character, to clear the land and establish an infrastructure. But 'when some 800 or 1000 families are seated there, the colony will be best filled up with youths and girls, which must be continually drawn over to supply the rooms of men-servants and maid-servants, which will marry away daily and leave their masters destitute'. Careful recruiting would rectify the imbalanced sex ratio and artificial demographic pattern. Early settlers would include 'good governors, able ministers, physicians, soldiers, schoolmasters, mariners and mechanics of all sorts', augmented by such 'handicraftsmen, as shoemakers, tailors, nay masons, carpenters and the like'.[24] Elaborating the list of 'what men be most fit for these plantations', William Wood called for husbandmen, carpenters, joiners, coopers, brickmakers, tilers, smiths, leather-dressers, gardeners, tailors, fishermen and fowlers. New England would provide opportunities for all.[25]

---

[20] *Ibid.*, pp. 152–67; *Mass. Recs.*, vol. 1, pp. 24–40, 383–5.
[21] *Chronicles*, pp. 152–3.
[22] *Ibid.*, pp. 152–3; *Mass. Recs.*, vol. 1, pp. 27–37.
[23] Higginson's letter in Thomas Hutchinson, *The Hutchinson Papers: A Collection of Original Papers Relative to the History of ... Massachusetts*, 2 vols. (Boston, 1865), vol. 1, p. 53.
[24] John White, 'The planters plea', in M.H.S. *The Founding of Massachusetts* (Boston, 1930), pp. 183, 168, 157.
[25] William Wood, *New England's Prospect*, ed. Alden T. Vaughan (Amherst, Mass., 1977), pp. 72–3.

After 1630 the emphasis shifted firmly in favour of a residential and agricultural settlement, peopled by free migrants and their families as well as by company employees. Extractive industries and commercial activities would figure in the balance, but New England could now be envisaged as a place of permanent habitation, needing carpenters to shape houses and craftsmen to replicate the material features of English village life. A demographically diverse colony such as this would require a more flexible mode of recruitment.

Under the leadership of Massachusetts Bay, however, New England was to be a colony with a difference. It would be properly furnished with all the requisite occupations for life and profit on the frontier, but it would also shine as a model of godly devotion and moral rectitude. The Massachusetts Bay Company wanted 'persons of worth and quality' to settle in New England to offset the poor and the disreputable. This was one of the reasons they advanced for transferring the Massachusetts charter across the ocean, as if the document itself would serve to lure respectable migrants.[26] The ideal migrant, as Thomas Dudley imagined him in 1631, would be 'endued with grace and furnished with means', combining spiritual and material resources. 'Godly men' would be welcomed, 'but they must not be of the poorer sort yet.'[27]

Bearing in mind the disciplinary problems of Virginia and Plymouth, the leaders of Massachusetts attempted to set strict standards for screening their colonial population. John White reviewed the old arguments, stretching back to Hakluyt, and recommended a vigilant quality control. 'It seems to be a common and gross error,' he wrote, 'that colonies ought to be emunctories or sinks of states, to drain away their filth.' Instead of 'men nourished up in idleness, unconstant, and affecting novelties, unwilling, stubborn and inclined to faction, covetous, luxurious, prodigal, and generally men habituated to any gross evil', the Massachusetts recruiters should look for people who were 'willing, constant, industrious, obedient, frugal, lovers of the common good, or at least such as may be easily wrought to this temper'.[28] New England would attempt to find, or make, men in the image of the saints.

The Massachusetts Bay Company considered the moral character and religious disposition of its servants to be at least as important as

---

[26] *Mass. Recs.*, vol. 1, p. 49.
[27] Dudley's letter in *Chronicles*, pp. 324–5. In a letter of July 1630 John Winthrop expressed similar concerns about screening out the poorer sort of migrant; *Winthrop Papers*, vol. 2, p. 306.
[28] White, 'Planters plea', p. 168.

their occupational ability. Company employees were subject to moral and religious screening. John Betts was to be inquired of, for example, 'not only of his ability, but of his deportment in his life and conversation'. A French physician came with 'good commendations both of his sufficiency and of his godly life and conversation'.[29] However, the company could never guarantee that the recruits would live up to expectations. Although they sought 'honest and able servants' for Massachusetts, they feared that 'too many are addicted' to swearing and other vices.[30]

Writing in 1629 with instructions and advice about a recent shipment of workers, the company hoped Governor Endecott would 'find many religious, discreet and well-ordered persons' among them. However, 'amongst such a number, notwithstanding our care to purge them, there may still remain some libertines'.[31] The problem lay both in the difficulties of recruiting and screening in England and in the bad examples already waiting in America. The rival Council for New England had never been very scrupulous in its screening of emigrants, while interlopers were often of an unsavoury character. Newcomers to Massachusetts complained of 'the prophane and dissolute living of divers of our nation', and found irregular traders and squatters on the Bay Company's land.[32] Plymouth Colony had struggled against reprobates for almost a decade, and the struggle was by no means won.

≈≈≈≈≈≈≈

John Winthrop spent much of the autumn and winter of 1629-30 recruiting the party who would emigrate with him to Massachusetts in the following spring. He directed this effort from London, employing family members and associates in the provinces, especially his eldest son. In October 1629, Winthrop dispatched 'all the late news from New England' to his family in Suffolk. 'I would have some of you read it to your mother,' he told John, Jr., 'and let Forth copy out the observations from the [☞], and the letter in the end, and show it [to] Mr. Motte and others that intend this voyage.' Winthrop distributed letters to 'others that have a mind to New England', urging them

[29] *Mass. Recs.*, vol. 1, p. 49.
[30] *Ibid.*, p. 406; *Chronicles*, p. 189
[31] *Mass. Recs.*, vol. 1, p. 393; *Chronicles*, p. 158.
[32] *Mass. Recs.*, vol. 1, p. 48. Throughout the seventeenth century the idea lingered that people and natural species alike were likely to degenerate in raw American conditions, away from the influence of civilization. See, for example, Cotton Mather, *Things for a Distress'd People to Think Upon* (Boston, 1696), p. 14.

'to read seriously over' the encouraging reports from Massachusetts. Circulating in manuscript and carried enthusiastically by word of mouth, Higginson's rosy 'True Relation' was finding its audience even before it appeared in print.[33]

The Winthrops' circle of associates and retainers, kinsmen and friends, operated as one of the primary pools for recruitment to New England throughout the 1630s. Providing a place in the New England expedition was treated like any other exercise of patronage. Friends, neighbours, kinsmen, tenants, servants and dependents were invited to join in. The family cast its net and considered the claims and merits of all it drew.

Though still busy in London, John Winthrop became increasingly responsible for the recruiting and vetting of prospective migrants from East Anglia. On 20 October 1629 Winthrop instructed, 'Let John enquire out two or three carpenters, and know how many of our neighbours will go, that we may provide ships for them.' On 12 November, 'Let John speak with Cole the constable of Boxford and tell him that I have gotten a place for his kinsman with Sir Richard Saltonstall, who will entertain him presently if he will come up.'[34] John Sampson wrote to Winthrop from Suffolk on 12 January 1630, 'I was willing my son Samuel should go the voyage with you upon the writing you showed me at your house.' A few days later John Winthrop, Jr., reported from the family home at Groton, 'Here was today a youth from Halstead to be entertained for New England.'[35]

About the same time Nathaniel Ward, rector of Stondon Massey in Essex, petitioned Winthrop on behalf of some deserving parishioners. 'I entreat you to reserve room and passage in your ships for two families, a carpenter and a bricklayer, the most faithful and diligent workmen in all our parts. One of them hath put off a good farm this week and sold all, and should be much damaged and discouraged if he finds no place amongst you; he transports himself at his own charge. There is also a pair of sawyers also specially laborious. All of them will come to you upon Monday or Tuesday; I pray let them discern your hearty desire of their company.'[36] Ward himself would move to Massachusetts three years later.

The Winthrops served as counsellors as well as recruiters for emigrants to New England. Some prospective migrants had difficulty reaching their decision, and then a hard time keeping to it. Thomas

[33] *Winthrop Papers*, vol. 2, pp. 156–7.
[34] *Ibid.*, pp. 161, 168, 185.
[35] *Ibid.*, p. 194.
[36] *Ibid.*, p. 192.

Motte, for example, was one well-wishing associate of the Winthrops who never made the voyage to New England. In 1629 he announced, 'My mind stands inclinable, though I hear of great rubs in the way ...I have many doubts and questions in the which I desire to be resolved.'[37] Samuel Borrowes wrote to Winthrop from Colchester about James Boosey, 'a friend of mine, that is willing to go this voyage for New England. He hath been inclined to that voyage a great while, but he came not to me with a resolution for to go till this morning ...and he desired me to write to you for to enter his name and his wife's'. Three weeks later Boosey had changed his mind. His friend wrote in embarrassment to Winthrop.

I am very sorry that I did meddle in the business about sending to your worship for them; had I thought that he would have proved so unconstant he should have writ himself. He tells me the reason he cannot go this voyage is that he had sold his commodities, and the party tells him since that he will not have them except he will stay for his money till after Michaelmas.

Boosey finally arrived in New England in 1635.[38]

The network expanded through East Anglia and beyond. James Woodyeates and his wife, who crossed over to Massachusetts in 1633 bearing a letter to Governor Winthrop from his kinsman by marriage Henry Paynter, were both former servants to Paynter and were already known to some settlers in New England.[39] A group of emigrants from Derbyshire in 1636 were recommended by their neighbour Edward Revell, who had been clerk to Winthrop's colleague Brampton Gurdon, and who may have been kinsman to John Revell, an early participant in Massachusetts affairs.[40] Edward Howes, John Winthrop, Jr.'s friend in London, recommended John Sandbrooke, a young lawyer's clerk, 'brother to Sarah, your sister Feke's maid'.[41] Robert Reyce, John Winthrop's old friend in Suffolk, was responsible for directing John Fiske to the colonies. Philip Forth, Winthrop's cousin through his first wife Mary Forth, recommended the son of a neighbour and kinsman, 'of an honest, plain and religious disposition'.[42] Robert Stansby, a Puritan minister in Suffolk, looked to New England not for himself but for his nephew, and not so much as a religious refuge as a place to work. He wrote to John Winthrop about the young man, 'He is both willing and able to work in husbandry, al-

---

[37] *Ibid.*, p. 97.
[38] *Ibid.*, pp. 184, 195; Savage, *Genealogical Dictionary*, vol. 1, p. 211.
[39] *Winthrop Papers*, vol. 3, pp. 109–10.
[40] *Ibid.*, p. 252.
[41] *Ibid.*, p. 132.
[42] *Ibid.*, pp. 394–5.

though he have been lately a clothier.'[43] And so the pool of prospective migrants expanded.

Nor was Winthrop alone in directing the campaign of promotion and recruiting. Proposals concerning New England circulated much farther afield than the lanes between London and Suffolk. Each of the assistants and officers of the Massachusetts Bay Company worked through their networks of friends and colleagues to spread the word and secure commitments. Throughout the British Isles there were pockets of people with an interest in the outpost at Salem and the expanding settlements in Massachusetts. Some had heard the pitch from the pulpit, whereas others possessed direct information from letters or by word of mouth. Godly congregations in Leicestershire and Lancashire had discussed the matter before the end of 1629, sending to London 'a dozen or thirteen queries which have been answered'.[44]

Francis Higginson, quick off the mark, advised his friends in Leicestershire to join him in New England. 'First, if you linger too long, the passages of Jordan through the malice of Satan may be stopped, that you cannot come if you would. Secondly, those that come first speed best here and have the privilege of choosing choice places of habitations.'[45] This was a compelling mixture of material and ideological incentives. Richard Saltonstall wrote home from Massachusetts in 1632 urging Emmanuel Downing,

Good sir, encourage men to come over. If gentlemen of ability would transport themselves they might advance their own estates, and might improve their talents and times in being worthy instruments of propagating the gospel to these poor barbarous people. I pray you send over by some of your east country merchants to get some few master workmen for the ordering of our potash work.[46]

Another glimpse of the recruiting process is provided in the Massachusetts Bay Company's introductions of

Richard Ewstead, a wheelwright, who was commended to us by Mr. Davenport for a very able man, though not without his imperfections... Richard Claydon, a wheelwright, recommended unto us by Dr. Wells to be both a good and painful workman and of an orderly life and conversation... Richard Haward and Richard Inkersall, both Bedfordshire men, hired for the Company with their families... Thomas Beard, a shoemaker, and Isaac Rickman, being both recommended to us by Mr. Simon Whetcombe.[47]

[43] *Ibid.*, p. 381.
[44] *Winthrop Papers*, vol. 2, p. 178.
[45] *Hutchinson Papers*, vol. 1, p. 52.
[46] H.M.C., *Twelfth Report*, pt. 1 (London, 1888), p. 449.
[47] The company's letters to Endecott, April and May 1629, in *Chronicles*, pp. 165, 177, 178, 186. Davenport was the Puritan minister at St. Stephen's, Coleman Street, and

Long-distance arrangements conducted by third parties did not always produce efficient results, particularly when the principals could not agree about terms and disbursements. It was to deal with such problems, among others, that Emmanuel Downing urged John Winthrop, Jr., to return to England for a visit in 1633, 'which would be a means to encourage some to remove hence to your plantation'.[48]

Men who had actually lived in New England, and who intended to go back there, often proved to be effective recruiting agents. John Wilson, the Suffolk clergyman who was one of the first settlers of Boston, made two return visits to England in the 1630s to meet with prospective migrants. Back home, according to Edward Johnson, 'Clothed in a countryman's habit, passing from place to place, [Wilson] declared to the people of God what great works Christ had already done for his people in New England, which made many Christian souls long to see these admirable acts of Christ.' Wilson may have been effective in soliciting the wavering godly, but he failed to persuade his own wife to join him in New England.[49] By the early 1640s, however, these combined efforts had drawn more than 20,000 men, women and children to New England.[50]

≈≈≈≈≈

Migration to New England continued throughout the second half of the seventeenth century, but with neither the volume nor the celebrity of the pre-civil war generation. A trickle of emigration from England continued, with most ships on the Atlantic taking with them a small complement of passengers. Some of the newcomers were related to established colonial families, some were New Englanders returning from a sojourn in England, some were imported as servants, while others were drawn by the same mixture of religious, financial and personal motives as the migrants of the 1630s.

A few of the New Englanders who had invested their careers in the

a future migrant to New England; Whetcombe was a London clothier with family and mercantile connections in Dorset, an investor in the New England Company and an assistant of the Massachusetts Bay Company. 'Dr. Wells' was most likely Thomas Weld (sometimes written Wells), the anti-Laudian vicar of Terling, and a Massachusetts migrant of 1632, here given a courtesy title beyond his degree.

[48] *Winthrop Papers*, vol. 3, p. 129.

[49] *Wonder-Working Providence*, pp. 84, 104, 142.

[50] Johnson estimated that some 21,200 men, women and children, 'as near as at present can be gathered', crossed over to New England 'to the year 1643'. They arrived in 198 ships, at a total passage cost of £95,000; *Wonder-Working Providence*, pp. 54, 61, 58. Johnson apparently had access to Winthrop's journal, and to other official and semi-official records of the colony.

Cromwellian revolution returned to the quiet of New England after their defeat in 1660. Samuel Maverick reported to Clarendon soon after the Restoration that 'many seditious factious persons' were preparing to leave for New England. Already, he noted, 'Above one hundred ... are gone hence in discontent,' while 'there are some hundreds intend for that place with their families this year ... five ships are already designed.' Among the first to flee were the regicides William Goffe and Edward Whalley.[51]

John Hull noted the arrival at Boston of the *Charles* with eighty passengers from London in July 1661, and later noted the arrival of the *Untried* and the *Society*, 'laden with goods and passengers'.[52] In June 1662 John Davenport noted that 'forty passengers are come', and 'Captain Pierce is coming with two or three hundred passengers' from England.[53]

A few dissenting congregations in England reported to their New England friends in 1662 'a desire to come into this country if they may have any encouragement from hence.' Dr. Thomas Goodwin, ousted president of Magdalene College, Oxford, was among those who 'had come over now if his wife had not opposed it'.[54] However, scant encouragement was forthcoming. Most English dissenters in the Restoration period preferred to stay put, seeing little of advantage for them in America.

A new flurry of interest in New England stirred among the dissenting community towards the end of Charles II's reign, but once again little came of it. Increase Mather's brother Nathaniel, a leading light among dissenters in Ireland, actively dissuaded his co-religionists from emigration. One of them, Andrew Jackson, reported to the Boston minister in 1683, 'Your brother Mr. Mather with us doth much cross the designs that many has of coming to your parts ... because he looks upon it as a deserting of the cause, and truly I am of his mind.'[55]

Despite their 'inclinations' towards emigration, Increase Mather's English correspondents usually found themselves 'delayed by Provi-

---

[51] 'The Clarendon papers', *Collections of the New York Historical Society, 1869* (New York, 1870), pp. 30–3, 46.

[52] (Hull), 'The diaries of John Hull', A.A.S., *Transactions*, 3 (1857), pp. 203, 204, 209.

[53] Isabel MacBeath Calder (ed.), *Letters of John Davenport* (New Haven, Conn., 1937), p. 198.

[54] *Ibid.* Goodwin sent a message on behalf of 'many men of considerable quality and estate, who have a desire to come into this country if they may have any encouragement from hence'. *Cf.* Mary Eldred's letter of 1668, Massachusetts Archives, vol. 57, p. 52, discussed in chapter 11, this volume.

[55] Boston Public Library MS. Am. 1502/5/11–12.

dence'.[56] The call was not clear. They were further stayed by the promise of toleration under James II, and then by the new political climate of the Glorious Revolution, as well as expanding business opportunities in Great Britain.[57] Young Homer Jackson was one who migrated in 1683, with motives and circumstances as complicated as those of any migrant of the 1630s.

> He was bred a scholar, but by reason of his too active spirit rendering him somewhat averse to a contemplative kind of life, and more inclinable to action, the discouragements also which lies upon the dissenting party weighing too much with unpoised spirits, he hath now resolved to go abroad the world, and see what may offer in a way with trade.[58]

Another prospective migrant, Daniel Hemingway, the Lancashire draper, was primed for New England in 1686 but changed his mind after the Declaration of Indulgence in 1687.[59]

As in the previous generation, the newcomers to New England in the second half of the seventeenth century were a motley crew who included scoundrels and opportunists as well as the people of God. Some lighted there to evade their creditors, or at least to slow the process of debt collection. Thomas Hales, for example, younger son of Sir Edward Hales, 'being extravagant went over to New England' in the 1670s, where he got into further financial difficulties. John Hull, who made the mistake of dealing with him, remarked, 'I had better have laid out my money here and run the adventure of sea and market than of such a slippery gentleman.'[60] On board the *Susannah and Thomas*, which reached Boston in 1685, were thirty passengers who were, according to a fellow-passenger, 'flying for safety upon the rout at Sedgemoor' after Monmouth's unsuccessful rebellion.[61]

A significant proportion of the settlers of New England came over as servants. Servants are strongly associated with the southern colonies, but little attention has been paid to their presence in New England.

---

[56] E.g. John Bailey to Increase Mather, June 1683, in 'Mather papers', M.H.S. *Collections*, ser. 4, vol. 8 (1868), p. 492.
[57] *Ibid.*, pp. 486–9.
[58] *Ibid.*, p. 42; Boston Public Library MS. Am. 1502/5/11–12.
[59] 'Mather papers', pp. 657–9.
[60] A.A.S. MSS. 'Letter book of John Hull', p. 436.
[61] John Dunton, *The Life and Errors of John Dunton* (London, 1818), p. 86. Dunton should only be read in light of the criticisms in Chester Noyes Greenough, 'John Dunton's letters from New England', *Publications of the Colonial Society of Massachusetts*, 14 (1911–13), pp. 222–56.

This section attempts to bring them into fresh focus. The free plant-ers, who paid their own transportation and earned an independent living in New England, often brought servants with them as members of their households. Other servants came over bound to serve the company, or a particular master, engaged for a specific task and term of years. John Winthrop wrote in 1630 that the colony needed 'but few servants, and those useful ones',[62] but a moderate demand for bound labour persisted through most of the seventeenth century.[63] There was plenty of work to be done. Substantial planters were ac-customed to having servants, and other landowning settlers needed servants or employees to work on their property. In this respect they were following established English customs. As many as 25 per cent of the working population of old England were servants, and the proportion in New England was probably no lower.[64]

A trade in servants arose, in which people were delivered to New England as human merchandise at no financial charge to themselves. Although they were outnumbered by the swarms of servants who shipped to other colonial destinations, servants formed a significant part of the early New England community.[65] Hired more for their labour than their religion, the servants contributed to the economic prosperity of the region and added to its social and cultural diversity as well. Servants were often at the centre of New England's moral and disciplinary problems.

Servants in New England could be field workers, domestic servants, or specialist artisans who worked exclusively for one employer. Usu-ally they served for three or four years, though sometimes more than twice that time. Women might be engaged in dairying, washing and housework, men in agriculture, metal work or other trades. In ex-change for their labour they received either room and board 'all found', or wages in lieu. Masters were responsible for their servants' clothing, diet, welfare, behaviour and education. Their terms and conditions of employment, and rights of redress when things went

---

[62] *Winthrop Papers*, vol. 2, p. 306.
[63] *Winthrop's Journal*, vol. 1, p. 112; David Galenson, *White Servitude in Colonial America: An Economic Analysis* (Cambridge, 1981), p. 126.
[64] Peter Laslett, *The World We Have Lost, Further Explored* (London, 1983), pp. 13–16; and Ann Kussmaul, *Servants in Husbandry in Early Modern England* (Cambridge, 1981), pp. 135–42.
[65] Galenson, *White Servitude*, pp. 82–6, 220–1; Richard S. Dunn, 'Servants and slaves: the recruitment and employment of labor', in Jack P. Greene and J. R. Pole (eds.), *Colonial British America: Essays in the New History of the Early Modern Era* (Baltimore, 1984), p. 160. See also Abbot Emerson Smith, *Colonists in Bondage: White Servitude and Convict Labor in America 1607–1776* (New York, 1971), pp. 3–86.

wrong, were based on English law and precedent, suitably modified to the colonial situation.[66]

Many servants, when they crossed the Atlantic, were attached to migrant households, but others were little more than cargo. Their sponsors clothed them, fed them, paid for their transportation, and either profited from the sale of servant indentures in America or employed them directly. Wealthy colonists paid to bring over prospective employees; English merchants recruited servants for export; the New England courts assigned unattached young men and women to suitable masters, and corrected them when they went astray.[67]

Most of these servants were young people, but a few were middle-aged or older, and some even had families of their own. Most New England servants lived in their masters' households, as did servants in old England, but again, a few appear to have had separate residences. In this respect they differed from the adolescent house servants and servants in husbandry, so familiar in England. Nor were they quite comparable to the indentured servants who populated Virginia, Maryland and Barbados. Their function was not primarily to bring in a crop, as plantation labour, but rather to assist their employers in a multitude of economic tasks. Amenable servants were sometimes exchanged between members of the colonial elite as favours. John Haynes of Connecticut gave John Winthrop, Jr., 'a widow woman of about forty, came from Ireland but was brought up with the English'. He particularly commended this servant for her 'care, pains and skill in dairying, washing, and the like'.[68]

Service was not necessarily menial, nor was it exclusively a matter for the poor. Well-connected young Englishmen might engage as New England servants, just as in England they often became apprentices. William Hooke, for example, once a minister in New England who became a preacher to Oliver Cromwell, sent his son Ebenezer to serve as a four-year servant in New England in 1658.[69] Servants in New England were dispersed through the settlements and diversified through the economy. They included poor youths glad of the op-

---

[66] Thomas G. Barnes (ed.), *The Book of the General Lawes and Libertyes Concerning the Inhabitants of the Massachusets* (1648, facsimile, San Marino, Calif., 1975), pp. 38–9. For examples of letters setting out terms of service, see *Winthrop Papers*, vol. 3, pp. 125, 126. Cf. Kussmaul, *Servants in Husbandry*, pp. 31–5.

[67] Charles J. Hoadly (ed.), *Records of the Colony and Plantation of New Haven, 1638–49* (Hartford, Conn., 1857), p. 60; *Essex Courts*, vol. 2, pp. 294–5; Smith, *Colonists in Bondage*, pp. 207–25.

[68] M.H.S. *Collections*, ser. 4, vol. 7 (1865), p. 465.

[69] *Ibid.*, p. 594.

portunity to better themselves and established craftsmen only waiting
to set up again as independent householders. Some probably had
faint idea what was happening to them. What they had in common
was the temporary forfeit of their freedom in exchange for passage
and employment in the New World.

The Winthrop papers provide rare glimpses of the recruiting of
servants for New England. John Winthrop, Jr., canvassed his friends
and acquaintances throughout the British Isles to help find suitable
colonists for New England, including servants. In addition to independent migrants who would pay their own way, Winthrop was looking for 'boys and young maids of good towardness' who would serve
as bound labour.[70] Some servants were engaged at the last minute, to
fill up space on the ship. In April 1630, for example, Edward Howes
informed John Winthrop, Jr., that the *Thomas and William* was loading
in London, bound for New England. 'If you know of any sturdy youths
that will go servants for six or seven year, they may now have entertainment of Mr. Hewson, or any other that will go at their own charge,
there is room in the ship.'[71]

In 1633 Edward Howes took pains to describe for John Winthrop,
Jr., the promising quality of one of the servants he was dispatching,
an Irish Catholic boy engaged for five years to look after the dogs.
'This is a very tractable fellow, and yet of a hardy and stout courage;
I am persuaded he is very honest . . . The fellow can read and write
reasonable well, which is somewhat rare for one of his condition, and
makes me hope the more of him.'[72] Robert Barrington sent over
servants to New England 'for the use of the common stock', and later
engaged servants for his own family's use. Other prominent supporters of Massachusetts dispatched their own servants as agents to
secure a share of New England's wealth. Sir Mathew Boynton, for
example, sent over servants 'to preserve the increase of my cattle'.
His consignment in 1636 included 'two servants, ten ewe sheep and
a ram'.[73] The servants were to look after the beasts, but since Sir
Mathew remained in London who would look after his men? Boynton
asked John Winthrop, Jr., to watch out, observing, 'You know what
need there is that servants should have eyes over them, especially
when they are at so far a distance from their master.' The good Sir
Mathew sent his servants with 'a year's wages beforehand', paid their

---

[70] *Winthrop Papers*, vol. 3, p. 126.
[71] *Winthrop Papers*, vol. 2, p. 297.
[72] *Winthrop Papers*, vol. 3, p. 134.
[73] *Ibid.*, pp. 208, 211, 247.

passage, and was even willing to pay their passage back to England at the end of their contract if they wished to return.[74]

Finding the right people and persuading them to cross the ocean was no easy matter. In 1633 Thomas Gostlin, a Winthrop kinsman in Suffolk, replied to John Winthrop, Jr., in New England, 'concerning the men servants that you write to me for to send you, which were two carpenters or one carpenter and the other a husbandman'. The recruiting was not going well, Gostlin continued, 'for carpenters I could get none, nor husbandmen such as were fit for you, but as for maids and a girl I could have sent you enough if my brother Downing would have paid for their passage, and therefore I have sent you but one'.[75] This was to be a common complaint, since few young people could be induced to leave their homeland, and those who were willing usually chose destinations other than New England.

Henry Jacie, a Puritan minister in Yorkshire, managed to locate 'some few' prospective servants in 1633, including a widow and her daughters, but he would not send them to New England without reassurance about their duties and terms of service in the New World. Sensibly enough, these prospective servants refused to budge unless satisfied 'what should be the wages, and for how many years tied, whether apparel found, who should provide for their shipping over, their journey thither, their diet while they stay for the wind or ships setting forth, and provision in the ship besides ship diet'.[76] These conditions were all open to negotiation and all could be subject to dispute.

Servants who were both suitable and willing were perennially hard to find. Robert Barrington, Edward Hopkins and Philip Nye – Puritan associates of John Winthrop, Jr., in London and Essex – dispatched further shipments of servants to Massachusetts in 1635 'for the use of the common stock'. Philip Nye apologized, 'We have sent you some servants but not so many as we purposed.'[77] Passengers on the *Bachelor* of that year included a dozen servants for Winthrop to dispose of as he saw fit. The *Bachelor* was a tiny bark of twenty-five tons, so the journey must have been miserable.[78]

Robert Keayne, a Boston merchant, reported in 1637 that his agents in England had found him 'a very good husbandman and his wife . . .

---

[74] *Ibid.*, pp. 247, 389.
[75] *Ibid.*, pp. 124–5.
[76] *Ibid.*, p. 126.
[77] *Ibid.*, pp. 208, 210, 211.
[78] For the *Bachelor* see *Winthrop Papers*, vol. 3, pp. 203–6.

for whom I have sent letters to come this next summer'.[79] Other merchants like John Tinker conducted more of a bulk trade. In 1640 Tinker shipped 'divers servants and goods to the value of £560' from London, with instructions to John Winthrop, Jr., 'so soon as my servants and other passengers that I am allied unto are landed, to let one of your servants provide some lodging for them at some of the neighbours' houses, and I shall give good satisfaction, until such time as they shall be disposed of.'[80] These servants were recruited in England, dispatched as a cargo, and then assigned to their new colonial masters by the ship's captain or by the undertaker's factors. Few of them made much mark on Massachusetts history unless they got into trouble or got religion.

In keeping with the old Elizabethan idea that colonies could serve as dumping grounds for the unwanted, the revolutionary government of the 1650s sent victims of its Scottish and Irish campaigns as involuntary servants to New England. In 1651 the *John and Sarah* left London with 272 Scottish redemptioners, destined for service in New England.[81] The government of Oliver Cromwell sent over shiploads of 'Irish youths' to be bound servants in New England in 1654.[82] These, however, should not be taken as typical, any more than the notorious 'rogues, whores and vagabonds' were typical of other transatlantic migrant streams.[83]

Some servants were sponsored by governments or philanthropic organizations, though most came over as a result of the efforts of private individuals. Among those arriving on one ship in the 1640s were 'twenty children and some other passengers out of England . . . and those children, with many more to come after, were sent by money given one fast day in London, and allowed by the Parliament and City for that purpose'.[84] These children would be taken up by colonial masters for terms of four to nine years, depending on their age. Others were sent by such groups as the Corporation for the Propagation of the Gospel in New England, which raised money to ship 'poor children' across the ocean. The corporation accounts for 1647 report £799 3s. 3d. 'laid out for the children's transportation', enough

---

[79] *Ibid.*, p. 519.
[80] *Winthrop Papers*, vol. 4, p. 251.
[81] William B. Trask (ed.), *Suffolk Deeds* (Boston, 1880–1906), vol. 1, nos. 5, 6.
[82] *Essex Courts*, vol. 2, p. 295.
[83] David Souden, ' "Rogues, whores and vagabonds": indentured servant emigrants to North America', *Social History*, 3 (1978), pp. 23–41.
[84] *Winthrop's Journal*, vol. 2, p. 96.

for 160 passengers.[85] The sponsored migration of servants to New England continued sporadically throughout the seventeenth century, though never so well organized as during the 1640s and 1650s.

George Cole, mayor of Dorchester, England, recruited young people 'who are at the charge of the town maintained', and sent them to business associates in New England after the Restoration. His shipment of 1664 included boys and girls on eight- or nine-year contracts.[86] John Hull of Boston took advantage of a visit home to England in 1662 to recruit some youngsters for service in New England. Congratulating himself on the deal, he wrote in his diary about 'several children I brought over, and all in health, and so disposed of them', except for one who was unfortunately drowned on the way.[87] Such accidents ate into the godly merchant's profits. In 1672 a group of dissenting ministers in London wrote to their colleagues in Boston, regarding 'sending of youths over to you for their education, we can say no more than this, but that where we find any inclined so to dispose of their children, we shall not be wanting to encourage it'.[88]

Fragments of correspondence and occasional cases before the Massachusetts courts point to the continuing effort by leading colonial families to find suitable workers in England. Humbler colonists needed servants too, and sometimes asked their friends and kinsmen at home to help find them. John Wollcott of Somerset wrote to his brother Henry in Connecticut in 1639, 'You wrote unto me to send you a labouring man or two and I have spoken unto divers to go,' but without success.[89] The evidence is scattered, but it speaks of a constant low-intensity recruiting drive, as well as repeated frustrations of that end. The chore of finding servants occupied the second and third as well as the first colonial generations, and brought a trickle of young Britons to New England throughout the seventeenth century. This activity also helped keep the idea of New England alive in the English provinces. The Winthrops were by no means the only ones involved in this business.

The Wyllys family of Hartford, Connecticut, for example, drew effectively on its English connections to obtain servants. In 1640 George Wyllys wrote from Bristol to his father in Connecticut, 'I have

[85] Guildhall Library, MS. 7938, 'Papers relating to the proceedings of the Corporation for Propagating the Gospel in New England' (transcript of Bodleian Library, Rawlinson MS. C 934).

[86] Dorset Record Office, B2/16/5, 'Dorchester Corporation minutes', 2 March 1663/4.

[87] 'The diaries of John Hull', *A.A.S. Transactions*, 3 (1857), p. 153.

[88] *Hutchinson Papers*, vol. 2, p. 161.

[89] 'Letter of John Wollcott', *N.E.H.G.R.*, 2 (1848), p. 373.

sent you a man, one Will Vaughan, a tailor, who was commended to me here, and I hope will prove an honest man and good servant.'[90] The following year he dispatched four more servants to New England, at wages of £3 to £4 15s. a year, including one Thomas Bass, who proved to be an exemplary employee. George Wyllys's accounts for 1641 show that he bought these servants clothing, paid five pounds each for their passage, and expended an extra 13s. 6d. for 'cheese, flour and other necessaries that the servants had aboard with them to use by the way'. Two maid servants followed in 1643.[91] George Wyllys, Sr. wrote his son, 'I would have you send me four or six youths such as Thomas Bass and two girls, for such time as I had him or longer. These maids you sent me the last year prove not as yet fit for me; I would have them such as have not been bred idly.' If possible, the servants should know how to read and should come from the Wyllys family's home area of Warwickshire.[92] Local servants from the old country were presumably more trustworthy and more amenable to the demands of their masters.

The Pynchon family of Springfield, Massachusetts, similarly recruited servants through kinsmen in England. In 1672 Joseph Pynchon, a former colonist resettled as a physician at Uxbridge, Middlesex, responded to requests to 'procure' servants for his father and uncle in New England.[93] Samuel Symonds of Ipswich, Massachusetts, also asked his kinsman John Winthrop, Jr., to look out for servants while he was in England in 1661: 'If you could procure a likely boy and girl, about fourteen years old apiece . . . you shall do us a very great courtesy. It is said about Yorkshire, or remote places, they may easily be had.'[94]

The task of recruiting for New England was never easy, especially after the Puritan-led migration of the 1630s came to an end. Samuel Symonds's stepson John Hall, a goldsmith in London, sent Francis Graves over in 1674 as a servant for his mother at Ipswich, Massachusetts, apologizing for the servant's diminutive stature: 'He is little indeed but will be growing; and he is to serve you the longer, viz. five years . . . I have been endeavouring to get a more staunch servant but the age is so corrupt that I can hardly find one honest who is willing

---

[90] 'The Wyllys papers . . . 1590–1796', *Collections of the Connecticut Historical Society*, 21 (1924), p. 11.

[91] *Ibid.*, pp. 17, 41, 52.

[92] *Ibid.*, p. 73.

[93] Carl Bridenbaugh (ed.), *The Pynchon Papers*, vol. 1, *Letters of John Pynchon, 1654–1700* (Boston, 1982), p. 109.

[94] M.H.S. *Collections*, ser. 4, vol. 7 (1865), p. 136.

to pass the seas.'[95] John Hall was apologizing again in 1681, 'I am sorry I could not according to my desire and endeavour as yet get servants for your self, which I fear may prove a matter of difficulty to do.' A year later Hall had still not fulfilled his commission. 'Samuel Eps and myself have been solicitous for a servant for you and much perplexed that as yet we cannot serve you in this matter.'[96] The few servants who were willing to move overseas at this time were much more likely to choose the island colonies or the Chesapeake than cold and troubled New England.

Some servants did not want to be in New England at all. In 1634 John Winthrop faced the problem of Abigail Gifford, a poor widow who, 'being kept at the charge of the parish of Willesden in Middlesex, near London, was sent by Mr. Ball's ship into this country'. Abigail was a reluctant migrant who found no happiness as a servant in Massachusetts. Winthrop found her to be 'sometimes distracted, and a very burdensome woman', and lost little time arranging for her to be shipped back home.[97] Homesickness and personal instability were not the only problems. In 1671 young Robert Collins was enticed onto the *Arabella* with an offer of sea-service at eighteen shillings a month, and an immediate eighteen shillings as soon as he came aboard. The master, one Richard Sprague, 'deluded, spirited [and] ketched' him and attempted to sell him as a servant in New England. Collins resisted, according to witnesses, and when the customs searchers came aboard at Gravesend he declared his unwillingness to go, but to no avail. Some weeks later Robert Collins found himself in Boston harbour and took his story to the Suffolk County Court. Although Sprague countersued, claiming for the expense of feeding the boy and for the cost of his passage, the court found for Collins and set him free.[98]

The New England elite demanded servants, but grieved over them

---

[95] A.A.S. MSS. 'Letters of John Hall', 26 September 1674. Little Francis Graves was later left five pounds in an English kinsman's will, and John Hall wrote again to Massachusetts to find out what had happened to him; 'Letters of John Hall', 29 September 1682. Hall and Graves were distantly connected, young Francis being the nephew of Samuel Hall who was John Hall's friend and 'adopted cousin'. John and Samuel Hall had both previously resided in New England, and used their transatlantic connections to facilitate the informal servant traffic, H. F. Waters, *Genealogical Gleanings in England*, 2 vols. (Boston, 1901), pp. 780–81; Abraham Hammatt, *The Hammatt Papers: the Early Inhabitants of Ipswich, Massachusetts, 1633–1700* (Ipswich, Mass., 1899), p. 360.

[96] 'Letters of John Hall', 30 March 1682.

[97] *Winthrop's Journal*, vol. 1, p. 144.

[98] S. E. Morison (ed.), *Records of the Suffolk County Court 1671–1680* (Boston, 1933), vol. 1, pp. 18–20, 43.

too. Nathaniel Ward of Ipswich, Massachusetts, feared moral contamination from the 'multitudes of idle and profane young men, servants and others, with whom we must leave our children'.[99] Declension set in from the very beginning; indeed it was inherent in the colonial recruiting strategy, and the ill choice of servants was partly to blame. Servants were more likely than free planters to fall into trouble, and to be fined, whipped or stocked for drunkenness, theft or profanity. The New Haven authorities were especially alarmed when servants gathered at night for a rowdy feast of venison pasties and plum cakes, and when a servant confessed that he did not understand prayer.[100]

Among many troubling instances, John Winthrop recorded the case of the unhappy servant in 1633 who, 'being reproved for his lewdness, and put in mind of hell, answered, that if hell were ten times hotter he had rather be there than he would serve his master. The occasion was because he had bound himself for divers years, and saw that if he had been at liberty he might have had greater wages'.[101] One of John Moody's servants at Charlestown, 'in his passion would wish himself in hell, and use desperate words', before eventually being found drowned.[102] News of such incidents inevitably found its way back home across the Atlantic, to mix with other strands of information and opinion about life in the New England colonies.

From the employers' point of view, servants were a valuable investment. Their time represented money, at a rate of £2 or more per year. In an inventory of the ironworks at Lynn, Massachusetts, taken in 1653, the labourers were valued along with the wheelbarrows and furnace equipment. There were thirty-five Scottish servants, 'all valued at £350' or £10 a head, an English boy with four years to serve, worth £8, and another for six years, worth £13.[103]

Disputes and complaints provide another window into the world of servitude in New England. A few examples will illustrate their condition. John Whittingham recruited the brothers Richard and Mathew Coy (aged thirteen and sixteen) in Lincolnshire, lodged them in London, and arranged their shipping to Massachusetts in 1638. He then sold them as servants to William Hubbard of Ipswich. Although the boys agreed (with their mother's consent) to serve for seven years,

---

[99] *Winthrop Papers*, vol. 3, p. 216.
[100] See, for example, Hoadly (ed.), *Records of the Colony and Plantation of New Haven*, pp. 26, 28, 38, 62, 65, 84 and *passim*.
[101] *Winthrop's Journal*, vol. 1, p. 103.
[102] Record Commissioners of the City of Boston, *Sixth Report*, 'Roxbury land and church records' (Boston, 1881), p. 78.
[103] M.H.S. MSS. 'Miscellaneous, bound', 1653.

their New England masters actually extracted more time from them. Richard served ten years and his elder brother eight.[104]

In 1637 Edward Rawson brought Richard Crane to work in Massachusetts making gunpowder. Crane was a specialist craftsman, aged above fifty, and he left his wife and five children in England to fulfil this obligation. Rawson was supposed to pay him four pounds a year, and provide for his wife and children. Three years later, missing his family and aggrieved because his master made him work in agriculture instead of munitions, Crane petitioned the governor for release from his indenture. The document apparently tied him for five years, though Crane protested, 'I am sure I agreed for no more than three.'[105]

John Watkins, a servant brought to New England by Walter Price, had no time to dispute the term of his indenture. He died within seven weeks of landing, much to his master's annoyance. Price petitioned the Essex County Court in 1641 to keep the dead servant's clothing, 'as he had been at charge for Watkins' passage, and had no service of him of value'. The servant's clothing was valued at £5 4s. 10d., which would just about offset the cost of the voyage.[106]

Two of Samuel Symonds's Irish servants, Will Downing and Phillip Welch, decided in 1661 that they had worked long enough and brought suit to be released from their contracts. They told the court, 'We were brought out of our own country, contrary to our own wills and minds, and sold here unto Mr. Symonds by the master of the ship, Mr. Dill,' in 1654. Seven years, they argued (correctly) was longer than the usual term of service in Barbados, though equal to the practice of apprenticeship in England. The court, however, inspected the deed of sale and determined that they still had 'several years yet due'.[107]

Finally, John Gifford, a Massachusetts merchant, induced Henry Dispaw and his son Henry, Jr., both potters of Horsmonden, Kent,

---

[104] *Essex Courts*, vol. 1, pp. 381–2; Richard A. Rutyna, 'Richard Coy of Essex County, 1625–1675: a biographical sketch', *Essex Institute Historical Collections*, 104 (1968), pp. 75–9.

[105] *Winthrop Papers*, vol. 4, pp. 105–6, 238–9. See also the case at New Haven in 1643, in which Margaret Bedford committed fornication and then ran away to get married before her term of service expired; Hoadly (ed.), *Records of the Colony and Plantation of New Haven*, pp. 88, 105.

[106] *Essex Courts*, vol. 1, p. 30. Two servants recruited by John Cogeswell in London in 1653 for delivery to New England found themselves at the centre of a dispute when their master died during the voyage. Cogeswell's heirs and executors disagreed who owned the servants and would use their time; Massachusetts Archives, vol. 39, pp. 527, 418, 493, 516.

[107] *Essex Courts*, vol. 2, pp. 294–5.

to emigrate to New England with their families in 1675. Gifford paid the fares and promised them accommodation and substantial wages in return for six years' exclusive service as potters. Within two years, however, the Dispaws found themselves impoverished, disenchanted and homesick. They petitioned the Essex County Court, if they 'cannot be relieved in their suffering condition, that they be transported back to England at the charge of those who brought them over'. A deal was a deal, though, and the court held the family to its contract.[108] In most of these cases the courts upheld the terms of the written contract or indenture, rather than custom or the servant's own recollection of the agreement.

On completing his term a servant could normally look forward to full membership in the economic community, and perhaps to church membership as well. He could compete for wages and land, although without guarantees of special treatment. An entry in the Boston town records for 1638 indicates how ex-servants might be treated if they were lucky. 'Thomas Pettit, having served with our brother Oliver Mellows this three years and a half, shall have a house plot granted unto him.'[109] Such grants were rare after the first few years of settlement. Most ex-servants lived obscure lives as wage-earners or small landowners, and many no doubt migrated elsewhere or returned to England. A few former servants, like Roger Clap, established themselves as New England patriarchs, but they rarely rose to prominence in the colony as did some of their contemporaries in the Chesapeake.[110]

By the close of the great migration in 1642 approximately 21,000 men, women and children had set out for New England. Besides the celebrated ministers and colonial leaders these migrants included hundreds of servants and 'handicraftsmen of all sorts'.[111] This section examines the occupations of the early planters of New England.

---

[108] *Essex Courts*, vol. 6, p. 82.
[109] Record Commissioners of the City of Boston, *Second Report*, 'Boston town records' (Boston, 1877), p. 22.
[110] 'Roger Clap's memoirs', in *Chronicles*, pp. 346–7, 366–7; Lois Green Carr and Russell R. Menard, 'Immigration and opportunity: the freedman in early colonial Maryland', in Thad W. Tate and David L. Ammerman (eds.), *The Chesapeake in the Seventeenth Century* (New York, 1979), pp. 206–42; Russell R. Menard, 'From servant to freeholder: status mobility and property accumulation in seventeenth-century Maryland', *William and Mary Quarterly*, ser. 3, vol. 30 (1973), pp. 37–64.
[111] *Wonder-Working Providence*, pp. 58, 248.

Unfortunately for the historian, at neither end of the migration process did local officials fully record people's comings and goings. Neither the English ports of embarkation nor the Massachusetts points of arrival kept track of the migrant population, although this was not for want of trying. It is therefore no easy task to reconstruct the volume of migrants or to gauge their social complexion. At the beginning of their enterprise in 1629 the Massachusetts Bay Company ordered 'that a due register be taken and kept from time to time of all the persons formerly sent over, or that shall hereafter come to the plantation, both of the names, and quality, and age, of each particular person'.[112] But no attempt was made to follow this instruction, and no such register is known to exist. Later in the seventeenth century the Boston selectmen took note of strangers and newcomers, and required bonds and sureties for intending settlers in their town. But these records are incomplete and unrepresentative, and are in any case too late to throw light on the great migration of the 1630s.[113]

Writing in the 1640s, Edward Johnson listed coopers, shoemakers, tanners, tailors, carpenters, joiners, glaziers, painters, gunsmiths, locksmiths, blacksmiths, nailers, cutlers, weavers, brewers, bakers, costermongers, feltmakers, braziers, pewterers, tinkers, ropemakers, masons, limemakers, brickmakers, tilemakers, cardmakers, turners, pumpmakers, wheelers, glovers, fellmongers, furriers, vintners, seamen, farmers and 'divers sorts of shopkeepers' among the Massachusetts population.[114] Johnson was in a good position to know the occupational profile of the colony, but he was more interested in the message of 'wonder-working Providence' than in accurate sociological relation. Until the end of the seventeenth century the New England economy was insufficiently diversified to sustain the variety of occupations Johnson enumerated, so he must have been referring to the trades that the migrants left behind in England. Most of these English tradesmen became American subsistence farmers.

The only direct evidence of the social and occupational status of the migrants comes from the passenger lists and customs records of the 1630s. These documents, too, are incomplete and problematic. Until 1635 the English government had no administrative machinery to record the passage of emigrants, and only fragments survive of the

[112] *Mass. Recs*, vol. 1, p. 400.
[113] Record Commissioners of the City of Boston, *Tenth Report*, 'Miscellaneous papers', (Boston, 1886), pp. 55–82; Boston Public Library, MS. q.BOS.679.1, 'Strangers bonds, 1679–1700'.
[114] *Wonder-Working Providence*, p. 248.

shipping records of the later 1630s. No lists are known to survive of embarkations for this period at Bristol, Falmouth, Plymouth, Dartmouth, Deal or any of the ports of northern England. We do, however, have several passenger lists from London, Sandwich, Southampton, Weymouth, Great Yarmouth and Ipswich, which shed some light on the migrants' social and occupational condition.[115]

At their best the port records list the names, age, place of origin, occupation, and family relationship of each passenger at the point of embarkation, although too often they only give names. An exceptionally detailed registration in 1637 produced entries like the following: 'April the 8th, 1637. The examination of John Baker, born in Norwich, Norfolk, grocer, aged 39 years, and Elizabeth his wife, aged 31 years, with three children: Elizabeth, John and Thomas, and four servants: Mary Alxarson aged 24 years, Anne Alxarson aged 20 years, Bridget Boulle aged 32 years and Samuel Arres aged 14 years, are desirous to go for Charles Town in New England, there to inhabit and remain.'[116]

The following analysis is based on records of passengers boarding the *Planter*, the *Increase*, and the *Hopewell* of London, the *James* out of Southampton, the *Hercules* out of Sandwich, and an unnamed vessel from Weymouth in 1635; passenger lists for the *John and Dorothy* of Ipswich, the *Rose* and the *Mary Anne* of Yarmouth, and an unnamed ship from Sandwich in 1637; and the *Confidence* out of Southampton in 1638. Between them these eleven vessels carried 966 passengers, including 242 men whose occupations are recorded. Our sample com-

---

[115] These lists are printed or discussed in John Camden Hotten (ed.), *The Original Lists of Persons of Quality . . . Who went from Great Britain to the American Plantations 1600–1700* (1874; reprinted, Baltimore, 1974), pp. xix–xxi, 35–132, 289–300; Charles Edward Banks, *The Planters of the Commonwealth* (Boston, 1930; reprinted, Baltimore, 1975), pp. 47–205; Charles Boardman Jewson (ed.), 'Transcript of three registers of passengers from Great Yarmouth to Holland and New England 1637–1639', *Norfolk Record Society*, 25 (1954), pp. 6–30; and *N.E.H.G.R.*, 2 (1848), pp. 108–10; 5 (1851), p. 440; 25 (1871), pp. 13–15; 75 (1921), pp. 217–27; and 79 (1925), pp. 107–9. The most valuable discussion is N. C. P. Tyack, 'Migration from East Anglia to New England before 1660', Ph.D. thesis, University of London, 1951; T.H. Breen and Stephen Foster, 'Moving to the New World: the character of early Massachusetts immigration', *William and Mary Quarterly*, ser. 3, vol. 30 (1973), pp. 189–222; Anthony Salerno, 'The character of emigration from Wiltshire to the American Colonies, 1630–1660', Ph.D. thesis, University of Virginia, 1977; Anthony Salerno, 'The social background of seventeenth-century emigration to America', *Journal of British Studies*, 19 (1979), pp. 31–52; and Virginia DeJohn Anderson, 'Migrants and motives: religion and the settlement of New England, 1630–1640', *New England Quarterly*, 58 (1985), pp. 339–83.

[116] Hotten (ed.), *Original Lists*, p. 289.

Table 1. *Occupational grouping of 242 migrants to New England, 1635–8*

Clergy and professionals 5 (2%)
(1 minister, 1 schoolmaster, 3 surgeons)
Yeomen 5 (2%)
Husbandmen 49 (20%)
Labourers 10 (4%)
Servants 50 (21%)
(adult males aged 18 and above, including one apprentice)
Textile trades 50 (21%)
(1 calenderer, 2 clothiers, 1 dornix weaver, 1 fuller, 1 hemp dresser,
5 linen weavers, 3 mercers, 2 ropers, 23 tailors, 11 weavers)
Wood trades 26 (11%)
(14 carpenters, 3 coopers, 4 joiners, 1 ploughwright, 4 sawyers)
Leather trades 22 (9%)
(5 cordwainers, 3 glovers, 11 shoemakers, 1 skinner, 2 tanners)
Food and drink trades 10 (4%)
(1 brewer, 2 butchers, 1 fisherman, 1 fishmonger, 1 grocer, 1 maltster,
3 millers)
Transport and distribution trades 9 (4%)
(2 carriers, 1 chandler, 2 merchants, 1 ostler, 2 seamen, 1 stationer)
Metal and building trades 6 (2%)
(1 cutler, 1 glazier, 1 locksmith, 2 masons, 1 painter)

Total, 242

prises roughly 5 per cent of the participants in the great migration but we have no way of knowing whether it is truly representative. A summary of these lists is given in the appendix to this chapter.

The majority of the migrants to New England travelled in family groups, including servants and young children. Of those whose age and sex is recorded 30 per cent were men aged eighteen and over, 21 per cent were adult women, 25 per cent were boys aged less than eighteen, and 24 per cent were young girls. Table 1 shows the occupational composition of the migrants aboard the eleven vessels. Apart from the absence of gentry at the top of the social scale and the underrepresentation of labourers and the very poor at the bottom, these emigrants were not very different in their social and occupational composition from the mainstream of the English population. Only one was a minister, although we know that more clergymen travelled on other vessels. John Youngs, a Suffolk clergyman, attempted to join the passengers on board the *Mary Anne* of Yarmouth in 1637, but he was 'forbidden passage by the Commissioners', so he and his family are not counted here.[117] A few ministers are said to have emigrated in disguise, while a sprinkling of gentlemen found their way to New England on other vessels. The few gentlemen who crossed the Atlantic usually came from minor gentry families in England – the Winthrops are a good example – but they readily assumed leadership positions in New England.

Relatively few yeomen were attracted to New England. Men of this status headed 5–15 per cent of English households, depending on the region, yet only 2 per cent of the adult male passengers in this sample were identified as yeomen. Yeomen were independent farmers, usually freeholders and often prosperous. On the whole they were more literate and lived in finer style than the poorer farmers or husbandmen. Husbandmen were more strongly represented, comprising 20 per cent of this group.[118] Labourers, usually poor and illiterate, and much more numerous than yeomen and husbandmen, were very thinly represented here. Only ten of the men whose occupations are given were described as labourers, and nine of them came together on the *James* in 1635. Migrants with agrarian occupations – yeomen, husbandmen and labourers – made up 26 per cent of this sample.

Of the men embarking on these eleven ships, 21 per cent worked in textiles, representing England's depressed dominant industry. Few of them were occupied at the elite end of the business, however, and the bulk were tailors, a notoriously poor group. Woodworkers, always in demand in New England, comprised 11 per cent of this sample. The rest belonged to a miscellany of trades and crafts, similar to the list enumerated by Edward Johnson. Altogether, 51 per cent belonged to artisan occupations.[119] The 'industrious sort of people', ordinary workmen with moderate to low social status, formed the core of the migration to New England. These people were by no means destitute (indeed most of them had money enough to pay their fares and set themselves up in the New World) but neither did they belong to the most prosperous or dynamic groups in English society. In order to succeed in America they would have to learn to be farmers and jacks of all trades.

[117] *Ibid.*, p. 294.
[118] On yeomen and husbandmen see David Cressy, *Literacy and the Social Order: Reading and Writing in Tudor and Stuart England* (Cambridge, 1980), pp. 125–7, and 'Describing the social order of Elizabethan and Stuart England', *History and Literature*, 3 (1976), pp. 38–41.
[119] Breen and Foster also stress the artisan preponderance in the Massachusetts migration, and seem to be surprised by it; 'Moving to the New World', pp. 197–9.

The passenger lists provide only a rough indication of the size of the servant contingent. Servants were sometimes clearly identified in the documents, but at other times their status can only be inferred. The *Hopewell, Planter* and *Increase* out of London in 1635 carried between them only twenty-two passengers identified as servants out of 314 registered embarkations, but there were in addition fifty-six single people associated with migrant households but bearing different surnames who were probably servants also (making a total of 25 per cent). Of the passengers on the *Hercules* of Sandwich in 1635, 22 per cent were servants, attached to six emigrant families. Thirty-five of the passengers on board the Yarmouth and Ipswich ships of 1637 were servants (19 per cent), including fifteen men aged eighteen or older. A reasonable estimate would be that some 20–25 per cent of the migrants bound for New England in the 1630s were servants, although this does not take into account the occasional additional shipments of servants aboard cargo vessels.

Sixty per cent of these servants were male. Not surprisingly, they were mostly young as well as single, like the bulk of the servants in early modern England. The mean age of male servants on the three London ships of 1635 was 19 (in an age-range of 12–30), while the mean age of female servants was 23 (range 11–65). Male heads of emigrant households were usually in young middle age, the mean being 34.7 years and the age range 20–63.

Migration to America formed part of a greater pattern of British population mobility in the seventeenth century; the choice of New England was only one among several available destinations. It is well to remember that the great migration, though special, was not unique, and that larger swarms of English migrants went elsewhere within the British Atlantic world. Estimates vary, but the best figures indicate that 69,000 emigrant Britons crossed the Atlantic in the 1630s, of whom only 21,000 went to New England.[120] Even at its peak the

[120] These figures, and those that follow, are based on David Souden, 'English indentured servants and the transatlantic colonial economy', in Shula Marks and Peter Richardson (eds.), *International Labour Migration: Historical Perspectives* (London, 1984), pp. 19–33; E. A. Wrigley and R. S. Schofield, *The Population History of England, 1541–1871* (Cambridge, Mass., 1981), pp. 223–7; Henry A. Gemery, 'Emigration from the British Isles to the New World, 1630–1700: inferences from colonial populations', *Research in Economic History*, 5 (1980), pp. 179–231; John J. McCusker and Russell R. Menard, *The Economy of British America, 1607–1789* (Chapel Hill, N.C., 1985), pp. 102–3, 214–27; Daniel Scott Smith, 'The demographic history of colonial New En-

Table 2. *Net migration to and from New England, 1650–1700*

1650s	1660s	1670s	1680s	1690s
3,154	8,298	1,336	− 1,484	− 17,355

settlement of New England accounted for just 30 per cent of the departing migrants, with most of the rest going to the Chesapeake and the Caribbean. Approximately 540,000 people left England during the period 1630 to 1700, of whom roughly 377,600 went to the New World. Many of the others migrated to Ireland to populate the Protestant plantations of Ulster, or to other places in Europe. New England was by no means the most favoured destination, attracting only 39,000 British migrants by the end of the seventeenth century. The vast bulk went south, including 116,100 to the Chesapeake and southern mainland colonies and 222,500 to the Caribbean.

Migration to New England did not entirely end after the depression of the 1640s, but continued on a much reduced scale. David Galenson has constructed a table of decennial estimates of net migration for the British mainland colonies in America between 1650 and 1780 that includes the figures for New England given in Table 2.[121] These are indicators of inflow and exodus, including movement between the colonies; the negative values for the 1680s and 1690s represent an out-migration from New England made possible by favourable demographic conditions in that region. Blessed with abundant land and a relatively healthy environment, New Englanders generally married earlier, lived longer and reared more children than their English contemporaries.[122]

Estimates of the overall colonial population are equally problematic, being based on inferences and projections as well as partial local censuses. The numbers vary according to the authorities consulted. The picture is complicated by the fact that the population never stood still. Some of the emigrants returned to England; others moved on to other parts of the Americas.

The white population of New England in 1630 has been estimated

gland', *Journal of Economic History*, 32 (1972), pp. 165–83; Terry Lee Anderson and Robert Paul Thomas, 'White population, labor force and extensive growth of the New England economy in the seventeenth century', *Journal of Economic History*, 33 (1973), pp. 634–61; and R. C. Simmons, *The American Colonies: From Settlement to Independence* (New York, 1976), p. 24.

[121] Galenson, *White Servitude in Colonial America*, p. 216.

[122] Smith, 'Demographic history of colonial New England', pp. 165–83.

Table 3. *New England's white population, 1630–1700*

1630	1640	1650	1660	1670	1680	1690	1700
1,800	13,500	22,400	32,600	51,500	68,000	86,000	91,000

at 1,800, encompassing the Plymouth settlers, the Massachusetts Bay people at Salem and Boston, and other stragglers and interlopers farther north. By 1640 the population had grown to 13,500. What, then, had happened to the participants in the great migration? If 21,000 people came over in the 1630s but only two-thirds of that number could be found at the end of the decade we must assume that some of the remainder died and the rest moved on or went home.[123]

Table 3 shows decennial population estimates for New England between 1630 and 1700.[124]

The total British American population at the end of the seventeenth century was 257,000, of whom just over one-third were in New England. By 1700 it is estimated that the Caribbean colonies had 35,500 Britons (extremely high mortality claimed most of the white immigrants); the southern colonies had 86,400; the middle colonies had 40,800 Britons besides Dutch, Germans and Swedes; and there were 3,200 Britons shivering in Newfoundland.[125] Population figures for the various colonies within New England are sketchy. One estimate gives 19,660 whites in Massachusetts in 1660, 7,955 in Connecticut, 1,505 in New Hampshire, and 1,474 in Rhode Island, making a total of 30,594. At the same time it is estimated that there were 562 blacks in New England. An estimate for forty years later gauges the Massachusetts white population at 70,000 in 1700, with 24,000 more in Connecticut, 6,000 in New Hampshire, and 6,000 in Rhode Island,

[123] On return migration see chapter 8, this volume. An alternative set of estimates, the Rossiter series, gives the population of New England in 1640 as 17,600; in Anderson and Thomas, 'White population, labor force and extensive growth', p. 636.
[124] The table is based on the Sutherland series, in Anderson and Thomas, 'White population, labor force and extensive growth', p. 636; Gemery, 'Emigration from the British Isles', p. 212; McCusker and Menard, *Economy of British America*, p. 103; and Smith, 'Demographic history of New England', p. 175, where the Rossiter figures are compared. The alternative estimates of New England's white population are 2,200 in 1630, 17,600 in 1640, 26,800 in 1650, 36,200 in 1660, 45,100 in 1670, 60,500 in 1680, 81,000 in 1690, and 104,300 in 1700.
[125] Simmons, *American Colonies*, p. 24.

plus 1,700 blacks in New England at large.[126] The 'mixed multitude' who were enticed, attracted or driven to New England had created a society with a population roughly equivalent to that of the English county of Dorset.

Appendix
Adult male passengers (18+) on selected ships to New England

Planter of London, 1635

carpenter	2	miller	2
carrier	2	ostler	1
husbandman	7	sawyer	2
glover	2	servant	6
labourer	1	shoemaker	2
linen weaver	1	stationer	1
mason	1	tailor	5
mercer	1	unknown	2
		Total	38

(plus 27 adult women, 36 boys under 18, 29 girls under 18; total, 130 passengers)

Hopewell of London, 1635

fishmonger	1	shoemaker	1
glazier	1	tailor	1
husbandman	5	unknown	10
miller	1	Total	20

(plus 10 adult women, 22 boys under 18, 16 girls under 18; total, 68 passengers)

Increase of London, 1635

butcher	1	mason	1
carpenter	2	ploughwright	1
clothier	1	sawyer	1
glover	1	servant	2
husbandman	9	surgeon	1
joiner	1	tailor	1
linen weaver	2	unknown	12
		Total	36

(plus 24 adult women, 30 boys under 18, 26 girls under 18; total, 116 passengers)

[126] J. Potter, 'The growth of population in America, 1700–1860', in D. V. Glass and D. E. C. Eversley (eds.), *Population in History* (Chicago, 1965), p. 638; Henry A. Gemery, 'European emigration to North America, 1700–1820: numbers and semi-numbers', *Perspectives in American History*, n.s., 1 (1984), p. 322.

Coming over

James of London, out of Southampton, 1635

carpenter	4	roper	2
cutler	1	sawyer	1
fisherman	1	servant	5
fuller	1	shoemaker	3
husbandman	1	skinner	1
labourer	9	surgeon	1
linen weaver	1	tailor	7
maltster	1	tanner	1
mercer	1	weaver	3
painter	1	Total	45

(plus 21 females, 17 males [ages unknown]; total, 83 passengers)

Hercules out of Sandwich, 1635

carpenter	1	schoolmaster	1
hemp dresser	1	shoemaker	2
husbandman	1	surgeon	1
mercer	1	tailor	3
merchant	1	yeoman	1
		Total	13

(plus 40 females, 42 males [ages unknown]; total, 95 passengers)

An unknown vessel from Weymouth, 1635

chandler	1	minister	1
clothier	1	servant	9
cooper	1	tailor	2
husbandman	7	weaver	1
joiner	1	unknown	9
		Total	33

(plus 22 adult women, 24 boys under 18, 24 girls under 18; total, 103 passengers)

John and Dorothy of Ipswich, and *Rose* of Yarmouth, 1637 (lists combined)

apprentice	1	joiner	1
carpenter	1	locksmith	1
cordwainer	2	mariner	1
dornix weaver	1	servant	10
grocer	1	weaver	4
husbandman	5	unknown	2
		Total	30

(plus 32 adult women, 22 boys under 18, 34 girls under 18, 1 unidentified; total, 119 passengers)

'A mixed multitude'

Mary Anne of Yarmouth, 1637

butcher	1	husbandman	2
calenderer	1	mariner	1
carpenter	1	servant	5
cooper	2	weaver	3
cordwainer	1	unknown	3
		Total	20

(plus 17 adult women, 15 boys under 18, 14 girls under 18, 2 unspecified; total, 68 passengers)

An unknown vessel from Sandwich, 1637

brewer	1	joiner	1
carpenter	2	shoemaker	1
cordwainer	2	tailor	3
husbandman	2	yeoman	3
		Total	15

(plus 19 females, 27 males, 15 unspecified [ages unknown]; total, 76 passengers)

Confidence of London, out of Southampton, 1638

carpenter	1	shoemaker	2
husbandman	10	tailor	1
linen weaver	1	tanner	1
merchant	1	yeoman	1
servant	12	unknown	6
		Total	36

(plus 19 adult women, 27 boys under 18, 26 girls under 18; total, 108 passengers)

3

'Reasons moving this people to transplant themselves': migrant motives and decisions

Emigration was often the result of a bundle of motives, a cluster of considerations, that funnelled into a specific decision. Sometimes the elements that *caused* an action were different from those the actor would choose to *explain* it. Religion often provided the language and the frame of reference to explain decisions that involved family, financial and incidental matters as well as the service of God. Often these factors were so tightly tangled as to defy unravelling. For some settlers religion was utterly unimportant; for others it was paramount. When we look beyond the Puritan apologists to the mass of ordinary migrants, the movement to New England appears untidy, fractured and complex rather than rational, purposeful and coherent. Since no single factor accounts for the transfer of so many people we should hesitate to call it a 'Puritan migration'. This chapter delves into the historiography of motivation and reviews the circumstances that took people to New England.

Arguments have raged about the respective roles of religious and economic factors in propelling the migrants. Although most historians agree that both spiritual and secular motives were involved, Puritanism continues to dominate the story. Arminianism, Laudianism, and Charles I's drive for Anglican conformity are identified as the goads that drove the Puritans to despair, and thence to America. New England, in this view, was a haven for religious dissidents and a laboratory for the development of 'true religion'. At the same time social and economic frictions, a collapsing cloth industry, widespread unemployment, agrarian unrest, disease and bad harvests are cited as motivating discontents on the secular side of the ledger. The migration to New England can then be seen as one response to the stresses in English society that soon afterwards erupted in the civil war and revolution. New

England, from this perspective, was a land of freedom and opportunity, albeit with a distinctive Puritan coloration.[1]

While acknowledging the complexity of purpose and motivation, prevailing opinion upholds the primacy of religious considerations. Though sensitive to secular and economic factors, modern history has tended to solidify rather than dislodge the characterization of the movement to New England as a 'Puritan migration'. A powerful consensus supports this position, embracing historians from the seventeenth to the twentieth centuries. A brief review of this historiography is in order before returning to the migrants themselves.

It did not take long for the Puritan elders to frame a highly selective history of the peopling of New England. The *General Laws* of Plymouth Colony, set down in 1636, revised in 1671, and regarded with veneration by the time they were published in 1685, took as a given fact that religion alone was 'the great and known end of the first comers in the year of our lord 1620'.[2] The Pilgrim story, shorn of its secular elements, became annexed to the larger religious history of New England. The Articles of Confederation of the United Colonies of New England, adopted in 1643, agreed that 'we all came into these parts of America with one and the same end and aim, namely, to advance the kingdom of our Lord Jesus Christ and to enjoy the liberties of the Gospel in purity with peace'.[3]

Edward Johnson similarly promoted the view that the settlers of the 1630s came only 'that they might enjoy Christ and his Ordinances in their primitive purity... their whole aim in their removal from their native country was to enjoy the liberties of the Gospels of Christ'. Remembering not the prosaic work of the Massachusetts Bay Com-

---

[1] The debate may be traced in James Truslow Adams, *The Founding of New England* (1921; reprinted, Boston, 1949); Samuel Eliot Morison, *Builders of the Bay Colony*, rev. ed. (Boston, 1964); Charles Edward Banks, *The Planters of the Commonwealth* (1930; reprinted, Boston, 1975); Nellis M. Crouse, 'Causes of the great migration 1630–1640', *New England Quarterly*, 5 (1932), pp. 3–36; Edmund S. Morgan, 'The historians of early New England', in Ray Allen Billington (ed.), *The Reinterpretation of Early American History* (San Marino, Calif., 1966), pp. 41–63; John T. Horton, 'Two bishops and the Holy Brood: a fresh look at a familiar fact', *New England Quarterly*, 40 (1967), pp. 339–46; T. H. Breen and Stephen Foster, 'Moving to the New World: the character of early Massachusetts immigration', *William and Mary Quarterly*, ser. 3, vol. 30 (1973), pp. 189–222; and Virginia DeJohn Anderson, 'Migrants and motives: religion and the settlement of New England, 1630–1640', *New England Quarterly*, 58 (1985), pp. 339–383. The discussion between Anderson and Allen in *New England Quarterly*, 59 (1986), pp. 406–24, appeared after this work was written.

[2] William Bradford, *History of Plymouth Plantation 1620–1647* (Boston, 1912), vol. 2, p. 239.

[3] *New-Haven's Settling in New England* (1656; reprinted, Hartford, Conn., 1858), p. 2.

pany or the orderly migration of ordinary people, Johnson only had eyes for oppressed saints, 'the people of Christ', and the dramatic flight of a handful of Puritan ministers. His rather breathless *History of New England*, better known as *Wonder-Working Providence*, set the tone and established the image for much subsequent description.[4]

Certainly by the 1670s, and perhaps as early as the 1640s, Puritan religious apologists had gained control of New England's history as a device to win pulpit points and to berate the rising generation. Samuel Danforth, preaching at Boston in 1670, reminded his audience that

the cause of your leaving your country, kindred and father's houses, and transporting yourselves with your wives, little ones and substance over the vast ocean into this vast and howling wilderness, was your liberty to walk in the faith of the Gospel with all good conscience, according to the order of the Gospel, and your enjoyment of the pure worship of God according to his institution, without human mixtures and impositions.[5]

Danforth gave an account of the first comers in the 1630s that was standard fare in later-seventeenth-century New England pulpits. 'To what purpose came we into the wilderness, and what expectation drew us hither? Was it not the pure and faithful dispensation of the Gospel and Kingdom of God?'[6]

Urian Oakes, three years later, picked up this theme of the 'errand into the wilderness' and saw God's purposes alone in the peopling of New England.[7] John Higginson echoed this view in the 1690s, seeing 'our fathers coming into these ends of the earth not upon any worldly design, but merely on account of religion'.[8] At the same time Nicholas Noyes asserted that 'the world knows that our predecessors did not leave their native soil, that *dulce solum patriam*, for better accommodations in worldly respects; they did not come into this wilderness for worldliness, but for Godliness' sake'.[9]

This refrain reached its highest pitch in the writings of Cotton Mather, for whom the first planters of New England were 'generous, notable, brave spirited men...choice grain from three sifted nations'.[10] This may be good sermonizing, but it is not good history. It

---

[4] *Wonder-Working Providence*, pp. 22, 35, 140; Sacvan Bercovitch, 'The historiography of Johnson's *Wonder-Working Providence*', *Essex Institute Historical Collections*, 104 (1968), pp. 138–61.

[5] Samuel Danforth, *A Brief Recognition of New Englands Errand into the Wilderness* (Cambridge, Mass., 1671), pp. 9–10.

[6] *Ibid.*, p. 17.

[7] Urian Oakes, *New-England Pleaded With* (Cambridge, Mass., 1673), pp. 17–22.

[8] Nicholas Noyes, *New-Englands Duty and Interest, to be an Habitation of Justice, and Mountain of Holiness* (Boston, 1698), epistle dedicatory by John Higginson.

[9] *Ibid.*, p. 46.

[10] Cotton Mather, *Things for a Distress'd People to Think Upon* (Boston, 1696), p. 15. *Cf.*

held up an unmatchable model of the first generation, compared to which their descendants inevitably fell short. One wonders how much of the anger and anxiety of the preachers of the second generation can be laid to their misreading of the history of the great migration. The worldliness, backsliding and declension that fuelled their jeremiads may have been chimera produced by a defective historical vision.[11]

Religious revivalism and provincial patriotism in the eighteenth century also deployed a selective account of the early migration. For Thomas Prince, preaching in Boston on the one hundredth anniversary of the Winthrop fleet, the great migration was much as Edward Johnson and Samuel Danforth pictured it. In old England the godly 'were censured, pursued, seized, imprisoned, fined, and suffered a world of hardship' for true religion. They therefore 'cast themselves and their children on the tumultuous ocean; and nothing can move them, so they may come into a wilderness, rude and hideous, to hear the voice of their teachers, become a covenant people of God, observe his laws, set up his tabernacle, behold his glory, and leave these things to their offspring forever'.[12] Prince, of course, was addressing their offspring, and was castigating them for their declension. His view of the great migration, which coloured his historical writing as well as his sermons, was as follows: 'Those who came over at first came hither for the sake of religion... they encouraged only the virtuous to come with and follow them... Such vast numbers were coming that the crown was obliged to stop them, or a great part of the nation had soon emptied itself into these American regions."[13] Each of these propositions is wrong.

One difficulty in tackling this topic is the risk of being overwhelmed by the eloquent, insistent and self-serving assertions of American Puritan authors. Preachers and ministers dominate the historical record, as they no doubt dominated their communities, but that does not mean that their interpretation of early New England history is correct. The colonial leaders had an interest in telling a partial and partisan story. Whether they were congratulating themselves on their godliness, chastising their sons for their backsliding, corresponding with

---

William Stoughton, *New-Englands True Interest* (Cambridge, Mass., 1670), p. 19; 'God sifted a whole Nation that he might send choice grain over into this wilderness.'

[11] For Puritan reactions to the crisis of 'declension' see Perry Miller, *Errand into the Wilderness* (1956; reprint, New York, 1964), pp. 1–15; and Sacvan Bercovitch, *The American Jeremiad* (Madison, Wisc., 1978).

[12] Thomas Prince, *The People of New-England Put in Mind of the Righteous Acts of the Lord* (Boston, 1730), pp. 24, 27.

[13] *Ibid.*, p. 29.

co-religionists or explaining themselves to suspicious English governments, the elders of New England had an investment in the story of the 'Puritan migration'. It is, of course, a wonderful story, often related in inspiring words. Its authors have laid a trail through the historical record that has commanded generations of pious attention.

James Truslow Adams attempted to bury the Puritan legend in 1921, when he challenged the traditional religious explanation of the great migration. 'The old conception of New England history, according to which that section was considered to have been settled by persecuted religious refugees, devoted to liberty of conscience, who, in the disputes with the mother-country, formed a united mass of liberty-loving patriots unanimously opposed to an unmitigated tyranny, has, happily, for many years, been passing.' Adams insisted that 'economic as well as religious factors played a very considerable part in the great migration'. He went so far as to argue that four out of five New Englanders were out of sympathy with the Puritan church and that 'even of the first thousand who came with Winthrop, it is probable that many were without strong religious motives; that few realized the plans of the leaders; and it is practically certain that the great bulk of them had never seen the charter'.[14]

Adams's social and economic explanation enjoyed a brief popularity, affecting even Charles Edward Banks, stalwart of the Massachusetts Historical Society. Banks had first taken the traditional line, seeing the majority of emigrants from East Anglia as Puritan individualists who sought 'an outlet for their repressed religious liberty'.[15] By 1930, however, Banks was popularizing Adams's explanation, which downplayed religious motivations. The settlers, he argued, were drawn by the prospect of land without landlords, and were fleeing the 'social slavery and degradation of the land system at home'.[16] Social and economic factors became uppermost, especially frustration with the 'manorial system' and the 'arbitrary government' of Charles I.[17]

This was too much for Samuel Eliot Morison, the great New England patriot-historian, who came down heavily against Adams. While acknowledging that 'economic motives weighed even with the more religiously minded', Morison insisted that 'the settlers of New England

[14] Adams, *Founding of New England*, pp. x, 122, 134–7, 144.
[15] C. E. Banks, 'English sources of emigration to the New England colonies in the seventeenth century', M.H.S. *Proceedings*, 60 (1927), p. 369.
[16] Banks, *Planters of the Commonwealth*, pp. 20–2.
[17] Charles Edward Banks, *The Winthrop Fleet of 1630* (1930; reprinted, Baltimore, 1972), pp. 13–14.

were predominantly Puritan'. They came from Puritan territory, notably East Anglia and the West Country, and belonged to the 'middle classes . . . the backbone of the Puritan movement'. Since they themselves, their leaders, their descendants, even their enemies, said they were Puritan, then Puritan they must have been.[18] This vigorous argument was accentuated in 1930 by celebrations for the tercentenary of the founding of Massachusetts.

Nellis Crouse attempted to adjudicate the dispute in 1932 in an essay on 'the causes of the great migration'. While giving some weight to economic factors such as disturbances in the textile industries and scarcity of grain, Crouse clearly associated the 'great migration' with 'the Puritan upheaval' and Laudian repression, and concluded that 'religion was the mainspring of the migration to New England'. The evidence that supports this conclusion, however, is drawn almost entirely from Puritan divines, especially John Cotton, John Davenport, Thomas Hooker and Thomas Shepard, and includes eight citations from the apologetic hagiography of Cotton Mather.[19]

As a coda to the discussion, making no concessions to the other side, Morison asserted in the magisterial *Oxford History of the American People* that 'Puritanism was responsible for the settlement of New England' and that 'the New England people, almost to a man, were English and Puritan'.[20]

The religious explanation of the 'Puritan migration' continues to dominate the writing of early American history, despite some eloquent cautions. 'Puritans' stride through the pages of popular New England history as if no one else was present. Indeed, it is rare to find references to early New England where the word 'Puritan' (invariably capitalized) is not used as a modifier. The colony was founded as a 'Puritan experiment', financed by 'Puritan merchants', peopled through a 'Puritan migration' or even a 'Puritan hegira'.[21] The settlers were 'Puritans' in flight from 'the terrors of Old England', although most English historians would have difficulty identifying those 'terrors'.[22] 'Puritans'

---

[18] Morison, *Builders of the Bay Colony*, pp. 380–6.
[19] Crouse, 'Causes of the great migration', pp. 8–15, 22–9, 36.
[20] Samuel Eliot Morison, *The Oxford History of the American People* (New York, 1965), pp. 61, 69.
[21] Francis J. Bremer, *The Puritan Experiment: New England Society from Bradford to Edwards* (New York, 1976), pp. 33–40; Carl Bridenbaugh, *Vexed and Troubled Englishmen 1590–1642*, rev. ed. (Oxford, 1976), pp. 434–41; Bernard Bailyn, *The New England Merchants in the Seventeenth Century* (1955; reprinted, Cambridge, Mass., 1979), p. 16.
[22] James M. O'Toole, 'New England reactions to the English civil wars', *N.E.H.G.R.*, 129 (1975), p. 245.

and 'the settlers of New England' are commonly conflated as if the one group signified the other.[23] The early settlers are said to have constituted a 'Puritan state' in a 'Puritan society', governed by 'Puritan political doctrine'.[24]

In his often-cited study of 'the Puritan hegira', Carl Bridenbaugh reports that the migrants of the 1630s 'shared a religious ideal, a sense of destiny, and a firm conviction that God wanted them to depart from their corrupt homeland and settle in the New England Canaan'.[25] For Bernard Bailyn too, 'The spirit of Puritanism' was 'the main force behind the movement as a whole.' Although religion was 'not the determinant in every decision to leave England', 'most' of the New England migrants were 'sympathetic to the cause of religious reform, feared persecution and sought a haven where they intended to build a godlier community'. The 'great migration' was a 'Puritan hegira' to a 'Puritan haven'.[26]

It is hard to escape the barrage of repetition. Rutman's study of Boston is subtitled 'a portrait of a Puritan town'. Powell's study of Sudbury, Massachusetts, is titled *Puritan Village*, although its subject is land division, not religion. Boorstin's survey of American history naturally begins with 'the Puritans of Massachusetts Bay'. Tindall's narrative history employs the word 'Puritan' seven times in its first three paragraphs on the founding of Massachusetts.[27] 'Puritan' New England stands firm in the textbooks as the standard counterpart to merely 'colonial' Virginia. 'Puritan studies' have become an established branch of American scholarship, finding in colonial New England some of the shaping forces of the American 'self'.[28]

---

[23] For example, Perry Miller (ed.), *The American Puritans, Their Prose and Poetry* (New York, 1956), p. ix.

[24] Miller, *Errand into the Wilderness*, p. 141.

[25] Bridenbaugh, *Vexed and Troubled Englishmen*, p. 434. James Axtell, *The School upon a Hill: Education and Society in Colonial New England* (New Haven, Conn., 1974), p. 4, praises Bridenbaugh's 'superb description of "the Puritan hegira" '.

[26] Bailyn, *New England Merchants*, pp. 46, 16.

[27] Darrett B. Rutman, *Winthrop's Boston: a Portrait of a Puritan Town, 1630–1649* (1965; reprinted, New York, 1972); Sumner Chilton Powell, *Puritan Village: the Formation of a New England Town* (Middletown, Conn., 1963); Daniel J. Boorstin, *The Americans: The Colonial Experience* (New York, 1958), p. 3; George Brown Tindall, *America: A Narrative History* (New York, 1984), pp. 60–1.

[28] Andrew Delbanco, 'The Puritan errand re-viewed', *Journal of American Studies*, 18 (1984), pp. 343–60, discusses the Puritans' 'initiating role in American culture'. Alan Heimert and Andrew Delbanco (eds.), *The Puritans in America: A Narrative Anthology* (Cambridge, Mass., 1985), present examples of 'Puritan utterance', 'the Puritan imagination', and 'the Puritan voice', as pointers to 'the American soul', pp. xi, 9, 15. Everett Emerson, *Puritanism in America 1620–1750* (Boston, 1977), p. 11, uses America's 'Puritan heritage' of 'capitalism and democracy' to reveal 'the American char-

'Reasons moving this people'

One can turn almost at random to recent work on early New England to find acceptance of the traditional 'Puritan' position. The leading article in the *William and Mary Quarterly* for 1984, for example, begins, 'The Puritan settlers of New England, *we know*, were driven by a sense of errand. They migrated in order "to study and practice true Scripture-Reformation", quitting an unregenerate England to work out in the wilderness "a due form of government both civil and ecclesiastical." ' The quotation in support of this position is taken from an exegesis of New England's second generation; what 'we know' about the migration of the 1630s is, in this case, refracted through an interpretive prism of the 1670s.[29]

The most level-headed account of the peopling of New England refuses to adopt the standard 'Puritan' explanation, but also steers clear of social or economic determinism. T. H. Breen and Stephen Foster, in an important article published in 1973, suggest that the debate involving Adams, Morison and their successors is hobbled by 'a question badly posed'. Preferring instead to recognize the variety of circumstances and the complexity of individual migrants' decisions, they conclude that 'the traditional either/or dichotomy – *either* religion *or* economics – makes no sense'. Breen and Foster lean heavily on the unpublished Ph.D. dissertation of Norman C. P. Tyack, 'Migration from East Anglia to New England before 1660'. 'Tyack's approach,' they judge, 'is open minded and well balanced, *but* his emphasis generally falls on the social and economic discontents of the migrants.' This 'but' indicates the tenacity of the religious interpretation.[30]

David Grayson Allen expands on Breen and Foster in his study of the settlement of five New England towns. Here migrant motives 'varied from a desire to engage in profitable economic pursuits to the hope of perfecting a conservative Puritan society in the wilderness'. But everywhere local and personal factors intervened, and 'so many modifying circumstances existed in each case that the significance of the single broad explanation is greatly reduced'.[31] Puritans were as

acter'. See also Sacvan Bercovitch, *Puritan Origins of the American Self* (New Haven, Conn., 1975).

[29] David M. Scobey, 'Revising the errand: New England's ways and the Puritan sense of the past', *William and Mary Quarterly*, ser. 3, vol. 41 (1984), p. 3; my emphasis.

[30] Breen and Foster, 'Moving to the New World', pp. 201, 189, my emphasis; N. C. P. Tyack, 'Migration from East Anglia to New England before 1660', Ph.D. thesis, University of London, 1951.

[31] David Grayson Allen, *In English Ways: The Movement of Societies and the Transferal of English Local Law and Custom to Massachusetts Bay in the Seventeenth Century* (Chapel Hill, N.C., 1981), pp. 89, 164.

complicated as any other human beings, and the closer one looks the more difficult it is to see any coherent pattern.

In a detailed examination of 'the character of emigration from Wiltshire', Anthony Salerno similarly finds it impossible to conclude whether religious or economic factors prompted removal to New England. Although Wiltshire, like East Anglia, experienced social and economic dislocations with the decline of the woollen industry, and suffered short-term distress from enclosures and disforestment, the emigrants of the 1630s did not come from the afflicted communities but rather from the more prosperous towns and the wood-pasture regions. Religious harassment does not seem to have been a factor in their leaving, nor were these migrants identifiable as Puritans or religious malcontents. Most of them were young artisans or servants.[32]

By contrast, Virginia DeJohn Anderson has recently placed religion once again at the centre in her explanation of migrant motives, concluding that the movement of the 1630s was, after all, a Puritan migration. 'Adherence to Puritan principles', she writes, 'became the common thread that stitched individual emigrants together into a larger movement.... Religious motivation is the only factor with sufficient power to explain the departure of so many otherwise ordinary families.... The majority of emigrants responded to a common spiritual impulse in moving to New England.'[33]

Anderson's presentation of the traditional position is likely to command widespread support, given America's predilection for a Puritan past. She argues, first, that Edward Johnson and the other seventeenth-century New England authors knew of what they wrote, so their characterization of the migration as religious should be taken seriously.[34] Next, she suggests that we may infer motivations from a study of social origins, as if knowing *who* the migrants were will tell us *why* they came. Anderson's study of a sample of passengers shows that most of them came in family groups and that few of them were economically distressed. They were not, so far as can be learned, casualties of agricultural or economic depression, so economic motivations cannot have been uppermost in their actions.[35] On the contrary, she argues, the religious mission of New England was well

---

[32] Anthony Salerno, 'The social background of seventeenth-century emigration to America', *Journal of British Studies*, 19 (1979), pp. 31–52; Anthony Salerno, 'The character of emigration from Wiltshire to the American colonies, 1630–1660', Ph.D. thesis, University of Virginia, 1977.
[33] Anderson, 'Migrants and motives', pp. 376, 379, 383.
[34] *Ibid.*, pp. 341–2.
[35] *Ibid.*, pp. 343–56, 364–73.

understood, and this inspired religious nonconformists to lean towards emigration. Examples can be found of future migrants in trouble with the episcopal authorities, and others with advanced spiritual
inclinations, and these are to be regarded as typical. Although the
migrants' religious history is obscure, and little evidence exists to reconstruct it, they are assumed to have been Puritans.[36]

Behind these arguments, however, lurks another motif, more a
matter of historical taste than of evidence. Anderson, like many historians, takes comfort in finding in the great migration 'a common,
reasoned response to a highly specific set of circumstances'. The religious explanation is orderly and coherent, and by implication pref-
erable to the suggestion that migrant motives were 'highly localized
... complicated and highly individualistic'. Anderson describes Breen
and Foster's and Allen's conclusions as 'disappointing' because they
are untidy, not because they are wrong.[37]

There is no reason to dismiss religion as a major causal factor in
the early migration to New England. Indeed, many of the leading
colonists were infused with the spirit of the Lord and saw His hand
in their every action. But whether the bulk of their followers were
Puritans, Separatists, Anabaptists, Anglicans or simply indifferent
Protestants is a matter of conjecture. If we wish to be free from the
grip of the Puritan legend, to attempt an unencumbered assessment
of the purposes and motivations of the ordinary migrants to New
England, we must read with scepticism the Puritan sermons, Puritan
jeremiads and the memorials of Puritan history that bulk so large. It
would be better to begin with the more candid assessments made by
some of New England's founders when they were not promoting their
plantations as landmarks in universal history.

Shrewd contemporary observers recognized the variety of motives
that took men and women to New England. William Bradford, though
he had no doubt about his own religious purposes, acknowledged the
broad range of factors that brought some other migrants to New
England in the 1620s and 1630s. The core of the Plymouth Pilgrims
came over 'for sundry weighty and solid reasons', but others chose
America 'out of any new fangledness or other suchlike giddy hu-

[36] *Ibid.*, pp. 374–81.
[37] *Ibid.*, pp. 341–3.

mour'.[38] Included among them were the people who caused so many problems in the early years of the colony.

Looking back from the 1640s, Bradford sought explanations for the spate of troubles in Plymouth Plantation. 'It may be demanded how came it to pass that so many wicked persons and profane people should so quickly come over into this land, and mix themselves amongst them, seeing it was religious men that began the work, and they came for religion's sake.' The answer lay in part in the continuing battle between light and dark, and in the inevitable corruption of human nature. 'When the Lord begins to sow good seed, then the envious man will endeavour to sow tares.' Moving down from this Manichaean plane, Bradford explained that the first settlers in the wilderness, faced with the enormous difficulty of clearing the land and planting a society, 'when they could not have such as they would, were glad to take such as they could'. So the settlers themselves were partly to blame for accepting among them people of unapproved character. Many of these newcomers proved to be 'untoward servants', who contributed their unruly stamp to the community.[39]

Promoters and recruiters in England also bore some responsibility for the moral and social blemishes of New England. According to Bradford,

Finding so many Godly-disposed persons willing to come into these parts, some began to make a trade of it, to transport passengers and their goods, and hired ships for that end; and then, to make up their freight and advance their profit, cared not who the persons were, so they had money to pay them. And by this means the country became pestered with many unworthy persons who, being come over, crept into one place or other.[40]

Finally, Bradford recognized that some of his new neighbours had come to New England unwillingly, or out of desperation. 'Many were sent by their friends, some under hope that they would be made better; others that they might be eased of such burdens, and they kept from shame at home that would necessarily follow their dissolute courses.' The result, not surprisingly, was 'a mixed multitude', a heterogeneous society that from the very beginning accommodated both the godly and the dissolute, the disciplined and the vicious. Bradford and other Puritan leaders of the first generation reconciled themselves to this disappointment, recognizing that 'a mixed multitude came into the wilderness with the people of God out of Egypt', while 'many

[38] Bradford, *History of Plymouth Plantation*, vol. 1, p. 52.
[39] *Ibid.*, vol. 2, p. 329.
[40] *Ibid.*, vol. 2, p. 330.

followed Christ for the loaves sake'.[41] Although the *purpose* of the colony was decidedly religious, its *people* were varied in their motives and characters.

John White, author of *The Planters Plea*, acknowledged the mixture of motives leading migrants to Massachusetts. Writing at the very beginning of the great migration, White shared Winthrop's dream of a godly commonwealth, but he had no illusions about the religious exclusiveness of Massachusetts or the spiritual purity of its members.

As it were absurd to conceive they have all one motive, so were it more ridiculous to imagine they have all one scope.... It may be private interests may prevail with some. One brother may draw over another, a son the father, and perhaps some man his inward acquaintance.... Necessity may press some, novelty draw on others, hopes of gain in time to come may prevail with a third sort; but that the most and most sincere and godly part have the advancement of the Gospel for their main scope I am confident.[42]

This was the confidence of a preacher and promoter, however, not the confidence of a sociological observer.

Thomas Dudley, deputy-governor of Massachusetts, also recognized that people came to New England 'for worldly ends' as well as spiritual ones. Dudley frowned on this secular element, and warned, 'If any come hither to plant for worldly ends, that can live well at home, he commits an error, of which he will soon repent him.' As for 'profane and debauched persons', who all too unfortunately seemed to gravitate to the American colonies, 'Their oversight in coming hither is wondered at, where they shall find nothing to content them.' If there was to be any choice in the matter, Dudley wished for 'godly men' who would come over 'out of religious ends', and blessed with substantial purses. His preferred planters would be Puritan householders, 'endued with grace, and furnished with means to feed themselves and theirs for eighteen months'.[43] But Dudley was enough of a realist to know that a substantial number would fall short of both the economic and the spiritual criteria.

Although some migrants thought hard and agonized long over their decision, others paid slender attention to the significance of their venture and crossed over in a casual or impulsive manner. It may be reassuring to think that people gave careful consideration to such a major undertaking as moving to America, and moved only on the most rational and wholesome of grounds, but the truth is sometimes

---

[41] *Ibid.*, vol. 2, p. 330.
[42] John White, 'The planters plea' (London, 1630), in M.H.S., *The Founding of Massachusetts* (Boston, 1930), pp. 182–3, 187.
[43] (Dudley), 'Dudley's letter to the Countess of Lincoln', in *Chronicles*, pp. 324–5.

messier. The author of *New Englands First Fruits* acknowledged this in 1643, and gave it as one reason why so many of the first settlers of Massachusetts were going back home. 'As some went thither upon sudden undigested grounds, and saw not God leading them in their way but were carried by an unstayed spirit, so have they returned upon as slight, heedless, unworthy reasons as they went.'[44]

Motives and circumstances were complex, rather than simple, and had as much to do with private hopes and frustrations, and opportunities of the moment, as with assessments of the comparative religious and economic prospects of England and America. Not only did New England draw different people with a variety of motives, it also attracted many individuals in whom a tangle of motives combined. The author of *Good News from New-England*, a Puritan tribute of 1648, knew this when he listed land, social mobility, economic independence, earnings and a thirst for novelty, as well as religion, among the 'reasons moving this people to transplant themselves and families to those remote parts'.[45]

Some Puritans insisted that missionary work among the Indians was as important a motive as their own religious freedom. Emmanuel Downing explained to Sir John Coke in 1633 that the planters of Massachusetts went 'some to satisfy their own curiosity in point of conscience, others, which was more general, to transport the gospel to those heathen that never heard thereof'.[46] Henry Dunster also counted missionary work as one of the 'special ends' that brought people to New England, where God led his Englishmen 'to spread the light of his blessed gospels to such as never heard the sound of it'.[47] Arguments of this kind served well to deflect criticism and to raise subscriptions, but they did not come close to the truth. Very few of the men and women involved in the great migration considered themselves missionaries, and conversion of the Indians never claimed more than a fraction of the Puritans' energies.[48] Writing at the time of the Pequot war, Philip Vincent noted that 'the propagation of the gospel was that precious jewel' for which the New England settlers had ventured so much. 'This I am sure they pretended, and I hope intended,'

---

[44] Henry Dunster and/or Thomas Weld, *New-Englands First Fruits* (1643; reprinted, New York, 1865), p. 46.

[45] 'Good news from New-England', in M.H.S. *Collections*, ser. 4, vol. 1 (1852), p. 197. The verse continues, 'but sure it is that godliness, and purity's deriding / moved many godly ones to seek a place of new abiding'.

[46] H.M.C. *Twelfth Report* (London, 1888), pt. 1, vol. 2, p. 38.

[47] *New-Englands First Fruits*, p. 19.

[48] See the works by Jennings, Kupperman, Salisbury, and Ronda cited in chapter 1, note 95.

Vincent added, as if their statements did not match his observations, for 'gain is the loadstone of adventures.'[49]

The leaders of Massachusetts, both lay and ecclesiastical, explained and justified their migration in religious terms. The journeys of Abraham and Moses provided models for understanding their own lives, and biblical passages about the wanderings of the people of Israel became a kind of code for describing the English movement to New England. John Cotton, Thomas Shepard, Thomas Hooker, Richard Mather and the other leading ministers understood their actions entirely in religious terms. They were living under God's eye and fulfilling His purposes. They saw themselves as actors in biblical history, often taking their script from Revelations as well as Genesis and Exodus. The religious dimensions of migrant motivation were complex, but the principal elements included alarm at the religious situation in England, hope for a purer religious environment across the ocean and a desire to participate in the fulfilling of the Scriptures.[50]

The migrant swarm of the 1630s certainly included people who felt threatened or exasperated by the religious policies of Charles I and the Laudian bishops. But only a handful had actually experienced religious persecution. Only 76 of the 10,000 or more ordained ministers in England joined the migration to New England, and of these only 47 had run into trouble with their episcopal superiors.[51] Several well-known Puritan divines – Thomas Hooker and Thomas Shepard, for example – were actually on the run from the episcopal authorities, whereas a few lay migrants like Michael Metcalf of Norwich took flight

---

[49] Philip Vincent, 'A true relation of the late battell fought in New England between the English and the Pequet Salvages', in Charles Orr (ed.), *History of the Pequot War* (Cleveland, 1897), pp. 109–11.

[50] For these well-known divines, see David D. Hall, *The Faithful Shepherd: A History of the New England Ministry in the Seventeenth Century* (1972; reprinted, New York, 1974); Michael McGiffert (ed.), *God's Plot: The Paradoxes of Puritan Piety, Being the Autobiography and Journal of Thomas Shepard* (Amherst, Mass., 1972); Robert Middlekauff, *The Mathers: Three Generations of Puritan Intellectuals* (New York, 1971); Frank Shuffelton, *Thomas Hooker 1586–1647* (Princeton, N.J., 1977); Larzer Ziff, *The Career of John Cotton: Puritanism and the American Experience* (Princeton, N.J., 1962); and Cotton Mather, *Magnalia Christi Americana*, 2 vols. (Hartford, Conn., 1820).

[51] Richard Waterhouse, 'Reluctant emigrants: the English background of the first generation of the New England Puritan clergy', *Historical Magazine of the Protestant Episcopal Church*, 44 (1975), pp. 473–88; Edward Johnson called the migrants 'the people of Christ that are (in England) oppressed, imprisoned, and scurrilously derided'; *Wonder-Working Providence*, p. 24.

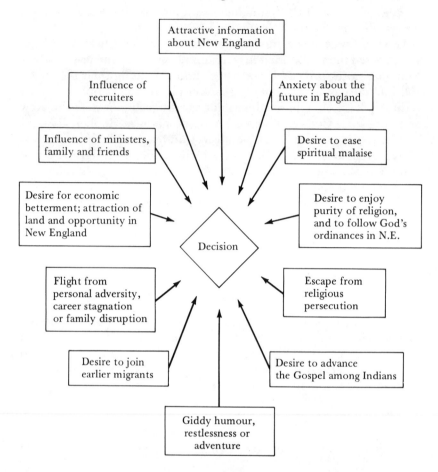

Figure 2. Motives and reasons: a dozen factors shaping migrants' decisions

after repeated collisions with the ecclesiastical apparitors.[52] Others had experienced harassment and frustration, or summons before the ecclesiastical courts. Some felt the rise of Laudian uniformity to be intolerable, and anticipated worse to come, but few were direct victims of its wrath. The Laudian Church of England was by no means as efficient or as monolithic as it has been painted, and most English Puritans were able to endure it.

In fact, the American Puritan memorial of oppression, imprison-

---

[52] Waterhouse, 'Reluctant emigrants', pp. 483–4; Anderson, 'Migrants and motives', p. 377.

ment and derision is a caricature of conditions in Caroline England. The standard story is that the movement for Protestant reform became stifled when Charles I promoted Laud and his Arminian associates to positions of power in the Church of England. Wielding episcopal authority, and using the diocesan courts and the Court of High Commission, these unyielding churchmen advanced a religious policy that restored altars, promoted kneeling, silenced sermons, enjoined the use of priestly vestments, profaned the sabbath, and demanded uniformity from ministers and laity alike. If it was bad enough that this regime promoted forms of worship that evoked the Mass and tokened a return to Rome, it was worse that the fashionable Arminianism that some of these bishops espoused downplayed predestination and other aspects of Calvinist theology, and elevated concepts of free will. In its theology, its worship and its discipline, the Anglican church had forfeited the Puritans' allegiance, so those who could escaped to New England.

The opponents of Mathew Wren, the Laudian bishop of Norwich, charged that the bishop's 'rigorous prosecution' was responsible for driving three thousand inhabitants of his diocese overseas. But many of these were textile workers who went to Holland rather than America, and Wren claimed that they had gone there for higher wages. In other words, it was economic betterment rather than religious scruples that took them into exile.[53] As to the charge that the New England migrants left to escape his episcopal persecution, Wren had two answers: first, that East Anglians had gone to New England before he took over as bishop in 1635, and second, that emigrants also left from other dioceses. Thus the migration could not simply be attributed to his strict administration. Furthermore, ecclesiastical discipline was not intolerable, so 'what needed they to go away when an appeal would have tied up the consistory court?' Wren added that 'he knows not any layman that was meddled with, nor any clerk deprived till he was said to have gone out of the land' in 1638.[54]

This exchange took place after the summoning of the Long Parliament, when Wren was fighting for his career and perhaps for his life, so we should discount the special pleading. But several of Wren's observations deserve to be taken seriously. First, there was much more traffic between East Anglia and Holland than between East Anglia and New England. For an unemployed cloth worker, especially one

[53] Bodleian Library, Tanner 68, 314.
[54] Bodleian Library, Tanner 314. 'Do not the two chief colonies in New England carry the title of Boston in Lincoln Diocese and Plymouth in Exeter?' Wren asked, referring to areas with less rigorous episcopal administration.

who was a zealous Calvinist, Holland was the natural and nearest place to build a new life. Wren was right to note that religious and economic motives were entwined, even if he was unduly dismissive of the Puritans.

Henry Dade, commissary to the bishop of Norwich in Suffolk, had charged in 1634 that the emigrants were 'either indebted persons or are discontented with the government of the church'. Sometimes they were both, for 'as soon as anyone do purpose to break, or is become much indebted, he may fly into New England and be accepted as a religious man for leaving of the kingdom because he cannot endure the ceremonies of the church'.[55] It does not take too much cynicism to wonder to what degree Dade and Wren might have been right.

Finally, Wren's attempt to disassociate strict episcopal administration from overseas migration correctly draws attention to the variable timing and incidence of 'Laudian pressure'. Much of the migration from the diocese of Norwich took place under Wren's predecessor Richard Corbet, who was lazy and good-natured, and under his successor Richard Montague, who was too old and tired to create much trouble. The East Anglian migrants of the Winthrop fleet in 1630 may have had many apprehensions, but they had virtually no direct experience of fierce episcopal discipline. By no means were all of Charles I's bishops Laudians, and Laud himself, Bishop of London since 1628, only took over at Canterbury in 1633. The official response to religious irregularity varied from diocese to diocese, and was modified by the personality of local government. The Church of England was an administrative patchwork, with innumerable loopholes for Puritan offenders.[56]

[55] P.R.O., SP16/260/17. For the rise and fall of Henry Dade see *Calendar of State Papers, Domestic, 1635*, p. 86; *1635–36*, pp. 47, 51, 98, 429; *1636–37*, pp. 260, 322, 420; *1637*, pp. 109, 143.

[56] Stephen Foster, 'English Puritanism and the progress of New England institutions, 1630–1660', in David D. Hall, John M. Murrin and Thad W. Tate (eds.), *Saints and Revolutionaries: Essays on Early American History* (New York, 1984), pp. 3–37, is sensitive to the variable timing of religious pressure and its impact on emigration. On the variable incidence of 'Laudian pressure', see N. C. P. Tyack, 'The humbler Puritans of East Anglia and the New England movement: evidence from the court records of the 1630s', *N.E.H.G.R.*, 138 (1984), pp. 91, 103; and Horton, 'Two bishops and the Holy Brood', pp. 339–46. On episcopal laxity in Richard Mather's diocese see B. W. Quintrell, 'Lancashire ills, the king's will and the troubling of Bishop Bridgeman', *Transactions of the Historic Society of Lancashire and Cheshire*, 132 (1983), pp. 69–70; and R. C. Richardson, 'Puritanism and the ecclesiastical authorities: the case of the diocese of Chester', in Brian Manning (ed.), *Politics, Religion and the English Civil War* (London, 1973), pp. 3–33. See also Archbishop Neile's report on the emigration

In the view of one revisionist historian, 'Laud pursued order and unity, not discord and division.'[57] If that is true, emigration seems an extreme and unusual response. The problem, of course, lay in the different concepts of order in early modern England. Puritans, too, sought order and unity, though not like that of the archbishop. The diocese of London continued to be tightly governed, using every disciplinary weapon in the Laudian arsenal, yet Puritanism flourished there notwithstanding. Thomas Shepard, Thomas Hooker, Thomas Weld and others were silenced in Essex and soon moved to New England, but many of their colleagues and lay supporters kept the struggle alive. Some of the most outspoken Puritans thought emigration to New England was a mistake. Lucy Downing was not alone in her optimism about religious developments in England in the 1630s. 'The chief incitement of our stay here, and that which justifies all others, is that God doth now as graciously and gloriously hold forth Christ and the word of reconciliation to us now here,' she wrote to John Winthrop in 1636.[58] Two years later she joined him in New England.

The religious motive was most clear-cut among Puritan clergymen who had been deprived of their licences to preach. John Cotton explained in a letter from New England in 1634:

God having shut a door against both of us from ministering to him and his people in our wonted congregations, and calling us, by a remnant of our people, and by others of this country, to minister to them here, and opening a door to us this way, who are we that should strive against God, and refuse to follow the concurrence of his ordinance and providence together, calling us forth to minister here?[59]

The circumstance of professional inhibition at home and the opportunity of religious liberty in New England together provided strong reasons for emigration.

The same was true for Richard Mather, an active Puritan preacher and lecturer in Lancashire, who was twice suspended for nonconformity in 1633. As his son Increase tells it,

No hope being left of enjoying liberty again in his native land, foreseeing also (*sapiens divinat*) the approaching calamities of England, he meditated a

---

of Ezekiel Rogers, 'whom I have laboured by the space of two years in sundry conferences to reclaim', in *Calendar of State Papers, Domestic, 1638–39*, p. 431.

[57] Kevin Sharpe, 'Archbishop Laud and the University of Oxford', in Hugh Lloyd-Jones, Valerie Pearl and Blair Worden (eds.), *History and Imagination* (New York, 1981), p. 161.

[58] *Winthrop Papers*, vol. 3, p. 278. See also Robert Reyce, *ibid.*, vol. 2, pp. 105–6; Sir Nathaniel Barnardiston, *ibid.*, vol. 4, p. 218; and White, 'Planters plea', p. 182.

[59] *Chronicles*, p. 439.

removal into New England. The principal arguments whereby he was convinced that he had a divine call to engage in so great and hazardous a design he drew up together and put into form.

Mather's decision was not easy, and it took much prayer and discussion to reach a resolution. His 'arguments tending to prove the removing from old England to New, or to some such like place, to be not only lawful but also necessary', stand as an articulate account of Puritan religious justifications.[60]

In Mather's view it would be right 'to remove from a corrupt church to a purer ... because by staying voluntarily in places corrupt we do endanger ourselves to be corrupted'. Emigration would remove him 'from a place where the truth and the professors of it are persecuted, unto a place of more quietness and safety' where he might 'enjoy all the ordinances of God'. 'To remove from old England to New is to remove from a place where the ministers of God are unjustly inhibited, to a place where they may more freely execute their functions' and 'from a place where are signs of fearful desolation, to a place where one may have well-grounded hope of God's protection.' [61] Buttressed by sixty-three scriptural citations, these arguments were discussion points among the local Puritan clergy and laymen. Additional encouragement came through correspondence with John Cotton and Thomas Hooker, the latter claiming of New England, 'There is no place this day upon the face of the earth where a gracious heart and a judicious head may receive more spiritual good to himself, and do more temporal and spiritual good to others.' [62]

With his career disrupted by the loss of his pulpit, and armed with other signs of God's providence, Richard Mather set sail for New England in 1635. But, notwithstanding his grandson Cotton Mather's account, he was not *fleeing* his homeland, he did not travel in disguise and there were no pursuivants on his tail. Like other passengers embarking at Bristol Richard Mather took the Oath of Allegiance, presented his certificate of conformity, and duly received a licence to pass the seas.[63]

Hundreds of prospective migrants, though inclined towards the New World, waited for a clear call before making their decision. Religious sentiments were sometimes jolted by secular events. A fi-

---

[60] Increase Mather, *The Life and Death of that Reverend Man of God, Mr. Richard Mather* (Cambridge, Mass., 1670), pp. 10–20.
[61] *Ibid.*, pp. 12–19.
[62] *Ibid.*, p. 20.
[63] 'Richard Mather's Journal' in *Chronicles*, p. 448; Cotton Mather, *Magnalia*, vol. 1, p. 406; B. R. Burg, *Richard Mather* (Boston, 1982), p. 15.

nancial crisis, career dislocation or a death in the family sometimes precipitated the move. John Fiske, for example, was stirred
by the death of his father to cross over to Massachusetts in 1637.
The death of the elder Fiske provided an inheritance that paid
for supplies and transportation, and may also have released the
son from a previously steadfast veto. Fiske had been a preacher,
but 'seeing the danger of the times' had turned to medicine. His
career was in flux when he arrived in New England bearing commendations for his piety and religion.[64]

Others hesitated until they accumulated more information or until
their inner torment was resolved. Like several of John Winthrop's
correspondents, and like Richard Mather in Lancashire, some needed
written proposals and arguments before they could see their call to
be clear. A report reached Massachusetts from Ireland in 1634 that
'there were many good Christians in those parts resolved to come
hither, if they might receive satisfaction concerning some questions
and propositions which they sent over'.[65]

Throughout the 1630s families and friends argued with intending
emigrants about the sense and consequences of their decision. In John
White's words, 'Some pity the exposing of their friends...unto so
many dangers and inconveniences; others, and the most part, scoff
at their folly; a third sort murmur and grudge that they are abandoned
and forsaken by them; and good men dispute the warrant of their
undertaking this work and will not be convinced.'[66] The proposal to
migrate to America had stirred similar agitation among William Bradford's separatist community before they took ship on the *Mayflower*.
Bradford recalled, 'It raised many variable opinions amongst men
and caused many fears and doubts amongst themselves.'[67] John
Winthrop's own friends tried hard to change his mind. 'All your
kinsfolks and most understanding friends will more rejoice at your
staying at home, with any condition which God shall send, than to
throw yourself upon vain hopes with many difficulties and uncer-
tainties.' Similar arguments must have been heard in other households
– we need you here, the risks are too great, stay home.[68]

Edward Johnson remembered that the call to join the Winthrop

---

[64] Robert G. Pope, *The Notebook of the Reverend John Fiske 1644–1675* (Salem, Mass.,
1974), p. xxxvii; Cotton Mather, *Magnalia*, vol. 1, p. 431; *Winthrop Papers*, vol. 3, p.
394.

[65] *Winthrop's Journal*, vol. 1, p. 127. The following year 'Mr. Wilson, being in Ireland,
gave much satisfaction to the Christians there about New England', *ibid.*; p. 164.

[66] White, 'Planters plea', p. 182.

[67] Bradford, *History of Plymouth Plantation*, vol. 1, p. 56.

[68] *Winthrop Papers*, vol. 2, pp. 105–6; vol. 3, p. 278; vol. 4, p. 218.

fleet raised a ferment of discussion all over England. 'The rumour ran through cities, towns and village. When those that were opposites heard it some cried one thing and some another, much like the tumult in the town hall at Ephesus.'[69] Johnson, as usual, exaggerated, but the vigorous recruiting activity of the Massachusetts Bay Company in the early 1630s made more Englishmen than ever aware of the possibilities overseas. Prospective migrants (of the sober rather than the giddy sort) continued to press for news and to seek clarification about conditions and prospects in New England.

James Hopkins of Wenham, Suffolk, a former neighbour of the Winthrops, wrote warmly in 1633 of his affection towards Massachusetts, and expressed a conditional interest in going over. 'If I cannot enjoy my liberty upon good terms as I have done I have a purpose to make myself a member of your plantation.... But if our peace be continued, which we desire for the good of our land, then we hold ourselves tied here, and dare not break loose till God set us loose.'[70] Sympathy with New England did not necessarily convert into a readiness to emigrate. Nor were conditions in England in the 1630s so desperate as to drive many people from hearth and home.

Decisions did not come easy, even for the celebrated Puritans who became so important in Massachusetts history. Many were dogged by frustration, stagnation and closure of career opportunities before reluctantly and sadly embracing New England. The majority of their colleagues and brethren, bearing similar crosses and faced with comparable reversals, chose to remain in England.[71] John Winthrop himself, it is worth recalling, was failing in his career as a lawyer before he became charged with the leadership of Massachusetts. Among the 'particular considerations' affecting his decision Winthrop noted, 'My means here are so shortened, now my three eldest sons are come to age, as I shall not be able to continue in this place and employment ...and if I should let pass this opportunity, that talent which God hath bestowed on me for public service were like to be buried.' Winthrop's confidence in God's guidance of his mission was intricately bound up with this second chance to make something of his life.[72]

That decisions were complicated is apparent in most of the cases for which any kind of evidence survives. Samuel Rogers, an Essex

[69] *Wonder-Working Providence*, p. 36.
[70] *Winthrop Papers*, vol. 3, p. 106, corrected from M.H.S. MSS. 'Miscellaneous, bound', 1633.
[71] Waterhouse, 'Reluctant emigrants', pp. 473–88.
[72] *Winthrop Papers*, vol. 2, pp. 125–6; Darrett B. Rutman, *John Winthrop's Decision for America: 1629* (Philadelphia, 1975), pp. 35, 105.

Puritan chaplain, received visits from the Massachusetts minister John
Wilson and gave serious consideration to the recruiter's call. Although
Rogers ultimately decided to stay in England, the entries in his diary
reveal some of the factors that bore on the prospective migrant's
decision. Several of Rogers's associates had already emigrated, per-
haps in response to Wilson's solicitation, and in March 1636 another
neighbour heeded the call. 'This day I part with honest G. Howe to
New England. Oh how precious is the company of the saints, and the
Lord rends them from us and gleans away the choice and full ears.'
The Essex Puritan community buzzed with 'good news from New
England'. Roger Harlakenden and James Howe wrote that 'things go
very well with them' in America. As for Rogers, 'New England, New
England is in my thoughts. My heart rejoices to think of it. Lord show
me thy way.' While New England appeared to be flourishing, old England was in trouble. Rogers prayed, 'Lord stay also with us; purge
our decaying estate. Lord preserve Thy commonwealth [which] is now
tottering. Lord preserve and convert our king.'[73]

Besides the frustration of the times, Rogers was also experiencing
a spiritual malaise, career stagnation, 'personal adversity' and difficulties with his father and stepbrother. He would seem to have been
ripe for joining the great migration. Rogers wrote in his diary in
September, 'I cannot go on faithfully in my particular calling. I cannot
see God clearly before me in any way. Lord, chart out thy way....
Shall I one day see New England?' Rogers wrestled with this problem
over several months, but finally set thoughts of America aside. In
January 1638 he accepted the vicarage of the parish of Great Tey,
Essex, under the patronage of his uncle Nehemiah Rogers, a Laudian
conformist. Another uncle, Ezekiel Rogers, had visited Samuel in 1636
while New England was on his mind, and he did go to Massachusetts,
emigrating in the summer of 1638.[74]

Another who considered emigration was the Yorkshire Puritan, Sir
William Constable, who was one of the principal landowners in Ezekiel
Rogers's district of Rowley. Constable planned to go to New England
in 1635, and went so far as to make arrangements to settle in Connecticut. Like many prospective migrants he was experiencing a crisis
in his affairs, personal, financial and political as well as spiritual. He
was interested in joining the godly commonwealth but eventually

[73] Kenneth W. Shipps, 'The Puritan emigration to New England: a new source on
motivation', *N.E.H.G.R.*, 135 (1981), pp. 87–8.
[74] *Ibid.*, pp. 88–93. Samuel's father, uncles and cousins were divines, though not all
were Puritans. *D.N.B. sub* Nehemiah Rogers; and John and J. A. Venn, *Alumni
Cantabrigienses* (Cambridge, 1922–7), pt. 1, vol. 3, pp. 478–80.

changed his mind about America and found solace in another direction by travelling on the Continent.[75]

Nathaniel Eaton, a schoolmaster in Essex, experienced the inner emptiness and spiritual agitation that often marked Puritans in the 1630s. At the same time his career lacked direction, and he was having difficulties with his pupils, their parents and his associates. Friends who were already resolved on New England 'intimated to me their resolutions to come hither, and they spent some time in reasoning about a common prayer book and church government. And before they had done I saw the truth and was persuaded to close with it, and so I resolved to come along with them'. Such was the explanation Eaton gave a few years later when applying for church membership at Cambridge, Massachusetts.[76]

John Sill, formerly of Newcastle, 'an ignorant place', at first resisted the call to New England. 'Being glued to the place, he considered whether it was not better to suffer than to cast himself upon dangers in flying.' Like many others of a godly bent, Sill thought that 'he should not stir till he saw the Lord leading him, and be contented to be where He will have him'. Eventually the call was clear, and by 1637 Sill was settled in Massachusetts.[77] Both Eaton and Sill were predisposed to be sympathetic to the New England way, but they were led to it only after hesitation, argument and doubt.

A vivid example of the decision-making process appears in the memoirs of Roger Clap. Clap, a twenty-year-old servant in Devonshire, had 'never so much as heard of New England' until he learned that a nearby clergyman and some followers had determined to go there. Roger was the youngest of five sons and faced limited prospects in old England. His autobiography, written for his children almost fifty years later, recalls the circumstances of his emigration.

My master asked me whether I would go. I told him, were I not engaged unto him I would willingly go. He answered me, that should be no hindrance. I might go for him, or for myself, which I would. I then wrote to my father, who lived about twelve miles off, to entreat his leave to go to New England; who was so much displeased at first that he wrote me no answer, but told my

---

[75] Allen, *In English Ways*, p. 28; J. T. Cliffe, *The Yorkshire Gentry from the Reformation to the Civil War* (London, 1969), pp. 306–8.

[76] George Selement and Bruce C. Woolley (eds.), *Thomas Shepard's Confessions* (Boston, 1981), pp. 56–7. Diocesan records show Eaton as curate and schoolmaster at Salcot Wigborough, Essex, in 1637; Guildhall Library MS. 9537/14. After a brief stint as the first president of Harvard, Eaton moved on to Virginia, and eventually returned to England; Morison, *Builders of the Bay Colony*, pp. 190–2; *D.N.B.*

[77] Selement and Woolley (eds.), *Thomas Shepard's Confessions*, pp. 44–7.

brethren that I should not go. Having no answer, I went and made my request to him; and God so inclined his heart that he never said me nay.[78]

Another autobiographer recalled the 'remarkable providence' that determined his emigration in the 1630s. John Dane was a tailor in Hertfordshire and became 'utterly forlorn in my spirit and knew not what to do'. After briefly considering an adventure in the Caribbean, he suffered a string of demoralizing experiences in England. 'I then bent myself to come to New England, thinking that I should be more free here than there from temptations.' Telling this desire to his parents,

My father and mother showed themselves unwilling. I sat close by a table where there lay a Bible. I hastily took up the Bible, and told my father if where I opened the Bible there I met with any thing either to encourage or discourage, that should settle me. I opening of it, not knowing no more than the child in the womb, the first I cast my eyes on was: Come out from among them, touch no unclean thing, and I will be your God and you shall be my people.

The text could not have been more appropriate if it had been rehearsed. Dane's entire family was impressed by this potent feat of bibliomancy, which struck them into an acquiescent silence. 'My father and mother never more opposed me, but furthered me in the thing, and hastened after me as soon as they could.' New England was supposed to free him from his religious morbidity, but, Dane confessed, 'I find here a devil to tempt and a corrupt heart to deceive.'[79]

James Cole of Whitechapel, Middlesex, was wracked by bad debts, a divided family, and spiritual distress in the years preceding his emigration to New England. In 1634 he separated from his wife and wrote to her of his 'sorrowful heart' and 'poor and miserable condition'. Nehemiah Wallington, Cole's spiritual counsellor, entreated him 'in the name of God, return, return', but the wanderer went on from Suffolk to Warwickshire, where he fell in with a godly congregation. At the end of November he wrote to his wife, 'Oh wife, that I could obtain such strength of faith that I might make poverty, shame, persecution, banishment, debts and all troubles not dreadful and harmful but useful and serviceable.' Then came the significant new thought: 'My Lord's desire is to employ me for New England.' Nehemiah Wallington tried to dissuade him from this call, urging 'you should be at

---

[78] 'Roger Clap's Memoirs', in *Chronicles*, pp. 346–7.
[79] John Dane, 'A declaration of remarkabell provedenses in the corse of my lyfe', in *N.E.H.G.R.*, 8 (1854), pp. 149–56.

Whitechapel with your wife', but Cole had made up his mind and soon he was crossing the Atlantic. Wallington himself briefly thought about joining him in the 1640s.[80]

Unfortunately, the majority of migrants left no such intimate record, so it is impossible to see into their minds. However, the likelihood is that their choices too were complex, difficult, and involved a variety of considerations including indecision and chance as well as spiritual anxieties or aspirations. The cases cited here all concern religious emigrants, people who may be identified as Puritans (though not all Puritans of the same stripe). They were literate, self-conscious writers of autobiographies, diaries and letters, and that feature immediately distinguishes them from the mainstream.[81] In most cases their testimony is retrospective and inspirational, allowing the authors to screen out the secular elements from their story. Yet even among these godly migrants it is clear that personal factors weighed in the balance. Rarely was the decision to emigrate based solely on an appraisal of England's religious or political situation or the prospects for church government in New England. Very often the 'call' coincided with a private spiritual crisis, a job loss, family problems or debt.

〰〰〰〰〰

Whereas religion drove Puritan ministers and lay enthusiasts to Massachusetts (providing, at least, the most explicit, the most accessible and certainly the most venerable interpretation of their actions), secular factors and even casual incidents guided the recruitment of others. It is not necessary to agree with John Smith, Henry Dade or Philip Vincent to recognize the private and secular components of migrant motivation. Disastrous harvests (especially in 1629 and 1630), a collapsing cloth industry, rising poor rates, popular disturbances and the recurrence of plague (in 1625 and in 1636–7) no doubt contrib-

---

[80] British Library, Sloan 922, ff. 94–107; Paul S. Seaver, *Wallington's World: A Puritan Artisan in Seventeenth-Century London* (Stanford, 1985), pp. 95–100, and personal communication.

[81] Margaret Spufford, 'First steps in literacy: the reading and writing experiences of the humblest seventeenth-century spiritual autobiographers', *Social History*, 4 (1979), pp. 407–35. Illiteracy rates among tradesmen and craftsmen in England at this time ranged from 30% to 50%, while overall male illiteracy was closer to 70%; David Cressy, *Literacy and the Social Order: Reading and Writing in Tudor and Stuart England* (Cambridge, 1980), pp. 72–95, 129–51. Seventeenth-century New England, experiencing literacy-specific migration and a relative concentration of tradesmen, had male illiteracy rates of less than 50%; Kenneth A. Lockridge, *Literacy in Colonial New England* (New York, 1974), pp. 13–26.

uted to the feeling that these were dark days.[82] Although there is no evidence to link these conditions directly with emigration, the cumulative miseries of Charles I's reign (no worse than those of Elizabeth's reign) may have inclined some people to move when the opportunity of New England beckoned.

Unaware that there would be either Plymouth separatists or Massachusetts Puritans, Captain Smith had written, 'I am not so simple to think that ever any other motive than wealth will ever erect there a commonwealth, or draw company from their ease and humours at home, to stay in New England.'[83] Time proved Smith wrong in this regard, but he also appreciated the intangible benefits that might attract people to America. Smith sketched these advantages in one of the earliest evocations of the American dream.

Here are no hard landlords to rack us with high rents or extorting fines, nor tedious pleas in law to consume us with their many years disputations for justice, no multitudes to occasion such impediments to good orders as in popular states... Here every man may be master of his own labour and land ...and if he have nothing but his hands he may set up his trade, and by industry grow rich.[84]

Religious and secular migrants alike might be affected by these views, which would compound rather than displace their other motivations.

Disreputable motives brought more than a handful of migrants to New England. Some were escaping prosecution, debts or vengeance at home, and accepted emigration as the lesser evil. In 1639 the inhabitants of Newbury, Massachusetts, pondered the problem of Walter Allen, a newcomer from Bury in England who had allegedly fathered two bastard children in the last five years. Allen 'came over hither because he could no longer abide in Bury', but he found life no sweeter in New England.[85] Other newcomers in the 1630s included Robert Wright, a sometime linen draper in Newgate market and after that a brewer on the Bankside and on Thames Street; he was allegedly wanted in London 'for clipping the king's coin'.[86] Another was 'Sir' Christopher Gardiner, adventurer, fraud and bigamist, who had abandoned two wives in London and was living in Massachusetts with

---

[82] The incidence of dearth, depression, plague and distress in Essex in the 1620s and 1630s is reviewed in William Hunt, *The Puritan Moment: The Coming of Revolution in an English County* (Cambridge, Mass., 1983), pp. 235–46. See also John Walter and Keith Wrightson, 'Dearth and the social order in early modern England', *Past and Present*, 71 (1976), pp. 22–42.

[83] John Smith, 'The general historie of Virginia, New-England and the Summer Isles' in Arber, *Smith*, p. 726.

[84] *Ibid.*, p. 710.

[85] *Winthrop Papers*, vol. 4, p. 97.

[86] (Dudley), 'Dudley's letter to the Countess of Lincoln', pp. 332–3.

Mary Groves, 'a known harlot'.[87] One more was William Schooler, a vintner of London, who not only had 'been a common adulterer, as he himself did confess', but 'had wounded a man in duel'. Schooler had fled first to the Low Countries before migrating to New England, abandoning his wife on the other side of the ocean. Despite the godly environment he ran further into crime in Massachusetts, and was hung for raping and killing a maidservant.[88]

Such notorious migrants were moved by neither religious purity nor economic opportunities. They demonstrate that New England, despite its religious orientation, played host to a diverse people with motives of all sorts. The migrant stream was mixed in its morality and circumstances, as Bradford and Winthrop well recognized. My intention in drawing attention to these disreputable colonists is not to substitute the secular for the religious, renegades for saints, but rather to illustrate the variety of personality and experience in a community that is still often presented as homogeneous, upright and dour. The Schoolers and Allens were no more typical than the Winthrops and Mathers.

Every ship to New England seemed to bring its complement of trouble-makers and ne'er-do-wells. Some were servants, whose motives remain enigmatic, while others were free migrants seeking adventure or profit. The *Fortune* reached Plymouth in November 1621, spilling ashore thirty-five new settlers, 'most of them were lusty young men, and many of them wild enough'. The settlers sent over on the *Anne* and the *Little James* in 1623 included some who were 'so bad as they were fain to be at charge to send them home again the next year'. Plymouth's neighbours at Thomas Weston's short-lived colony contained 'lusty men . . . so base in condition, for the most part, as in all appearance not fit for an honest man's company'. The rowdy outpost at Merry-Mount attracted 'all the scum of the country' and set a bad example to the rest of New England.[89]

Massachusetts was no more immune to unsuitable migrants than was Plymouth. Although led by Puritans, the passengers of the Winthrop fleet and their successors included hundreds who were drawn by other than godly considerations. Those who came over with economic or private motives could not be counted on to behave as saints. Many – perhaps 20 per cent – were simply brought

[87] *Ibid.*, pp. 333–5.
[88] *Winthrop's Journal*, vol. 1, p. 236.
[89] Bradford, *History of Plymouth Plantation*, vol. 1, pp. 231, 316–17, 271; vol. 2, p. 5. *Cf.* Michael Zuckerman, 'Pilgrims in the wilderness: community, modernity, and the Maypole at Merry Mount', *New England Quarterly*, 50 (1977), pp. 255–77.

over as servants, engaged as manpower rather than as future church members. Their masters, too, included men who would never qualify for church membership. The 'sifted grain' clearly needed additional winnowing.

Friction between the godly and the reprobate first appeared on board ship, when servants and ill-disciplined passengers had to be whipped for swearing, stealing or worse. To the horror of the Puritans, 'five beastly sodomitical boys' were found engaged in vicious practices on board the *Talbot* in 1629.[90] The Devil was everywhere, even in New Canaan, and his work was a constant test for the vigilance and discipline of the saints. To read John Winthrop's journal is to enter a world of cosmic conflict, of God's providence and Satan's wiles, in which New England became as much a battleground as a refuge. The culture of 'licence' and the culture of 'discipline' faced each other in New England and often came into conflict, just as they did in old England. The task of the 'reformation of manners', which busied the elite even before the Protestant Reformation, took on a new urgency as the leaders of New England endeavoured to create, or maintain, their cherished 'city upon a hill'.[91]

Unsuitable and unregenerate settlers repeatedly violated the godly calm of New England. Problems of profanity, drunkenness and tobacco-puffing stained the winter of 1632. 'Wicked persons', not only servants, brought down upon themselves the 'evident judgement of God' as well as the outrage of the Puritan leaders.[92] The early court records teem with incidents of irreligion, drunkenness, profanity, lechery and worse. In one of the most extreme cases, George Spencer was charged at New Haven with 'prophane, atheistical carriage, in unfaithfulness and stubbornness to his master, a course of notorious lying, filthiness, scoffing at the ordinances, ways and people of God', culminating in his bestiality with a pig. An anxious committee of ministers asked him 'whether he did use to pray to God. He answered, he had not since he came to New England, which was between four or five years ago'. Spencer admitted that he had scoffed at the Lord's

---

[90] *Chronicles*, p. 231.
[91] *Winthrop's Journal*, *passim*; Daniel Vickers, 'Work and life on the fishing periphery of Essex County, Massachusetts, 1630–1675', in David D. Hall and David Grayson Allen (eds.), *Seventeenth-Century New England* (Boston, Mass., 1984), pp. 84, 112–15. For the 'reformation of manners' in England, see Keith Wrightson, *English Society 1580–1680* (London, 1982), pp. 168–70, 205, 210–15; Margaret Spufford, 'Puritanism and social control?' in Anthony Fletcher and John Stevenson (eds.), *Order and Disorder in Early Modern England* (Cambridge, 1985), pp. 41–57; and David Underdown, *Revel, Riot, and Rebellion: Popular Politics and Culture in England 1603–1660* (Oxford, 1985).
[92] *Winthrop's Journal*, vol. 1, pp. 82, 103, 112, 115.

day, calling it Lady's day, but denied all the rest. However, he could not gainsay the record of his bad character, or the evidence of a monstrous piglet, to which he allegedly showed a telling paternal resemblance. George Spencer was executed at New Haven in April 1642.[93]

The battle saw victories as well as defeats, which may explain how New England developed as a Puritan society despite the flaws and exceptions in the 'Puritan migration'. Conceiving the settlement in religious terms, the leaders constantly struggled to bring their population into conformity with their ideals. The colonies were organized and controlled by the godly party, who once they were in power began to make their own rules. Puritan magistrates and Puritan ministers dominated social and political life. The Puritan alliance between court house and pulpit created a religious culture unparalleled in the English-speaking world. Secular migrants, who had chosen New England for social or economic reasons, found themselves at a distinct disadvantage if they did not join a church. Church membership, a visible symbol of belonging, paved the way for social, political and economic success. A conversion experience, and the ability to testify to it, became the prerequisite for admission to a church. Under the pressure of powerful Puritan preaching, in an environment dominated by Puritan magistrates, it would not be surprising if a sizeable proportion of the settlers experienced 'conversion'. Whether shallow and hypocritical or deeply passionate, Puritanism grew more readily in the environment of New England than back home.

New England saints could be hewn from the most unlikely material. In 1633 Edward Howes offered John Winthrop, Jr., the challenge of converting a young Roman Catholic (the Irish servant brought over to tend the dogs) and preparing him for Massachusetts church membership.

I hope with God's grace he will become a good convert. *Converte gradatim.* Sir, I dare boldly say it is as much honour for you to win this fellow's soul out of the subtilist snares (Rome's politic religion) of Satan, as to win an Indian's soul out of the Devil's claws . . . As for his fitness to be a member of your church, it's well if the Lord work it in three or four year, yet he can do it sooner if he please.[94]

The promoters of the Massachusetts ironworks apologized for the roughness of the workers sent over in 1648, yet hoped that they too

---

[93] Charles J. Hoadly (ed.), *Records of the Colony and Plantation of New Haven, 1638–49* (Hartford, Conn., 1857), pp. 65–73.
[94] *Winthrop Papers*, vol. 3, p. 134.

might be reformed and perhaps converted. 'Notwithstanding all our care we have been necessitated to send some for whose civilities we cannot undertake, who yet we hope by the good example and discipline of your country, with your good assistance, may in time be cured of their distempers.'[95] The reformation of manners was the prelude to the infusion of the Holy Spirit.

The process began in England as the migrants assembled, and continued forcefully aboard ship. The Atlantic crossing, eight or more weeks at sea, was a time for religious socialization when Puritan migrants tested their faith and gave instruction and example to the others. A further religious blossoming occurred in New England, which even embraced some of the hardy reprobates. John Cotton and his cohorts hammered away from their pulpits, with the result that 'some were converted, others much edified'. Affected by Cotton's preaching, and perhaps also considering the social advantages of identifying with the dominant party, 'Divers profane and notorious evil persons came and confessed their sins, and were comfortably received into the bosom of the church.' Other godly ministers in New England reported similar success in turning 'divers lewd persons' into 'good Christians'.[96] Such efforts would have been supernumerary if Puritanism was already well established.

It is no surprise, then, that many of the planters of New England moved into the Puritan fold, even if they had previously been hovering outside its doors. A burgeoning religious consciousness developed in New England that was not merely the product of migration. The evidence for this includes church membership, the adoption of Congregationalism by people who had previously been Anglicans, and the rise in the selection of godly names. Roger Clap, the Devonshire servant who became a New England patriarch, fathered ten sons and four daughters. The early children, born in the 1630s, had ordinary names like Samuel, William and Elizabeth, but the children born in the 1640s and 1650s were named Experience, Waitstill, Preserved, Hopestill, Thanks, Desire, Unite and Supply. This choice of names may signify a deepening of Clap's religious experience in his second decade in New England, coincident with a further evolution of Puritanism in New England's decades of crisis.[97]

---

[95] *Winthrop Papers*, vol. 5, p. 209.
[96] *Winthrop's Journal*, vol. 1, pp. 116, 126.
[97] Savage, *Genealogical Dictionary*, vol. 1, p. 390. For a more systematic treatment of this topic see Daniel Scott Smith, 'Child-naming practices, kinship ties, and changes in

As the colonies became established further opportunites developed to draw people over to New England. Some came over to join their families, or to take up estates, with motives quite different from those of the first comers. Husbands sent for wives, brothers sent for siblings, and members of the younger generation followed in their wake. Colonial relatives solicited some who might not otherwise have left home. In their case the pull to the plantations owed less to an autonomous interest in America and more to the call from a kinsman. Those who responded might be called 'passive migrants', to distinguish them from the first comers who wrestled with spiritual or personal decisions.

Roger Clap's autobiography provides a rare view of this family chain migration. Having settled in New England, Clap wrote home to his family encouraging them to follow him over. 'I wished and advised some of my dear brethren to come hither also; and accordingly one of my brothers, and those two that married my sisters, sold their means and came hither.' A brother, two sisters, two brothers-in-law and three cousins followed Roger Clap to Massachusetts in the 1630s.[98]

The Boston merchant Robert Keayne also arranged for his wife's brother, John Mansfield, to migrate to New England in 1635. By Keayne's account Mansfield was a trouble-maker and ne'er-do-well who looked to New England as a refuge from his creditors rather than a place for religious development. 'I sent him over into New England when his life was in some hazard,' Keayne remembered. 'I paid his passage and some of his debts for him in England, and lent him money to furnish himself with clothes and other necessaries for his voyage.' Mansfield would have had no interest in New England were it not for his kinsman's offer.[99]

Augustine Clement of Dorchester, Massachusetts, invited his wife's sister to Boston in 1638 by offering her a share in the proceeds of premises to be sold in Berkshire, 'if she shall come away for New England'. To make it easier for her, Clement instructed his friend, a Boston merchant who was returning to England, to 'advise, help and assist the said Margaret in making and buying provisions for the passage and transportation of herself, her servants and estate and goods, over the seas into these parts of New England, according to

family attitude in Hingham, Massachusetts, 1641 to 1880', *Journal of Social History*, 18 (1985), pp. 541–66, esp. pp. 543–5.

[98] [Clap], 'Roger Clap's memoirs', p. 354.

[99] Record Commissioners of the City of Boston, *Tenth Report* (Boston, 1886), p. 25.

his best skills and ability'. Clement's friend, John Tinker, was to help dispose of the English property and to receive five pounds for his services, 'whether the said Margaret come over to New England or no'.[100]

In the same spirit William Wilson, who had established himself in Boston by 1638, sent for his mother to come over from England. Wilson also engaged John Tinker to dispose of some land in Lincolnshire and apply the proceeds 'towards the bringing over, passage and provisions of Alice Wilson, mother of the said William, into these parts of New England, if she please to come'.[101] Such arrangements were not unusual among migrants to New England, and are common among immigrant communities throughout the world today.

Still more English men and women were offered opportunities in New England by the terms of a dying colonist's will. It was not uncommon for a settler to attempt to reunite his family, or secure a son's or kinsman's succession to his New England property, by specifying that a bequest was conditional on the legatee's moving to New England. Bequests of this sort appeared in wills of the middle decades of the seventeenth century, as the first generation of settlers began to die.

William Homes, making his will in 1649, promised farmland at Scituate, Massachusetts, 'unto my sister-in-law Margaret Webb, alias Homes, the late wife of my brother Thomas Homes, and to Rachel Homes and Bathsheba Homes, two other daughters of my said brother, all now living in London, if they hereafter come over into New England'.[102] John Bayley of Newbury, Massachusetts, two years later, left an annuity of six pounds to his wife and sums of money to his children, *provided they come over hither to New England*. Bayley's executor was to pay for their passage. But if they ignored this opportunity and 'do not come over hither' they were to be virtually disinherited, with just five shillings apiece.[103] In 1653 William Denning of Boston left half his estate to his son Obediah on condition that he come to New England. But 'in case he doth not come personally into the country, then I give unto said son twenty shillings and no more'.[104]

---

[100] Edward E. Hale (ed.), *Note-Book Kept by Thomas Lechford . . . 1638 to . . . 1641* (Cambridge, Mass., 1885), pp. 6–10.
[101] *Ibid.*, pp. 23, 256–8.
[102] *Suffolk County Wills: Abstracts of the Earliest Wills upon Record in the County of Suffolk, Massachusetts* (Baltimore, 1984), p. 103.
[103] *The Probate Records of Essex County, Massachusetts*, vol. 1 (Salem, Mass., 1916), p. 145.
[104] *Suffolk County Wills*, p. 52.

Obediah would have to consider whether his inheritance was worth the cost (intangible as well as financial) of moving to New England.

These inducements to migration were not always successful. Not everyone leaped at the opportunity of a legacy in America, especially if its value was small or if they had pressing concerns or better prospects at home. Not everybody wanted to be a colonial American. Some, indeed, were quite adamant about remaining in England. A Massachusetts court in 1649 forgave John Bayley for living apart from his wife, he 'having used sufficient means to procure his wife over from England, and she utterly refusing to come, shall not be constrained to go over to her, using still what means he may to get her over'. Dozens of families were similarly divided because key members refused to risk their lives in New England.[105]

It bears repeating that the vast majority of Englishmen were indifferent to colonial America, that most of those who did emigrate went to colonies other than New England and that the participants in the peopling of New England were moved by a mixture of motives. Religion was obviously important, especially in the minds of the leaders and preachers, but secular and circumstantial motives were blended in and sometimes came to the fore. English historians are no longer comfortable describing the events of the 1640s as a 'Puritan revolution', and some have attempted to expunge the word 'Puritan' from their vocabulary.[106] In the same spirit, unless firm evidence can be found to tie the migration directly to Puritan religion, and to show the primacy of Puritan concerns in the bulk of the movement to New England, terms like 'Puritan migration' and 'Puritan hegira' should be dropped from discussions of seventeenth-century Anglo-American history.

[105] *Essex Courts*, vol. 1, p. 166, and other examples pp. 123–4, 159, 166, 207, 360.
[106] Patrick Collinson, 'A comment: concerning the name Puritan', *Journal of Ecclesiastical History*, 31 (1980), pp. 483–8.

4

'Needful provisions': the cost
of emigration

Having made up one's mind to emigrate, how much did it cost to go to New England in the seventeenth century? How much money did a family need to establish itself in the New World? How much for transportation and how much for equipment and supplies? What additional resources were necessary to complete a successful move? These questions shift the discussion from matters of motive (why certain people left England) to matters of opportunity (who could afford to go). To what extent did the *cost* of transatlantic migration constrain the peopling of New England? If costs presented obstacles to intending migrants, what ways could be found around them? The purpose of this chapter is to consider the expenses involved in moving to New England, and to set those costs in their social context.

Psychological costs and opportunity costs should also be added to the ledger, although they are virtually impossible to compute. A price had to be paid for the disruption of family, employment and prospects, and for the privation endured on board ship and in the early stages of resettlement. Emigration involved sacrifice, at least in the short run, as John Robinson and William Brewster recognized when considering their move to New Plymouth. 'We shall much prejudice both our arts and our means by removal; who if we should be driven to return, we should not hope to recover our present helps and comforts, neither indeed look ever for ourselves to attain unto the like in any other place during our lives.'[1] A calculation of prospects must have been part of the emigrant decision process, as well as a counting of available cash.

Moving people, animals, foodstuffs and equipment from England to America was a major logistical undertaking for the colonial planners

---

[1] William Bradford, *History of Plymouth Plantation 1620-1647* (Boston, 1912), vol. 1, pp. 76–7.

as well as for individual migrants. Looking back from the middle of the seventeenth century, Edward Johnson estimated the total investment that had gone into the creation of New England.

> The passage of the persons that peopled New England cost ninety-five thousand pounds; the swine, goats, sheep, neat and horse, cost to transport twelve thousand pounds besides the price they cost; getting the food for all persons for the time till they could bring the woods to tillage amounted unto forty-five thousand pounds; nails, glass and other iron-work for their meeting houses and other dwelling houses, before they could raise any means in the country to purchase them, eighteen thousand pounds; arms, powder, bullet and match, together with their great artillery, twenty-two thousand pounds: the whole sum amounts unto one hundred ninety-two thousand pounds, beside which the adventurers laid out in England.[2]

Although other passages in Johnson's history are written for their moral and rhetorical effect, this account of the cost and numbers does not appear to be exaggerated. Johnson probably obtained his figures from Governor Winthrop, who made his manuscript history and papers available to interested parties.[3] If we go along with Johnson's account of the expenses, and if we accept his figure of 21,000 migrants by the early 1640s, we can estimate the overall per capita outlay. Transportation, according to this calculation, cost £4 10s. per person; the entire enterprise was achieved at a little over £9 per head. The share for a six-person household would come to £54.

Evidence from other sources indicates that individual and family expenditures were often somewhat higher. The passage across the Atlantic normally cost £5 per head, although other fares of £4–14 were recorded, depending on the availability of shipping and the desired level of comfort. In 1629 the leaders of Plymouth Colony paid £550 to bring over a party of thirty-five settlers from Leyden. Their passage cost almost £16 a head, which seems an exhorbitant amount, but included transportation from Holland to England and additional expenses en route.[4] Later that year the Massachusetts Bay Company proclaimed a standard tariff, £5 for adults, two-thirds fare for children aged eight to twelve, half-fare for children four to eight, one-third fare for infants under four, and 'sucking children not to be reckoned'.[5]

Francis Higginson observed in 1630, 'The payment of the trans-

---

[2] *Wonder-Working Providence*, pp. 54-5. Identical figures, probably from the same source, appear in 'expenses of the first plantation of New England', H.M.C., *Report on the Pepys Manuscripts Preserved at Magdalene College, Cambridge* (London, 1911), p. 270.

[3] A newsletter from New England, dated 24 December 1645, notes that 'Mr. Winthrop the elder writes particular passages of the country every day in a book which he freely communicates to any'; Beinecke Library, Yale University, Osborne Files.

[4] Bradford, *History of Plymouth Plantation*, vol. 1, p. 67.

[5] *Mass. Recs.*, vol. 1, p. 65.

portation of things is wondrous dear, as five pounds a man and ten pounds a horse and commonly three pounds for every ton of goods.'[6] The same year John Winthrop mentioned the expenditure of £16 10s. to transport a man, his wife and servant, £11 for their goods, and £15 2s. to ship a cow.[7] Massachusetts Bay Company officials calculated standard transatlantic freight charges at £4 a ton in 1629.[8] Francis Borrowes laid out £5 for passage and £4 a ton for freight for his son Samuel's journey to New England in 1630, remarking that the baggage 'will not be above half a ton or three-quarters at the most'.[9] Captain Pierce, a friend to New England, 'would have no less than five pounds a passenger', and required another 2s. 6d. for the services of his ship's surgeon.[10] Wealthy migrants who wished to travel in style could pay an additional £1 10s. for a cabin; they might also engage a steward, usually a fellow-emigrant, to look after their needs and comforts.[11]

At the peak of the great migration in the 1630s a family of five would pay from £30 to £50 for the passage to New England, 'and so more or less as their number and expenses were'.[12] Walter Price paid £5 in 1641 to bring over a servant, and the same cost of passage was quoted in 1645.[13] During the 1650s, when the philanthropic New England Company was engaged in shipping children, the managers estimated £5 a head to send servants to the colony, besides the expense of their clothing and maintenance.[14] Rates increased somewhat in the second half of the the seventeenth century, but a £5 fare was still possible. The volume of commercial shipping between England and New England expanded after 1660, but the number of emigrant passengers declined. In 1680 the master of the *Unity* charged £24 to transport Henry Lilly and his wife as cabin passengers from London to Boston.[15]

---

[6] Thomas Hutchinson, *The Hutchinson Papers* (Boston, 1865), vol. 1, p. 53.
[7] *Winthrop Papers*, vol. 2, p. 306.
[8] *Chronicles*, p. 187.
[9] *Winthrop Papers*, vol. 2, p. 183.
[10] *Winthrop Papers*, vol. 3, p. 125.
[11] Edward E. Hale (ed.), *Note-Book Kept by Thomas Lechford... 1638 to... 1641* (Cambridge, Mass., 1885), p. 325; Charles J. Hoadly (ed.), *Records of the Colony and Plantation of New Haven, 1638-49* (Hartford, Conn., 1857), p. 33.
[12] Bradford, *History of Plymouth Plantation*, vol. 2, p. 67.
[13] *Essex Courts*, vol. 1, p. 27; *The Probate Records of Essex County, Massachusetts* (Salem, Mass., 1916-20), vol. 1, p. 13; Massachusetts Archives, vol. 100, pp. 6, 88.
[14] Guildhall Library, MS. 7938.
[15] *Essex Courts*, vol. 8, p. 31. For comparison, the cost of transportation between Newcastle and London at the end of the seventeenth century was £4 10s. by public coach, £15 by private coach.

The earliest migrants barely knew what to pack, what to expect, or how to conduct themselves on their way to America. Ill-equipped newcomers to Plymouth in the 1620s received courteous greetings and Christian charity, but they almost overwhelmed the marginal food resources of the young settlement.[16] The difficulties of the Winthrop party on their arrival in 1630 were attributed to their 'coming over so rawly and uncomfortably provided, wanting all utensils and provisions which belonged to the well-being of planters'.[17]

Fresh additions to early Massachusetts were a liability rather than an asset unless they came well supplied. As John White correctly observed in 1630, New England lay beyond the reach of 'the poorer sort' who could not bring their own comestibles; 'without such provisions they will be found very unwelcome to such as are already planted there'.[18] James Hopkins put it well when he wrote to his friends in New England in 1633, 'Your first going was hard and fatal to many of your company, partly through want of experience, not knowing how to furnish yourselves for such a voyage; but God surely had an over-ruling hand, who by hard beginnings teacheth people to cleave the closer unto him."[19]

Close cleaving was no doubt of prime importance, but subsequent settlers also learned from the problems and mistakes of the first pioneers. Within a few years a body of knowledge had been assembled to pepper prospective migrants with advice. Christopher Levett recommended the new planter to bring food supplies for eighteen months, 'so that he shall take benefit of two seasons before his provision be spent'. Thomas Dudley wanted only settlers 'furnished with means to feed themselves and theirs for eighteen months'.[20] This was a sensible precaution when the first colonists were struggling to survive but was unnecessary after the success of subsistence agriculture in the early 1630s. John Dane related, 'I brought a year's provision with me,

---

[16] Bradford, *History of Plymouth Plantation*, vol. 2, pp. 67–8.
[17] William Wood, *New England's Prospect*, ed. Alden T. Vaughan (Amherst, Mass., 1977), p. 28.
[18] John White, 'The planters plea', in M.H.S., *The Founding of Massachusetts* (Boston, 1930), p. 183. John Dudley similarly concluded that the poorer sort 'are not yet fitted for this business'; *Chronicles*, p. 325.
[19] *Winthrop Papers*, vol. 3, p. 105, corrected from M.H.S. Mss., 'Miscellaneous, Bound'.
[20] Christopher Levett, 'A voyage into New England begun in 1623 and ended in 1624', in James Phinney Baxter, *Christopher Levett, of York, the Pioneer Colonist in Casco Bay* (Portland, Maine, 1893), p. 139; *Chronicles*, p. 325.

but I soon parted with it,' trading and sharing with neighbours.[21] Once survival was assured, equipment became a more important part of an emigrant's baggage than food.

Francis Higginson advised his friends:

Before you come . . . be careful to be strongly instructed what things are fittest to bring with you for your more comfortable passage at sea, as also for your husbandry occasions when you come to land. For when you are once parted with England you shall meet neither with taverns nor alehouses, nor butchers, nor grocers, nor apothecaries' shops to help what things you need, in the midst of the great ocean nor when you come to land.[22]

However obvious it was that the earliest colonists had to start virtually from scratch, it was salutary to remind them that talk of the 'wilderness' was not entirely metaphoric. If they wanted to live like Englishmen, the planters would have to ferry essential tools and commodities from home. Higginson continued:

Therefore be sure to furnish yourselves with things fitting to be had before you come, as meal for bread, malt for drink, woollen and linen cloth, and leather for shoes, and all manner of carpenters' tools, and a good deal of iron and steel to make nails and locks for houses, and furniture for plough and carts, and glass for windows, and many other things which were better for you to think of them than to want them here.[23]

Within a few years, however, Massachusetts was well organized, even booming. By the end of the 1630s English merchants regarded New England as a valuable market for their goods, no longer an outpost requiring a lifeline of supply. Boston became a nodal point in a commercial network linking Newfoundland, Long Island, the Chesapeake region, the Caribbean, western Spain, the British Isles and rural New England. John Winthrop, Jr., observed in 1660, 'It is not now as in our beginnings, when we were necessitated to bring with us provisions sufficient for a long time.'[24]

Before he left England in 1630 John Winthrop counselled his companions what to bring and how to prepare for their great adventure. Although he had never yet seen America, Winthrop had urgently collected information from anybody with overseas experience. Recruits to Massachusetts naturally looked to Winthrop for advice. Robert Parke wrote to him from Lincolnshire, 'I do purpose to go with you and all my company. . . . I would desire you to give me directions

---

[21] John Dane, 'A declaration of remarkabell provedenses in the corse of my lyfe', *N.E.H.G.R.*, 8 (1854), p. 154.

[22] *Hutchinson Papers*, vol. 1, p. 54.

[23] *Ibid.*, p. 54.

[24] M.H.S. *Collections*, ser. 5, vol. 8 (1882), p. 65.

what household I shall take with me, and for how long we shall victual us.''[25]

Several printed lists apeared to answer the kind of question posed by Robert Parke. Published catalogues enumerated the equipment and provisions thought most useful for an intending settler in New England. A broadsheet entitled *Proportion of Provisions Needfull for Such as Intend to Plant Themselves in New England, for One Whole Yeare*, 'Collected by the Adventurers, with the advice of the Planters', appeared in 1630. Francis Higginson prepared 'a catalogue of such needful things as every planter doth or ought to provide to go to New England', which appeared as an appendix to his *New-Englands Plantation*, thrice reprinted in 1630. John Josselyn reproduced Higginson's list with some additions and modifications. William Wood devoted a chapter of his valuable book on New England to 'what provision is to be made for a journey at sea, and what to carry with us for our use at land'.[26]

The 1630 broadsheet is remarkable for its sensitivity to the varying power of the planters' purses. While listing the ideal equipment, it also indicated various non-essential items 'the poorer sort may spare'. Poorer migrants might dispense with the boots, pistol, building hardware, pickled meat, aquavitae and salt that their more prosperous neighbours were expected to take. Every item on the check-list had its price.

Victual	£	s.	d.
Meal, one hogshead	2	0	0
Malt, one hogshead * +	1	0	0
Beef, one hundredweight*		18	0
Pork pickled, 100 or Bacon 74 pound*	1	5	0
Peas, two bushels		8	0
Greats, one bushel		6	0
Butter, two dozen		8	0
Cheese, half a hundred		12	0
Vinegar, two gallons		1	0
Aquavitae, one gallon*		2	8
Mustard seed, two quarts		1	0
Salt to save fish, half a hogshead*		10	0
	£7	11s.	8d.

[25] *Winthrop Papers*, vol. 2, p. 213.
[26] *Proportion of Provisions Needfull for Such as Intend to Plant Themselves in New England, for One Whole Yeare* (London, 1630; copy at Lincoln Cathedral); Francis Higginson, 'New-Englands Plantation', in M.H.S., *Founding of Massachusetts*, pp. 95–7; John Josselyn, *An Account of Two Voyages to New England* (Boston, 1865), pp. 14–20; Wood, *New England's Prospect*, pp. 69–72.

'Needful provisions'

These things thus marked * the poorer sort may spare, and yet find provisions sufficient for supplying the want of these.

+ Of which the poorer sort may spare to the greater part, if they can content themselves with water in the heat of the summer, which is found by much experience to be as wholesome and healthful as beer.

Apparel

Shoes, six pair	16	0
Boots for men, one pair*	9	0
Leather to mend shoes, four pound	5	0
Irish stockings, four pair	4	6
Shirts, six	14	0
Handkerchiefs, twelve +	4	0
One sea cape or gown, of coarse cloth	16	0
Other apparel as their purses will afford		
£3	8s.	6d.

+ Which for the poorer sort may be of blue calico; these in summer they use for bands.

Tools which may also serve a family of four or five persons

One English spade	1	4
One steel shovel	1	4
Two hatchets	2	8
Axes 3. One broad axe and two felling axes	5	8
One wood hook	1	0
Hoes 3. One broad of nine inches, and two narrow of five or six inches	3	4
One wimble, with six piercer bits	1	6
One hammer		8
Other tools as men's several occupations require, as hand saws, whip saws, thwart saws, augers, chisels, frows, grindstones, etc.		
	17s.	6d.

As for bedding, and necessary vessels for kitchen uses, men may carry what they have, less serving the turn there than would give contentment here.

For building

Nails of all sorts*		
Locks for doors and chests*		
Gimmals for chests*		
Hooks and twists for doors*	£3 0s.	0d.

* According to the proportion of the house intended to be built.

Arms

One musket, rest and bandolier
Powder, ten pound
Shot, sixteen
Match, six pound

One sword			
One belt			
One pistol, with a mould*	£2	0	0

For fishing

Twelve cod hooks		2	0
Two lines		4	0
One mackerel line and twelve hooks			10
28 pounds of lead for bullets and fishing lead		3	3

	The total:	£17	7s.	9d.

Out of which take that which the poor may spare, having sufficient in that which the country affords for needful sustentation of nature		£ 7	4s.	8d.
Remains for their charge besides transportation	£10	3s.	1d.

Though for the more convenient and plentiful accommodation of each planter it were to be desired that they carried the provisions of victuals above said, if their estates would reach thereunto, yet they may, having means to take fish and fowl, live comfortably that want all the rest, meal for bread only excepted, which is the staff of life.[27]

John Josselyn augmented Higginson's list of necessary items, adding such useful things as a hat to the list of apparel, a file, locks, chains and ironware to the tool kit, and a mortar, bellows, lantern and farm implements to the household equipment. Moreover, he priced each item, making his list comparable to the 1630 broadsheet.

Victuals for a whole year to be carried out of England for one man, and so for more after the rate.

	£	s.	d.
Eight bushels of meal	2	0	0
Two bushels of peas		6	0
Two bushels of oatmeal		9	0
One gallon aquavitae		2	6
One gallon of oil		3	6
Two gallons of vinegar		2	0
	£3	3s.	0d.

[Higginson also included one firkin of butter.]

Apparel for one man

One hat		3	0
One Monmouth cap		1	10
Three falling bands		1	3

[27] *Proportion of Provisions Needfull.*

'Needful provisions'

Three shirts		7	6
One waist coat		2	6
One suit of frieze		19	0
One suit of cloth		15	0
One suit of canvas		7	6
Three pair of Irish stockings		5	0
Four pairs of shoes		8	0
One pair of canvas sheets		8	0
Seven ells of canvas to make a bed and bolster		5	0
One coarse rug		6	0
	£4	9s.	7d.

Arms

One armour complete, light		17	0
One long piece	1	2	0
One sword		5	0
One belt		1	0
One bandolier		1	6
Twenty pound of powder		18	0
Sixty pound of shot or lead, one pistol and goose shot		5	0
	£3	9s.	6d.

If half of your men have armour it is sufficient so that all have pieces and swords.

Tools for a family of six

Five broad hoes		10	0
Narrow hoes		6	8
Five felling axes		7	6
Two steel handsaws		2	8
Two handsaws at five shillings a piece		10	0
One whip saw		10	0
A file, a rest			10
Two hammers		2	0
Three shovels		4	6
Two spades		3	0
Two augers		1	0
Two broad axes		7	4
Six chisels		3	0
Three gimlets			6
Two hatchets		3	6
Two frows to cleave pail		3	0
Two hand bills		3	4
Two pickaxes		3	0
Nails of all sorts	2	0	0
Three locks and three pair of fetters		5	10
Two curry combs			11
A brand to brand beasts			6

A chain and lock for a boat	2	2
A coulter weighing ten pound	3	4
A hand vise	2	6
A pitchfork	1	4
One hundredweight of spikes, nails and pins	2	5	0
A share	2	11

£9   6s.   0d.

Household implements for a family of six

One iron pot	7	0
One great copper kettle	2	0	0
A small kettle	10	0
A lesser kettle	6	0
One large frying pan	2	6
A small frying pan	1	8
A brass mortar	3	0
A spit	2	0
One gridiron	2	0
Two skillets	5	0
Platters, dishes and spoons of wood	4	0

£4   1s.   2d.

Spices

Sugar, pepper, cloves, mace, cinnamon, nutmegs, fruit   12s.   1d.

Wooden ware

A pair of bellows	2	0
A scoop		9
A pair of wheels for a cart (if you buy them in the country they will cost 3 or 4 pound)	14	0
Wheelbarrow you may have there, in England they cost	6	0
A great pail in England will cost		10
A boat called a canoe will cost in the country, with a pair of paddles, if it be a good one	3	0	0
A short oak ladder in England will cost but		10
A plough	3	9
An axletree		8
A cart	10	0
A casting shovel		10
A shovel	2	4
A lantern	1	3

£5   1s.   9d.

The total: £30   3s.   1d.

Higginson also advised that various other things were 'necessary to be taken over to this plantation, as books, nets, hooks, lines, cheese, bacon, kine, goats, etc.' His original list included two piercers and a grindstone, which Josselyn omitted.[28]

These lists are useful for giving standard English values to the various items an emigrant family was expected to provide. They remind us that the settlement of New England was a matter of axes and saws, pitchforks and kettles, as well as ideas and opportunities. Comparison with the items found in probate inventories on either side of the Atlantic would show the accuracy of these valuations, and might indicate how completely the migrants maintained the material culture of their homeland.

Basing their calculations on the 1630 broadsheet an emigrant family (of the poorer sort) could estimate the cost of provisioning themselves thus: foodstuffs at £3 16s. a head (say £15 for a family of six including young children); apparel at £2 per person (say £6 for a family using hand-me-downs); basic household tools, 17s. 6d.; arms £2; fishing kit, 10s. 1d. The total: £24 7s. 7d. Transportation at £5 pounds a head, including a discount for young children, would run to another £25. A modest migrant family, then, intending to set itself up independently in New England, would need at least £50 for transportation and equipment, even before contemplating the cost of purchasing land. This sum is remarkably close to the estimate based on Edward Johnson's figures.

The Higginson/Josselyn catalogue appealed to a wealthier and higher-status migrant. With suits of frieze and cloth, and neck bands instead of handkerchiefs, he would outdress and outrank his humbler neighbour. Josselin's list includes enough gear for a fully-equipped country kitchen and sufficient agricultural equipment for a yeoman-like farming establishment.

Foodstuffs, by this calculation, came to £3 3s. a head (say £12 12s. for a family of six), plus 12s. 1d. for delectables, sugar, fruit and spices. Clothing worked out at £4 9s. 7d. per person (say £12 for an unostentatious family). Arms cost £3 9s. 6d. Household equipment came to £4 1s. 2. Tools for a family of six came to £9 6s., with another £5 1s. 9d. to be laid out (mostly in America) for wooden wares. According to these figures an emigrant family would need £47 2s. 6d. to establish itself comfortably in New England, almost twice as much as a family 'of the poorer sort'. Add at least £25 for the family's transportation, £4 for freight and incidental expenses along the way,

---

[28] Higginson, 'New-Englands Plantation', pp. 95–7; Josselyn, *Account of Two Voyages,* pp. 14–20.

and it appears that a family wishing to set up according to Josselyn's specifications would need to lay out close to £80.

Within a few years the majority of these items could be purchased in New England, either locally manufactured or from the estates of people who had died or returned. But they were more expensive than similar items obtained in England. Although it was no longer so vital for migrants to transport tools and household stuff, they were still urged to bring as much as they could manage. Writing in 1634, William Wood advised that newcomers could sell surplus clothing, tools and victuals at a good profit, and he especially recommended Irish stockings, warming pans, glassware, and good wines as items that were in demand. Wood suggested that 'a stock of an hundred pound' would enable one to live comfortably in New England, but the cost of livestock (either transported at £15 per cow or purchased from established settlers), seed, land and the myriad incidental expenses of emigration would consume that sum very fast.[29]

The surviving port books sometimes indicate the value of the goods and supplies migrants took with them to New England. When the *Recovery* of London left Weymouth for Massachusetts in 1632, the customs officials noted the possessions of twenty-six households, 'all planters and have carried with them divers sorts of household stuff, apparel, and other provisions for the necessary use of themselves, their wives, children and servants, all which provisions are valued at their cost and their worth here'. The total came to £920 6s. 8d., an average of over £35 per household. Whether this was an accurate and honest valuation, and whether it covered everything the migrants took with them, is not clear. The particulars of this assessment are unfortunately 'unfit for production' at the Public Record Office, but the entry for the *Speedwell* out of Weymouth in 1637 is useful in showing the varying degrees of wealth and preparation among migrants to New England.[30]

Elizabeth Poole, travelling to New England with two friends and fourteen servants, took provisions valued at £101 2s. 6d., and shipped additional supplies worth £131 10s. 1d. on an accompanying vessel. She had seventeen mouths to feed and was evidently planning to do

[29] Wood, *New England's Prospect*, pp. 71–2, 68. When Stephen Dummer and his family were preparing to go to New England in 1638, they assembled two hogshead of beef, five of meal, four of bacon and malt, two firkins of beer, and six cheeses; P.R.O. CO.1/9/101/1.

[30] P.R.O. E.190/875/8; E.190/876/11. See also A.D.M.G., 'Ships, merchants and passengers to the American Colonies 1618–1668', P.R.O typescript (1982).

it in style.[31] Next in order of wealth, according to the customs valuation, was Walter Harris who, with his wife, six children and three servants, took goods worth £47 7s. Henry Cogan, with his wife and servants, had household goods and supplies on board the *Speedwell* to the value of £31 15s. Like Elizabeth Poole, however, he divided his freight and sent goods worth as much again on another vessel. Other passengers travelled light. Giles Richard, with his wife, three children and two servants, had goods valued at £27 6s. John Crocker's goods were worth £14 16s., and the provisions and stores of Thomas Cooke, his wife and three children were worth only £6. Henry Webb, with eight dependents, was valued at just £6 17s. The average value of an emigrant family's stores on board the *Speedwell* was £26, or just over £4 a head. If these Weymouth passengers were typical of those going to New England in the period of the great migration, it appears that some of them were less well equipped than the colonial managers thought desirable.

〜〜〜〜〜〜

The outlay required for supplies and transportation – £5 to transport a single person across the Atlantic, £25 or thereabouts to move a family, £50 for basic household equipment and shipping, and a total of £100 or more to transplant to a respectable yeoman status in New England – can be better appreciated by considering it in relation to the distribution of wealth and incomes in England at the time of the great migration. The figures that follow will be more indicative than comprehensive. They are based on account books, probate inventories and other documents that point to the financial resources of families at different social levels.

Gentlemen commanded incomes ranging from several hundred to several thousand pounds. Such people were more likely to be involved in New England as sponsors or investors than as actual migrants. The parish gentry, members of the local elite, a few of whom did go to New England, often commanded incomes in the range of £200–300 a year, and might have landed estates valued in the thousands.[32]

Beneficed clergy received stipends ranging from £10 to £100 a year. The median salary for a vicar in the West Midlands in 1650 was £42

[31] Elizabeth Poole, single and aged thirty-eight in 1637, became one of the original proprietors of Tecticutt, alias Taunton; James Savage (ed.), *The History of New England from 1630 to 1649, by John Winthrop* (Boston, 1853), vol. 1, pp. 302–3.
[32] Keith Wrightson, *English Society 1580–1680* (London, 1982), p. 25.

2s. 8d., and the average rector had a living of £78.[33] Curates, lecturers and chaplains were much less secure. But stipends alone did not account for the whole of a minister's resources. Crops and credit mattered as much to a country clergyman as ecclesiastical salaries, and fees of various kinds supplemented the regular income. This is made clear in the case of Ralph Josselin, whose remarkable diary permits a close examination of his economic circumstances. With a living of £24 a year as vicar of Earls Colne, Josselin also worked glebe land worth £5 a year in the early 1640s. By 1650 Josselin's acreage had grown to provide him with £27 a year, and more acquisitions of property brought his agricultural income to around £40 in the mid-1650s and twice that sum after the Restoration.[34] Josselin also supplemented his income by serving as a schoolteacher. Grammar school masters in the seventeenth century were lucky if they drew stipends of £20, but many of them made additional income from boarders and fees, and some supplemented their livelihood by farming. Freelance teachers, and ushers or undermasters, scratched a more precarious living.[35]

Yeomen's incomes might ordinarily amount to £40–60 a year, although annual profits of £100 or more were not uncommon. In 1613 the Berkshire yeoman Robert Loder showed a profit of £185 15s. 7d. after spending £12 a head to feed his family and servants.[36] Yeomen, who were usually freeholders, had a considerable amount of wealth tied up in land. Ralph Josselin's land cost from £4 to almost £15 an acre, with nominal values of 17s. to 19s. per acre per year.[37] At these rates an East Anglian yeoman with fifty acres might derive £45 a year from agriculture. If he sold his land he might realize anything from two hundred to seven hundred pounds, and would have, in addition to any savings, a comfortable nest-egg to begin anew in New England.

Husbandmen were considerably less well off. A husbandman who leased thirty acres might command an income of £27 or a profit of only £14 or £15 in a normal year. If subsistence alone cost him £11 his disposable surplus would be little more than £3 or £4 a year.[38] As a tenant farmer he would have little to gain by giving up his land, although leaseholds had a residual value. Analysis of probate inven-

---

[33] Patrick K. Orpen, 'Schoolmastering as a profession in the seventeenth century: the career patterns of the grammar schoolmaster', *History of Education*, 6 (1977), p. 186.

[34] Alan Macfarlane, *The Family Life of Ralph Josselin* (Cambridge, 1970), pp. 38, 57–63.

[35] David Cressy, 'A drudgery of schoolmasters: the teaching profession in seventeenth-century England', in W. R. Prest (ed.), *The Professions in Early Modern England* (London, 1987).

[36] Wrightson, *English Society*, pp. 32–3.

[37] Macfarlane, *Family Life of Ralph Josselin*, pp. 38, 60–61.

[38] Wrightson, *English Society*, p. 33.

Table 4. *The social distribution of wealth in Stuart England*

Occupation/status	N	Mean probate wealth (£; 1640 values)	Standard deviation
Merchants	22	1,293.2	1,850.8
Knights	11	1,145.7	961.2
Esquires	69	657.8	831.3
Gentlemen	298	329.3	346.9
Mercers	13	282.2	450.0
Tanners	31	235.2	239.0
Maltsters	12	202.6	177.5
Yeomen	1,071	195.0	232.3
Clergy	234	186.3	171.7
Glovers	13	169.0	392.5
Butchers	52	146.5	213.3
Innkeepes	21	140.1	154.1
Chandlers	10	111.9	176.9
Bakers	33	104.5	103.1
Weavers	78	97.9	119.7
Millers	38	85.7	134.0
Shoemakers	26	84.2	105.6
Husbandmen	470	80.0	77.6
Locksmiths	10	77.9	52.7
Blacksmiths	44	68.8	65.0
Cordwainers	11	56.8	52.3
Shepherds	31	55.2	63.6
Masons	25	48.7	42.6
Carpenters	51	46.6	56.3
Nailers	29	39.7	28.8
Wheelwrights	10	39.4	22.1
Tailors	52	36.1	30.5
Bricklayers	11	29.9	26.5
Labourers	103	27.9	35.5

tories shows an average husbandman to have had an estate of movable goods worth £80, whereas an average yeoman (if such existed) had movables worth £195, in addition to his freehold land. The mean probate wealth of yeomen, husbandmen and men of other ranks and occupations in seventeenth-century England is shown in Table 4.[39]

Farming families measured their income both in cash and in kind. Their profits varied with the success of the season. The balance be-

[39] The table is based on my analysis of 2,879 inventories from fourteen English counties; sources and procedures are described in Cressy, *Literacy and the Social Order: Reading and Writing in Tudor and Stuart England*, pp. 137–41, 226–7.

tween the amount reserved for subsistence and the proportion sent to market varied with the household, the holding, the area and the year. Capricious weather upset calculations. Bumper harvests meant falling prices, good for consumers but potentially devastating to producers. Dearth, on the other hand, might be crippling to the community at large but beneficial to the farmer with grain in hand.

Labourers, who rarely show up among migrants to New England, worked for a shilling a day and were lucky to find work all year. A regularly employed labourer in southern England could earn no more than £12 a year in the early seventeenth century, and would more likely bring in £8 or less. Probate inventories of labourers' estates shows their mean value as less than £28.[40]

It is extremely difficult to calculate the wealth, income or purchasing power of the rest of the population. England in the 1630s enjoyed a mixed economy, firmly based on agriculture but becoming increasingly diversified with processing, manufacturing and trade. Husbandmen took on by-employments in leather trades, woodwork and building. Tailors and tanners, clergymen and schoolmasters, also engaged in farming. A web of credit created financial interdependence. Foreign wars might close down the market for cloth exporters, and cast cloth workers into unemployment, while military procurement brought profits elsewhere. Commercial incomes varied with the success of investments, demand, supply, prices and a variety of economic and intangible considerations. For tradesmen and craftsmen, making a living was not as predictable as earning a salary. Indeed, for most people in Stuart England, for those who worked the land or worked with their hands, the concept of an 'annual income' would have little meaning. It would be better to inquire whether families grew enough or sold enough to cover their expenses, and to ask how much was left over for discretionary spending. The liquidity, or potential liquidity, of wealth was an important matter for prospective migrants to New England.

Income figures are elusive, and they mask a multitude of differences. Other kinds of evidence are needed to reconstruct the scale of wealth in order to evaluate the relative expense of emigration. One source that lends itself to this effort is probate records. Probate inventories list the movable goods of the deceased, attaching values to each item in order to protect the heirs and executors from fraud. Inventories survive by the thousand from the various probate juris-

---

[40] Wrightson, *English Society*, p. 34. Servants, whose masters provided room and board, earned from two to five pounds a year.

dictions. English inventories did not include the value of land – real estate – but they usually listed household goods, crops and livestock, cash on hand and debts owing and due. The omission of land is a serious defect and leads to an undervaluation of the estates of land-owners like gentlemen and yeomen. Another problem arises since the inventories were made post-mortem, and there is no telling how much wealth might have been divested earlier, or what other resources the person commanded in his prime. However, the valuation of goods and chattels does provide a reasonable indication of the resources available for emigration, so long as we do not put too much weight on them.

Table 4 displays the English social order, anatomized by movable wealth at death. The table is based on an analysis of 2,879 probate inventories from fourteen counties. All sums are converted to 1640 values. Crude though it is, with large standard deviations, the table gives a rough categorical indication of the occupational groups whose members could afford to move to New England.[41] Gentlemen, yeomen, clergymen and superior tradesmen with estates of £150 or more could probably raise enough money without difficulty, even without liquidating their land. Such people could readily set themselves up in the style to which they were accustomed. For husbandmen and middle-ranking tradesmen, the move would more likely involve a greater struggle, leaving a slender margin unless they had financial help from another source. A shoemaker with goods to the value of £84 would have little left over after equipping and transporting his family to New England. Carpenters, so much in demand in Massachussets, had an average probate wealth of £46 12s., which would barely cover gear and shipping. Tailors and other poorer workers, like labourers, would need subsidies, or else they would arrive in New England in debt.

New England was not built on bondage, like the Chesapeake colonies, but a considerable number of free migrants must have arrived with obligations or debts. Seventeenth-century emigrants did not necessarily have to find all the passage money themselves. Some were subsidized by employers or were sponsored by wealthy neighbours, friends or kinsmen. Intending migrants who could not lay hands on fifty pounds might nonetheless find benefactors or partners who were

[41] See note 39, this chapter.

willing to pay part of their fare. The Massachussetts Bay Company paid the passage of men on its payroll, such as the surveyor Thomas Graves, ministers Francis Bright and Francis Higginson, and the mineral workers recruited in 1643. The company similarly allowed twenty pounds towards outfitting Francis Bright's family and thirty pounds for Francis Higginson's somewhat larger household, over and above their travel costs and maintenance expenses.[42] Francis Higginson himself urged the wealthier supporters of New England to subsidize the passage of the poorer brethren, 'to help them with your purses only to convey them hither with their children and families'.[43]

Subsidized passages were sometimes available through the agency of Puritan benefactors or mercantile sponsors, but there was no standard way to obtain this assistance. Emmanuel Downing sponsored the migration of several of his Suffolk tenants and neighbours in the 1630s.[44] The Winthrop family displayed similar seigneurial generosity among its local clientele; James Boosey and his wife quite naturally expected John Winthrop to undertake half the costs of their passage to New England in 1630.[45] Once the colony was established, Boston grandees began to provide similar patronage on an occasional or piecemeal basis, bringing over kinsmen, servants or friends of friends. Robert Keayne, for example, covered the migration expenses of his brother-in-law in 1637.[46]

Migrants who were willing to become servants for three to five years could more readily find sponsors for their voyage. William Wood explained, 'If any cannot transport himself, he may provide himself of an honest master and so may do as well.'[47] Passage in exchange for service did not require indentures, and did not necessarily bind the parties for a term of years. Goodman Spencer was promised £5 10s. towards the passage of himself and a child to New Haven by serving as 'steward at sea' to Mr. George Lamberton. When Spencer died en route his duties (and wages) were taken over by another passenger, Roger Allen.[48]

In 1631 a fraternal organization, the Company of Husbandmen, came into being to help some 'very honest, plain, downright dealing people' emigrate to New England. The company raised money and

---

[42] *Chronicles*, pp. 208, 212.
[43] *Hutchinson Papers*, vol. 1, pp. 52–3.
[44] *Winthrop Papers*, vol. 3, pp. 124–5.
[45] *Winthrop Papers*, vol. 2, pp. 184, 195. See also Isaac Lovell to John Winthrop in 1637, *Winthrop Papers*, vol. 3, p. 409.
[46] Record Commissioners of the City of Boston, *Tenth Report*, (Boston, 1886) p. 25.
[47] Wood, *New England's Prospect*, p. 73.
[48] Hoadly (ed.), *Records of . . . New Haven*, p. 33.

pooled resources to bring over Englishmen who could not otherwise afford the fare. John Aste, a mealman, put up ten pounds for John Smith, while Nathaniel Mereman went over 'upon the adventure of Peter Wouster'. 'There is also a very poor Yorkshireman, his name is Peter Banester; he hath made such extraordinary moan to come over that Mr. Bachellor and Mr. Dummer hath had compassion and paid his passage.' Another associate, John Kirman, 'seeing the company is not able to bear his charges over, he hath strained himself to provide provision for himself and his family, and hath done his utmost endeavour to help over as many as possible'.[49]

Most migrant families scrambled for cash to meet the cost of transportation and supplies. They raised loans or liquidated their holdings, called in their credits or sold off their stock. Recruits for New England could be found 'making sale of such land as they possess, to the great admiration of their friends and acquaintance'.[50] A dispute in Chancery brings one such set of preparations into view.

When Edmund Tapp began to close down his farm at Bennington, Hertfordshire, in preparation for moving to New England in 1637, his landlord initially gave his 'consent and good liking' to Tapp's arrangements. 'The said Edmund Tapp made his intended journey known, that he intended to go thither with his family to dwell above three years before he went, and made provision for his said intended journey, and the same was commonly talked of amongst his neighbours and kindred before he went.' Grain was still growing in the fields in the spring of 1637, and Tapp sold the unharvested crop to a neighbouring yeoman, Richard Barber. The sale of 'divers parcels of corn then growing upon the premises, and other goods' including 'instruments of husbandry' realized the handsome sum of £786 4s. 8d., more than enough for a comfortable relocation in New England. Not all this money came into Tapp's hands at once, however. Barber, the purchaser, was supposed to pay by instalments, so Tapp left various bills and bonds with his brother and a friend, along with letters of attorney to collect the money and dispatch it to New England 'when Edmund should write for the same'. This seems to have been a conventional transaction, but we would know nothing about it had not Barber complained that Tapp had got the better of the deal. He brought a suit in Chancery, which required depositions from both sides of the Atlantic, and which was still going strong in 1640.[51]

[49] *Winthrop Papers*, vol. 3, pp. 67–71.
[50] *Wonder-Working Providence*, p. 51.
[51] P.R.O. C2/Chas I/B86/3, C2/Chas I/B93/34. Tapp was a tenant-at-will to Sir Charles Caesar. He left England owing £2 6s. in unpaid Ship-Money.

Some of the more prosperous and foresightful migrants, especially those who owned land, mortgaged their English holdings, or turned over the collection of rents and revenues to agents or relatives. This gave them a continuing economic interest in old England as well as a flow of income and resources to fall back on if they ever returned. Others simply sold everything they had. John Fiske, for example, sold his inheritance and converted his property into tools and provisions before setting off with his family for New England.[52] Thomas Hale liquidated everything and 'had almost £200 when he began to make his provision for this voyage' in 1637. His kinsman Francis Kirby wrote to Winthrop, 'I suppose the greatest half is expended in his transportation and in such necessaries as will be spent by him and his family in the first use; the lesser half I suppose he hath in money and vendible goods, to provide him a cottage to dwell in and a milch cow for his children's sustenance.'[53]

While individual migrants busied themselves with their private preparations their leaders learned about shipping and victualling, calculated the costs of freight and storage, located seamen and suppliers, and lobbied their associates in government and business for political and financial support. Francis Higginson advised future migrants to pool their funds to buy or hire a ship for the voyage. 'A little more than will pay for the passage will purchase the possession of a ship altogether.'[54] The suggestion was well intentioned, but carrying it out would have strained the resources of most planters beyond their capacity. For a well-connected and well-organized group, however, leasing or chartering a ship could be a calculated investment. In 1637, for example, a party of Londoners leased the *Hector*, an almost-new ship of 250 tons, for their emigrant voyage to New England.[55] The shipping interests of some prosperous New Englanders, which were to figure so importantly from the middle of the seventeenth century, began with their first outward passage.

The *Talbot*, the 300-tonner that took Francis Higginson's party to Salem in 1629, leased for £150 a month; John Josselyn estimated that

---

[52] Robert G. Pope, *The Notebook of the Reverend John Fiske 1644–1675* (Salem, Mass., 1974), p. xxxvii; Cotton Mather, *Magnalia Christi Americana* (Hartford, Conn., 1820), vol. 1, p. 431.
[53] *Winthrop Papers*, vol. 3, p. 410.
[54] *Hutchinson Papers*, vol. 1, p. 53.
[55] Isabel MacBeath Calder (ed.), *Letters of John Davenport* (New Haven, Conn., 1937), p. 5.

a vessel of 150 tons with twenty-six mariners and twelve guns cost £120 a month in 1638. The ship would be needed for a minimum of four months, requiring an investment of £500–600, and considerably more if there were delays. Extra wages, supplies, insurance, port dues and unforeseen contingencies added to the expense. Crewmen's wages were more than £1 per month, £2 for the mate and £4 10s. for the master. Victuals for the crew ran to almost a £1 per head each month.[56]

Overall costs for a transatlantic charter with a crew of twenty-five could easily run to eight hundred pounds or more. If one hundred passengers between them contributed five hundred pounds in fares and another three hundred for freight and livestock, the investors could meet their expenses on the outward journey alone, if all went well. There was even room for profit if the ship carried commodities for sale in New England and came home, as most did, with a cargo from Newfoundland, Virginia or the islands.[57]

Purchasing a ship incurred greater risk than leasing but held out the promise of long-term financial rewards. In 1632 the London agents of the Massachusetts Bay Colony purchased the *Thomas*, renamed it the *Richard*, and fitted it out for service in New England. Unfortunately, this particular vessel 'proved unseaworthy and was forced back into port', a reminder of the unpredictable complications of shipowning.[58]

Preparations for the departure of the Winthrop fleet in 1630 involved months of negotiation, provisioning and fund-raising. The Massachusetts Bay Company invested hundreds of pounds in biscuits and barrelled meat. Thomas Keen, wholesale baker of Southwark, contracted to deliver '15,000 biscuits of the coarser sort', 5,000 white biscuits, and two hogsheads of rusks by the end of January 1630. The white biscuits were to be 'sweet and good wheat, well baked according to the patterns delivered'. Mr. Stretton, butcher of East Cheap, prepared thirty hogsheads of beef, six hogsheads of pork, and two

---

[56] *Hutchinson Papers*, vol. 1, p. 53; *Winthrop Papers*, vol. 3, pp. 203–4; *Essex Courts*, vol. 8, p. 77; *Essex Courts*, vol. 9, p. 25. For detailed schedules of crews' wages see *Archives of Maryland* (Baltimore, 1883–1937), vol. 51, p. 474, and *ibid.*, vol. 66, p. 301.

[57] Bernard Bailyn, *The New England Merchants in the Seventeenth Century* (1955; reprinted, Cambridge, Mass., 1979), pp. 80–6. For typical charter arrangements see Josselyn, *Account of Two Voyages*, p. 13; Vincent B. Redstone, 'Notes on New England voyages', *N.E.H.G.R.*, 104 (1950), pp. 16–19; George Carrington Mason, 'An Atlantic crossing in the seventeenth century', *American Neptune*, 11 (1951), p. 37; *Archives of Maryland*, vol. 66, p. 299; *ibid.*, vol. 67, p. xxxi; *ibid.*, vol. 69, pp. 126–30.

[58] Robert E. Moody (ed.), *The Saltonstall Papers, 1607–1815* (Boston, 1972), vol. 1, p. 12.

hundred neats' tongues for the Winthrop fleet.[59] (A hogshead was a cask of 100 to 140 gallons' capacity; neats were oxen, bullocks or other cattle.) So well was this dry meat preserved that John Winthrop could write from Massachusetts eight months later, 'The beef we had of Mr. Stretton is as sweet and good as if it were but a month powdered.' [60] This was not just a compliment to the London butcher but also a token that the venture would succeed. Provisions from England formed a vital part of the colonists' rations in the first few years. Later, as New England became self-sufficient, the settlers enjoyed a plentiful, varied and affordable food supply, but in the earliest years reliable supplies from home made up the margin between sufficiency and starvation, on board ship and ashore.

Provisioning a ship for an emigrant voyage was a complicated and expensive undertaking. The organizers had to coordinate purchasing, delivery, quality control and stowage of victuals and stores. Merchant captains, already experienced by the 1630s in fitting and provisioning for long-distance voyages, usually took charge of the details, with colonial investors and company officials looking over their shoulders. Cargo manifests, drawn up to satisfy customs officials (and therefore inherently untrustworthy), give some indication of the provisions taken on board. The *Mary Rose* of Bristol, a vessel of 180 tons bound with 120 passengers to New England in November 1639, reported a typical lading:

20 quarters of meal
60 dozen of shoes
20 kinderkins of butter
30 hundredweight of cheese
10 barrels of powder
500 weight of small shot
80 dozen of candles
30 hogsheads of meal
30 hogsheads of oatmeal
10 hogsheads of peas
100 weight of pewter
1000 weight of soap
20,000 nails of all sorts
clothes for the passengers, viz:
   shirts, caps, stockings, beds and hamackos
4 tons of Spanish and French wines
2 tons of vinegar
1 ton of hot waters in cask, bottles and cases.[61]

---

[59] *Winthrop Papers*, vol. 2, pp. 171–2.
[60] *Ibid.*, p. 309.
[61] P.R.O. PC2/51, ff. 25–25v, also ff. 120–120v, 126v, 157; N. C. P. Tyack, 'English

Other vessels carried oil, malt, raisins, ironware, pewter, coal, cloth, etc., besides livestock, passengers and their effects, and miscellaneous supplies.

Migrant families quickly learned what was useful to them in the new country. Those who could afford the fare could usually afford to equip themselves adequately. Borrowing, skimping and saving, and a willingness to endure present hardship for future reward, brought New England within reach of the modest artisan and husbandman. Grants of land turned many of them into incipient yeomen, although others floundered and went home.[62] Early New England was well supplied, and its residents were able, within a few years, to replicate many of the familiar features of English rural life. What the colony lacked, as a result of selective migration, was the perennial English problem of poverty and beggars.

exports to New England, 1632–1640: some records in the Port Books', *N.E.H.G.R.*, 135 (1981), pp. 213-38.

[62] Sumner Chilton Powell, *Puritan Village: The Formation of a New England Town* (Middletown, Connecticut, 1963), pp. 83–97, 189–90; Kenneth A. Lockridge, *A New England Town: the First Hundred Years*, exp. ed. (New York, 1985), pp. 71–3; David Grayson Allen, *In English Ways: the Movement of Societies and the Transferal of English Local Law and Custom to Massachusetts Bay in the Seventeenth Century* (Chapel Hill, N.C., 1981), pp. 31–2, 65, 111, 128–9.

5

'Promiscuous and disorderly departing out of the realm': the control of emigration

Leaving England was not simply a matter of making a decision and raising the necessary cash. Prospective emigrants needed permission to depart the realm, and had to clear a series of administrative hurdles before they could set off for America. The regulations governing emigration pre-dated the seventeenth century, but became most elaborate at the time of the first large-scale movement to New England in the 1630s. Official interference applied no matter what the emigrant's destination, but extra layers of difficulty were placed in the way of people leaving for Massachusetts.[1] However, as this chapter will show, government controls were more in the nature of political and bureaucratic irritants than serious impediments to migration.

As subjects of the Crown, rather than free citizens of the world, the movements of all Englishmen fell within the purview of the king. As soon as there was serious talk of establishing a colony overseas the government stepped in to scrutinize and control its prospective population. In 1607, the year of the Jamestown settlement, James I renewed the traditional mediaeval restriction 'forbidding all persons save great lords, true and notable merchants, and the king's soldiers to leave the realm' without express permission. A royal proclamation forbade 'any to leave the realm, other than soldiers, merchants, mariners and their factors and apprentices, without special licence of the king or four of his Privy Council'.[2] The Crown reserved the right to

---

[1] The *Expedition*, bound for Virginia in July 1633, was delayed by searchers and her passengers subjected to the oaths of allegiance, so that she lost her wind; Peter Wilson Coldham (ed.), *English Adventurers and Emigrants, 1609-1660* (Baltimore, 1984), p. 42. Passengers to Maryland were similarly stayed;*Archives of Maryland*, vol. 3 (Baltimore, 1885), p. 23.
[2] Robert Steele (ed.), *Tudor and Stuart Proclamations* (Oxford, 1910), p. 121.

control departures out of the realm, and invoked this proclamation again in 1630 to justify the licensing of migrants to New England.[3]

In the early years, however, before the settlement of New England became an issue in Caroline religious politics, regulation of emigration was primarily a matter of protecting commercial investments. Regulatory initiatives stemmed from the colonial companies themselves and were buttressed by government action. During the 1620s the Council for New England obtained privileges for its own colonizing activities but sought tighter government control of interlopers in order to safeguard its monopoly. As a commercial collective with designs on the territory north from Massachusetts Bay, the Council for New England enjoyed a royal patent 'prohibiting all other his [majesty's] subjects not Adventurers or Planters to frequent those coasts'. Nevertheless, as the Council complained in 1622, 'sundry and irregular persons . . . have this last year sent and gone into those parts . . . to the hindrance and great prejudice of the plantation'. Agreeing that interloping by 'sundry and irregular persons' could not be countenanced, the Privy Council issued a proclamation 'prohibiting all persons to resort unto the coasts of New England contrary to his majesty's said royal grant'.[4]

During its brief life the Council for New England hatched several ingenious schemes to populate its distant territory. Although it achieved very little in the way of actual colonization, it did explore in detail the bureaucratic procedures involved in regulating emigration. The council dreamed up a mountain of paperwork and pro forma instructions that set the tone for what came later. In 1623 they ordered that 'no ship shall be henceforth set out by any . . . but they shall first take licence from us the said Council'. Furthermore, any ship's captain or master transporting passengers

shall likewise, upon pain of such penalties as the said Council shall think fit to inflict, deliver or cause to be delivered unto the clerk of the said Council a true note or inventory . . . of all the names, surnames, trades, professions and faculties of all passengers, together with an invoice or inventory, signed also by the proprietor, of all such goods, cattle, arms, munitions, and provisions whatsoever intended to be thither transported.[5]

Not only was the clerk to the council supposed to register and file this extensive documentation, but he was also charged with copying

---

[3] *Ibid.*, p. 192.
[4] A.A.S. MSS., 'Records of the Council for New England, 1622–23', pp. 40–1; *Acts of the Privy Council, Colonial Series, 1613–1680*, (hereinafter, *A.P.C., Colonial*) (London, 1908), p. 55.
[5] A.A.S. MSS., 'Records of the Council for New England', pp. 40–2.

every list and inventory for use when unloading the cargo in America. The intent was to protect the company, the officers and the passengers themselves against fraud, and to make sure that all persons and articles were accounted in a comprehensive bill of lading. But, needless to say, this rigorous bureaucratic task was never performed. Captains and colonists had enough to do without filling in forms, and these instructions from London were ignored.

In practice neither the Privy Council nor the Council for New England could effectively control movement to New England. West Country fishermen had long frequented the New England coasts and were not going to let high-placed Londoners interfere with their livelihood. The Council for New England bluffed and expostulated, but the fishermen came and went as they pleased. Putting their best face on the matter, the council explained 'that it is not the Council's meaning to stay or hinder any from going to New England in fishing voyages, so as they will conform themselves to such orders as are concluded and agreed on by the Council'.[6] In principle, anyone engaging in the Atlantic traffic and anyone moving to New England would do so only on official terms and with the council's permission. Despite the limitations of their power, the New England investors and the government officials who supported them insisted on the principle of control.

The Massachusetts Bay Company inherited some of the procedures and concerns of the Council for New England. It too wished to maintain control of the emigration to its American territory and to vet and to view every person crossing over. Like the Council for New England, Bay Company officials had a penchant for paperwork that was not entirely satisfied. In May 1629 they addressed a letter to John Endecott, already in New England, 'desiring...that a due register be taken and kept, from time to time, of all the persons formerly sent over, or that shall hereafter come to the Plantation, both of the names and quality and age of each particular person, and for whom or by whom they are sent over'. At the same time they requested 'a perfect register of the daily work done' by every colonist, 'a copy whereof we pray you send unto us once every half year'.[7] Documentation of this sort would, of course, be invaluable for reconstructing the social and economic history of early New England, but it does not exist. The

---

[6] *Ibid.*, p. 25.
[7] 'The Company's second general letter of instructions to Endecott', in *Chronicles*, p. 175; *Mass. Recs.*, vol. 1, pp. 400, 401, 405.

company's instructions were ignored, as were so many other demands for reports and details in this period.

Much to the chagrin of the Council for New England, King Charles in 1628 granted the Massachusetts Bay Company the right 'to take, lead, carry and transport... all such and so many of our loving subjects, or any other strangers that will become our loving subjects and live under our allegiance, as shall willingly accompany them in the same voyages'.[8] This gave the company a valuable freedom to recruit and to ship whomsoever it liked, notwithstanding the Jacobean proclamation and the pre-existing monopolies. Understandably, the Council for New England felt threatened by this privilege, which undercut its own exclusive patent. As a result the early 1630s saw a political tussle over shipping and emigration, in which the agents of the competing New England factions lobbied members of the Privy Council to intervene on their behalf. Ordinary migrants might be sped or stayed, according to the current clout of their leaders and spokesmen.

Emigrant vessels bound for Massachusetts Bay were periodically stayed until they displayed a licence from the Council for New England. When John Humphrey, one of the original patentees of the Massachusetts Company, protested that this harassment violated law and equity, his temerity only won him a rebuke from the council and a rereading of their orders of 1622. To underscore its point the Council for New England in 1632 reiterated that 'no ship, passengers or goods be permitted to be transported for New England without licence from the President and Council or their deputy or deputies'.[9] Migrants to New England were faced with a shifting flurry of paperwork and regulations, the weight of which varied with the political fortunes or administrative adroitness of their sponsors.

Recalling the proclamation of 1607, the Crown ordered in 1630 that no passengers should take ship from the western ports, from Workington to Bristol, unless they could show an appropriate licence or passport. Clerks and commissioners were appointed to prepare these documents. At this time the government wanted only to know the names and status of those departing the realm, and was not overly exercised about their religion.[10] Regulating emigration was still primarily a matter of commercial protectiveness and political convenience. Beliefs and ideology were not at issue. The official

---

[8] 'The Royal Charter', in M.H.S., *The Founding of Massachusetts* (Boston, 1930), pp. 40–1.

[9] 'Records of the Council for New England', A.A.S. *Proceedings* (1867), p. 111.

[10] Steele (ed.), *Tudor and Stuart Proclamations*, pp. 189–92.

impediments at first were designed to protect the security of the realm or the business and political interests of the colonial projectors, rather than to make it more difficult for Puritans to go to America. Not until the mid-1630s did the government impose religious checks on people departing the realm.

Only in 1634, after several thousand Englishmen and women had crossed over to New England, did the government of Charles I expand its procedures of control. By this time the Bay Colony had more enemies than friends in high places in London. Critics seized on rumours about the high-handedness of the Puritan regime and used complaints by disgruntled returners to support their case against the Massachusetts charter. The Council for New England had been thwarted, but its principals, Sir Ferdinando Gorges and Captain John Mason in particular, continued to lobby against Massachusetts on all occasions.[11]

Citing 'the frequent transportation of great numbers of his majesty's subjects out of this kingdom to the plantation called New England, whom divers persons know to be ill affected and discontented, as well with the civil as ecclesiastical government', the government sought to bring New England under tighter rein. The Privy Council claimed that 'such confusion and disorder is already grown there, especially in point of religion, as beside the ruin of the said plantation cannot but highly tend to the scandal both of the church and state here'.[12] One solution was to attack the Massachusetts charter directly, another was to harass emigration; both tactics were deployed.

In February 1634 the Privy Council stayed shipping to New England, delaying a dozen ships in the Thames and at Ipswich. The emigrant vessels were allowed to depart only after all passengers on board had taken the oaths of supremacy and allegiance and after the captains promised that they would hold daily services in accordance with the Book of Common Prayer of the Church of England.[13]

Laudian regulatory control was reaching towards America. In April Archbishop Laud became chairman of the newly-created Commission for Foreign Plantations, and the pressure against New England mounted. Bay Colony officials protested that the new licensing procedure and its associated delays 'hath impoverished the planters and merchants . . . the voyages of the ships have by that means been hindered, the passengers' estates much weakened'. That, of course, was

[11] Andrews, *Colonial Period*, vol. 1, p. 417.
[12] *A.P.C., Colonial*, p. 199.
[13] *Ibid.*, pp. 199–201.

the intent, and Laud was not moved by the petition. Nor was he impressed by a recitation of the 'liberties granted to the planters of New England'.[14]

In December 1634 the Commission for Foreign Plantations alerted port officials in London: 'It appeareth that great numbers of his majesty's subjects have been and are every year transported into those parts of America which have been granted by patent to several persons, and there settle themselves, some with their families and whole estates.' Among these migrants, they claimed, were 'many idle and refractory humours, whose only end is to live as much as they can without the reach of authority'.[15]

Such behaviour was clearly insufferable. The government therefore framed a 'careful and effectual order for the stopping of such promiscuous and disorderly parting out of the realm'. Henceforth, anyone intending to leave England needed a testimonial from a minister regarding his religious conformity and conversation, had to swear the oath of supremacy (acknowledging Charles I as supreme head of the Church of England) and the oath of allegiance (pledging undivided loyalty to the king), and had to provide attestations to their economic status from two justices of the peace. Anyone wealthy enough to be a subsidy payer needed a special licence from the king's commissioners. Prospective migrants had to collect this documentation and present it to the port officials before they could leave, paying sixpence each for their permits. The officials were supposed to list the names and qualities of everyone who departed, and submit their records twice yearly to the commissioners.[16]

Some of this paperwork survives. A record of the control process can be found in 'a register of the names of all the passengers which passed from the Port of London for one whole year ending at Christmas 1635'.[17] This register includes emigrants bound for Virginia and Barbados as well as New England. Adult males had to take the oaths of supremacy and allegiance regardless of their destination. On 2

[14] *Calendar of State Papers, Colonial, 1574–1666* (London, 1860), pp. 192, 194–5; Everett Emerson (ed.), *Letters from New England: The Massachusetts Bay Colony, 1629–1638* (Amherst. Mass., 1976), pp. 121–3.

[15] 'Commissioners of Plantations to the Lord Warden of the Cinque Ports', in H.M.C. *Thirteenth Report*, pt. 4 (Rye Corp.) (London, 1892), p. 95.

[16] *Winthrop Papers*, vol. 3, pp. 180–1. The searchers at Gravesend received sixpence per passenger, 'commonly called head-money', as a 'perquisite and benefit belonging to their places'; P.R.O., PC2/48, f. 228v.

[17] *A.P.C., Colonial*, p. 206; John Camden Hotten (ed.), *The Original Lists of Persons of Quality... Who Went from Great Britain to the American Plantations 1600–1700* (1874; reprinted, Baltimore, 1974), pp. 35–145.

April 1635 the port officials entered, 'These under-written names are to be transported to New England imbarqued in the *Planter*, Nicholas Trerice master, bound thither; the parties have brought certificate from the minister of St. Albans in Hertfordshire and attestations from the Justices of Peace according to the Lords' order.' Thirty-eight names follow, with more added on later dates as the passengers came aboard. Similarly on 9 April, 'In the *Elizabeth* of London, master William Stagg, bound for New England: these under-written have brought certificate from the minister of Hawkhurst in Kent, and attestation from two Justices of Peace, being conformable to the Church of England and that they are no subsidy men,' followed by the names and ages of James Hosmer, clothier, his wife, children and servants. So it continues throughout the year.[18] Records like these make possible the reconstruction of the social and demographic structure of the great migration essayed in Chapter 2.

Richard Mather gives an emigrant's-eye view of how the registration was carried out on board the *James* at Bristol in May 1635.

This day there came aboard the ship two of the searchers, and viewed a list of all our names, ministered the oath of Allegiance to all at full age, viewed our certificates from the ministers in the parishes from whence we came, approved well thereof, and gave us tickets, that is licences under their hands and seals to pass the seas, and cleared the ship, and so we departed.[19]

Such scrutiny may have been a tedious business, but there is no hint that Mather or his companions were fleeing in secrecy from an oppressive regime.

A stiffer regulatory climate was embodied in a royal proclamation of July 1635, 'to restrain the king's subjects from departing out of the realm without licence'. Though not specifically directed at migrants to New England, since it restricted travel to any foreign territories, the new order gave port officials a further opportunity to intimidate Massachusetts-bound migrants. 'Owners, masters, or mariners of any ships' were forbidden to transport passengers beyond the seas unless the passengers had produced, and the port officials had authenticated, a special licence from the Privy Council and secretary of state.[20] Among the elements that led to this regulation was nervousness about the tense international situation. The year 1635 was the year of French intervention in the Thirty Years War. At home it was a time of height-

[18] Hotten, *Original Lists*, pp. 45, 53–4.
[19] 'Richard Mather's Journal' in *Chronicles*, pp. 448–9.
[20] James F. Larkin (ed.), *Stuart Royal Proclamations*, vol. 2, *1625–1646* (Oxford, 1983), pp. 462–4; *Calendar of State Papers, Domestic, 1635–36*, p. 175.

ened militia preparations, and the extension to the inland counties of Ship-Money.

Although the government made clear its intention to control migration to New England, it was still quite easy to evade both the letter and the spirit of the law. In practice, the regulations were softened by the human frailty of the men entrusted with enforcement and by the ingenuity of those bent on evasion. Indeed, the tighter regulations of 1635 were said to have been imposed 'because those who were charged to examine the original passports, for some slight gain, allowed forged ones to pass'.[21]

The colony's agents worked hard to subvert as well as circumvent the official procedures. The government learned of 'John Harwood, a merchant at Mile End Green a factious dangerous independent and the common factor for all the merchants trading especially to New England', who 'uses constantly to cover and disguise the ships, goods and persons of those of that opinion in their voyages and passages, so as the officers of the customs, etc. at Gravesend and other places are by his interest and money corrupted to slip the oaths which otherwise ought to be tendered to all persons going out'.[22]

Charles I employed more than two hundred customs officers in ports around the country, and for every strict official there were others notorious for their laziness or corruption.[23] Like many bureaucratic operations, the activities of the customs service could be measured in waves, with periods of rigorous enforcement interspersed with periods of apathy and inefficiency. Even the crack-down of 1635 left gaps. Despite the intent of the Privy Council, a customs search could be a fairly perfunctory business, with plenty of opportunity for tips, bribes, drinks, gifts and turning of blind eyes.

Emmanuel Downing reported to John Winthrop, Jr., in 1635 that Massachusetts-bound migrants could leave London without too close an inspection.

There is one at the custom house appointed to receive certificates and give discharges to all such as shall go to the plantation. Some that are going to New England went to him to know what they should do. He bade them bring him any certificate from minister, churchwardens or Justice, that they were honest men, and he would give them their pass. They asked him what subsidy

---

[21] Larkin (ed.), *Stuart Royal Proclamations*, vol. 2, p. 463n.
[22] P.R.O., SP. Domestic and Foreign, Miscellaneous, no. 26. This John Harwood was most likely a kinsman to the Henry Harwood who sailed with the Winthrop fleet, and to George Harwood who was one of the original undertakers of the Massachusetts Bay Company.
[23] G. E. Aylmer, *The King's Servants: The Civil Service of Charles I* (London, 1961), pp. 125, 478–9.

men should do. He answered that he could not tell who were subsidy men, and would discharge them upon their certificate.[24]

Government policy towards emigration fluctuated with the pressure brought to bear on the Privy Council by the enemies of the Bay Colony. The subject was not one that Charles or Laud, by themselves, found consistently interesting. The pressure relaxed somewhat in 1636, to be reapplied the following year. Migrants who left at different times, and from different ports, would therefore have different experiences to report. John Winthrop attributed the ease of emigration in 1636 to the providential death of Captain John Mason of the Council for New England, an implacable enemy of Massachusetts, who, with Gorges, was 'the chief mover in all the attempts against us'. In 1636, 'the Lord taking him away, all the business fell on sleep, so as ships came and brought what and whom they would without any question or control'.[25] Winthrop's observation supports the opinion that the control of emigration had more to do with attacks on the Massachusetts charter than with the government's concern about who actually left England. The regulations were not designed simply to harass Puritans.

By the spring of 1637 the proceedings against the Massachusetts charter were coming to a head, so it is not surprising to find a new wave of regulations at that time. A new proclamation requiring stricter inspection of emigrants' licences and certificates was issued on 30 April, just a few days after the council secured a judgement that the charter could be vacated and a few days before they ordered the attorney-general to deliver the patent for New England to Laud's Commission for Foreign Plantations.

The King's most excellent majesty being informed that great numbers of his subjects have been and are every year transported into those parts of America which have been granted by patent to several persons, and there settle themselves, some of them with their families and whole estates; amongst which numbers there are also many idle and refractory humours, whose only or principal end is to live as much as they can without the reach of authority; his majesty having taken the premises into consideration, is minded to restrain for the time to come such promiscuous and disorderly departing out of the realm.

In practice, this prohibition was no more effective than any previous attempt to control the flow of overseas migrants.[26]

Mounting disquiet at Whitehall about the state of affairs in New England (and at home too) prompted the issue of additional regu-

[24] *Winthrop Papers*, vol. 3, p. 195.
[25] *Winthrop's Journal*, vol. 1, p. 181.
[26] *A.P.C., Colonial*, p. 217; Larkin (ed.), *Stuart Royal Proclamations*, vol. 2, pp. 555–6.

lations in 1638. 'His Majesty and the Board taking...into consideration the frequent resort to New England of divers persons ill-affected to the religion established in the Church of England and to the good and peaceable government of this state,' and 'well knowing the factious disposition of the people, or a great part of them, in that plantation, and how unfit and unworthy they are of any support or countenance from hence,' set out 'to restrain the transporting of passengers and provisions to New England,' and thereby to punish them by hobbling their trade. This time the government placed the burden on shipowners and their agents rather than individual migrants. Henceforth, 'all merchants, masters and owners of ships...with passengers for New England' had to obtain a special licence from the Privy Council before they could depart, and such licences could be withheld for arbitrary reasons.[27]

The effect was to outrage the merchant community and to clog the Thames and the Downs with delayed shipping. Shipowners protested that singling out the traffic to New England was damaging as well as unfair. Ships bound for Massachusetts might come home by way of Newfoundland, Virginia or the Spanish islands, and the export of emigrants was just the first leg of a developing triangle trade. The new restrictions, said the merchants, would 'deprive the kingdom of much trade, the importation of much money, his majesty of much custom, and many ships and seamen of employment'.[28]

As before, the Privy Council blew hot and cold, and in any case lacked the policing powers to enforce the proclamation. Some ships were inconvenienced and missed a good wind, but the regulations were more symptomatic of Privy Council hostility to Massachusetts than a serious handicap to the peopling of New England. John Winthrop recorded with satisfaction at the end of 1638, 'Many ships arrived this year with people of good quality and estate, notwithstanding the Council's order that none should come without the king's licence; but God so wrought that some obtained licence and others came away without.' The customs officials, according to Winthrop, were swayed by divine providence; they 'never made search for any goods, etc., but let men bring what they would without question or control. For sure the Lord awed their hearts'.[29] Perhaps what really happened is that someone awed their pockets, or simply distracted their attention.

From 1638 onwards the government was preoccupied with the Scot-

---

[27] P.R.O., PC2/49, f. 38; Larkin (ed.), *Stuart Royal Proclamations*, vol. 2, p. 610.
[28] A.P.C., *Colonial*, pp. 248–9.
[29] *Winthrop's Journal*, vol. 1, p. 271.

tish rebellion, the revolt against Ship-Money, and a developing political crisis at home, and could pay no more than periodic and perfunctory attention to its problem with New England. Some ships were detained, but most set sail without undue interference. Searchers were more concerned to intercept embargoed foodstuffs, in time of dearth, than to ferret out runaway Puritans, and even in this their effort was uneven. When James Alexander, the constable of Mansbridge Hundred, Hampshire, was ordered to stop victuals going to New England in 1638 he flatly refused to co-operate, 'whereby his majesty's business was neglected and hindered'.[30]

The old notion, still not buried, that Puritan migrants to America had to escape from Charles I's England through an underground network, is seriously wrong. Hardly any of the families involved in the great migration were actually fleeing from persecution. Edward Johnson's characterization of their departure, 'hunted after as David was by Saul', is utterly misleading.[31] It is true that a few radical preachers like Thomas Hooker, Thomas Shepard and Hugh Peter assumed false names or slipped aboard the emigrant vessels after the searchers and customs officers had left, but these were exceptional. Nearly everyone else left openly, and found little to hinder them in the regulatory procedures. For most people the controls were not burdensome, and their enforcement was erratic.

Diocesan officials were no more consistent in their attitude to emigration than were customs searchers or privy councillors. Early in 1634 Henry Dade, commissary to the archdeacon of Suffolk, wrote a fawning letter to Archbishop Laud, complaining about the laxity of local control of New England-bound migrants planning to depart from Ipswich. Requesting that Laud not tell the bishop of Norwich that he had written, Dade listed his objections to the peopling of New England.

If they are suffered to go in such swarms out of this kingdom it will be a decrease of the king's majesty's people here, an increase of the adversaries to the episcopal state [there]...and also will be an overthrow of trade.... Lastly it may abate the awefulness of the subjects of his majesty, for that they having of their own country and religion out of the king's dominions upon any discontent may fly to New England, from whence they cannot be advocated by reason of the largeness of that continent. And in every of these ways I am

---

[30] *Calendar of State Papers, Domestic, 1637–38*, p, 411. Negotiations for the staying and releasing of New England shipping can be traced in the Privy Council Registers, P.R.O., PC2/49, ff. 41v, 48, 169; PC2/50, ff. 1v, 7v, 260; PC2/51, ff. 25, 120. See also Leo Francis Stock (ed.), *Proceedings and Debates of the British Parliaments Respecting North America*, vol. 1, *1542–1668* (Washington, D.C., 1924), p. 109.

[31] *Wonder-Working Providence*, p. 25.

persuaded that such liberties of transporting of people will much endamage this kingdom, except that the plantation of New England suffer some great disaster.[32]

Dade's hostility to New England was founded on the view that the mere existence of the Puritan plantation posed a threat to domestic episcopal discipline. Others, including many of the bishops, held different opinions. Dade may have been thinking of his own bishop Corbet (Wren's predecessor at Norwich), when he told Laud, 'I am not of their mind who think it not material how many of such persons shall go out of this land, except they shall carry with them their breeders.'[33] Dade wanted the Puritan leaders punished; others in the government and ecclesiastical hierarchy were content to see them gone.

Indeed, some officials were only too happy to see the backs of the noisiest and most persistent trouble-makers. Stephen Goffe, a government agent in Holland, wrote in 1634 to Gilbert Sheldon, chaplain to Lord Keeper Coventry, expressing sarcastic satisfaction at John Davenport's difficulties with the Delft congregation. 'I doubt not but we shall be delivered from this plague too, and he will make for New England, whither Mr. Cotton . . . and Mr. Hooker are safely arrived, as they say here, by special extraordinary prosperous winds.'[34] In his report to the king on the condition of the Province of Canterbury in 1636 Laud recorded, 'In Norwich one Mr. Bridge, rather than he would conform, hath left his lecture and two cures, and is gone into Holland.' To which Charles made the marginal notation, 'Let him go, we are well rid of him.'[35]

In 1637 Archbishop Laud received a letter from John Bramhall, bishop of Derry in Ireland, reporting that 'the leaders of our nonconformists were all embarked for New England'. Bramhall added with apparent satisfaction, 'This church will quickly purge herself of her peccant humours if there be not a supply from thence.' When another Puritan emigrant group turned back after encountering severe Atlantic weather Laud wrote, ' 'Tis great pity the ringleaders . . .

---

[32] P.R.O., SP16/260/17.

[33] *Ibid.* Dade publicly stated that 'he knew the king and his council would be glad that the thousands who went to New England were drowned in the sea'; *Calendar of State Papers, Domestic (C.S.P.D.), 1635*, pp. 86, 518. Dade over-reached himself in his battle with the Ipswich Puritans, and found himself first hauled before the High Commission and then out of a job; *C.S.P.D., 1635–36*, pp. 47, 51, 98, 429; *C.S.P.D., 1636–37*, pp. 260, 322, 420; *C.S.P.D., 1637*, pp. 109, 143.

[34] P.R.O., SP16/260/13. Davenport, vicar at St. Stephen, Coleman Street, London, before ministering to his Dutch congregation, moved to New England in 1637.

[35] W. Scott and J. Bliss (eds.), *Works of . . . William Laud*, vol. 5 (Oxford, 1853), p. 340.

fell short of New England.'[36] Similarly in 1638 Laud corresponded with Strafford, the Lord Deputy in Ireland, 'I could not but smile at first when I saw how ready you were to stop the New Englanders, that they might plant with you, and presently after how glad you are to be rid of them, and let them go. For certainly wherever they come they'll root out that which is better than what they plant.'[37] Like Pharaoh with the Israelites (which is how some of the migrants saw themselves), Charles was willing to let his people go.

The Parliamentary regime of the 1640s was generally sympathetic to New England but was no less insistent on regulations. In August 1643 the House of Commons ordered 'all that shall desire to pass beyond the seas, with their wives, children or families' to 'first address themselves to the Committee at Haberdashers' Hall and bring testimony'. This was an all-encompassing regulation, aimed primarily at *émigrés* leaving civil war England for refuge in Europe but also affecting those going to America. The *Sarah*, bound for New England, was stayed as a result. Parliament insisted, however, that they did 'not intend by the general order of restraint of persons going beyond sea to restrain any ships, persons or goods going to New England, or to any other the English plantations', so the *Sarah* was allowed to depart.[38]

The procedure changed little during the rest of the seventeenth century, except that the traditional oaths were dropped during the Interregnum. Searchers and customs men continued to board ships bound for Massachusetts, registering the passengers and inspecting the cargo, although the pace of migration to New England fell off sharply after 1640. In 1651, for example, three customs officials at Gravesend searched the *John and Sarah* and registered 272 passengers before clearing them for their voyage to New England.[39] George Fox, the Quaker, who had more than his share of hostile treatment from government officials, observed similar activity on board the *Industry* in 1671. Although the searchers had already examined the passengers at Gravesend, below London, they insisted on a second enumeration at Deal. Fox wryly noted that the customs officials came aboard 'to peruse packets and get fees'.[40] The Gravesend searchers similarly

---

[36] H.M.C., *Report on the Manuscripts of the late R. R. Hastings* (London, 1947), vol. 4, pp. 73, 75.
[37] Scott and Bliss (eds.), *Works of ... William Laud*, vol. 7 (Oxford, 1860), p. 448.
[38] Stock (ed.), *Proceedings and Debates ... Respecting North America*, pp. 199, 207.
[39] W. B. Trask (ed.), *Suffolk Deeds* (Boston, 1880), vol. 1, nos. 5, 6. Most of these passengers were Scottish redemptioners consigned as servants in New England.
[40] George Fox, *Journal* (London, 1694), pp. 349–50.

came aboard the *Arabella* in 1671, 'to take notice of the names of the passengers'.[41] By this time official scrutiny of departures to New England, and to other places beyond the seas, was a matter of routine. But American Puritan memorialists were already recalling their departure for New England as a special providential deliverance, and their ease of exit as another of God's blessings.

[41] S. E. Morison (ed.), *Records of the Suffolk County Court 1671–1680* (Boston, 1933), vol. 1, p. 20.

6

'The vast and furious ocean': shipboard socialization and the Atlantic passage

At last, with all decisions and preparations in hand, the migrants can leave for New England. Although most accounts of this period slip quickly from descriptions of conditions in England to resettlement in America, without much consideration of the intervening journey, it will be argued here that the Atlantic crossing was a vital formative part of the colonizing experience.

English emigrants and travellers who journeyed to America in the seventeenth century underwent a crucial seasoning process, a *passage* in several senses of the word. Whether they shipped to the Chesapeake or sailed to the island colonies or New England, the voyagers experienced travails that could not be met on dry land. For many of the travellers the crossing was not simply a matter of transportation but rather a primary occasion for seasoning and testing, bonding and socialization, a rehearsal and preparation for community life in the wilderness. Puritans in particular, among those sailing to New England in the 1630s, perceived their journey as a series of tests and revelations. Emigrants with a heightened religious sensibility taught fellow-passengers how to interpret and internalize the trauma of the ocean passage. Although voyagers to other destinations may have seen similar sights and experienced similar hardships, the New England Puritans were unique in supplying a coherent framework for understanding, remembering and giving significance to their ocean passage. It is worth recalling that two of the most important documents in early American history, the 'Mayflower Compact' and Winthrop's 'Model of Christian Charity', originated on board ship.

Earlier versions of parts of this chapter appeared in 'The vast and furious ocean: the passage to Puritan New England', *New England Quarterly*, 57 (1984), pp. 511–32, and 'Puritans at sea: the seventeenth-century voyage to New England', *Log of Mystic Seaport*, 36 (1984), pp. 87–94. I am grateful to the editors of these journals for permission to incorporate this work.

'The vast and furious ocean'

Battling the Atlantic, bound for New England, the voyagers encountered terrors, witnessed marvels and earned a store of salt-grained memories that endowed them with the cachet of veterans. The ocean adventure left an indelible mark that irrevocably offset their experience from that of landsmen who stayed at home. The journey tried their endurance and challenged their health. It also made manifest God's power and mercy, which confirmed or expanded the Puritan providential view of the world. Puritans found confirmation of their faith in the course of the ocean passage, and the journey to New England sometimes hastened or consolidated the religious conversion of others. Migrants whose religion was unformed or unimportant to them at the time of embarkation might become much more amenable to New England godliness by the time they reached the Massachusetts shore. No wonder that New England sermonists employed such evocative maritime imagery; no wonder that the Puritan memorialists presented the first comers to New England as heroes who had braved a troublesome sea.[1]

Most of the ships that took passengers to New England were converted merchantmen with limited facilities for human freight. Wine traders were said to be most desirable, since they were sweeter smelling and tightly caulked. Others were pressed into service from the fishing fleet or the collier's trade. The *Mary Rose*, a Bristol ship of 180 tons, had engaged in the Spanish wine trade and Newfoundland fishing before being chartered for New England in 1639.[2] Few vessels were rated at more than 250 tons, with overall dimensions rarely exceeding a hundred feet. The *Warwick*, a typical ocean trader of the 1640s, measured eighty feet in length, twenty-three feet nine inches in beam, and was rated at 186 tons. John Winthrop's flagship, the *Arbella*, at 350 tons was unusually grand, befitting the governor of a new plantation, but its consorts, the *Talbot*, *Ambrose* and *Jewel* had more modest dimensions. The *Hercules* of Plymouth at 150 tons, the *Providence* of Barnstable at 160 tons and the *Elizabeth* of Dartmouth at 200 tons were more typical of the ships hauling emigrants and goods across the Atlantic in the 1630s.[3] The *James*, which carried Richard Mather's party from Bristol in 1635, was not much bigger, with a 220-ton rating.

[1] *Wonder-Working Providence*, pp. 25, 52, 56, 57.
[2] P.R.O., PC2/51, f. 25.
[3] R. C. Anderson, 'Lists of men-of-war 1650–1700, part 1, English ships, 1649–1702', *Society for Nautical Research Occasional Publications*, 5 (1935), pp. 2–4, 62–3; *Winthrop Papers*, vol. 2, p. 239. Other ships of the 1630s are listed in the Port Books, P.R.O., E/190, *passim*. For calculations of tons and tonnage see William A. Baker, *Colonial Vessels: Some Seventeenth-Century Sailing Craft* (Barre, Mass., 1962), p. 25.

Coming over

The *New Supply*, which took John Josselyn to New England in 1638, was a splendid 300-tonner, with 164 passengers on board.[4] Passengers, cargo and crew shared less than fifteen hundred square feet of decking and a hold in which a person could barely stand.

Some of the ships were frighteningly small and must have offered a miserable passage. The *Sparrowhawk*, which beached at Cape Cod in 1626, was barely forty feet in length. The *Margaret and John* of London, sailing to New England in 1630, was rated at forty tons, the same as the *William* of Barnstable in 1631 and the *Truelove* of Bideford in 1636. The *Bachelor*, shipping servants to Massachusetts in 1635, was a tiny bark of twenty-five tons.[5]

Larger vessels appeared on the Atlantic later in the period, not for the convenience of passengers but to accommodate the profitable cargoes of timber, fish, oil and wine that the merchantmen picked up from Newfoundland or the Spanish islands on their way home. Passengers' quarters involved temporary partitions of lumber and canvas, with cots and hammocks in whatever space was available. Gentlemen were lucky to find cabins. Personal chests and casks were stowed below, along with the animals and cargo, but most passengers kept a box or bundle of sea clothes and extra provisions to hand. Whatever motivated the movement to America, the voyage itself would be memorable for its discomforts, dankness and fetid odours.

English migrants to North America often approached their journey with apprehension and fear. Stories of storms and wrecks effectively dissuaded some prospective migrants from voyaging to America; others battled anxieties as they encountered the strange and terrifying world of the sea. Before the great migration of the 1630s only professional travellers, merchants and mariners knew the ropes of bluewater sailing. Although they were an island race, all living within eighty miles of the shore, the English, like most agrarian peoples, had shunned the sea and had little familiarity with its ways. Very few Englishmen of the seventeenth century had spent a night on a coastal vessel, and most had never been to sea at all. Some had never even seen a ship. Even coastal communities were normally oriented inland unless forced to face the water for fishing or defence. Ordinary people

[4] [Mather], 'Richard Mather's journal' in *Chronicles*, p. 453; John Josselyn, *An Account of Two Voyages to New England* (Boston, 1865), p. 5.
[5] *Ye Antient Wrecke: Loss of the Sparrow-Hawk in 1626* (Boston, 1865); P.R.O. E.190/947, 949; *Winthrop Papers*, vol. 3, p. 203. See also Charles Deane, 'Remarks on the small size of ships used in crossing the Atlantic, 1492–1626', M.H.S. *Proceedings*, 8 (1865), pp. 465–6.

travelled by land, picking their way along the ancient ridge routes or taking to the mud or dust of the ill-made roads.

The ocean was another matter, unknown and therefore feared. To the popular imagination the ocean suggested hazard and uncertainty. It conjured an alien and frightful environment of commotion and discomfort, fraught with 'daily expectations of swallowing waves and cruel pirates'.[6] Apprehensions about 'the casualties of the seas, which none can be freed from' and 'the length of the voyage... such as the weak bodies of women and other persons worn out with age and travail... could never be able to endure', had turned some of William Bradford's associates away from the Pilgrim venture.[7] Similar concerns dissuaded some prospective emigrants to Massachusetts. 'Good workmen... are fearful to go to sea for fear they shall not live to come to your land, but were it not for the danger of the seas you might have enough,' explained John Wollcott, describing the difficulty of attracting migrants to Connecticut in 1639.[8] William Cutter, writing from Newcastle in 1654, explained that 'truly the sad discouragement in coming by sea is enough to hinder' him in joining his family in New England.[9]

Preparing to die as they committed themselves to the deep, travellers customarily made their wills when embarking on an ocean crossing. Richard Swayne was so fearful when he emigrated to New England in 1635 that he distributed his family on four different vessels. Other families became separated when stay-at-home wives refused to follow their emigrant husbands, choosing to be rather 'a living wife in England than a dead one in the sea'.[10]

Much of this thalassophobia was overblown. Remarkably few people drowned on the way to New England, and many found the journey more exhilarating than tormenting. As some colonial promoters

---

[6] *Wonder-Working Providence*, p. 52.

[7] William Bradford, *History of Plymouth Plantation 1620–1647* (Boston, 1912), vol. 1, p. 56. Bradford's friends had good reason to be apprehensive after hearing Robert Cushman's report of the desperate voyage of 1618 in which 130 people died; Cushman to the Leyden Congregation, 8 May 1619, in William Bradford, *Of Plymouth Plantation 1620–1647*, ed. Samuel Eliot Morison (New York, 1963), pp. 356–7.

[8] [Wollcott], 'Letter of John Wollcott', *N.E.H.G.R.*, 2 (1848), p. 373.

[9] 'Dunster papers', M.H.S. *Collections*, ser. 4, vol. 2 (1854), p. 196.

[10] Edward E. Hale (ed.), *Note-book kept by Thomas Lechford... 1638 to... 1641* (Cambridge, Mass., 1885), pp. 18-19, for John Newgate's will in 1638; M.H.S. MSS., 'Miscellaneous, bound', for Edmund Jacklin in 1672. For the Swayne family see Savage, *Genealogical Dictionary*, vol. 4, p. 235. The phrase is from John Dunton, *The Life and Errors of John Dunton* (London, 1818), pp. 91–2, but the sentiment was not uncommon. Cf. *Wonder-Working Providence*, pp. 51, 84.

pointed out, open-water sailing was much less hazardous than coasting.[11] William Wood reassured prospective emigrants that 'whosever
put to sea in a stout and well-conditioned ship, having an honest
master and loving seamen, shall not need to fear but he shall find as
good content at sea as at land.... A ship at sea may well be compared
to a cradle rocked by a careful mother's hand, which though it be
moved up and down is not in danger of falling'.[12]

Most ships arrived safely. Available statistics confirm Christopher
Levett's encouraging estimate that 'once in seven years a ship should
be cast away, which is more than hath been usual, for I dare say that
for every ship that is cast away in those voyages there is a hundred
which cometh safe'.[13] In fact, of 198 recorded voyages bringing settlers
to New England in the 1630s only that of the *Angel Gabriel* ended in
disaster, and even then most of the passengers survived. Losses there
were, as merchants and insurers knew to their cost, but very few
seventeenth-century shipwrecks involved emigrants. The most dangerous voyage was the one back to England, where the rocks at the
mouth of the Channel devoured ships by the dozen.[14] Smallpox and
dysentery took their toll, but transatlantic travel was generally health-
ier in the 1630s than in the centuries of mass emigration that
followed.[15]

Nonetheless, most travellers prepared for the worst and measured
their actual experience at sea against their bleakest expectations. The
devout found refuge in prayer, comforted by the omnipresence of a
God who was 'Lord of sea and land'. 'If he did not watch over us, we
need not go over sea to seek death or misery, we should meet it at

[11] Sir Robert Gordon, *Encouragements for Such as Shall Have Intention to be Under-Takers
in the New Plantation* (Edinburgh, 1625), sig. D.
[12] William Wood, *New England's Prospect*, ed. Alden T. Vaughan (Amherst, Mass., 1977),
p. 70.
[13] Christopher Levett, 'A voyage into New England begun in 1623 and ended in 1624',
in James Phinney Baxter (ed.), *Christopher Levett, of York, the Pioneer Colonist in Casco
Bay* (Portland, Maine, 1893), p. 136.
[14] For example, the *Lyon* foundered in the Chesapeake in 1632 after delivering her
passengers to New England; Robert E. Moody (ed.), *The Saltonstall Papers*, vol. 1
(Boston, 1972), p. 121n. The *Mary and Jane* was lost homewardbound in 1633;
Winthrop's Journal, vol. 1, p. 153. For vivid accounts of shipwrecks see Richard Steere,
A Monumental Memorial of Marine Mercy (Boston, 1684), pp. 4–6, and 'Edward Rhode's
journal', Maryland Historical Society MS. 1699, p. 58. See also Violet Barbour, 'Marine risks and insurance in the seventeenth century', *Journal of Economics and Business
History*, 1 (1928–9), pp. 561–96.
[15] *Cf.* the severe mortality among eighteenth- and nineteenth-century migrants, reported in John Duffy, 'The passage to the colonies', *Mississippi Valley Historical Review*,
38 (1951–2), pp. 29–32, and Philip Taylor, *The Distant Magnet: European Emigration
to the U.S.A.* (New York, 1971), p. 140.

every step, in every journey; and is he not a God abroad as well as at home?'[16] In the providential world-view of most Puritans, every crashing wave carried the breath of God and every league of distance was a step towards heaven. Puritans interpreted their safe arrival in America as a signal of providential deliverance, mere completion of the journey confirming God's presence in their venture. Non-Puritans could take comfort in the confidence of the elect.

The passengers not only had to adjust to the novel conditions of the ship and the ocean but also had to get to know each other. Although some had journeyed in groups from their homes in the country and many had made the decision to leave in the company of relatives and friends, others, servants in particular, came singly or with none of their immediate family. Emigrants congregated from various parts of England and rarely had a chance to take stock of their travelling companions before they assembled on board. Even the Winthrop fleet, the best organized of all collective departures, contained hundreds who were strangers to one another. According to John White in 1630, 'There passed away about 140 persons out of the western parts from Plymouth, of which I conceive there were not six known either by face or fame to any of the rest.'[17] Rather than being a tight-knit conspiracy, as some enemies alleged, White argued that the exodus to New England represented the separate desires of a heterogeneous movement, a story confirmed by the surviving passenger lists. The *Elizabeth and Anne* outbound from London in 1635, for example, carried 104 passengers from Worcestershire and Surrey, Middlesex and Kent. The *Abigall*, which left for New England a month later, registered 175 passengers from Bedfordshire and Northamptonshire, as well as from the Thameside counties of Middlesex and Kent. Each group brought its distinctive local heritage and patterns of experience, which sometimes endured in New England.[18]

Whether they came from Lancashire or Hampshire, the West Country or East Anglia, the emigrants created a new, if temporary, community on board. For some, their time at sea represented a first communal experience, an important preparation for the community discipline of early New England. The long weeks on the Atlantic could

[16] *Winthrop Papers*, vol. 2, pp. 198, 209, 219. Cf. Proverbs 30:4, and Job 28:5.
[17] John White, 'The planters plea', in M.H.S., *The Founding of Massachusetts* (Boston, 1930), p. 186.
[18] John Camden Hotten, *The Original Lists of Persons of Quality* (1874; reprinted, Baltimore, 1984), pp. 57–100; David Grayson Allen, *In English Ways: The Movement of Societies and the Transferal of English Local Law and Custom to Massachusetts Bay in the Seventeenth Century* (Chapel Hill, N.C., 1981).

be spent comparing past experiences, establishing useful connections, and sounding religious beliefs. Active Puritans spent much of their time teaching and converting. Others found time to question and to think. Alliances that shaped subsequent behaviour in America sometimes owed their origin to the enforced close company of the Atlantic passage. Strangers became acquaintances, acquaintances became firm friends (and sometimes enemies). Passengers took stock of their shipmates' characters and reputations while sharing duties, diet and danger. Aboard the *Griffin* in 1634, Anne Hutchinson allured some shipmates and alarmed others with her intense religiosity. Edmund Brown, a correspondent of Sir Simonds D'Ewes, 'found some company of worth' aboard the *Thomas and Frances* in 1638, and shared a mess with Emmanuel Downing. Thomas Lechford, in the same company, recalled conversations 'on shipboard' that continued on land.[19]

Roger Clap found his future wife among fellow-passengers on the *Mary and John*. Thomas Noyes married Mary Haynes, who had been his shipmate on board the *Confidence*. Edward Winslow, a *Mayflower* passenger, married Susanna White, widow of William White, 'who had been his companion in the ship'. Thomas Bittlestone, who died at Cambridge, Massachusetts, in 1643, left twenty shillings in his will to 'Mr. Fordham who came over in the ship with me'.[20] Undoubtedly there were other kin connections, neighbourly relationships and networks of interaction that could be traced to social bonding on the journey. Future research may discover whether free English migrants on their way to New England remembered fellow-travellers in the same way as slaves bound for Virginia regarded their shipmates as fictive kin.[21]

The traditional social hierarchy continued in force at sea, but modified in ways that anticipated the beginnings of a different social order in New England. The migrants took with them a truncated social structure, much more socially homogeneous than any they had known

[19] David D. Hall (ed.), *The Antinomian Controversy, 1636–1638* (Middletown, Conn., 1968), pp. 6, 317, 339, 365, 370, 382; Everett Emerson (ed.), *Letters from New England: The Massachusetts Bay Colony, 1629–1638* (Amherst, Mass., 1976), p. 226; Hale (ed.), *Note-Book Kept by Thomas Lechford*, p. 45.

[20] [Clap], 'Roger Clap's memoirs', in *Chronicles*, p. 367n.; Savage, *Genealogical Dictionary*, vol. 3, p. 299, and vol. 4, p. 599; *Suffolk County Wills* (Baltimore, 1984), p. 14. Some of these people were already acquainted before their journey, and their marriages sometimes occurred several years after, so the point should not be stretched.

[21] Herbert G. Gutman, 'Afro-American kinship before and after emancipation in North America', in Hans Medick and David Warren Sabean (eds.), *Interest and Emotion: Essays in the Study of Family and Kinship* (Cambridge, 1984), pp. 247–8.

at home. The uppermost ranks of English society seldom graced an emigrant vessel, and the ships bound for New England rarely carried common labourers or the very poor. Participants in the great migration ranged from minor gentry and clergy down to craftsmen and husbandmen, and their servants were not necessarily of lowlier origins. Although social relationships on board continued to reflect the established modulations of degree, rank and status, important sectors of the traditional social order were missing.[22]

Servants continued to obey their masters, artisans deferred to yeomen, and tradesmen still acknowleged the superiority of gentlemen, but the special circumstances of the floating regime conspired to diminish traditional attributes of social standing. Rank and status usually reflected one's occupation or 'addition', but during the journey all conventional economic activities were suspended. The captain held absolute authority and was free to override the respect that accompanied English social position. Gentlemen and their families enjoyed more spacious quarters, but their rank could not buy them a safer or a speedier passage. Listlessness, privation and fear touched all sectors of the shipboard community, regardless of social distinctions. Everyone was, quite literally, in the same boat.

Betwixt and between the Old World and the New, the passengers could be likened to participants in a protracted *rite de passage*, enjoying an intensive form of *communitas* while separated from their normal regime. The ship became a liminal space, floating free of conventional considerations.[23] Even the tyranny of time was transformed, since the daily round at sea had nothing in common with the rhythms of a Suffolk village or a London street. Such conditions, involving fellowship in adversity and the pursuit of common goals, are well known to intensify group cohesiveness and group commitment, so it is not far-fetched to imagine a bonding among Atlantic travellers of the kind that is found among veterans of other intensive group experiences. Confined for eight to twelve weeks or more to a tiny wooden world, the travellers were thrust into intimacies that might never have developed on land.[24]

---

[22] See chapter 2.

[23] *Communitas* and 'liminality' are discussed in Victor W. Turner, *The Ritual Process: Structure and Anti-Structure* (Chicago, 1969), pp. 94–130, and *Dramas, Fields and Metaphors: Symbolic Action in Human Society* (Ithaca, N.Y., 1974), pp. 166–9, 200–4, 321–33.

[24] On group experiences see I. L. Janis, 'Group identification under conditions of extreme danger', in Dorwin Cartwright and Alvin Zander (eds.), *Group Dynamics:*

Coming over

≈≈≈≈≈≈

The travellers' first impression at the port of embarkation was the strangeness of it all. Arriving at Bristol in May 1635, Richard Mather 'found things very unready, and all on heaps, many goods being not stowed, but lying on disordered heaps here and there in the ship'.[25] Skeins, coils and tangles of rope hung with mysterious complexity. Unfamiliar nautical tackle and the puzzling seafarer's vocabulary sparked both wariness and curiosity. Later in the seventeenth century Ned Ward remarked, with dark facetiousness, that the ship had enough rope to remind a man of the gallows, which was only of comfort if one preferred hanging to drowning.[26] Edward Taylor and his companions found the sailors' activity with ropes and canvas so absorbing that they quite forgot to say their morning prayers.[27]

Delay was endemic to the start of an ocean voyage. Almost every migrant group became resigned to a period of waiting – waiting for instructions from the ship's owners or undertakers, clearance by customs officials and searchers, approval of harbour authorities, the gathering of a protective convoy and, above all, waiting for a favourable wind. The time called for the saints to talk of patience, and for others to divert themselves as best they could. During the 1630s, when a regular traffic ferried emigrants to New England, at least three or four weeks commonly elapsed between passengers' first coming aboard and the ship's departure.[28] Delay and dispiritment provided an early test for the migrants' fortitude and character. Thomas Shepard waited almost eight weeks at Ipswich in 1634 for the *Hope* to prepare for its abortive voyage to New England, and then faced further frustration as heavy seas forced the vessel back against the shore. The *Defence*, the vessel that eventually took Thomas Shepard to New England, began gathering its passengers as early as 20 June 1635, but did not sail before 10 August.[29] Richard Mather's party had journeyed overland from Lancashire to Bristol in 1635, and then had to wait

---

Research and Theory, 3rd. ed. (New York, 1968), pp. 80–90; and Charles A. Kiesler, *The Psychology of Commitment: Experiments Linking Behavior to Belief* (New York, 1971).

[25] 'Richard Mather's journal', in *Chronicles*, p. 448.

[26] Ned Ward, 'A trip to New-England', in George P. Winship (ed.), *Boston in 1682 and 1699* (Providence, R.I., 1905), p. 34.

[27] [Taylor], 'Diary of Edward Taylor', M.H.S. *Proceedings*, 18 (1880–1), p. 7. Taylor crossed the ocean in 1668 but his observations would equally have applied in the 1630s.

[28] See Hotten, *Original Lists*, pp. 44–144.

[29] Michael McGiffert (ed.), *God's Plot: The Paradoxes of Puritan Piety, Being the Autobiography and Journal of Thomas Shepard* (Amherst, Mass., 1972), pp. 57–60, 63, and Hotten, *Original Lists*, p. 90.

Figure 3. 'Dockside'. Detail from Wenceslaus Hollar, *Navium Variae Figurae et Formae* (London, 1647). By permission of The Huntington Library, San Marino, California (RB 313969 H 2449).

153

through most of April and May for their ship to be readied and for the rest of the company to assemble.[30]

Delays caused by failures of the wind were intensely frustrating. One emigrant vessel of 1636 left Gravesend on 1 June but by 30 August had gone no farther than the Isle of Wight. An observer reported, 'This will fall exceeding heavy to divers in the ship who had made some provision for their livelihood in New England; they will be enforced to spend it before they go, and all for the want of a constant east wind. They have had the wind for a day or two and then brought back again.'[31] Ships out of London commonly found themselves windbound at the Downs, between the mouth of the Thames and the straits of Dover. Even departures from western ports could be frustrated by the capricious westerlies of the Atlantic wind system. Richard Mather's group aboard the *James*, for example, became stuck off Bristol for more than a week and were then blown around the Bristol Channel and windbound for twelve days at Milford Haven before finally thrusting out into the ocean.[32]

Political winds could further complicate the start of a voyage, and the ship could be mired in a tangle of orders and instructions more fickle and debilitating than any contrariness of the weather. Government agencies periodically imposed fresh regulations on departing vessels or enforced unexpected embargoes on all traffic to New England. Customs bailiffs blocked the departure of the *Francis* and the *Elizabeth*, preparing to sail from Ipswich to Boston in 1634. It took two weeks of negotiation before the vessels were free of this particular entanglement, and another two months before they actually set sail. Similarly, the *James* was stayed three months in 1640 'to the great prejudice and exceeding great discouragement of the passengers'.[33]

Delay was expensive as well as dispiriting. Travellers who had prepared psychologically for an overseas adventure instead found themselves cooped in a crowded seaport, either already on board a vessel whose bilges were beginning to fester, or ashore in rented lodgings.

---

[30] 'Richard Mather's journal', p. 448.
[31] *Winthrop Papers*, vol. 3, p. 296.
[32] 'Richard Mather's journal', pp. 451–8.
[33] *Acts of the Privy Council, Colonial Series, 1613–1680* (London, 1908), pp. 199, 201, 206; Leo Francis Stock (ed.), *Proceedings and Debates of the British Parliaments Respecting North America* (Washington, D.C., 1924), vol. 1, pp. 113, 107–9. Ships were further delayed by the periodic visits of the king's pressmen, who had first claim on their crews; see Francis Higginson, 'A true relation of the last voyage to New England', in M.H.S., *The Founding of Massachusetts* (Boston, 1930), pp. 63–5; Isabel MacBeath Calder (ed.), *Letters of John Davenport* (New Haven, Conn., 1937), p. 5; and Charles A. LeGuin, 'Sea life in seventeenth-century England', *American Neptune*, 27 (1967), pp. 133–4.

Each day of delay cost from sixpence to several shillings or more, depending on style and status, and this added to the cost of emigration.[34] Emigrants might well complain, like Robert Cushman waiting for the leaky and mis-named *Speedwell*, 'Our victuals will be half eaten up, I think, before we go from the coast of England.'[35] Some travellers seized the opportunity for a final stroll ashore or passed the time with local sightseeing. Some diverted themselves in taverns, and felt the censure of their more sanctimonious fellow travellers. A few consulted dockside astrologers who sold them prognostications for the voyage. Delay also allowed waverers a final chance to change their minds, like the workmen recruited for the ironworks in Massachusetts who jumped ship at the Isle of Wight.[36]

At last, after all the false starts, postponements and delays, the ship could be on its way. Casting off signified a momentous break with old England. Bursts of trumpets, rounds of shot, flaring of flags, and waving of hats and hands accompanied the vessel from the harbour to catch the wind and the tide. Passengers who were caught ashore had to hurry, and some even managed to miss the boat. This was the fate of the hapless Henry Winthrop, who missed the *Arbella* in 1630. Precipitous sailing almost stranded Edward Taylor at Plymouth and John Barnard at Portsmouth. Only energetic rowing in a commandeered longboat allowed Barnard and his companions to catch the *Buckingham*, which had already started on its voyage to New England.[37]

No one could say how long the voyage would take. Everything depended on the unpredictable Atlantic weather and the success of ship and crew in contending with it. Five-week passages were recorded, but such speedy crossings were remarkable. Eight to twelve weeks was more usual, with the average passage taking ten and a half weeks. The *James* out of Southampton took barely five and a half

---

[34] For typical expenses ashore in 1633, see *Archives of Maryland*, vol. 3 (Annapolis, 1885), p. 24.

[35] Bradford, *History of Plymouth Plantation*, vol. 1, p. 142.

[36] 'Richard Mather's journal', pp. 451–4; Dunton, *Life and Errors*, pp. 87-8; *Winthrop Papers*, vol. 3, p. 296, and vol. 4, pp. 36–7. Thomas Gilmett, a London haberdasher, set out for New England in 1632 but was apparently so unnerved by an accident that damaged the *Elizabeth* at Pendennis, Cornwall, that he left the ship and was still in England to testify in a damage suit about the incident in 1637; Peter Wilson Coldham (ed.), *English Adventurers and Emigrants, 1609–1660* (Baltimore, 1984), pp. 88, 36. Francis Rogers, awaiting a convoy later in the Stuart period, reported, 'We had much idle time on our hands, having many amours and intrigues'; in Bruce S. Ingram (ed.), *Three Sea Journals of Stuart Times* (London, 1936), p. 218.

[37] *Winthrop Papers*, vol. 2, p. 244; 'Diary of Edward Taylor', p. 8; (Barnard), 'Autobiography of the Rev. John Barnard', in M.H.S., *Collections*, ser. 3, vol. 5 (1836), p. 209.

weeks to reach Boston in 1635, but another *James* out of Bristol in the same year spent twelve weeks at sea before reaching New England.[38] Sometimes things went terribly wrong, and the journey lengthened to the point of disaster. The passengers on the *Sparrow-hawk* had 'no water, no beer, nor any wood left, but had burnt up all their empty cask... they feared they should be starved at sea or consumed with diseases' before they finally ran aground on Cape Cod.[39] Another poor ship limped into Boston harbour in 1636 after twenty-six weeks at sea, eighteen weeks from land to land. Tormented by contrary winds, a Bristol vessel spent twenty weeks at sea before making land, and its starving company was lucky to land at Barbados before continuing to New England.[40]

Two routes were available, the northern route via the banks of Newfoundland or the southern route via the Azores and Barbados. Some ships seem to have tramped their way around the Atlantic, going as far north as the Faroes, or south to the Canaries, to pick up supplies. The northern route might be quicker, though colder, but ran the hazard of fogs and shoals. The southern route could be so hot that leaks resulted from shrinking timbers and melting pitch. Springtime was the favoured time of departure. As Fitz-John Winthrop later explained, 'It will be difficult to adventure upon the coast of New England' if delayed after August, 'and then it must be deferred till February or the beginning of March.'[41] Like the earlier explorers, most migrants made their first direct acquaintance with New England in high summer.

From the very beginning the voyage offered opportunities for a providential and self-congratulatory view of the world. In the confusion of departure there were inevitably minor collisions as cables dragged or spars and rigging came foul. Superstitious travellers interpreted these mishaps as ill omens for the voyage, but the devout, like Richard Mather, attributed survival to 'the guidance of God and his care over us'.[42] Errors of navigation, achievements of seamanship

[38] Crossing times are calculated from forty-four seventeenth-century voyages from England to New England where the dates of departure and arrival are known.

[39] Bradford, *History of Plymouth Plantation*, vol. 2, p. 13; *Ye Antient Wrecke.*

[40] *Winthrop's Journal*, vol. 1, p. 200; Cotton Mather, *Magnalia Christi Americana* (Hartford, Conn., 1820), vol. 2, pp. 298–9.

[41] Einar Joensen (ed.), *Tingbókin 1615–54* (Tórshavn, 1953), pp. 297–8 (I owe this reference to Jonathan Wylie); M.H.S. *Collections*, ser. 5, vol. 8 (1882), p. 324; Coldham, *English Adventurers and Emigrants*, p. 121. On the seasonal advantages of various routes see William S. Powell, *John Pory, 1572–1636: The Life and Letters of a Man of Many Parts* (Chapel Hill, N.C., 1977), p. 83.

[42] 'Richard Mather's journal', p. 453.

and the fickleness of the weather could all be seen as manifestations of divine will. A safe arrival in New England could be attributed to serviceable ships and a hard-working crew, but thanks were directed primarily to God for a signal preservation. Skilful sailors could be regarded simply as 'instruments' of God's mercy, and deliverance from drowning could be taken as proof that the Puritans indeed had Christ by their side. John Cotton explained, 'The safety of mariners' and passengers' lives . . . lieth not on ropes and cables . . . but in the name and hand of the lord.'[43]

Richard Mather automatically attributed the success of his voyage to 'the goodness of our God . . . the blessing of God. Our gracious God (blessed and forever blessed be his name!) did save us all alive'.[44] Thomas Shepard saw God's 'unspeakable rich mercy' in escape from a tempest. 'This deliverance was so great that I then did think if ever the Lord did bring me to shore again I should live like one come and risen from the dead.'[45] Coming safe to land was akin to being born again.

Puritans laid this on heavier than most, but it is worth pointing out that they had no monopoly of godliness and were not the sole pur-veyors of providentialism. The company aboard the *Alexander*, bound for the Antilles in 1631, held prayers three times a day, and the Catholic Sir Henry Colt gave thanks to God for Divine 'favour and benefit'. The Anglican Thomas James, serving Charles I in the icy north Atlantic, similarly gave 'praise to God for his merciful delivery of us', and named his landfall 'the Harbour of God's Providence'.[46]

When secular migrants travelled in the company of religious en-thusiasts they could easily acquire godly habits by example and by exhortation. This might be called the Puritan osmosis syndrome. In-cidents of all sorts proved occasions for Puritan recruitment, godly instruction or religious reinforcement. Whenever a minister was on board he took command of religious instruction and daily devotions. Some ships carried several clergymen, but most had none. Thomas Shepard worked the mariners while John Norton led the passengers in prayer on board the *Hope* of Ipswich. Those on board the *Defence*

---

[43] John Cotton, 'A brief exposition upon Ecclesiastes', quoted in Peter N. Carroll, *Puritanism and the Wilderness: The Intellectual Significance of the New England Frontier, 1629–1700* (New York, 1969), p. 39.
[44] 'Richard Mather's journal', pp. 476–8.
[45] McGiffert (ed.), *God's Plot*, p. 60.
[46] 'The voyage of Sir Henry Colt', in V. T. Harlow (ed.), *Colonising Expeditions to the West Indies and Guiana, 1623-1667* (London, 1925), pp. 57, 65; Thomas James, *The Strange and Dangerous Voyage of Captaine Thomas Iames* (London, 1633), pp. 6, 7, 11, 12 and *passim*.

'were refreshed with the society of Mr. Wilson and Mr. Jones, by their faith and prayers and preaching'.[47] Richard Mather and Daniel Maud shared religious duties on board the *James,* enjoying 'the fellowship of divers godly Christians in the ship, and by means of our constant serving God morning and evening every day'.[48] Similar roles were played by lay Puritans in the 1630s and by the Nonconformists who travelled to New England after the Restoration.

Practising their religion beyond the eyes of bishops and apparitors, in a primitive shipboard environment that could not possibly accommodate traditional liturgical forms, the Puritans demonstrated the power and simplicity of reformed Protestantism. The Privy Council ordered in 1634 that shipboard worship should follow 'the Book of Common Prayers established in the Church of England', but there was nothing it could do to enforce the ruling.[49] This was just another Laudian gesture, annoying but without teeth. Ministers conducted services at sea without the paraphernalia of vestments and altars, a practice that foreshadowed the purity of the ordinances in New England.

On board ship, if never before, the travellers discovered the spiritual dominance of the Puritan leaders. The vessel provided a felicitous environment for the making of Puritans. The journey saw the consolidation of the faithful, the drawing in of the wavering and perhaps, in reaction, the hardening of the unregenerate. Religious activists appealed to a captive audience. After eight weeks of exposure to Puritan ministration and propaganda, the emigrants might find the preachers' message hard to resist. Ordinary laymen, with little else to do, engaged in prolonged discussions about the merits of episcopacy and congregationalism. Debate on board the *Griffin* focussed on the nature and means to grace and salvation. Some Puritan ministers even gained converts among the hardbitten crew.[50]

Godly travellers gave thanks for their success in converting fellow-passengers. A group of Puritan ministers bound for America in 1636 'were very instrumental in the converting of many souls'. Though all seemed lost when their vessel was disabled by 'a desperate leak' and a broken rudder, the ministers took credit for saving the ship through

[47] McGiffert (ed.), *God's Plot,* pp. 60, 63.
[48] 'Richard Mather's journal', p. 479.
[49] *Acts of the Privy Council, Colonial, 1613–60,* pp. 200–1.
[50] *Wonder-Working Providence,* p. 62; Hall, *Antinomian Controversy,* p. 382; Thomas Lechford, *Plain Dealing, or News from New England,* ed. Darrett B. Rutman (New York, 1969), introduction; Thomas Shepard, 'Election sermon in 1638', *N.E.H.G.R.,* 24 (1870), p. 366.

prayer. 'This looks like life from the dead to these poor men who had received but a little before a sentence of death.' In such circumstances it was easy to herd frightened passengers into the Puritan fold, especially when it became clear that the new religious conformity would be vital to prospects in New England.[51] We may never know what proportion of the emigrants were uncommitted in their religion when they embarked at London or Southampton, but it is likely that several hundreds more had cleaved to God's cause by the time they came ashore at Salem or Boston.

After the novelty and tension of departure, the journey itself could be anticlimactic. The weeks were marked by seasickness, monotony, boredom, bad weather and a steadily deteriorating diet. Passengers had long stretches of time for discourse and contemplation, and plentiful opportunity to observe the wonders of the deep. In confined space and insanitary conditions, with wet bedding and festering bilges, they might frequently regret the decision that had taken them from a familiar shore.

Ships setting out for New England often associated briefly with vessels bound for other parts of the world. As they gathered at the Downs or sailed down the Channel they might fall alongside stately East Indiamen, southern wine traders, Newfoundland fishermen or elements of the Virginia servant/tobacco fleet. Sometimes conditions allowed ship-to-ship visiting, giving the New England-bound passengers a vivid introduction to global commerce.

Since the waters at the mouth of the Channel were notoriously infested with predators, the various English ships usually formed convoys to secure their mutual defence. These conveys might be informal groupings, lasting no more than a few days, or they could be organized flotillas with pre-arranged rules for signalling and carefully defined structures of command. Signals with ensigns and topsails communicated particular intentions, and at night the ships carried lights on their mizen shrouds to indicate their position. Two lights meant trouble, perhaps a leak or a problem with the rigging. In fog the crews fired shots or banged drums in order to maintain contact. Working across the Atlantic in 1635 the *James* stayed close to the slower *Angel Gabriel*, not out of affection but because the crew felt safer in the

[51] Robert Fleming, *The Fulfilling of the Scriptures* (London, 1669), p. 283; James Janeway, *Mr. James Janeway's Legacy to His Friends: Containing Twenty-Seven Famous Instances of God's Providence in and about Sea Dangers and Deliverances* (London, 1675), pp. 9–14.

Figure 4. 'Atlantic freighter, 1629'. From Josef Furtenbach, *Architectura Navalis* (Ulm, 1629).

company of the *Angel*'s superior weaponry. Richard Mather noted that the *James* 'went sometimes with three sails less than we might', in order to keep pace with its consort, but the loss of time was compensated by the improvement in security.[52]

Every ship was armed. The *Angel Gabriel* carried 'fourteen or sixteen pieces of ordnance', sufficient to hold off a lightly-armed marauder but not enough to wage serious battle. Winthrop's *Arbella* carried twenty-eight guns. The *New Supply* of 1638 boasted a score of sacres and minions that could fire five-pound shot over 520 paces at point blank. Although formidable to landsmen with limited experience of weaponry, these arms were puny compared to the calverins and demi-calverins of the men-of-war. A fighting ship could hurl shot weighing eighteen pounds or more over almost half a mile. Smaller guns, like falcons and falconets, were useful only for salutations.[53]

Without weapons or a protective convoy an emigrant ship lay exposed to the attentions of pirates. Dunkirk rovers, Dutch capers, Irish raiders, and French, Flemish and Spanish privateers all preyed on English commercial shipping. English royalist privateers added to the problem in the 1640s and 1650s. Most feared of all were the Islamic Sallee-men, 'Turkish' raiders from Algiers, who were not content with plunder but also took Christians as slaves. Lady Mary Eden wrote anxiously to John Winthrop in 1636 about her emigrant cousin, 'I hear there were two ships taken by the Turk, and I am afraid they are in one of them.'[54] Every unidentified sail produced palpitations, since all strange ships were presumed hostile until proved friendly.

The crew of Winthrop's *Arbella* jumped to battle stations when suspicious sails appeared in the Channel. Women and children huddled below decks while the male passengers and crewmen drilled with muskets. 'Our captain caused the gun room and gun deck to be cleared, all the hammocks were taken down, our ordnance loaded, and our powder chests and fireworks made ready.' The ship's company assembled for prayer. Anxious minutes passed as the vessels closed in expectation of a fight. Fortunately, this scare proved to be a false alarm, and 'our fear and danger was turned into mirth and friendly entertainment'.[55]

Others were not so lucky. The *Charles*, the *Success* and the *Whale* barely scraped into Plymouth in 1631 after Dunkirkers ravaged them

[52] *Winthrop Papers*, vol. 2, pp. 239, 247, 249, 257; 'Richard Mather's journal', p. 459.
[53] Josselyn, *Account of Two Voyages*, p. 5; John Smith, 'An accidence, or the path-way to experience, necessary for all young seamen', in Arber, *Smith*, vol. 2, p. 801.
[54] *Winthrop Papers*, vol. 3, p. 237.
[55] *Winthrop Papers*, vol. 2, pp. 242–3.

on their return from New England. The *Charles*, 'a stout ship of 300 tons', was 'so torn that she had not much left of her whole above water'.[56] Although actual attacks on New England-bound vessels were rare, the expectation of danger was ever present. Stories about pirates and other enemies heightened the tension, so that Puritan emigrants were inclined to attribute an incident-free passage to divine protection.

Nearly every emigrant was seasick. Indeed, there is hardly an account of transatlantic travel in the seventeenth century that fails to mention 'spewing' and the unaccustomed discomfort of the passengers. Pitching and rolling produced an unpleasant novelty, with miserable effects. Passengers on the *Talbot* in 1629 reacted badly to 'the tossing waves of the western sea'. Richard Mather's party aboard the *James* was similarly afflicted. 'The ship danced, and many of our women and children were not well, but seasick and mazy and light in their heads, and so could scarce go without falling.' Seasickness so reduced Edward Taylor on his journey to New England that on some Sundays it kept him from his religious duties. The Quaker leader, George Fox, crossing the Atlantic in 1671, was unusual in not falling victim to seasickness when all around him were indisposed, but he attributed this to the damage already done to his internal organs by repeated imprisonments.[57]

Seasickness was no joking matter. It sapped the travellers' strength and weakened their morale. For some migrants the experience was distressing enough to dissuade them from ever going to sea again. Ingenious remedies appeared, including 'conserve of wormwood', and a concoction of sugar, tragacanth, cinnamon and ginger, made up into gilded pills. The best remedy was activity and exercise. The symptoms rarely persisted for more than a week or two, unless the weather was especially boisterous. On board the *Arbella* in 1630 seasick victims were brought on deck to play a game with a rope stretched from the steerage to the mainmast, to 'sway it up and down till they were warm, and by this means they grew well and merry'.[58]

Whereas the sailors were in their element in this tossing and bobbing world, working the ship and making their living, the emigrants were

---

[56] *Winthrop's Journal*, vol. 1, p. 59; *Chronicles*, p. 330.
[57] Higginson, 'True relation', p. 64; 'Richard Mather's journal', p. 449; 'Diary of Edward Taylor', p. 9; George Fox, *Journal* (London, 1694), p. 351. See also Bradford, *History of Plymouth Plantation*, vol. 1, p. 149; *Wonder-Working Providence*, p. 57; and LeGuin, 'Sea life in seventeenth-century England', p. 126. Animals also suffered from seasickness, compounding the stench and misery on board.
[58] Josselyn, *Account of Two Voyages*, p. 15; *Winthrop Papers*, vol. 2, p. 246.

simply in transit. According to Captain John Smith, many mariners 'care not much whether the passengers live or die', so long as the freight has been paid, 'for a common sailor regards not a landman, especially a poor passenger'.[59] A social and cultural gulf separated the emigrants from the seamen, and this further facilitated the passengers' bonding. Differences in social position, expertise and even vocabulary kept them realms apart.

Passengers and crew had different standards of behaviour and different senses of orderliness as well. Captain Milborne of the *Arbella* complained to John Winthrop that 'our landmen were very nasty and slovenly, and that the gun deck where they lodged was so beastly and noisome with their victuals and beastliness as would much endanger the health of the ship'.[60] The journey provided an unexpected but salutary taste of maritime discipline. Passengers soon learned that 'a commander, when at sea, is a marine deity; his will is his law and the power of punishing solely in his hands'.[61] Some seventeenth-century captains terrorized their passengers in an 'inhuman and unchristian manner', while others 'made it their only study to dispute with tempests'. A few, like William Pierce, who ferried shiploads of migrants to New England in the 1630s, were godly seamen, in strong sympathy with the leaders of the Bay Colony. Some were blasphemous tyrants, early Ahabs, who would as readily dump their human cargo at the first convenient haven as see them safely ashore at Boston. Captain Squeb, 'a merciless man', dropped Roger Clap and his fellow-migrants at Nantasket Point in 1630 'and left us to shift for ourselves in a forlorn place in this wilderness'.[62]

Puritan emigrants endured the mockery and profanity of sailors who had no sympathy for the enterprise that was taking them to New England. Seamen were more often amused than awed at the presence of clergymen on board.[63] The passengers on the *Mayflower* had been troubled by

a proud and very profane young man, one of the seamen, of a lusty, able body, which made him the more haughty; he would always be condemning the poor people in their sickness, and cursing them daily with grievous execrations, and did not let to tell them that he hoped to help to cast half of them overboard before they came to their journey's end, and make merry

---

[59] Smith, 'Advertisments for the unexperienced planters', in Arber, *Smith*, vol. 2, p. 953.

[60] *Winthrop Papers*, vol. 2, p. 247.

[61] Ward, 'A trip to New England', p. 35.

[62] *Essex Courts*, vol. 8, pp. 29–31; Dunton, *Life and Errors*, p. 88; 'Roger Clap's memoirs', pp. 350, 348.

[63] LeGuin, 'Sea life in seventeenth-century England', p. 113.

with what they had; and if gently reproved, he would curse and swear most bitterly.[64]

The *Talbot* in 1629 had a similiar hostile crewman, 'a notorious, wicked fellow' who 'mocked at our days of fast, railing and jesting against Puritans'. Thomas Miller, pilot and mate of the *Hector* in 1636, made no secret of his opinion that the emigrants were 'all rebels and traitors'. John Josselyn, himself not a Puritan, noted the tension between the sailors and the 'sectaries' on board the *New Supply* in 1638. Mariners on the *Mary Rose* in 1640 'would constantly jeer at the holy brethren of New England'.[65] Friction with such 'reprobates' served further to solidify the godly travellers' view of themselves as an elect.

Remarks and gestures that the crew found merely amusing could be deeply offensive to Puritan sensibilities. Some sailors perhaps even deliberately exaggerated their coarseness in order to bait and antagonize the more squeamish or sanctimonious passengers. 'Obscene, smutty, bawdy talk' of the sort Cotton Mather likened to 'so much filthy bilge water' was a hallmark of sailors in the seventeenth century, as much as any other time.[66] Was it normal behaviour or deliberate provocation when the ship's cook of the *Unity* 'behaved so rudely and profanely in swearing, singing base songs, and drunkenness'?[67] The foul-mouthed crew, Satan's companions, became another lasting memory of the ocean crossing. Instead of praying, like decent Christians, the sailors often sang during storms and hurled curses in the face of inclement weather. Some seamen even argued that prayer in time of storm was sure to bring bad luck.[68]

Puritan travellers could preach and pray, or stop their ears, but they could do little to reduce the banter and profanity of the shipboard environment. The remedy lay with the Lord, and sometimes He spoke to the saints' satisfaction. The profane young man on the *Mayflower* was smitten with a deadly disease and was himself the first corpse to be jettisoned. Bradford interpreted this circumstance as 'a special work of God's providence' and a warning to others. 'Thus his curses light on his own head; and it was an astonishment to all his fellows, for they noticed it to be the just hand of God upon him.'[69] A similar

---

[64] Bradford, *History of Plymouth Plantation*, vol. 1, p. 149.
[65] Higginson, 'True relation', p. 70; John Noble (ed.), *Records of the Court of Assistants of the Colony of the Massachusetts Bay, 1630–1692*, 3 vols. (Boston, 1901–28), vol. 2, p. 63; Josselyn, *Account of Two Voyages*, p. 11; *Winthrop Papers*, vol. 4, p. 270.
[66] Cotton Mather, *The Sailours Companion and Counsellor* (Boston, 1709), p. 39.
[67] *Essex Courts*, vol. 8, p. 31.
[68] Robert Ralston Cawley, *Unpathed Waters: Studies in the Influence of the Voyagers on Elizabethan Literature* (Princeton, N.J., 1940), pp. 194–5, 197, 203.
[69] Bradford, *History of Plymouth Plantation*, vol. 1, p. 149.

fate befell the wicked fellow aboard the *Talbot*. Francis Higginson positively gloated as he reported the death of this enemy of godliness.[70] Separatists and Puritans were not in the least surprised when calamity caught up with their antagonists; victory over the coarse and unregenerate only stiffened their sense of moral superiority. When the irreligious crewmen of the *Mary Rose* were blown up by their own gunpowder while carousing in Boston harbour in 1640, John Winthrop saw their fate as a 'judgment of God upon these scorners of his ordinances'. John Endecott concurred that the destruction of the *Mary Rose* clearly indicated the reward for 'atheistical passages and hellish profanations of the Sabbath and deridings of the people and ways of God'.[71] The certainty of the Puritans in their opinions, and the remarkable events that seemed to confirm them, must have had a potent effect in bringing religious waverers to their side.

Puritan travellers also preached against the sailors' superstitions. Cotton Mather took up the refrain from his seventeenth-century predecessors in castigating the 'paganish superstitions or any magical ceremonies which have been used in some of our vessels. To be afraid of sailing on such or such a day because 'tis an unlucky day, or to practice rites of sorcery for the good of the voyage, is a thing that ill becomes professed Christians'.[72] Seamen employed magical formulae to conjure the wind or to quell a storm, and consulted an elaborate folklore for interpreting omens. Sea-birds, sea-creatures, and unusual natural phenomena provided clues to the outcome of the voyage. Porpoises signalled 'the forerunner of a gale of wind', and dolphins betokened storms. St. Elmo's fire, a candlelike effect that sometimes appeared in the rigging, was 'commonly thought to be a spirit'. One flame was an ill omen, but two indicated safety.[73] Seamen refused to sail with those they considered unlucky, and in two horrifying incidents in the 1650s (on voyages to the Chesapeake, not New England) they threw overboard women they considered to be witches.[74] Crew-

---

[70] Higginson, 'True relation', p. 70.
[71] *Winthrop's Journal*, vol. 2, pp. 9–10; *Winthrop Papers*, vol. 4, p. 270.
[72] Cotton Mather, *Sailours Companion*, p. vi.
[73] LeGuin, 'Sea life in seventeenth-century England', pp. 131–2; Ingram, *Three Sea Journals*, p. 144; Clayton C. Hall (ed.), *Narratives of Early Maryland, 1633–1684* (New York, 1910), p. 31; 'Diary of Edward Taylor', pp. 10, 11; Josselyn, *Account of Two Voyages*, p. 8; Dunton, *Life and Errors*, 89; Cawley, *Unpathed Waters*, pp. 201–2.
[74] *Archives of Maryland*, vol. 3, pp. 306–8, vol. 41, pp. 327–8. Hall (ed.), *Narratives of Early Maryland*, p. 141; Coldham, *English Adventurers and Emigrants*, p. 164. The 'Jonah' syndrome also led a ship bound for England to jettison the offensive Massachusetts Remonstrance as a means to quell a raging storm; John Child, *New-Englands Jonas Cast up at London* (London, 1647), ed. W. T. R. Marvin (Boston, 1869), p. 27.

men on Thomas Shepard's storm-driven *Hope* became convinced that their vessel was bewitched, 'and therefore made use of the common charm ignorant people use, nailing two red-hot horse shoes to their main mast'.[75] Ordinary countrymen among the passengers would find nothing strange in this, for did they not ring bells to drive away thunder and make straw effigies to ensure good harvests? To the Puritans, however, these beliefs signified irreligious ignorance, part of the uncompleted agenda of the Reformation.[76]

However imperfectly the Puritans understood meteorology they knew that witchcraft did not normally cause storms. Rather, the raging sea expressed God's power and glory, provoked perhaps by combat with the Devil. Passengers to New England were shocked by the fury of Atlantic storms. Edward Johnson recalled 'hideous waves' in the 'dreadful and terrible ocean'. Francis Higginson remembered a night of darkness and terror when 'the wind blew mightily, the rain fell vehemently, the sea roared and the waves tossed us horribly'. In the worst of weather the passengers were battened below the hatches, imprisoned in the holds, for their own safety. Lights went out, cooking was impossible, chests and equipment were bounced and broken, and the ship seemed out of control.[77]

Puritan writers never tired of telling how prayer had silenced these storms or brought deliverance when all seemed lost. When 'the Lord sent a most dreadful and terrible storm of wind from the west' against the *Hope* in 1634, Thomas Shepard and the other ministers on board began devotions, and 'immediately after prayer the wind began to abate'. Escape came with 'the Lord showing his dreadful power toward us and yet his unspeakable rich mercy'.[78] Although the Puritans' trust in providence and the mariners' belief in magic might appear to have much in common, their natural philosophy divided them still further into mutually uncomprehending factions.

Along with storms came leaks, accidents and injuries. The Pilgrims on the *Speedwell* believed that 'if we had stayed at sea but three or four hours more she would have sunk right down'. Only strenuous bailing and pumping enabled them to limp back to England. One of

---

[75] *Chronicles*, p. 536n.
[76] Keith Thomas, *Religion and the Decline of Magic* (New York, 1971), esp. chs. 2, 4, 5, 6, and 9.
[77] *Wonder-Working Providence*, pp. 133, 49; Higginson, 'True relation', p. 67.
[78] McGiffert (ed.), *God's Plot*, p. 60; 'Richard Mather's journal', p. 478. For more vivid accounts of Atlantic storms see Herbert F. Ricard (ed.), *Journal of John Bowne 1650–1694* (New Orleans, 1975), pp. 2–4; [Michel], 'Report of the journey of Francis Louis Michel', *Virginia Magazine of History and Biography*, 24 (1916), pp. 11–12; Ingram, *Three Sea Journals of Stuart Times*, p. 145.

Figure 5.   'The vast and furious ocean'. Wenceslaus Hollar, 1665, bound
with *Navium Variae Figurae et Formae* (London, 1647). By permission of The Huntington Library, San Marino, California (RB
313969 H 2449).

the emigrant ships of 1633 leaked so badly it had to put in to the
Azores for emergency repairs. The *Defence*, bound for New England
in 1635, was 'very rotten and unfit for such a voyage', and took in
water in every storm.[79] Bad stowage, misplaced ballast or inappro-
priate sails caused swamping. Poor construction or weak caulking
allowed water to seep into the bilges even under calm conditions, and
a dangerous inundation was likely when the weather became rough.
Sometimes the pumps were in constant demand, and occasionally they
would not work because they were blocked by rubbish or by carpen-

[79] Bradford, *History of Plymouth Plantation*, vol. 1, pp. 137–8;*Winthrop's Journal*, vol. 1,
p. 103; Shepard, *God's Plot*, p. 63.

ters' shavings.[80] Passengers found water below decks immeasurably disconcerting, and often imagined the danger to be greater than it was.

Storm damage necessitated ingenious repairs. After a storm struck Bradford's *Mayflower*, 'One of the main beams in the midships was bowed and cracked', and was repaired with 'a great iron screw the passengers brought out of Holland.' This may have been part of a printing press, sacrificed to secure the integrity of the ship. The *Hopewell* bringing John Norton to New England in 1635 became so shaken by the waves that the crew had 'to undergird the ship with the cable, that they might keep her sides together'. Similarly, the *Fox* could only complete its voyage in 1646 with three hawsers bound round below the keel to keep its boards from splitting. Bad weather cracked the fore mast of the *New Supply* in 1638 and left its main mast 'twisted and shivered'.[81] Clothing, bedding, animal hides and sail cloth would be stuffed into cracks to hold leaks.

If a leak endanger the ship, what care is there to find it, and stop it! How nimbly is the sheet lead, or the plug wrapped in canvas, applied, when the leak may be easily come at! If it be below among the ground timbers, or hooks, and there may be hope to stop it within board, with what solicitude then do they sink down their bag, and their various mixtures of tallow, and coals, and other things! If it be over-low, and yet there be hope to stop it, without board, how solicitously do they sink their bag with oakum or ropeyarn, that the indraught may lodge in that port-hole of death! What prayers are to be made in such perils by sea![82]

Before they reached New England the emigrants learned makeshift survival skills that would later serve them well in frontier conditions. Nevertheless, the Puritans among them attributed deliverance to the providence of God, rather than the hard work of the mariners. When an emigrant ship in 1636 'met with great distress of weather, which broke off the rudder', the ministers on board claimed that prayer and preaching, rather than ingenuity and sweat, brought them through the crisis.[83]

Bruises and minor injuries were common. 'The shaking of the ship in a violent storm' threw Margaret Shepard off balance and 'her head was pitched against an iron bolt'. A physician aboard the *Hannah and*

---

[80] Janeway, *James Janeway's Legacy*, pp. 9–10; S. E. Morison (ed.), *Records of the Suffolk County Court 1671–1680* (Boston, 1933), p. 830; Steere, *Monumental Memorial*, p. 5.

[81] Bradford, *History of Plymouth Plantation*, vol. 1, p. 150; Cotton Mather, *Magnalia Christi Americana*, p. 264; George Carrington Mason, 'An Atlantic crossing in the seventeenth century', *American Neptune*, 11 (1951), p. 40; Josselyn, *Account of Two Voyages*, p. 8.

[82] Cotton Mather, *Sailours Companion*, p. 48.

[83] Robert Fleming, *The Fulfilling of the Scriptures*, p. 283.

Elizabeth treated people for bruised and broken fingers, a broken shin, cut and blistered hands, and for the impact of a rusty nail. Poor Richard Becon, a passenger on the *James*, 'lending his help to the seamen at the hauling of a cable, had the cable catched about his arm, whereby his arm was crushed in pieces and his right hand pulled away, and himself brought into doleful and grievous pain and misery'.[84] Nor was this the worst that could happen. John Howland fell into the sea from the *Mayflower*, but happily became tangled in ropes and was pulled back to safety. Not so lucky was the sailor on the *Lyon* 'who in a tempest having helped to take in the spritsail, lost his hold as he was coming down, and fell into the sea, where, after long swimming, he was drowned'. The *Lyon* also lost a carpenter who was swept to his death while caulking a port, and a passenger fell from the *Griffin* while fishing. In the same way the sea also claimed Samuel Gaylor, an indentured servant who 'fell overboard and was lost by the way' coming to New England in 1662.[85] Fortunately, tragedy of this kind was rare, but tales of such episodes contributed to the passengers' state of apprehension.

Much more common was the spectre of sickness and contagion. The cold and dampness of the ship, cramped and insanitary living conditions, and the rigours of diet and motion could accelerate the course of an illness in someone who was already infected, and reduce the resistance to disease of the rest. The *Elizabeth Dorcas* reached New England in 1634, 'having a long passage, and being hurt upon a rock at Scilly, and very ill victualled, she lost sixty passengers at sea and divers came sick on shore'.[86] This was the greatest passage mortality among the seventeenth-century voyages to New England.

Typhus and dysentery, flux and bloody flux, could ravage a ship's company, but the greatest concern was reserved for smallpox. Smallpox hit the *Talbot* in 1629, and four-year-old Mary Higginson died of the disease within two weeks of leaving England. Her funeral at sea was 'a terror to all the rest as being the beginning of a contagious disease and mortality'.[87] Elements of the Winthrop fleet suffered similarly. John Pond, who sailed to New England in 1630, reported to his father, 'We were wonderful sick as we came at sea with the small-

---

[84] McGiffert (ed.), *God's Plot*, pp. 63–4; *Essex Courts*, vol. 7, p. 304; 'Richard Mather's journal', p. 475.

[85] Bradford, *History of Plymouth Plantation*, vol. 1, p. 151; *Chronicles*, p. 330; *Winthrop's Journal*, vol. 1, pp. 92, 105; [Hull], 'The diaries of John Hull', A.A.S. *Transactions*, 3 (1857), p. 153.

[86] *Winthrop's Journal*, vol. 1, p. 128.

[87] Higginson, 'True relation', pp. 65–6. *Cf.* Duffy, 'Passage to the Colonies', pp. 28–31.

pox. No man thought that I and my little child would have lived, and my boy is lame and my girl too; and there died in the ship that I came in fourteen persons.'[88] It was a miserable introduction to America.

Edmund Brown reported that 'when we had been three weeks at sea the contagious pox struck in amongst us, yet ordered by the Lord's power, as if it had not been infectious'. Thirty people were stricken by the disease on board the *Thomas and Frances* but only 'one or two died'. A servant on board the *New Supply* exhibited smallpox symptoms just a week out from London in 1638, and ten days later the victim was dead. Two more passengers died of smallpox before the ship reached Boston, and another died of consumption.[89] Well might the travellers wonder who would be next as they saw the corpse knotted in a shroud with lead weights at each end. Prayers and salutations accompanied the body into 'the bowels of the great Atlantic sea'.[90] No marker but the memory of fellow-passengers honoured these ocean casualties. In the midst of this were occasional births at sea, happy events, of which the most famous is John Cotton's son Seaborn. There were also moments of despair, as when Peter Fitchew attempted suicide on board the *Champion*.[91]

Few voyages were as healthy as that which brought Richard Mather and his family to New England. 'Fevers, calentures, smallpox, and such diseases as have afflicted other passengers, the Lord kept from among us, and put upon us no grief in our bodies but a little seasickness at the beginning.'[92] But even on this blessed journey the passengers suffered from scurvy. Deficiency disease was a natural accompaniment to long weeks at sea. Hundreds of migrants suffered scurvy symptoms, aching joints, painful gums, and general lassitude. Nor were professional sailors immune. The lack of fresh vegetables and vitamins in the shipboard diet could weaken anyone after ten or twelve weeks, and scurvy was almost inevitable if the voyage took longer. The master of the ill-fated *Sparrowhawk* lay 'sick and lame of the scurvy' and could not come on deck. Scurvy hit passengers on the *Talbot* after only six weeks at sea, and many who arrived with Winthrop were suffering from the disease. Some were so weakened that they could not carry their baggage ashore. A land diet brought most sufferers back to health, but in the early years of New England fresh

[88] *Winthrop Papers*, vol. 3, p. 19.
[89] Josselyn, *Account of Two Voyages*, pp. 6, 9, 13.
[90] Higginson, 'True relation', p. 65; Smith, 'Accidence', p. 797.
[91] *Winthrop Papers*, vol. 2, pp. 257, 259, vol. 3, p. 139; *Suffolk County Wills*, p. 116.
[92] 'Richard Mather's journal', p. 477.

food stocks were limited and some people died of scurvy after their voyage had ended.[93]

Remedies were legion, and most had the sense to include fresh lemons. Captain John Smith prescribed 'the juice of fresh lemons for the scurvy' as early as 1626. John Winthrop advised his wife, 'Remember to bring juice of lemons to sea with thee, for thee and thy company to eat with your meat as sauce.'[94] One enterprising New Englander was fined five pounds in 1631 'for taking upon him to cure the scurvy by a water of no worth nor value which he sold at a very dear rate'.[95] A concoction of scurvy-grass with saltpetre and nutmeg was believed to be excellent physic. Scurvy-grass (*Cochlearia officinalis*) was of dubious value but easily found; lemons were effective but dear. As part of a food parcel for her emigrant son, Muriel Gurdon sent over in 1636 a 'conserve of scurvy grass and some syrup of lemons'. John Josselyn advised travellers to carry lemon juice among their personal supplies. The valuable lemons were more likely to be kept by the ship's surgeon than the cook, to be treated as medical supplies rather than as food. On board the *New Supply* a servant 'was whipped naked at the capstan with a cat of nine tails, for filching nine great lemons out of the surgeon's cabin, which he eat rind and all in less than an hours time'.[96] At least he had some notion of antiscorbutic diet supplements, no matter what damage he inflicted on his digestive system.

The shipboard diet included dried bread and biscuits, oatmeal pottage and buttered peas, salted eggs, salted fish, bacon and cured meats, neats' tongues in bran or meal, 'bag pudding' made with raisins and currants, and perhaps some fruit or cheese, all of it subject to spoilage. The undertakers provided basic rations, included in the price of the passage, but migrants were advised to take extra supplies and delicacies for their private use. Cooking was performed at an open fire, insulated from the timbers by a bed of sand, but weather conditions often made it too dangerous. Live animals provided eggs, milk and fresh meat for special occasions. One enterprising migrant of 1640, 'having a milch cow in the ship as he came over sold the milk to the passengers for 2d. the quart', a rate John Winthrop regarded as ex-

[93] Bradford, *History of Plymouth Plantation*, vol. 2, pp. 13, 89, 113n.; Higginson, 'True relation', pp. 68, 74; *Wonder-Working Providence*, p. 65; *Chronicles*, p. 313.
[94] Smith, 'Accidence', p. 804; *Winthrop Papers*, vol. 3, p. 20.
[95] *Mass. Recs.*, vol. 1, p. 83.
[96] *Winthrop Papers*, vol. 2, pp. 303–4, vol. 3, p. 258; Josselyn, *Account of Two Voyages*, pp. 9, 14.

cessive.[97] Water and beer accompanied the dry food, sometimes supplemented by wine and strong spirits. One passenger complained, 'Our supply of water stank very much and our beer was like mud because of the slovenly negligence of those who should have taken care of it.' Another grumbled that the drink was 'either very salt or as thick as pudding', although the sailors assured him that this was quite normal.[98]

Fascinating novelties distracted the passengers from the rigours of life at sea. By venturing into 'this element of water',the ocean traveller obtained a privileged view of God's creation. Many of the emigrants to New England comforted themselves with the expectation that their journey would indeed show them special glimpses of God. The Bible seemed to promise as much, for 'they that go down to the sea in ships, and do business in great waters, these men see the works of the Lord and his wonders in the deep'.[99] Passengers delighted in the unfamiliar creatures, 'which, though common at sea, may be a subject of wonder to such as are home-bred'.[100]

Voyagers thrilled to 'the strange fish which we saw there, some with wings flying above the water, others with manes, ears, and heads, and chasing one another with open mouths like stone horses in a park'. Francis Higginson remarked on the strange fish – bonitos, carvels, grampuses, sunfish and whales – that inspected the rolling *Talbot*. Other travellers noted albacores or tunny, calamaries or squid, jellyfish, flailfish, torpedofish, swordfish, sharks and threshers. To Richard Mather, 'It was a pleasant thing to behold the variety of fowls and mighty fishes.'[101] A virtual aquarium of exotic creatures disported itself to demonstrate the diversity of God's creation so far from English waters.

John Winthrop's company 'saw a whale who lay just in our ship's way, the bunch of his back about a yard above water; he would not shun us, so we passed within a stone's cast of him as he lay spouting up water'. Edward Taylor also saw whales, and listened to their 'rough,

[97] *Winthrop's Journal*, vol. 2, p. 20.

[98] Jasper Danckaerts, *Diary of Our Second Trip from Holland to New Netherland, 1683* (Upper Saddle River, N.J., 1969), p. 26; *Essex Courts*, vol. 8, p. 30; LeGuin, 'Sea life in seventeenth-century England', pp. 114–7; 'Report of the journey of Francis Louis Michel', p. 10.

[99] John Cope, *A Religious Inquisition* (London, 1629), p. 59; Psalms 107 and 136.

[100] John Cordy Jeaffreson (ed.), *A Young Squire of the Seventeenth Century* (London, 1878), p. 179.

[101] Christopher Levett, 'A voyage into New England', p. 85; Higginson, 'True relation', p. 68; 'Richard Mather's journal', p. 479; Josselyn, *Account of Two Voyages*, pp. 7, 9, 12.

Figure 6. 'Wonders of the deep'. From Josef Furtenbach, *Architectura Navalis*
(Ulm, 1629).

hoarse noise, blothering in the water'.[102] Whales naturally prompted
pious thoughts about the biblical Jonah, and curiosity about the capacity of the belly of this great 'fish'. Journal after journal treats of
the dashing of dolphins and porpoises. Richard Mather and friends
'saw with wonder and delight an innumerable multitude of porpoises
leaping and playing about the ship'. The Puritans were moved to

[102] *Winthrop Papers*, vol. 2, p. 252; 'Diary of Edward Taylor', p. 11.

prayers of gratitude, 'so marvellous to behold are the works and wonders of the Almighty in the deep'.[103]

Some of these creatures, as well as being a stimulus to the imagination, provided a welcome supplement to the limited shipboard diet. John Josselyn found shark meat 'very rough grained, not worthy of wholesome preferment', but fried porpoise agreed with him more. 'It tastes like rusty bacon or hung beef, if not worse; but the liver boiled and soused in vinegar is more grateful to the palate.'[104] Richard Mather enjoyed porpoise with gusto. 'The flesh of them was good meat, with salt, pepper and vinegar; the fat like bacon, the lean like bull-beef.' Harpooning porpoises and hauling them aboard was 'marvellous delightful recreation.' The dead cetacean reminded Mather of a butcher's hog, which 'being opened upon the deck had within his entrails, as liver, lights, heart, guts, etc., for all the world like a swine'. Quite what Mather expected to find is unclear, but it was evidently reassuring, so far from land, to discover the familiar viscera of a mammal. Opening the porpoise 'upon the deck in view of all our company was wonderful to us all, and marvellous merry sport, and delightful to our women and children'. The slaughter took on the atmosphere of a country fair, providing a valuable respite from the shipboard routine.[105]

After weeks of isolation a new mood gripped the ship's company as they came closer and closer to land. The crew became occupied with soundings, and all on board became aware of the approaching shore.[106] A tradition arose that the passengers would make up a prize for the first person to spy land. Mariners became alert to changes in the air and water, and the passengers soon learned to pick up the clues. Some believed they could actually smell New England before it came into view.[107] Sharp eyes watched for flotsam, seaweed, or sea-birds that were welcome harbingers of the shore. Excitement gripped Edward Taylor's company in 1668 when a dead butterfly was noticed floating on the water, surely a sign that America was near.[108] Finally,

[103] 'Richard Mather's journal', pp. 463, 467.
[104] Josselyn, *Account of Two Voyages*, pp. 9, 8.
[105] 'Richard Mather's journal', pp. 460–7. *Cf.* Ingram, *Three Sea Journals*, p. 151.
[106] 'Autobiography of the Rev. John Barnard', p. 211; *Winthrop Papers*, vol. 2, p. 261; Danckaerts, *Diary*, p. 31.
[107] Josselyn, *Account of Two Voyages*, p. 163; *Good News From New England*, p. 199; John Clayton, 'A letter . . . to the Royal Society', in Peter Force (ed.), *Tracts and Other Papers Relating . . . to the Origin, Settlement, and Progress of the Colonies* (Washington, D.C., 1844), vol. 3, p. 5. *Cf.* John Milton, *Paradise Lost*, Book 4, lines 160ff.
[108] 'Diary of Edward Taylor', p. 11.

gun salutes greeted the travellers as they hove into Boston harbour. Dry land never felt so fine.

Incoming vessels were usually met by a pilot boat and were escorted to anchor below Castle Island. With land so close the moment was ripe for celebration, but in 1637 a hailing shot misfired and, in an unfortunate introduction to America, 'killed a passenger, an honest man'.[109] Less disturbing but still unpleasant was the tongue-lashing some passengers received from Mary Oliver, who was sentenced to prison in 1639 'for her speeches at the arrival of some newcomers'.[110] For most newcomers the next few days would be spent in rediscovering their land legs, greeting friends and kinsmen, making introductions and arrangements for permanent settlement, and exchanging their English truck for items vital in the new environment. Sometimes passengers continued to live for a week or more on board their ship, until they had secured shore accommodation.[111] Strangers were closely watched, and were supposed to present themselves to the local authorities for vetting and clearance.[112]

With such memorable experiences behind them, it is no wonder that New England Puritans made the ocean a powerful emblem in their sermons and literature. Increase Mather, writing of the many 'eminent deliverances of providence' that befell his father, Richard Mather, insisted that 'the most remarkable and memorable of all other was that which happened to him on the mighty waters'. The settlers of New Haven (a name with both nautical and providential connotations) acknowledged God's protection that had brought them 'over the great deeps'.[113] Puritan ministers, recognizing the distinctive seasoning that accompanied the Atlantic passage, obtained didactic and rhetorical mileage from the experience. Thomas Shepard reminded Massachusetts settlers in 1638, 'The Lord hath brought you by a strong hand and brought you and blessed you, and he hath when you cried to him saved

[109] *Winthrop's Journal*, vol. 1, pp. 222–3.
[110] *Essex Courts*, vol. 1, p. 12.
[111] *Note-Book Kept by Thomas Lechford*, p. 165.
[112] Record Commissioners of the City of Boston, *Second Report* (Boston, 1877), 'Boston town records', pp. 10, 11, 12; *Tenth Report* (Boston, 1886), 'Admissions to the town of Boston, 1670–1700', pp. 55–82.
[113] Increase Mather, *The Life and Death of that Reverend Man of God, Mr. Richard Mather* (Cambridge, Mass., 1670), p. 31; *New-Haven's Settling in New England* (1656; reprinted, Hartford, Conn., 1856), p. 1.

you from sins, from storms.' To have come so far, and to have endured so much, was surely a sanctifying and a winnowing experience from which great things could be expected. The crossing itself became a metaphor for conflict against worldly corruption. Images of a storm-tossed vessel readily suggested the Christian in a sea of sin. Without discipline and vigilance, 'the sins of men are like raging sea, which would overwhelm all'. This conventional image was especially potent to those, like Shepard himself, who had recently 'passed through the waves . . . and stood many a week six inches from death'. John Norton, who had shipped with Shepard in 1635, touched a similar chord, invoking memories of 'continual tossings in stormy seas'.[114]

Thomas Hooker identified religious error as 'a ship that is foundered in the midst of the main ocean without the sight of succour, or hope of relief'. Worldly temptations threatened the course of New England like 'violent and boisterous winds and raging waves'. Peter Bulkeley admonished the faithful at Concord in 1646, 'He that rests on works . . . is like a wave of the sea, tossed and tumbled up and down, and finds no rest.'[115] Early Massachusetts congregations could readily respond to this echo of a journey that they had all recently completed. Every adult in New England before the 1650s was a veteran of the ocean passage.

The second generation, reared in New England, knew less of this maritime experience. Urian Oakes reminded them how their fathers had 'cast, not their bread, but themselves and their families upon the great waters, to venture all upon the mere mercy of God'. Richard Mather, in his farewell sermon, exhorted his Dorchester congregation to take special care of the rising generation, to prevent them being 'swept away and drowned in the waters and waves of the sea'. His son, Eleazer Mather, likened the second generation to 'unskilfull passengers', who lacked the seasoning of their elders. He asked them, 'What think you of a vessel at sea that springs a leak, and takes in water apace, and mariners some dead, many sick, a few left to keep pump going, are they not in danger to sink and perish in the waters?'[116]

In the same way the ancient idea of the ship of state took on new meaning to those who had ventured their lives on the Atlantic ocean.

[114] Thomas Shepard, 'Election sermon in 1638', p. 366; Carroll, *Puritanism and the Wilderness*, pp. 41, 39.
[115] Carroll, *Puritanism and the Wilderness*, pp. 38, 39.
[116] Urian Oakes, *New-England Pleaded With* (Cambridge, Mass., 1673), p. 22. Richard Mather, *A Farewell Exhortation to the Church and People of Dorchester* (Cambridge, Mass., 1657), p. 9; Eleazer Mather, quoted in Emory Elliott, *Power and the Pulpit in Puritan New England* (Princeton, N.J., 1975) p. 18.

Storm waves threatened not just individual sinners but the entire enterprise of New England. The Massachusetts Remonstrants of 1646 warned those 'at the helm of these plantations' to deal with 'storms and tempests'. 'Those who are under decks, being at present unfit for higher employments, may perceive those leaks which will inevitably sink this weak and ill-compacted vessel.'[117] Thomas Shepard similarly warned New England, 'The ship is sinking.' 'Alas,' wrote Samuel Danforth, 'the times are difficult and perilous; the wind is stormy and the sea tempestuous; the vessel heaves and sets, and tumbles up and down in the rough and boisterous waters, and is in danger to be swallowed up.' The journey itself was a rehearsal and reference point for the early history of New England.[118]

[117] Michael Walzer, *The Revolution of the Saints* (Cambridge, Mass., 1965) pp. 180–1; Child, *New-Englands Jonas Cast up at London*, pp. 8–9.
[118] Thomas Shepard, *Wine for Gospel Wantons* (Cambridge, Mass., 1668), p. 12; Samuel Danforth, *A Brief Recognition of New Englands Errand into the Wilderness* (Cambridge, Mass., 1671), p. 21. See also Roger B. Stein, 'Seascape and the American imagination: the Puritan seventeenth century', *Early American Literature*, 7 (1972), pp. 21–5; and Albert E. Stone, 'Sea and the self: travel as experience and metaphor in early American autobiography', *Genre*, 7 (1974), pp. 279–306.

7

'Occasions in England': debts, obligations and inheritances across the ocean

Although most colonists looked forward (and westward), and got on with the task of rebuilding their lives in America, they were never entirely free of reminders and claims of the old country. In place-names, in law and custom, in memory, and in the partial replication of the home society, old England was ever present. Through politics, religion and trade, as well as family relationships and the vagaries of inheritance, the homeland continued to beckon. Many migrants never intended to settle permanently in New England, and a surprising number went home. Others who stayed in America nonetheless continued to receive news, handle business, and sustain contacts across three thousand miles of water. This chapter, and those that follow, will show how English affairs repeatedly intruded themselves on the early New Englanders.

Simply crossing the ocean did not necessarily sever kinship or community responsibilities, nor did emigration to America eliminate English legal or familial obligations. New Englanders, just like other Englishmen, were subject to the claims of courts, creditors, lessees and heirs. The transatlantic distance may have frustrated some suits and slowed others, but a remarkable amount of business followed the colonists across the ocean. Early migrants to New England brought with them their existing entanglements in the legal, financial and testamentary systems of old England. It was not at all unusual for colonial settlers to deal with properties, debts and obligations 'here or in England'.[1]

A simple matter involving Boston minister John Cotton shows how ordinary obligations could follow a migrant to New England. Cotton

---

[1] *Suffolk County Wills: Abstracts of the Earliest Wills upon Record in the County of Suffolk, Massachusetts* (Baltimore, 1984), p. 48.

had been appointed an overseer of a neighbour's will at home in Lincolnshire. But in 1638, 'because I remain by the good providence of God in these parts of New England', and because the probate still required his attention, Cotton appointed a deputy to proceed 'as effectively to all intents and purposes as if I myself were there present in England'.[2]

Financial obligations were common. In 1640, for example, a court at New Haven bound Thomas Saule 'in the sum of twenty pounds' to 'satisfy the just demands of Humphrey Spinage whensoever he shall be called to account about a claim which the said Spinage doth make in the behalf of one of London'.[3]

In a more complicated case, Edmund Tapp, a New England resident since 1637, was sued in Chancery in 1640 by his former landlord in Hertfordshire. The suit involved disputed accounts, undischarged obligations, and the usual mixture of allegations and countercharges, requiring the taking of depositions on both sides of the Atlantic. The depositions reveal not only what was involved in leaving old England but also the complications that could arise from a less than clean break. The landlord, Sir Charles Caesar, an expert in manipulating the English legal system, now sided with his new tenant and claimed that Tapp had 'estranged and absented' himself from the premises, and was thereby responsible for their decay. It took a deposition from New England, signed by the magistrates of New Haven, and testimony from Tapp's loyal brother in Hertfordshire, to establish that he had not departed from his tenancy in a disorderly manner. Despite the distance separating the parties, and the problems of communication, the suit proceeded to an orderly resolution. The parties in New Haven handled the Chancery documents just as they would in any remote part of England.[4]

Leases and lands, legacies and liens, bonds and releases, guardianships, executorships and dowers in the homeland, all demanded the attention of New England settlers. Thomas Lechford's Boston notebooks of the late 1630s and William Aspinwall's notarial registers of the 1640s record dozens of arrangements concerning legal matters in England. There was hardly a problem that ingenuity, patience and good will could not solve. Lechford and

---

[2] Edward E. Hale (ed.), *Note-Book Kept by Thomas Lechford... 1638 to... 1641* (Cambridge, Mass., 1885) (hereinafter, Lechford *Notebook*), p. 32.
[3] Charles J. Hoadly (ed.), *Records of the Colony and Plantation of New Haven, 1638–49* (Hartford, Conn., 1857), p. 41.
[4] P.R.O., C2/Chas I/B93–34, B86/3.

Aspinwall, and others like them, set up the paperwork and registered agreements to lighten the burden or maximize the advantage for their New England clients.[5]

Although most colonists attempted to liquidate their holdings at home before settling in New England, a surprising number continued to own land or hold leases in old England. Others acquired additional transatlantic holdings through inheritance. New Englanders maintained estates in old England because they had been unable to sell before emigrating, because they valued the English property as a source of income, because it provided them with insurance should their transatlantic venture come to an end, and because owning something in England kept alive the notion that they had not entirely cut off their roots. Land ownership can serve psychological as well as economic purposes.

Several of the leading New England families augmented their income through rents from property in England. John Cotton, for example, drew rent from a 'house and garden in the market-place of Boston in Lincolnshire', which came to him through his wife.[6] Katherine Coytmore, widow, of Charlestown, Massachusetts, in 1638 appointed 'attorneys, baylies and receivers' in England 'to receive my rents out of my lands in Sutton in Suffolk for me and in my name'.[7] The Whittinghams of Ipswich, Massachusetts, had lands, houses and tenements at Southerton, Lincolnshire, that produced a useful sum of money in the 1640s despite some 'arrearages'. The Lanes of Malden, Massachusetts, collected rent from land in Yorkshire, where Job Lane's cousin, John Dickinson of Gildersome, Yorkshire, acted as agent.[8] The Wyllys family of Hartford, Connecticut, collected £5 a year from the rent of a house and shop at Stratford-upon-Avon, and a total of £199 in 1640 from other tenants in England. George Wyllys, Jr., continued to act as the family agent, apologizing in 1644 and 1646 for the difficulty in collecting the full amount because of the disruptions of civil war.[9] The Pynchons of Springfield, Massachusetts, also drew rent from land in England. In 1672 the New England-born

---

[5] Lechford *Notebook*, pp. 4–7, 10–14, 16, 18, 20, 32, 35, 131, 133, 135, *passim*; Registry Department of the City of Boston (ed.), *Aspinwall Notarial Records from 1644 to 1651* (Boston, 1903), pp. 5, 7, 11, 50, 88, *passim*.

[6] *Suffolk County Wills*, p. 43.

[7] Lechford *Notebook*, p. 35.

[8] *The Probate Records of Essex County, Massachusetts* (Salem, Mass., 1916), vol. 1, p. 104; W. H. Whitmore (ed.), 'Lane family papers', *N.E.H.G.R.*, 11 (1857), pp. 109–10.

[9] 'The Wyllys papers ... 1590–1796', *Collections of the Connecticut Historical Society*, 21 (1924), pp. 10, 27, 64, 86.

Joseph Pynchon was looking after the family property near Uxbridge, Middlesex. Writing from Springfield, John Pynchon counselled his son in England, 'You speak of tenants complaining, etc. It hath always been so.'[10]

It was not only the New England gentry who had the means and the will to guard their property interests in England. Ephraim Hunt, blacksmith of Weymouth, Massachusetts, authorized a returning New Englander in 1646 to collect 'all rents or arrearages', from his land in Buckinghamshire, 'with power to rent the same for a year, and to sue, etc., and to commence any actions in any court of record' against the former tenants.[11]

Sometimes the rent fell in arrears. But property-owners in New England were not necessarily more inconvenienced than any other absentee landlord who might have been living in London. Samuel Sewall wrote to an English cousin, John Stork, in 1687, 'I depend on you for getting my small rent and remitting of it to cousin Hull.' And as a precaution he wrote the same day to cousin Edward Hull asking him to check on cousin Stork.[12]

Colonists returning to England could inspect their properties and check on their tenants and agents first hand. They could also act as visiting stewards or bailiffs for kinsmen, neighbours and friends. John Hall, stepson of Samuel Symonds of Ipswich, Massachusetts, crossed over to England in 1662 in pursuit of a legacy, but while there promised, among other things, to 'collect my mother's rents in Sarum'. Hall never returned to New England, but for the next twenty years sent back detailed accounts of the Salisbury tenements. In effect, he served as agent for the Symonds' English properties.[13]

John Hall based himself in London, corresponded actively with kinsmen in Wiltshire and Essex, and went down occasionally to Salisbury to deal directly with the tenants. His letters to his mother and stepfather in New England provide an unusual glimpse of the rent-collecting efforts of a minor absentee landlord. In 1663 Hall calculated that the income from the Salisbury rentals for the last four years amounted to £62 8s. 2d. One of the tenants was severely in arrears, but 'there is not any here that can, by law, force him out, for Mr.

[10] Carl Bridenbaugh (ed.), *The Pynchon Papers*, vol. 1, *Letters of John Pynchon, 1654–1700* (Boston, 1982), p. 109.
[11] *Aspinwall Notarial Records*, p. 50. *Cf.* 'Lane family papers', p. 109.
[12] [Sewall], 'Letter book of Samuel Sewall', M.H.S. *Collections*, ser. 6, vol. 1 (1886), pp. 52, 60.
[13] A.A.S. MSS. 'Letters of John Hall'.

Worcester's letter of attorney died with him'. William Worcester was John Hall's previous stepfather, a minister at Salisbury, Massachusetts, who died in 1662.[14]

Equipped with a fresh letter of attorney from New England, John Hall began to straighten out his mother's English affairs. He proved himself a competent property manager who actually enjoyed collecting rents. He wrote to his mother in 1665, 'Indeed, whilst I am single 'tis but a recreation to travel once a year to Sarum, though it cost me not less than thirty shillings besides my horse'. Instead of sending all the receipts as cash, Hall often sent his mother English luxury or fashion items that she requested, all carefully costed in his accounts. As he explained to his stepfather Symonds, 'Even reckonings makes long friends.'[15]

In 1667 some of the Salisbury tenants fell into arrears again. John Hall explained, 'I have sent letters but they signify nothing without my personal appearance, and some tenants refuse to pay without they first see my face.' As far as the tenants were concerned, it made little difference whether their landlord was in London or Massachusetts. Additional problems arose in 1677 and 1682, but in most years the money flowed smoothly from Wiltshire to New England. Hall was tenacious in looking after his mother's financial affairs, although he remarked in one letter, 'The matter is but a worldly thing.'[16]

This transplanted New Englander even handled transatlantic philanthropy. His adopted cousin, Samuel Hall, sometime resident of Massachusetts but now a Londoner, left charitable legacies to his former American neighbours in his will of 1681 – fifty pounds to the poor of Massachusetts who had suffered by the Indian wars, fifty pounds to the Boston poor who had suffered from fire, and cloth for the poor of Newbury, Hampton and Amesbury in New England. John Hall arranged for the discharge of these obligations.[17]

Emigration may have impaired, but did not foreclose, the operation of the English inheritance system. Parents, uncles, brothers and cousins in England sometimes designated their colonial relations as major, minor or residual heirs to an estate some three thousand miles distant. Robert Rice of Preston, Suffolk, for example, made provision in his will of 1639 for 'my loving brother-in-law Samuel Appleton, gentle-

---

[14] 'Letters of John Hall', 11 March 1663; *Probate Records of Essex County*, vol. 1, pp. 403–6.
[15] 'Letters of John Hall', 17 and 22 March 1665.
[16] *Ibid.*, 7 May 1667, 16 March 1677, 28 September 1682.
[17] *Ibid.*, 23 May 1681; Henry F. Waters, *Genealogical Gleanings in England* (Boston, Mass., 1901), pp. 780–2.

man, now dwelling at Ipswich in New England'.[18] Richard Barnes of Marlborough, Massachusetts, received legacies from his mother and grandmother in England in 1646, seven years after he migrated to New England. John Caffinch of Tenterden, Kent, but formerly of Connecticut, left his house and land in England to his wife and children who were still in New Haven. Should they fail to come back to England they would forfeit the inheritance, which would then go to Caffinch's English nieces. Roger Allen, 'now living in New England', inherited the estate of his father, James Allen of Bedfordshire, blacksmith. Francis Graves, who had gone as a servant, inherited five pounds from his uncle's will.[19]

In a sad twist to this pattern, one Richard Browne, after thirty years in the colonies, heard of his father's death and hastened home to West Haughton in Lancashire to claim his inheritance. Arriving in 1666, he found that his father had passed his estate to his younger brother, who had sensibly remained in England, leaving poor Richard 'destitute of all relief'.[20] In another case a homesick New England wife *invented* a legacy that necessitated her return to England. 'For some time Katherine Hitchbourne had importuned her husband to let her come home to England but he would not consent.' She then engaged a scrivener 'to continue a letter, ostensibly directed to her from a person in London, to the effect that she had inherited a house at Stratford Bow in England, and that she must come with her daughter to take possession'. Moved more by greed than compassion, Daniel Hitchbourne allowed his wife to return to England to take up her non-existent inheritance. The details are extant because the case came to the notice of the Lord Mayor's court in London in 1669.[21]

At the same time, will makers in New England sometimes left property to relations in the old country, remembering kinsmen who had never left England or those who had returned. Richard Ellis, who died in New England in 1639, left forty-five shillings to be sent to kinsmen in England. Sarah Dillingham, widow of Ipswich, Massachu-

---

[18] Waters, *Genealogical Gleanings*, pp. 94–5.
[19] John Noble (ed.), *Records of the Court of Assistants of the Colony of the Massachusetts Bay 1630–1692*, vol. 3 (Boston, 1928), p. 20; Waters, *Genealogical Gleanings*, p. 546; Savage, *Genealogical Dictionary*, vol. 1, p. 328; George Sherwood, *American Colonists in English Records, First Series*, (London, 1932), p. 47; 'Letters of John Hall', 30 March 1682. For more examples see Sherwood, *American Colonists . . . First Series*, pp. 46, 48, 49; *American Colonists in English Records, Second Series* (London, 1933), pp. 119, 120, 127, 129, 156; Waters, *Genealogical Gleanings*, pp. 3, 7, 10, 23, 142.
[20] Lancashire Record Office, QSP/284/5.
[21] Peter Wilson Coldham (ed.), *Lord Mayor's Court of London Depositions Relating to Americans 1641–1736* (Washington, D.C., 1980), p. 35.

setts, left her entire estate to her daughter Sarah, but if Sarah died it was to go to 'my mother, brethren and sisters . . . now living in England'. Edward Skinner, in his will of 1641, awarded half the proceeds of the sale of his house and lands in Cambridge, Massachusetts, to Robert Ibbit 'of Cambridge in old England'. Thomas Bittlestone, also of Cambridge, Massachusetts, left 'one third of my estate to be given to my natural kindred in old England' in his will of 1640.[22]

In 1640 Elizabeth Cartwright of Salem bequeathed 'my bed, my bolster and two pillow-beres with a blanket and a coverlet unto Elizabeth Capon my sister in Walberswick in Suffolk'. Such a gift of household stuff was not much use to one so many miles away. It may have been a simple sisterly gesture, unless Elizabeth Capon was soon expected to arrive in New England.[23] Moses Paine of Braintree, Massachusetts, left property in New England and 'goods and debts in old England, if they may be recovered'. William Potter of Roxbury similarly left £6 13s. 4d. to his sister-in-law and nephews in England.[24]

Probate records in England and New England contain a scatter of such cases throughout the seventeenth century. Most bequests, of course, were made within the immediate nuclear family, whose members were usually nearby, but enough examples are found to show the vitality of a social system, a testamentary system and a kinship system that engaged participants on either side of the ocean.[25] A few more cases will drive the point home. George Alcock of Roxbury, Massachusetts, provided in his will of 1640 for his 'debts to be paid in old England and in new'. Roger Harlakenden, gentleman, late of Earls Colne, Essex, distributed property on both sides of the Atlantic. One Boston merchant, Robert Keayne, left a hundred pounds to his kindred in England; another, Peter Lidget, left cash legacies to his 'sister Mary Smith's two children' in Essex, the money to be paid in London. Mary Norton died in 1678 leaving her estate to cousins in England, the proceeds 'to be paid here in Boston in New England money'.[26] Bequests were made in both directions, as if emigration made little difference. Collecting these awards sometimes tried the

---

[22] *Suffolk County Wills*, pp. 1, 2, 14; *Probate Records of Essex County*, vol. 1, p. 4.
[23] *Probate Records of Essex County*, vol. 1, p. 12.
[24] *Suffolk County Wills*, pp. 14–15, 51.
[25] See chapter 11, this volume.
[26] *Suffolk County Wills*, pp. 3, 6–8; 'Last will and testament of me, Robert Keayne', in Record Commissioners of the City of Boston, *Tenth Report* (Boston, 1886), p. 50; Waters, *Genealogical Gleanings*, p. 79; A.A.S. MSS. 'Letter book of John Hull', p. 387. See also *Essex Courts*, vol. 2, p. 174. vol. 3, pp. 17, 62, 71, vol. 4, pp. 249, 447; *Probate Records of Essex County*, vol. 1, pp. 46, 55; Coldham, *Lord Mayor's Court*, pp. 4, 5, 8 and *passim*.

patience and tested the ingenuity of the beneficiaries, but few of the legacies went astray.

In fact, it was none too difficult to send money or discharge obligations across the Atlantic in the seventeenth century. Merchants did it all the time, and poorer and humbler settlers copied their techniques. Legacies, debts and rents could be collected simply by writing, or by using kinsmen, travellers, or attorneys as proxies. The connections were sometimes slow and tortuous, interrupted by deaths and retarded by distance. But the system provided for eventual payment and satisfaction. When Ralph Sprague of Charlestown heard of a legacy in England after his wife's father died in 1638, he instructed an English lawyer to collect the inheritance, deduct his fees and send the residue to New England.[27] A typical release of 1638 stated,

I Samson Shotton of Mount Woollaston in New England, planter, do hereby acknowledge that I have received of my brother Anthony Shotton of Cropston in the county of Leicester, yeoman, the sum of four score and ten pounds of lawful money of England, given and bequeathed unto me as a legacy by the last will and testament of Thomas Shotton late of Cropston aforesaid, our father.[28]

Matters were not always so smooth. When the Bigg brothers of Kent made bequests to their colonial kinsmen in 1638 and 1642, they triggered a round of 'uncomfortable differences' between the Fosters and Stowes of Massachusetts that lasted until 1653. The difficulty lay not in transmitting the legacy across the Atlantic but in deciding which of the competing New Englanders should receive the money.[29] Testamentary suits, which were commonplace in old England, sometimes expanded to involve distant emigrant relations and overseas jurisdictions. The Massachusetts courts had no difficulty assigning the estates of intestates to heirs who lived in England.[30] The Particular Court at Hartford, Connecticut, was similarly solicitous of the rights of legatees and creditors, no matter which side of the Atlantic they inhabited. In 1643, for example, dealing with the estate of the late Thomas Marshfield, the court ordered that 'such creditors from old England as may challenge and make proof of any just debts from the said Marshfield' had fourteen months in which to make their claims. This was ample time for necessary documents to go to England and back.[31]

Yet another occasion requiring New Englanders to deal with old

---

[27] Lechford *Notebook*, p. 37.
[28] *Ibid.*, p. 16.
[29] Waters, *Genealogical Gleanings*, p. 23.
[30] *Essex Courts*, vol. 1, p. 57.
[31] 'Records of the Particular Court of Connecticut 1639–1663', *Collections of the Connecticut Historical Society*, 22 (1928), p. 23.

England was when they purchased the property of colonists who had gone back home. Migrants returning to England did not always settle their affairs before leaving, just as those first going to America sometimes hung on to their English holdings as a way of keeping their options open. In the depressed land market of the 1640s it was hard to find a buyer in New England, and the owners who had left the colonies often had to negotiate from a distance and at a disadvantage when they finally decided to sell. Papers and signatures would once again make their way back and forth across the Atlantic.

In 1645, for example, James Marshall 'of Exeter in old England' disposed of his four and a half acres at Dorchester, Massachusetts. In 1646 William Roberts, wine-cooper of Middlesex, 'in old England', sold his house and land in Massachusetts to William Kilcop, sieve-maker of Charlestown. A few years later James Garret, mariner, of Wapping near London, agreed to sell property at Charlestown, Massachusetts, 'that is my former dwelling house', to Samuel Beadle, planter. Beadle was to pay thirty-six pounds, in cash or commodities, spread over a three-year period. In 1660 Hugh Peter, who remained in London, sold his farmland in Massachusetts to Marblehead fisherman John Devereux, using a Salem merchant to collect and transmit the money.[32] In each transaction the ensuing correspondence elaborated ties between the colony and the homeland.

If New Englanders wished to call in their debts or dispose of their assets in old England they usually sent instructions to agents or relations back home. Matters too complicated to be handled by correspondence required assigning a power of attorney, and sometimes necessitated resolution by the courts.[33] Power of attorney could be given to a trusted friend or kinsman on the spot in England or to a colonist going home. William Aspinwall registered two dozen such letters of attorney a year, relating to estates in England, during the 1640s.[34]

Several New Englanders financed their travel back to England with the commissions they earned for such service. In 1638, for example, when Augustine Clement of Dorchester, Massachusetts, wanted to sell his property and dispose of his leases at Wokingham, Berkshire, he engaged his friend, John Tinker of Boston, who was returning to

---

[32] Record Commissioners of the City of Boston, *Fourth Report* (Boston, 1880), 'Dorchester town records', p. 53; *Third Report* (Boston, 1878), 'Charlestown records', pp. 102, 141; Essex Institute, Curwen Papers, vol. 4.

[33] *Essex Courts*, vol. 1, pp. 102, 146, 332, 412; vol. 2, pp. 12–21.

[34] *Aspinwall Notarial Records, passim.* Aspinwall registered 24 in 1645, 21 in 1646, 28 in 1647. For more examples see *Essex Courts*, vol. 7, p. 146, vol. 9, pp. 476–8.

England, to handle the negotiations. Part of the proceeds of the sale was to be applied to bringing over Clement's sister Margaret to join him in New England, and a smaller part was Tinker's fee. Tinker agreed 'diligently and faithfully' to make the sale on Clement's behalf, and was promised five pounds for his pains.[35] In 1640 the Boston blacksmith, Thomas Scudamore, similarly granted power of attorney to Henry Hazard, mariner, and William Prigge, yeoman, 'to sell and dispose of one messuage or tenement in Westerley (Gloucestershire), and to bring over his wife and children'. Scudamore estimated his English property to be worth fifty pounds, which would more than cover the cost of his family's passage.[36]

Again, many more examples could be cited, but a couple will suffice. Thomas James of Salem authorized letters of attorney in 1645 to recover a debt and to sell a parcel of land at Earls Barton, Northamptonshire. John Coggeshall of Ispwich, Massachusetts, had power of attorney when he went over to England in 1652 to sell some land for a friend. The negotiations were successful, and Coggeshall had the money in hand when he died on the voyage back to New England the following year. We only know about this transaction because Coggeshall's heirs and the original landowner both laid claim to the money, and the dispute spilled over into the courts.[37] The overall impression is of a thicket of transactions, as dense and complicated as in any other English region.

The application of these colonial powers of attorney can sometimes be traced in English records. At Great Ormesby, Norfolk, in 1644, for example, Thomas Harward, yeoman, sold three acres of land 'by virtue of a certain writing or letter of attorney unto me by and from one William Moulton of Hampton in New England, yeoman'. Moulton had migrated to New England in 1637 as a twenty-year-old servant and inherited the land a few years later after the death of his father. The estate was not large enough to come home for, but the cash from its sale would be useful in New England.[38]

By the end of the seventeenth century there were enough people in the colonies who had inherited land in England to make it worthwhile for speculators to visit New England, cash in hand, to offer to buy them out. Fitz-John Winthrop, who had himself just recently

---

[35] Lechford *Notebook*, pp. 4–10.
[36] *Ibid.*, pp. 256–8.
[37] *Aspinwall Notarial Records*, p. 7; Massachusetts Archives, vol. 39, p. 481, 493, 516, 527.
[38] Norfolk Record Office, Accn. 21.8.81, R152 C; Norwich Archdeaconry Wills; Ormesby St. Margaret parish register; Savage, *Genealogical Dictionary*, vol. 3, p. 249.

returned to Massachusetts from England, reported in 1698 the presence of 'Mr. John Clarke, a Hertfordshire man, who is lately come from England to visit some relations as well as to purchase some small pieces of land in England belonging to some persons here'.[39]

An alternative device for disposing of property in England was the conditional conveyance. A colonist with land in England would convey it to someone about to return there, on the condition that he sold it at the best price and remitted the proceeds. This was worth a fee of one to five pounds. In 1638 William Wilson of Boston conveyed three and a half acres of meadow at Donnington, Lincolnshire, to John Tinker, 'upon this special condition that the said John Tinker shall sell the premises...unto some person or persons in England for as much money as he by his best skill and endeavours can get'.[40] A variant strategy was to convey the land to a kinsman who would then collect rents and remit a share of the proceeds to New England. This is what Jachin Reyner of Rowley, Massachusetts, did in 1660 after becoming heir to some property in Yorkshire.[41]

In the last resort a colonist might save up enough money to cross back over the Atlantic to settle his affairs himself. John Flute, a servant at Saugus, Massachusetts, in the 1630s, sought permission through his mother for his release from his contract, 'to come over and settle his estate [in England] and if he will he shall return thither again'. George Wyllys returned from Connecticut in 1639 in order to sell his father's 'lands in Warwickshire'. John Hall went from Massachusetts to England in 1662 to untangle his inheritance. William Hubbard returned to England in 1678 when 'some matters of consequence about his temporal estate there necessitated him to engage in this voyage'.[42]

Networks of credit and debt extended across the Atlantic, linking English and colonial associates, heirs and executors. Literate and influential colonists who continued in touch with their kinsmen in England often served as facilitators of these transoceanic negotiations and deals. In 1639 John Winthrop was asked to help secure a debt due from the migrant Robert Howen to a former associate in London. The request came from his 'brother' George Jenney, who was married to the sister of Winthrop's second wife, who had died in 1615. Increase

---

[39] M.H.S. *Collections*, ser. 5, vol. 1 (1871), pp. 355–6.
[40] Lechford *Notebook*, pp. 23–4.
[41] 'Lane family papers', pp. 105–9.
[42] *Winthrop Papers*, vol. 4, p. 237; 'Wyllys papers', p. 6; 'Letters of John Hall'; 'Mather papers', M.H.S. *Collections*, ser. 4, vol. 8 (1868), p. 91.

Mather similarly furthered William Hubbard's business through a letter to his English 'cousin' Jonathan Tuckney.[43] The kinship dimensions of these transatlantic relationships will be explored in Chapter 11.

In 1671 a Mr. Howes of Massachusetts wished to collect a legacy due to him from his grandfather who had died in Buckinghamshire. Not having the time, the inclination or the resources to collect it in person he requested his neighbour John Hull to write to Hull's kinsmen in England for help in the matter. Meanwhile Howes pursued his legacy from another direction. Hearing that Harlakenden Symonds was preparing to visit England, he commissioned the traveller to act on his behalf. Symonds must have advertised his intended visit to England, and his willingness to serve as attorney, since at the same time he also promised to collect a legacy of one hundred pounds due to Henry Bennet.[44]

Samuel Sewall wrote from Boston to his kinsman Edward Hull in London in 1686, 'A neighbour of mine, William Needham, is willing to give his brother Andrew Needham in Hoggin Lane, London, five pounds... wherefore I desire you and order you to pay.' Five years later, when the colonial William Needham died, Sewall transmitted a bequest of fifty pounds to Needham's kinsmen in England. By this time Andrew Needham was dead, but Sewall's London agent searched out his son Thomas Needham, a cutler, 'at the Sun and Bible on London Bridge'. We can only guess at Thomas Needham's reactions to this legacy from an uncle in America.[45]

Similar practices obtained in the other direction. Thomas Peeke, a linen draper of Colchester, Essex, empowered Thomas Firmin to collect debts due to him from James Browne of Charlestown, Massachusetts, in 1650. William Wilkins, labourer, of Chesham, Buckinghamshire, engaged a neighbour with cousins in Massachusetts to help him collect the five pounds willed to him in 1658 by his father, who had migrated to New England. In 1689 Nathaniel Randall, 'being now out of his time with his master' in England, took matters into his own hands and shipped to Massachusetts, 'to see what is left for him of his uncle William Morton's estate'. His first order of business was to introduce himself to his cousin Charles Morton, a prominent minister in Boston. Randall was associated with English Nonconformists

---

[43] *Winthrop Papers*, vol. 4, p. 197; 'Mather papers', p. 91.
[44] A.A.S. MSS. 'Letter book of John Hull', pp. 45, 66; *Essex Courts*, vol. 4, p. 84.
[45] 'Letter book of Samuel Sewall', pp. 32, 119, 130.

and American Puritans, and so might be considered a religious migrant, but it is obvious that his primary consideration was economic betterment.[46]

Despite the miscellaneous character of the evidence, it is clear that financial ties and legal obligations linked families in England and New England throughout the seventeenth century. The links were strongest during the first generation, but might be consolidated or renewed in the second. New England merchants have long been understood as members of an active Atlantic community; probates, debts, bonds and other business also drew other New Englanders into the circle, and directed their attention back home. These entanglements most often touched the propertied classes, the yeomen and the elite, but even servants and labourers could be involved.

[46] *Aspinwall Notarial Records*, p. 350; 'Lane family papers', p. 105; M.H.S. *Collections*, ser. 5, vol. 1 (1871), p. 436.

8

'A hankering desire for old England': homesickness, return visits and back migration

For every shipload of passengers arriving in Massachusetts a cluster of travellers was waiting at the dock to go home to old England. This phenomenon is barely recognized in standard accounts of American history, which tend to treat the New World as an irresistible and permanently-attracting magnet. Yet in the seventeenth century, as in every other period of America's history, there has been a trickle of back migration, sometimes rising to an appreciable tide. Migration theorists talk of 'return migration', 'reflux migration' and even 'retromigration' to describe the movement of migrants back to their land of origin. Ravenstein in the nineteenth century formulated the law that 'each main current of migration produces a compensating counter current', and events of the twentieth century continue to bear him out. How well known is the estimate that of the sixteen million European immigrants to the United States in the early twentieth century as many as one in four returned home?[1]

One purpose of this chapter is to draw attention to the homeward movement from New England in the seventeenth century, as a further indication of linkage and interaction between the colony and the old country. I am concerned not only with those well-known university men who returned to take part in the English revolution but also with ordinary people whose motives for return were more mundane or more complex. Some colonists went back to England on specific business, intending to return to America as soon as possible. Others deliberately turned their backs on the New World. An untold number of New Englanders thought hard and long about the possibilities of resettlement but finally remained in America. This chapter tries to take note of their yearnings.

---

[1] George Gmelch, 'Return migration', *Annual Review of Anthropology*, 9 (1980), pp. 135–6.

The evidence for back migration is patchy and haphazard, and does not lend itself to quantification. Just as migrants were not supposed to leave England without due registration, and none was to settle in Massachusetts without approval, so they were not supposed to leave the colonies without official permission. But no documention survives of this process, even if such control was ever attempted.[2] The scale of the return migration is a matter of conjecture. But when we hear of ships returning to England with a dozen, thirty, forty or seventy passengers at a time, and when so many colonial records refer to settlers 'now living in England', it does not seem unreasonable to estimate a back migration of several thousand souls during the 1630s and 1640s. As many as one in six of the migrants to New England may have either permanently or temporarily returned home.

Population estimates also throw some light, albeit indirectly, on return migration in the seventeenth century. It is generally accepted that 21,000 or more men, women and children left England for New England during the decade of the great migration. Yet modern estimates of the English population of New England in 1640 range from 13,500 to at most 17,600. These figures are not robust, but they are the best we have. Since the migrant families included many wives of child-bearing age and a good number of marriagebale daughters and female servants, and since New England is credited with an unusually favourable demographic environment, we might expect the final population figures to be higher. Death from natural causes, starvation, disease, accidents and Indian attacks would deplete the totals, but not to the level of our estimates. Only further migration can reconcile the numbers. Some New Englanders moved on in the New World, to Long Island, and points south, but the rest probably found their way back home. The last decades of the seventeenth century also saw a net migration *from* New England.[3]

For many migrants, including some Puritan leaders, New England was a temporary stopping point rather than a final destination. For some it was a place in which to shelter while a storm of ungodliness raged over Caroline England. For others their godly commonwealth

---

[2] *Mass. Recs.*, vol. 1, p. 88.
[3] Henry A. Gemery, 'Emigration from the British Isles to the New World, 1630–1700: inferences from colonial populations', *Research in Economic History*, 5 (1980), pp. 200, 212; Terry Lee Anderson and Robert Paul Thomas, 'White population, labor force and extensive growth of the New England economy in the seventeenth century', *Journal of Economic History*, 33 (1973), p. 636; John J. McCusker and Russell R. Menard, *The Economy of British America, 1607–1789* (Chapel Hill, N.C., 1985), pp. 103, 214–27; David Galenson, *White Servitude in Colonial America: An Economic Analysis* (Cambridge, 1981), pp. 214–16.

would be a model for the reconstruction of religion and society in old England, should such an opportunity occur. For Puritans like these the attraction of New England faded with the calling of the Long Parliament, the outbreak of civil war, and the prospect of godly reformation at home. For those who could afford the move, and who had not put down deep roots in America, returning to old England in the 1640s was an attractive option.

Leaving the colonies at any time, like leaving England in the first place, involved a host of personal motives and public circumstances. Changes in the political and religious climate in England explain much of the back migration of the 1640s, but homesickness, family duties, or the chance of an inheritance also induced people to brave the Atlantic once again. It is another 'law' of migration that those who have made one major move are predisposed to keep on moving. People who moved to New England for secular reasons might be prompted by other secular factors to move yet again. Some people were unhappy in early America, blaming the weather, the soil, the church or the government for their own failure to thrive. Others yearned for an England that was cosier, more sociable, more exciting or more familiar than Massachusetts. Enhanced by distance and re-shaped by nostalgia, old England made inroads on the memory and imagination. While most settlers made the best of their new environment, swallowing their frustration while building a future, others, usually those with better resources, acted on their discontent, their fancy or their sense of call to the mother country, and went home.

Removing to England was no light undertaking. Single men might work their passage, if a ship was short of hands, but normally the journey required money. Shippers still charged five pounds a head for the Atlantic crossing, no matter which direction, and there were other expenses involved in uprooting and resettling.[4] During the 1630s a planter who proposed to return could usually make a profit by selling land, housing or equipment to newcomers, but in the depressed economy of the 1640s and 1650s those leaving New England risked a loss. Robert Keayne of Boston warned his son in 1653, 'If he shall have an intent to remove himself into England...he will be forced to sell his land it may be for half the value of it.'[5] Returners were subject to psychological costs as well as out-of-purse expenses.

---

[4] Harlackenden Symonds paid £16 10s. for a trip to England and back in 1675, but travelled as a gentleman; *Essex Courts*, vol. 6, p. 222.
[5] 'Last will and testament of me Robert Keayne', in Record Commissioners of the City of Boston, *Tenth Report* (Boston, 1886), p. 19.

Loss of face, recognition of mistakes, or a feeling that life was passing them by might complicate the decision.[6]

At least half a dozen of the famous *Mayflower* passengers went back to England, though not all at once. Humility Cooper 'was sent for into England, and died there'. Desire Minter 'returned to her friends ...and died in England'. Bartholemew Allerton, Richard Gardiner, William Latham and Gilbert Winslow also resettled permanently in England.[7] For every returner there must have been several more who gave it thought.

Plymouth Colony had a considerable turnover of population in its early years. The evidence does not permit any calculation of rates and numbers, but we are left with an impression of hesitation and rootlessness in that 'mixed multitude'. Although the celebrated Pilgrim Fathers had the dedication and staying-power of heroes, others, including some of their friends and co-religionists, took ship at the first opportunity. Some left by their own accord, others were warned out or sent back. Among them were 'some of those that came over on their particular and were returned home'.[8]

Plymouth's early neighbours were even less permanently rooted. Most of the 'lusty men' of Thomas Weston's colony, who settled in some disorder close to Plymouth in the early 1620s, eventually found fishing vessels to return them to England.[9] Similarly, the colonists of Robert Gorges's settlement in Massachusetts soon dispersed, making their way to Virginia or home to England.[10] Thomas Morton, who loved New England, also returned after ten years in the colony, hounded by the 'cruel schismatics' of Plymouth.[11] The more articulate of these failed settlers were to trouble the Massachusetts Bay Company for a dozen years.

The miseries of the Massachusetts Bay settlement at Salem in 1629 were compounded, in Edward Johnson's view, by the colonists' sense of isolation and homesickness. Some of them sank into a haze of lethargy, alcohol and tobacco, 'and that which added to their present distracted thoughts, the ditch between England and their now place

---

[6] Gmelch, 'Return migration', pp. 141–3.
[7] William Bradford, *History of Plymouth Plantation 1620–1647* (Boston, Mass., 1912), vol. 2, pp. 401–10.
[8] *Ibid.*, vol. 1, p. 362.
[9] *Ibid.*, vol. 1, pp. 271, 296–7.
[10] *Ibid.*, vol. 1, pp. 336–7.
[11] Thomas Morton, *New English Canaan...or an Abstract of New England*, ed. Charles Francis Adams, Jr. (Boston, 1883), pp. 107, 345.

of abode was so wide, that they could not leap over with a lope-staff'.[12] The arrival of the Winthrop fleet brought not only leadership and fresh supplies but also a chance to go home. Francis Bright, one of the ministers recruited by the Massachusetts Bay Company in 1629, was among those who took the first available ship back to England.[13]

Hundreds returned from New England in the 1630s. Numerically this back migration was offset by the thousands of fresh arrivals, but the defection was a blow to the colony's self-esteem. Some were actually expelled from New England, but most made up their minds to depart while the going was good. Robert Parke, who had petitioned John Winthrop to be allowed to join his expedition to New England, returned in 1630, only to reconsider and migrate once again to New England in 1639.[14] Some two hundred members of the original Winthrop fleet left New England in 1630, almost as soon as they had arrived. They went, in Thomas Dudley's judgement, 'partly out of dislike of our government, which restrained and punished their excesses, and partly through fear of famine'. 'Missing of their expectations,' these colonists 'returned home and railed upon the country.' By 1631 most of them were back in England spreading 'clamours . . . as variable as their humours and auditors'. So powerful was the negative impression spread by these returners that Edward Howes reported to John Winthrop, Jr., the rumour of 1632 that 'you are all coming home'.[15]

John Pond's letter to his father in March 1631 captures the desperation and disappointment of some of these early settlers. 'I think that in the end if I live it must be by my leaving, for we do not know how long this plantation will stand.' Pond saw eighty or more fellow-migrants pack up their belongings and depart, 'and as many more would a come if they had wherewithall to bring them home'. Pond himself was willing to give New England a chance, but was ready to go home if conditions had not improved by Michaelmas.[16]

Dozens of short-term colonists sailed home on the *Lyon*, the first vessel to reach Massachusetts in 1631. Among those leaving that year were Arthur Tyndal, John Winthrop's brother-in-law, John Revell, one of the undertakers for the joint stock of the company, and William

[12] *Wonder-Working Providence*, p. 45.
[13] *Chronicles*, p. 316.
[14] *Winthrop Papers*, vol. 2, p. 213.
[15] *Chronicles*, p. 315; William Wood, *New England's Prospect*, ed. Alden T. Vaughan (Amherst, Mass., 1977), p. 67; John Smith, 'Advertisements for the unexperienced planters', in Arber, *Smith*, vol. 2, p. 954; *Winthrop Papers*, vol. 3, p. 94.
[16] *Winthrop Papers*, vol. 3, pp. 17–19.

Vassall, one of the company assistants. Their departure, like the removal of other educated and influential men in the 1640s, was an expensive loss.[17] The *Lion's Whelp* deposited eight passengers in New England in 1632 but took ten more on board for the return voyage. Thirty migrants sailed back to England on the *Elizabeth Bonadventure* in 1633. Another ship was ready to leave for England early in 1637, 'and many passengers in it'. The *Adventure* carried eighty passengers home from New England in 1652.[18]

The passage back to England was often more perilous than the western voyage, with the danger from privateers outmatched by the danger of rocks and strong currents at the mouth of the Channel. Several of the ships carrying returners had a hard time of it, the *Charles*, the *Success* and the *Whale* limping into Plymouth after scraping with Dunkirkers and the *Ambrose* becoming dismasted and in need of towing to Bristol. The *Mary and Jane* was wrecked on its return passage to England in 1633.[19]

To the Puritans, of course, such upsets were the marks of Providence, a judgement on the weakness of those who turned away from God's colony. There is at least a trace of smugness in Winthrop's remark of 1631 that 'of those that went back in the ships this summer, for fear of death or famine, etc., many died by the way and after they were landed, and others fell very sick and low'.[20] A terrible fate befell the Austin family, discontented returners of 1638 who were taken into Turkish slavery on their way home to England. This was surely another sign of the displeasure of the Lord with those 'who have spoken ill of this country, and so discouraged the hearts of his people'.[21] Severe judgements also fell on some of those who deserted the colony in the early 1640s. Returners were beaten by storms at sea and stalked on shore by hardship, madness and plagues, much to the steadfast saints' satisfaction.[22]

Massachusetts expelled notorious trouble-makers to the neighbouring territories of Rhode Island and New Hampshire, and returned the most incorrigible to England. Expulsion was an expensive

[17] *Winthrop Papers*, vol. 2, p. 303; *Chronicles*, p. 316. Vassall, a restless traveller, went back to Massachusetts in 1635, returned again to England eleven years later, and finally removed to Barbados.

[18] Peter Wilson Coldham (ed.), *English Adventurers and Emigrants, 1609–1660* (Baltimore, 1984), pp. 37–8, 141, 151; *Winthrop's Journal*, vol. 1, pp. 104, 209.

[19] *Winthrop's Journal*, vol. 1, pp. 59, 100.

[20] *Ibid.*, vol. 1, p. 58.

[21] *Ibid.*, vol. 2, p. 11.

[22] *Ibid.*, vol. 2, pp. 82–4; Cotton Mather, *Magnalia Christi Americana* (Hartford, Conn., 1820), vol. 1, pp. 257–8.

and awkward business but one that was designed to purge the commonwealth of infection. The colony had to bear the costs of repatriation. John and Samuel Browne, a 'factious and evil conditioned' pair, were sent back 'against their wills, for their offensive behaviour' after only six weeks in New England in 1629, and Massachusetts dispatched six more rejects back to England in 1631 as 'unmeet to inhabit here'.[23] Expulsion was the last resort, after warnings, fines and other punishments had failed.

People too weak, indigent or friendless to thrive in New England might also qualify for repatriation. Invalid servants and fatherless children in particular were liable to be sent home if they became a burden to the colony. Abigail Gifford, a widow, 'being found to be sometimes distracted, and a very burdensome woman', was sent home in 1634. The three orphan children of Christopher Young of Wenham, Massachusetts, were to be transported 'over sea into our native country, unto Great Yarmouth in Norfolk in old England', where they had grandparents who might care for them.[24] In 1654 the Commonwealth of Massachusetts transported Elizabeth Avis, 'a poor lame maid' who was costing her master four shillings a week and who 'much desireth to go for England to her friends'. John Brandon, a servant abandoned by his master after being injured in the Indian war, petitioned in 1676 to be sent back to England to his mother 'and other relations with whom he might be maintained'.[25] Like the rest of the returners of the seventeenth century, these casualties of the colonization process added their tales to the pool of information, and served as living links between New England and the homeland.

People who were dissatisfied with New England, or who decided that old England offered them more, were not the best advertisement for the colonies. Yet these returners had a powerful influence on English opinion about America, and helped shape the social relations between the colonies and the motherland. Someone who had actually been to America could be regarded as a witness, an expert, even if the view he or she offered was remorseful, biased or hostile. The Massachusetts leaders themselves recognized this when they attempted to control the backflow of migration. John Cotton warned a group of 'our brethren ... going to England' in 1630 against the consequences of malicious or damaging testimony. Again in 1637 he instructed returners not to spread unfavourable reports about the

---

[23] *Chronicles*, pp. 287, 290; *Mass. Recs.*, vol. 1, p. 83.
[24] *Winthrop's Journal*, vol. 1, p. 144; *Essex Courts*, vol. 1, pp. 121, 154.
[25] Massachusetts Archives, vol. 9, p. 23, vol. 69, p. 40.

colony.[26] The authorities were not quite sure what to do with disgruntled settlers like Thomas Lechford, whose return to England might hurt the Bay Colony's reputation. Lechford observed in 1640, 'I am not of them, in church or commonweal. Some bid me be gone, of which I am some sort glad; others labour with me to stay, fearing my return will do their cause wrong.' A year later Lechford had made up his mind 'to visit my friends in England', and to carry on his struggle with the Boston leaders through the medium of the London press.[27]

The returners were by no means all failed colonists, easy quitters or renegades from the New England way. Thomas Dudley believed that most of them 'purpose to return to us again if God will'.[28] Nor was this simply a pious hope. Dozens of early settlers left New England in order to reunite their families, to recruit for Massachusetts, or to wind up their affairs in England, before planting themselves permanently in America. Many accomplished their goals and came back to New England within a few years, while others became delayed or entangled in their homeland. Edward Johnson, for example, who sailed with the Winthrop fleet in 1630, was among those who went home in 1631; he spent five years in England before sailing again to Massachusetts with his wife and seven children. John Wilson, the minister, went home in 1631 to try to persuade his wife to accompany him to New England. Unsuccessful, he crossed over again in 1632, returned once more to England, and made his third and final voyage to America in 1635. Wilson spent most of his time away proselytizing for the Bay Colony, and was more successful with co-religionists than with his wife.[29] George Alcock, deacon of Roxbury, 'made two voyages into England upon just calling thereunto, wherein he had much experience of God's preservation and blessing'. Augustine Clement of Dorchester, Massachusetts, went home to England in 1636 to deal with his property in Berkshire, but he was back in New England in 1637. Edmund Gurdon was called back to England in 1637 to take up a copyhold in Suffolk, but with every intention of returning to Massachusetts.[30]

[26] Cotton Mather, *Magnalia*, vol. 1, p. 257.
[27] Edward E. Hale (ed.), *Note-Book Kept by Thomas Lechford...1638 to...1641* (Cambridge, Mass., 1885), pp. xxiii, xxvii, 275.
[28] *Chronicles*, p. 337.
[29] *Wonder-Working Providence*, pp. 6, 84, 104; *Winthrop's Journal*, vol. 1, pp. 61, 164.
[30] 'Roxbury land and court records' in Record Commissioners of the City of Boston, *Sixth Report* (Boston, 1881), p. 76; Hale (ed.), *Note-Book Kept by Thomas Lechford*, p. 4; *Winthrop Papers*, vol. 3, p. 387. Dozens more examples could be cited.

News of the Scottish war in 1638 and the calling of a parliament in 1640 caused some of the more ambitious and dutiful colonists 'to think of returning back to England'.[31] English Puritans called for the return of the godly emigrants, and a hundred or more responded. These included some of the best and the brightest, talent the colony could ill afford to lose. It has been estimated that 'nearly half of the colonies' intellectual leaders' left between 1640 and 1660.[32] English friends and sympathizers counselled New Englanders that their duty lay in the homeland rather than America. 'Now, blessed be God, the times be much changed here,' wrote James Sherley from Surrey in May 1641, 'I hope to see many of you return to your native country again and have such freedom and liberty as the word of God prescribes.'[33]

Yet the motives and circumstances of returning New Englanders could be as ambivalent as those that took them to America in the first place. Hanserd Knollys and Thomas Larkham, for example, who had been rivals in the ministry at Northam (alias Piscataqua), abandoned New England to do service as chaplains in the Parliamentary army. At first glance these men appear as conscientious Puritan ministers, drawn to God's work in the glory days of the 1640s. But closer inspection reveals them to have been *failures* in New England, misfits in the godly commonwealth, who departed America in a cloud of scandal and recrimination. The revolution in England afforded them an opportunity to make something of their lives, after making only blunders and enemies in New England.[34] Other returners, too, can be shown to have been acting on opportunity as well as conscience.

Thomas Lechford, the lawyer, was not so much drawn to the new possibilities of revolutionary England as repulsed by the exclusiveness and hypocrisy of the New England Puritans. 'Not agreeing to this new discipline,' he wrote, 'I have suffered.... I am kept from the sacrament and all place of preferment in the commonwealth, and forced

[31] *Winthrop's Journal*, vol. 2, p. 19.
[32] William L. Sachse, 'The migration of New Englanders to England, 1640–1660', *American Historical Review*, 53 (1948), pp. 251–78; Harry S. Stout, 'University men in New England 1620–1660: a demographic analysis', *Journal of Interdisciplinary History*, 4 (1974), pp. 394, 397–400; Harry S. Stout, 'The morphology of remigration: New England university men and their return to England, 1640–1660', *Journal of American Studies*, 10 (1976), pp. 151–72.
[33] Bradford, *History of Plymouth Plantation*, vol. 2, p. 295.
[34] Nathaniel Bouton (ed.), *Documents and Records Relating to the Province of New Hampshire*, vol. 1 *1623–1686* (Concord, N.H., 1867), pp. 122–4; Francis J. Bremer, *The Puritan Experiment: New England Society from Bradford to Edwards* (New York, 1976), p. 87.

to get my living by writing petty things.' Lechford returned to England in 1641 after a fruitless struggle with Massachusetts' religious and civic innovations. He also left his wife in America. Within months of his return to England, Lechford published a sharply critical account of Massachusetts, and he was still licking his wounds several years later. John Cotton recalled of Lechford, 'When he came to England the bishops were falling, so that he lost his friends and hopes both in old England and New.'[35]

Massachusetts dispatched Hugh Peter, Thomas Weld, William Hibbins and John Winthrop, Jr., on a political mission to England in 1641, and they travelled with 'other passengers to the number of forty'.[36] Only Hibbins and Winthrop ever found their way back to Boston. Hugh Peter became a celebrated chaplain in the parliamentary army, relishing his role as an associate of Lord General Cromwell. Although Peter repeatedly assured his friends of his intention to return to New England, he never made it back. He was eventually executed as a regicide.[37] Thomas Weld became active in England as a Puritan preacher and commissioner for New England charities in England. Although he spoke well of the colony, and wrote pamphlets on its behalf, he never crossed the ocean again.[38]

Hundreds of New Englanders joined these agents and divines in England during the momentous years of the Long Parliament and the Interregnum. The pacing and timing of their return were roughly synchronized with the receipt of good and bad news from old England. Among university-educated men there was a surge of returns in 1641 and 1642, then a falling off until a new peak in 1650.[39]

New Englanders were further disturbed in these years by economic dislocation. The end of the great migration, compounded by the outmigration of the returners, led to 'the sudden fall of land and cattle, and the scarcity of foreign commodities and money, etc.' This put some of them in a restless mood, and more decided to return to England. John Winthrop was furious, but he could not stem the haem-

---

[35] Thomas Lechford, *New-Englands Advice to Old England* (London, 1644), pp. 56–8, 69, 73; John Cotton, *The Way of Congregational Churches Cleared* (London, 1648), p. 71; *Suffolk County Wills: Abstracts of the Earliest Wills upon Record in the County of Suffolk, Massachusetts* (Baltimore, 1984), p. 350.

[36] *Winthrop's Journal*, vol. 2, p. 32; Raymond P. Stearns, 'The Weld-Peter mission to England', *Publications of the Colonial Society of Massachusetts*, 32 (1934), pp. 188–246.

[37] *Winthrop Papers*, vol. 5, pp. 30, 102; Raymond P. Stearns, *The Strenuous Puritan: Hugh Peter 1598–1660* (Urbana, Ill., 1954).

[38] 'Roxbury land and court records', p. 170; Roger Howell, *Puritans and Radicals in North England* (Lanham, Md., 1984), pp. 83–111.

[39] See articles by Sachse and Stout, cited in note 32, this chapter.

orrhage of defection. 'Much disputation there was about liberty of removing for outward advantages, and all ways were sought for an open door to get out at; but it is to be feared many crept out at a broken wall.'[40]

The early 1640s may have been the only time in New England history when immigrants were outnumbered by people returning in the opposite direction. Increase Mather observed that 'since the year 1640 more persons have removed out of New England than have gone thither'.[41] The ships of 1643 took 'many passengers, men of chief rank in the country'. Two more ships sailed to England in 1644, one with thirty, the other with seventy returning migrants. Young Harvard graduates looked to England for their future employment, in a reversal of the brain drain of the 1630s. More good colonists went home in 1645, including some 'of our best military men, and entered into the Parliament's service'.[42] Nathaniel Mather reported from London in 1651, 'Here is great encouragement for any to come over ... I cannot but sincerely wish from my very heart that all my good friends in New England were also here with myself.'[43] The easy entry that some New Englanders made into English pulpits and positions of authority was a further inducement for others to come home.

So substantial was the back migration of 1640–2, when vigorous settlers abandoned Massachusetts to take part in the revolutionary developments at home, that the movement damaged the moral credit of New England. The depletion in manpower posed psychological problems for the colony that identified itself with God's cause. 'Why do so many come away from thence?' asked the author of *New-Englands First Fruits*, an apologetic tract of 1643. The answer, it was claimed, lay in the variability of human nature, and had nothing to do with the alleged faults of New England. Some, the pamphlet explained, intended to go back to New England as soon as they had accomplished the 'special business and purpose' that took them to England, whereas 'of them that are come hither to stay ... some of the wisest repent them already and wish themselves there again'. Nor were all the returners men of wisdom or high principle. 'As some

[40] *Winthrop's Journal*, vol. 2, pp. 82–4. On the crisis in the New England economy see also Thomas Lechford, *Plain Dealing, or News from New England*, ed. Darrett B. Rutman (New York, 1969), p. 113; Marion H. Gottfried, 'The first depression in Massachusetts', *New England Quarterly*, 9 (1936), pp. 655–78.

[41] Increase Mather, *A Brief Relation of the State of New England, from the Beginning of that Plantation to this Present Year, 1689* (London, 1689), p. 5.

[42] *Winthrop's Journal*, vol. 2, pp. 152, 207, 250, 253. Cf. *Winthrop Papers*, vol. 5, pp. 89, 94, 137, 244.

[43] 'Mather papers', M.H.S. *Collections*, ser. 4, vol. 8 (1868), pp. 3, 4.

went thither upon sudden undigested grounds, and saw not God leading them in their way, but were carried by an unstayed spirit, so have they returned upon as slight, heedless, unworthy reasons as they went.' Others could not endure 'the strict government in the commonwealth or discipline in the church', and so New England was better off rid of them; 'as Ireland will not brook venemous beasts, so will not that land vile persons and loose lives'. This was remarkably similar to the Laudian bishops' view of the great migration.[44]

English friends of New England knew that the colonies were in trouble. Hannah Dugard, writing from Warwickshire in 1646 to a kinswoman in Connecticut, noted that 'there is not any speech or inclination in any that I hear of towards New England, but rather an expectation of some from thence'.[45] Hundreds of returning colonists became reunited with their families in England during this time. Still more made plans to return, but for one reason or another failed to accomplish them. News reached William Bisbey in London in 1646 that his son-in-law Samuel Martyn and daughter Phoebe, of Wethersfield, Connecticut, 'were purposed to come over' to England. Given the uncertainty of the English political situation, Bisbey advised against it. 'I hope they are not so foolish to spend £40 or £50 upon a slender occasion, nor so flush with money.'[46]

Robert Seeley, an original member of the Winthrop fleet and a veteran of the Pequot wars, who was by 1646 lieutenant of artillery at New Haven, obtained 'liberty of the court to go for England, although a public officer'. He had tried several times to resign his commission, and in November 1646 he managed to sell his town house and land. But for reasons that remain unclear – perhaps community pressure – Seeley changed his mind. In November 1649 the New Haven court recorded that Seeley was 'now resolved to stay here and follow his trade of shoemaking, and shall not remove unless the town be satisfied that God by his providence calls him away'. Deprived of the opportunity to take part in England's civil wars, Seeley went on to serve against the Dutch in New Netherlands and Long Island.[47]

So common was the return to England during the 1640s and 1650s that colonists making their wills at this time often inserted clauses to

---

[44] Henry Dunster and/or Thomas Weld, *New-Englands First Fruits* (1643; reprinted, New York, 1865), p. 46. For the Laudian bishops see chapters 3 and 5.
[45] 'The Wyllys papers . . . 1590–1796', *Collections of the Connecticut Historical Society*, 21 (1924), p. 91.
[46] *Ibid.*, p. 88.
[47] Charles J. Hoadly (ed.), *Records of the Colony and Plantation of New Haven, 1638–49* (Hartford, Conn., 1857), pp. 275–6; Savage, *Genealogical Dictionary*, vol. 4, p. 49.

cover the contingency of their legatees' or executors' being gone. Robert Turner, a Boston shoemaker, made provision for alternate overseers to his will of 1651 in case those first named 'remove to old England'. Robert Keayne hopefully appointed Edward Winslow an overseer of his will of 1653, 'if he return back to abide in New England'. William Halsted left most of his estate to his brother Henry, but 'in case he should go to England of his own accord' the inheritance was stymied.[48] The venerable John Cotton left his estate in Massachusetts to his wife and children, but 'if they shall transplant themselves from hence into old England', they would forfeit the inheritance, which would then go to Harvard College and the free school in Boston. This was, perhaps, a form of blackmail to keep the family tied to New England. Mrs. Cotton was happy to oblige; she stayed in Massachusetts to marry Richard Mather.[49] Thomas Richards of Weymouth, Massachusetts, was confident that his son John would came back from England, making him principal heir and overseer of his will of 1650. John Richards was still in England when his father died, however, and the other heirs sought permission to alter the arrangements, 'in case of his not returning'.[50]

A large number of returners intended but a temporary visit to England but allowed themselves to be diverted into permanent resettlement. Returning on errands, to fetch wives, settle estates, collect inheritances or serve God, they became so enmeshed in life in the homeland that it became impossible for them to sail to America again. William Wood left New England in 1633, intending to return. Soon after arriving in England he published *New England's Prospect*, one of the most influential guides to the colony, but there is no evidence that he ever went back to New England.[51] George Wyllys, Jr., left Connecticut in 1639 to dispose of some lands in Warwickshire and to find himself a wife. 'I desire much to be with you', he assured his family in New England, but he became so busy with English affairs that he never saw them again.[52] Herbert Pelham, back in London in the 1640s, assured John Winthrop he would rather be in New England, 'but we have not the disposing of our time, nor appointing the bounds of our habitation'.[53] Ben-

---

[48] *Suffolk County Wills*, pp. 37, 25; 'Last will and testament of me Robert Keayne', p. 51.
[49] *Suffolk County Wills*, p. 43.
[50] *Suffolk County Wills*, p. 105; Savage, *Genealogical Dictionary*, vol. 3, p. 533.
[51] Wood, *New England's Prospect*, pp. 3–6.
[52] 'Wyllys papers', pp. 6, 19.
[53] *Winthrop Papers*, vol. 5, p. 157.

jamin Gostlin similarly apologized for not returning to Massachusetts, explaining in 1640, 'I am in so good employment and in so hopeful a way that I should be much blameable if I should thrust myself out of it.' Richard Storer could not go back to New England, he explained in 1643, because he was prevented by the illness of his wife. George Alsop sailed from Massachusetts in 1650, called by 'the weightiness of his occasions in England'.[54] Returners like these, who became ministers, merchants, soldiers, shopkeepers, innkeepers and artisans in London and the provinces, were often the most enthusiastic advocates of New England. We find them collecting news, writing letters, arranging shipping, greeting American travellers, and providing tips and introductions for those still preparing to emigrate. Perhaps they felt guilty about abandoning New England.

Dozens of well-connected New Englanders of the younger generation found England too comfortable or too profitable to leave. Among those returning in the Cromwellian era were John Winthrop's son Stephen, Francis Higginson's son Nathaniel, and Robert Keayne's son Benjamin. All followed careers in the army. They were followed by such young gentlemen as John Hall, stepson to deputy-governor Samuel Symonds, Joseph Pynchon, son of the greatest man in western Massachusetts, and Samuel Mather, son of the celebrated Dorchester minister. Hall set up as an Islington goldsmith, Pynchon developed his career as a Middlesex physician, and Mather became a Nonconformist preacher in London and Ireland.[55]

Migrants who resettle in their homeland often feel wistful for the place they have left behind, and New Englanders who returned to old England were no exception.[56] The New England merchant Nehemiah Bourne, back in London in 1640, wrote, 'I ... have looked many times toward that good land, and not altogether without some breathings and longings ... I hope this long abstinence will make me set a higher price upon New England.' The Bourne family eventually resettled in New England after the Restoration.[57] 'Ah, sweet New England!' exclaimed Hugh Peter from his English billet in 1647, as he promised once more, and promised in vain, to return to Massa-

---

[54] *Winthrop Papers*, vol. 4, pp. 216, 375; M.H.S. *Collections*, ser. 5, vol. 1 (1871), p. 374.

[55] *Winthrop Papers*, vol. 5, p. 13; M.H.S. *Collections*, ser. 4, vol. 7 (1865), p. 399; 'Last will and testament of me Robert Keayne', p. 20; A.A.S. MSS. 'Letters of John Hall'; Carl Bridenbaugh (ed.), *The Pynchon Papers*, vol. 1 Letters of John Pynchon, 1654–1700 (Boston, 1982), pp. 99, 108; 'Mather papers', p. 549.

[56] Gmelch, 'Return migration', p. 145.

[57] *Winthrop Papers*, vol. 4, pp. 213–14; *cf. Winthrop Papers*, vol. 5, p. 244.

chusetts.[58] Stephen Winthrop, who was also in England in 1647, wrote to his father in Boston, 'It has pleased God to [thwart] all my purposes and endeavours to come back to New England at present.' He immediately took a commission in the parliamentary army. Three years later he assured his family, 'I expect not to settle in England, but to return amongst you.' As a Cromwellian soldier, Stephen Winthrop wrote to his stepbrother about his untended affairs in America, 'Truly I do value what I have there, for could I be assured of my health I think I should come away immediately, for I have no health here.' But he was still in England when he died in 1658.[59]

Emmanuel Downing, who made several trips back and forth across the Atlantic, confided in 1655, 'I do not give over thoughts of New England'. Still in London two years later, Downing again focussed his thoughts on the colonies: 'I value those things more, it may be, than some do, and think New England may have its times to flourish again.'[60] But New England would have to flourish without him.

Likewise John Hall, the Islington goldsmith, was haunted by New England, but he could not bring himself to return there. For Hall, who was born in America, Massachusetts was 'my native country' and 'the land of my fathers' sepulchres'. He acknowledged 'a hankering desire for New England', but the best he could do was to purchase (by proxy) a small piece of Massachusetts meadowland, 'for I would faine have some interest in New England'.[61]

John Hall's mild homesickness for New England was the obverse of the feelings of his father's generation. We also have the testimony of a younger New Englander, Benjamin Lynde, the Harvard-educated son of a Boston merchant, who crossed over to England in 1692 to complete his studies at the Middle Temple. Lynde wrote to his brother in New England, 'I look back oft to my pleasant country, my dear friends and acquaintance, and upon my little patrimony there.' Seven years later he was back in Massachusetts, launched on a successful American legal career.[62]

Homesickness, in its most acute form, is a psychological disorder presenting physiological symptoms. 'Hectic fever, constipation or diar-

---

[58] *Winthrop Papers*, vol. 5, p. 158.
[59] *Ibid.*, p. 174; M.H.S. *Collections*, ser. 5, vol. 8 (1882), pp. 212, 214.
[60] M.H.S. *Collections*, ser. 5, vol. 8 (1882), pp. 216, 218.
[61] A.A.S. MSS. 'Letters of John Hall', 3 May 1664, 28 May 1674, 25 August 1673.
[62] F. E. Oliver (ed.), *The Diaries of Benjamin Lynde* (Boston, 1880), p. 4.

Figure 7.   Richard Mather. Courtesy, American Antiquarian Society.

rhoea, delusions and even convulsions' have affected its sufferers. One eighteenth-century author went so far as to claim that home-sickness 'could wither a man to a skeleton'. Milder variations, including wistfulness, nostalgia, and disorientation, may have underlain the early history of New England, and may have been a common syndrome on the frontier.[63] 'Mary hath been very weak and low . . . and doth intreat you of your motherly affection to send for her home. . . . I doubt some part of the cause of her sickness and slow mending might be her affection to you and her long absence from you,' wrote John Hull in 1672 on behalf of a newcomer to Boston.[64]

Displacement, homesickness and a yearning for the attractions of the old country affected some of the most solid-seeming colonists. John Dunton reported that some of the first planters were still 'be-

---

[63] Charles Zwingmann, 'The nostalgic phenomenon and its exploitation', in Charles Zwingmann and Maria Pfister-Ammende (eds.), *Uprooting and After* (New York, 1973), pp. 20–21. See also Isaac Frost, 'Home-sickness and immigrant psychoses', *Journal of Mental Science* 84 (1938), pp. 801–47.
[64] A.A.S. MSS. 'Letter book of John Hull, 1670–1685', p. 42.

Figure 8.   Increase Mather. By permission of The Massachusetts Historical Society.

witched' by the name of their native country, 'ever, to their eightieth year, still pleasing themselves with hopes of their returning to England'.[65] Dunton is not the most reliable witness and his testimony is often dismissed. In this matter, however, there is strong evidence that

[65] John Dunton, *The Life and Errors of John Dunton* (London, 1818), pp. 128–9.

he was right, even if he exaggerated the point for effect. Even those members of the elite who resisted the call back to England in 1640 were sometimes troubled by home thoughts from abroad.

New England ministers and politicians, as well as humbler planters, had periodic fixations on 'our dear native country'. Writing his autobiography in the 1640s, Thomas Shepard could not forget 'lamenting the loss of our native country, when we took our last view of it' a decade earlier. William Hooke appealed in 1640 to the 'special ties and engagements' that bound the colonists to old England, a land with 'many a dear friend and countryman abiding'.[66] Richard Mather 'once had serious thoughts of returning to England', according to his son Increase. Mather's old congregation in Lancashire requested that he come back, but his new church at Dorchester, Massachusetts, would not relinquish him. Instead, Mather wrote 'an heart-melting exhortation' to his 'dear countrymen of Lancashire', expressing 'no small grief' at their continuing separation.[67] John Davenport, minister at New Haven, also wanted to go home. He confided to John Winthrop, Jr., in 1654, 'Now I see my call to be clear, to hasten, with the consent of the church, for my native land.' But that consent was not forthcoming, so Davenport, like his colleague Richard Mather, remained in New England.[68] Ann Eaton, wife of the governor of New Haven, was even more desperate to move. Falling out of sympathy with the New Haven Puritans, she became estranged from her husband, and 'dreamed of going back to England'.[69]

Members of the younger generation who were born in New England or brought there as children naturally enjoyed a different relationship with the old country. England for them was not so much a place of memories as a place of ancestors and history. Yet occasional references suggest that they too might develop a strong interest in old England.

---

[66] Michael McGiffert (ed.), *God's Plot: The Paradoxes of Puritan Piety, Being the Autobiography and Journal of Thomas Shepard* (Amherst, Mass., 1972), p. 63; William Hooke, *New Englands Teares, for Old Englands Feares* (London, 1641), pp. 17, 10.

[67] Increase Mather, *The Life and Death of that Reverend Man of God, Mr. Richard Mather* (Cambridge, Mass., 1670), p. 25; Richard Mather and William Tompson, *An Heart-Melting Exhortation Together with a Cordiall Consolation. Presented in a Letter from New England, to their Dear Countreymen of Lancashire* (London, 1650), pp. 1, 3, 4, 10. The call from Toxteth was appealing, but by the early 1640s Mather had hit his stride. He had encountered many frustrations in New England, especially in his first year, and may have considered returning in 1636; B. R. Burg, *Richard Mather* (Boston, 1982), p. 30.

[68] Isabel MacBeath Calder (ed.), *Letters of John Davenport, Puritan Divine* (New Haven, Conn., 1937), pp. 90, 91, 95.

[69] Lilian Handlin, 'Dissent in a small community', *New England Quarterly*, 58 (1985), pp. 196–9.

Boston's Daniel Quincy 'hath a great mind to see England', so his cousin recorded in 1676. Samuel Sewall, who was brought to New England in 1661 at the age of nine, developed a yearning 'to see my native country while some that I know are there'. This was the itch that brought Sewall to England in 1688 for an eleven-month visit.[70]

The prospect of resettling in England preyed on the minds of two of New England's most illustrious statesmen, John Winthrop, Jr., and Increase Mather. Each made repeated Atlantic crossings, and each came close to rededicating their careers to the old country.

John Winthrop, Jr., who had already made trips to England on colony business in the 1630s and 1640s, was pressured to return once again in the 1650s. Hugh Peter urged him in April 1652, 'You should come hither where you might many ways live comfortably.' Peter repeated his invitation in October: 'You should come hither with your family for certainly you will be capable of a comfortable living in this free commonwealth.'[71] Sir Kenelm Digby wrote to Winthrop in 1655, 'I hope it will not be long before this land, your native country, do enjoy your much desired presence...Where you are is too scanty a stage for you to remain too long.' A year later Digby was still pressing Winthrop to return. It was only a matter of time.[72] With several members of his family already in England, and a godly regime in power, the home country seemed especially attractive. But the collapse of the Protectorate did not extinguish all enthusiasm for old England. In 1660 John Winthrop, Jr., counselled his son Fitz-John to continue in England, where conditions were better 'for your future good and enabling you for future employment, than could be attained here'.[73]

Finally in 1661 John Winthrop, Jr., sailed to England for the third time, spending seven months there in a hectic round of family and-public business. His aunt Lucy Downing rejoiced that 'God hath brought you safe into your native land, and to a small remnant of your relations'. Before returning to America Winthrop enjoyed conversations with the English virtuoso community including founding members of the Royal Society.[74] Nor was this the last time old England weighed heavily on John Winthrop, Jr.'s mind. He maintained an extensive transatlantic correspondence, with an appetite for English

---

[70] 'Letter book of John Hull', p. 293; Samuel Sewall to Increase Mather, 'Mather papers', p. 520.
[71] M.H.S. *Collections*, ser. 3, vol. 10 (1849), pp. 113–14.
[72] *Ibid.*, pp. 5, 16.
[73] M.H.S. *Collections*, ser. 5, vol. 8 (1882), p. 69.
[74] M.H.S. *Collections*, ser. 5, vol. 1 (1871), pp. 51, 99. See also Robert C. Black III, *The Younger John Winthrop* (New York, 1966), pp. 216–45.

news, and he considered returning there in 1670 and again in 1675. Return to the home country remained an option, even if it was not to be followed. After Winthrop abandoned preparations for his departure in 1675 his neighbour Joseph Eliot confessed to being 'glad for the sake of the public of your having laid aside your thoughts of England for the present'. He died in Boston eight months later.[75]

Richard Mather's youngest son, Increase, had the most ambivalent relationship with old England. Renowned as one of the generation who 'invented New England',[76] Increase Mather was persistently troubled by the desire to build his career in old England. Born in Massachusetts in 1639, he first crossed the Atlantic to England in 1657, 'having myself a marvellous inclination and bent of spirit that way'. He spent four years in England, visiting his brother, travelling, talking, preaching and praying, before returning to his famous father in the colonies. England seems to have made a great impression on Increase Mather, for in 1662, though just married and settled in the church at Boston, he recalls, 'I had also a great desire to return to England, if liberty for Nonconformity should there be granted.'[77]

The Clarendon Code soon blocked this ambition, and Increase became bound up with Massachusetts affairs. But England still occupied a niche in his mind. Thwarted in local church politics, he confided to his diary in June 1664, 'Motions to resolve to go to England again and suffer there more under prelacy rather than to stay in New England to suffer under them that are looked upon as godly.'[78] This is a remarkably revealing admission. Increase's yearnings persisted, and two years later in June 1666 he made note of his 'secret prayer ... that He [God] would remove me out of Boston to England, and there dispose of me where I might have many to do good unto, and where I might have opportunity to follow my studies and increase learning, and where I might have suitable encouragement in outward respects, and not be distracted in the work of the Lord'. Far from being indifferent to England, as is commonly suggested, Increase Mather saw the old country as a metropolis of opportunity and as a place of respite from the interminable bickerings of New England.[79]

[75] M.H.S. *Collections*, ser. 5, vol. 8 (1882), pp. 137, 168–9; M.H.S. *Collections*, ser. 5, vol. 1 (1871), p. 431.
[76] Robert Middlekauff, *The Mathers: Three Generations of Puritan Intellectuals* (New York, 1971), pp. 96–111. See also Kenneth B. Murdock, *Increase Mather, the Foremost American Puritan* (Cambridge, Mass., 1926), pp. 59, 190–210, 262–86, 346–7, 386–7.
[77] [Mather], 'The autobiography of Increase Mather', ed. M. G. Hall, A.A.S. *Proceedings*, 71 (1961–2), pp. 281, 286, 287.
[78] A.A.S. MSS. 'Increase Mather's diary', 22 June 1664.
[79] *Ibid.*, 2 June 1666. *Cf.* Middlekauff, *Mathers*, pp. 75, 104.

'A hankering desire for old England'

For the next quarter of a century, as Increase Mather was building his reputation as a minister and administrator in Boston, he continued to read about England and to exchange letters with kinsmen and associates there. In 1688 he was chosen to represent Massachusetts in the charter negotiations in London, and came happily ashore in England, as he says, 'after twenty seven years absence'.[80] Increase Mather spent three exciting years in England from 1688 to 1691, hob-nobbing with the great, bowing to King James and then to King William, discoursing with friends, hearing sermons and buying books, as well as pressing the business of the charter. He seems to have relished his own celebrity status as a New England divine and head of Harvard College. England appeared to offer a broader arena for his talents. Increase actually considered *staying* in England, but allowed himself to be persuaded by a manipulative letter from his son Cotton. 'Have you indeed come to resolution of seeing New England no more? I am sorry for the country, the college, your own church ... I am sorry for your family ... for myself ... for my dear father too, who is *entered into temptations* and will find snares in his resolutions.'[81] Thus admonished, Increase Mather returned to Boston.

Though reunited with his family, and finding satisfaction in his ministerial duties, Increase still could not shed thoughts of old England. God or the colony might once again require his services there, a prospect he viewed with mixed feelings. In October 1693, 'I was much melted with apprehensions of my being returned to England again.' The likelihood 'of returning to England' still intrigued him the following March, although he confessed that 'the thought of absence from my family, and most of all the thoughts of absence from my son Cotton, is very grievous to me'.[82]

The thought would not leave him. Increase felt more 'persuasions' towards England in the spring of 1696, noting, 'I cannot think of going from my relations here without much reluctancy. So that if I return to England it must be purely and only to do greater service for Christ than in New England I am capable of.'[83] Again in 1703 Increase Mather marvelled at 'the strange persuasions I have had concerning my doing service for the Lord again in England. I know not what to think of it. Such things are often from angels'. Though 'so stricken in years, as that I am indisposed to travel and rather

---

[80] 'Increase Mather's diary', 16 May 1688.
[81] [Mather], 'Diary of Cotton Mather', M.H.S. *Collections*, ser. 7, vol. 7 (1911), pp. 137, 140; original emphasis.
[82] 'Autobiography of Increase Mather', pp. 345, 347, 349.
[83] *Ibid.*, p. 350.

desireous to die where I am', Increase was willing to go where God called him, especially if the call was to England.[84] In 1715, in his seventy-sixth year, Increase Mather again declared his willingness to cross the ocean, this time to deliver an address to King George. He reported 'the great desire I have to do some service for Christ in England once more before I die'.[85]

These private thoughts were an important thread in Increase Mather's life, although there is no mention of them in Middlekauff's study of the Mather family. England seems to have been a low-grade obsession, which periodically became acute. In his will, dated 1719, Increase Mather remembered his son Samuel, who had permanently removed to old England, and remarked somewhat enviously, 'He liveth where he may furnish himself with variety of books.'[86] One wonders how many other New Englanders of the second generation shared this persistent attachment to their fathers' country?

Homeward yearnings seem to have dried up by the third generation. But through most of the seventeenth century there were colonists in New England whose emotional identity involved looking east across the ocean. The incidence of these feelings is virtually impossible to measure, although it is important to recognize them. Whether they were more common among women or men, the young or the old, servants or free migrants, the prosperous or the poor, and whether colonists with dense kinship networks felt differently from people who were relatively isolated, is a subject for further research. Some no doubt detached themselves easily and thought no more about the old country. Others longed to return, and as many as one in six of the migrants may actually have gone home. One consequence of this back migration was the presence in English towns and villages of several thousand people with direct experience of New England.

[84] *Ibid.*, p. 352.
[85] *Ibid.*, p. 360.
[86] *Suffolk County Wills*, p. 62. Increase Mather died in 1723.

9

'A constant intercourse of letters':
the transatlantic flow of information

Correspondence, intermittent, painful and slow, bonded people in England and New England together, and helped them to maintain a sense of shared family membership and common national identity. In London and provincial England, and throughout the New England colonies, literate correspondents kept up an outpouring of affection along with an exchange of news. Even illiterates could sometimes participate in the long-distance communication that forms the subject of this chapter.

Arranging a payment, requesting a favour, inquiring after the circumstances of a co-religionist or kinsman, all could be done by mail. Letters provided an emotional lifeline, a cord of communication, that stretched across the wide ocean to inform, comfort or persuade kinsmen and friends on the other side. The leading families of New England engaged in a prolific transatlantic correspondence, consuming reams of imported paper and using gallons of home-made ink. Lesser lights also struggled to stay in touch, regularly, occasionally or perhaps only once in a lifetime. Most people wrote only when necessity moved them, to deal with a crisis; others wrote frequently, for pleasure or out of duty. Letter-writers often sent news of their neighbours and common associates, thereby broadening the network of contact. One correspondent of 1645 closed his letter from New England with the assurance that 'Mr. Leader, in whose house I sojourn at Boston, remembers his love to you and desires to be excused for neglecting to write to you according to his promise'. Someone else's letter was the next best thing.[1]

Every ship carried correspondence, and several hundred of the letters sent between England and New England in the seventeenth

---

[1] Beinecke Library MSS., Yale University, Osborne Files, 'Newsletter describing English settlements in New England ... December 1645'.

century survive. Having come so far they were, perhaps, treated with extra care; that they served as a link across vast distance may have been a factor in their preservation. Letters from afar were 'not common nor cheap', according to Thomas Dudley, and he knew that his own letter from Massachusetts in 1631 would be highly valued when it passed from hand to hand in England. Lucy Downing told her brother in 1636, 'How acceptable your so affectionate letter is to me, it is like the overflowings of Nilus, which enricheth the land and fertileth it for a year after.' John Hall's letters from London were lovingly filed by the Massachusetts branch of his family to be reread at leisure.[2]

James Cudworth of Scituate, Massachusetts, found letters from London in 1634 'put a great deal of quickening life and edge into my affections'. William Ellis wrote from Boston to his Quaker friends in Yorkshire, 'Though I be far separated from you in body, yet neither length of time nor distance of place hath hitherto cast you out of my remembrance.' Letters allowed their familiarity to continue. When Fitz-John Winthrop crossed over to London in 1658, his father in New England instructed him in the importance of correspondence. 'You should omit no opportunity of writing. Your mother will also be much troubled that most others that have relations here have written to their friends, and she cannot hear of any from you. You should write by every way that offers.' In the same vein William Gilbert wrote longingly from Boston in 1680 for English family news and 'a more particular account of our friends who are living and who are dead... Pray neglect no opportunity of writing unto me, if you did but know how welcome your lines was to me, I doubt you would not.'[3]

Family members in England placed a similarly high value on transatlantic correspondence. Johanna Tuttle, writing to her daughter in New England in 1656, allowed, 'The letter I received from you lay by me as a cordial which I often refresh myself with.' Hannah Dugard wrote from Warwickshire to her cousin Mary Wyllys at Hartford, Connecticut, in 1648 expressing disappointment that some of their correspondence had miscarried, 'but it is a comfort that they come to hand any time, being such a distance'. Nathaniel Mather, a member of an avid letter-writing family, took comfort in 1651 from 'a constant

---

[2] [Dudley], 'Dudley's letter to the Countess of Lincoln', in *Chronicles*, p. 303; *Winthrop Papers*, vol. 3, p. 278; A.A.S. MSS. 'Letters of John Hall'.

[3] Everett Emerson (ed.), *Letters from New England: The Massachusetts Bay Colony, 1629–1638* (Amherst, Mass., 1976), pp. 139–40; James Backhouse (ed.), *The Life and Correspondence of William and Alice Ellis* (London, 1849), p. 92; M.H.S. *Collections*, ser. 5, vol. 8 (1882), p. 46; *Essex Courts*, vol. 9, p. 478.

intercourse of letters' from New England that reached him in London.[4]

Many of the surviving letters include expressions of love, duty, respect or condolence, along with news or instructions about practical affairs. They usually end with valedictions that, though formulaic, express remembrance and affection for a circle of distant kin. Emmanuel Downing, for example, closed his letter to John Winthrop, Jr., in 1633, 'With my daily prayers for you and yours, with my love to your self and your good wife, I take leave and rest your loving uncle.' William Bisbey saluted a kinsman in Connecticut in 1640, 'Loving brother, my best respect remembered to you and my sister, the like from my wife, and all our cousins.' Rosamund Saltonstall, writing in 1644 to an emigrant brother she had not seen in thirteen years, concluded, 'Dear brother farewell, only remember me and I shall never forget you, your truly affectionate sister.'[5] These letters gave the authors an opportunity to enumerate, address and show respect towards associates and kinsmen. Their tone often displays tenderness rather than mere conventional obligation.

From the very beginning of settlement, fishermen, seamen, merchants and returning migrants ferried letters home to England. Edward Winslow and Emmanuel Altham provided an irregular courier service from Plymouth Colony in the 1620s, and other news crossed the ocean on ships by way of Virginia, the island colonies, or Newfoundland. When the *Talbot* and the *Lion's Whelp* returned from Massachusetts in 1629, they carried various letters along with the manuscript of Higginson's 'True relation' and 'all the late news from New England'. News by word of mouth gained corroboration through being set in writing. Word of John Winthrop's safe arrival in the New World in June 1630 reached his family in East Anglia in August, 'by a ship that came to Bristol from the plantation in New Plymouth'. Winthrop himself wrote to his wife on 16 July, more than a month after landing, 'that thou mayest know that yet I live and am mindful of thee'; this letter probably reached Suffolk in September.[6]

[4] *Essex Courts*, vol. 2, p. 173; 'Wyllys papers', *Collections of the Connecticut Historical Society*, 21 (1924), p. 106; 'Mather papers', M.H.S. *Collections*, ser. 4, vol. 8 (1868), p. 3.

[5] *Winthrop Papers*, vol. 3, p. 137; 'Wyllys papers', p. 11; Robert E. Moody (ed.), *The Saltonstall Papers, 1607–1815*, vol. 1, *1607–1789* (Boston, 1972), p. 137.

[6] Sydney V. James, Jr. (ed.), *Three Visitors to Early Plymouth . . . John Pory, Emmanuel Altham and Isaack de Rasieres* (Plymouth, Mass., 1963), pp. 23–39, 53–9; William Bradford, *History of Plymouth Plantation 1620–1647* (Boston, 1912), vol. 1, pp. 231, 383; *Winthrop Papers*, vol. 2, pp. 156, 157, 301–2, 311.

Every year throughout the 1630s returning vessels brought back news and correspondence as well as trade goods and homeward-bound travellers. Returning migrants made excellent couriers, even if they did not always bring good news. John Winthrop's brother-in-law, Arthur Tyndal, carried letters for members of the family when he left New England in 1630. When a friend was bound for England in 1635, Israel Stoughton took the opportunity to write a letter, 'Though as yet we have not a ship come nor know not certainly whether we shall, only we hear of many and hope the best.' In the same year James Howe and Roger Harlakenden wrote that 'things go very well with them' in Massachusetts. Their letters carried successfully to Samuel Rogers, an Essex clergyman, who reported 'good news from New England' in the spring of 1636.[7] John Tinker carried packets of letters back to England on board the *Mary Anne* in 1638. Other informal couriers included Peter Gardner, a yeoman of Roxbury, Massachusetts, who carried letters to London in the 1640s, and William Payne and Harlakenden Symonds in the 1670s.[8]

Although they might have to wait months for a ship, and could never anticipate how long the mail would take to reach its destination, early migrants in fact had little difficulty exchanging messages with family and friends in England. John Rogers wrote home in 1630 'so lamentable a letter' as to alarm his friends and kin. John Pond sent a similar sad letter home aboard the *Lyon* in 1631, describing the scarcity and disease of the frontier settlement. Roger Clap wrote more optimistically, asking his father for supplies and inviting his brothers and sisters to join him. Thomas Weld wrote enthusiastically about New England to his former parishioners in Essex. John Gallop wrote to his former neighbours in Dorset asking them to send him twelve dozen cod lines.[9] Ralph Josselin, the rector of Earls Colne, received a letter 'out of New England' in 1646 from his former neighbour and fellow-minister Thomas Shepard, telling 'of the welfare of that plantation, for which the name of the Lord be praised'. Josselin also corre-

---

[7] *Winthrop Papers*, vol. 2, p. 303; [Stoughton], 'A letter of Israel Stoughton, 1635', M.H.S. *Proceedings*, 58 (1924–5), p. 450; Kenneth W. Shipps, 'The Puritan emigration to New England: a new source on motivation', *N.E.H.G.R.*, 135 (1981), pp. 87–8, 91.

[8] Edward E. Hale (ed.), *Note-Book Kept by Thomas Lechford . . . 1638 to . . . 1641* (Cambridge, Mass., 1885), pp. 8, 10; Massachusetts Archives, vol. 15A, pp. 11–12; Boston Public Library MSS. Am. 1502/v2/34; A.A.S. MSS. 'Letter book of John Hull', p. 45; *Essex Courts*, vol. 6, pp. 84, 222; M.H.S. MSS. 'Miscellaneous, bound', Deposition of Ephraim Fellows, October 1675.

[9] *Winthrop Papers*, vol. 2, p. 316; *ibid.*, vol. 3, pp. 17–19, 87; 'Roger Clap's memoirs', in *Chronicles*, pp. 351, 354; Emerson (ed.), *Letters from New England*, pp. 94–8.

sponded with 'my friend Mr. [John] Haynes in N.E.', writing to him in 1648 in the care of 'a maid servant to Thomas Prentice'. Josselin also had cousins in New England with whom he kept in touch.[10]

The Winthrop family kept up an extensive correspondence, dealing with agents and friends in London, keeping up with their English kindred, answering the queries of prospective migrants and responding to requests from the friends or kinsmen of fellow-settlers. Ninety-three of the many letters addressed to John Winthrop from the English side of the Atlantic survive from the period 1630–40, of which thirty-two were written by kinsmen. From the same period there survive eighty-nine overseas letters to his son, John Winthrop, Jr., including dozens from his scientific friends in London and sixteen from relatives.[11] Writing protectively about the elder Winthrop, Richard Saltonstall remarked in 1632, 'I fear he hath too many letters.'[12]

The power and flexibility of correspondence testified to the practical value of literacy. But illiterates were not necessarily excluded; they too could participate in transatlantic communications. Motivation – the desire to communicate – was more important than mere technical skill. As many as two-thirds of the men and four-fifths of the women in mid-seventeenth-century England were illiterate to the degree that they could not write their own names. New England enjoyed superior literacy, due to the social selection and religious orientation of the migration, but at least two-fifths of the male colonists and two-thirds of the women were similarly illiterate in the seventeenth century.[13] The advantages of literacy were manifest, but its absence was not necessarily debilitating. People who had never learned to read could obtain help from a literate neighbour, while those who could not write might readily employ a scribe to set their words on paper. Physicians, clergymen, shopkeepers, schoolmasters, indeed, anyone in the community known to be adept with a pen, could be pressed into service on behalf of the less educated.

Thomas Lechford charged one shilling to pen letters from Boston in the late 1630s. John Barton, the Marblehead physician, charged the same amount for letters in the 1670s. Roger Lowe, a Lancashire

---

[10] Alan Macfarlane (ed.), *The Diary of Ralph Josselin 1616–1683* (London, 1976), pp. 56, 134, 196, 239, 277, 35, 39, 419, 421.
[11] *Winthrop Papers*, vols. 2, 3, 4, *passim.*
[12] *Saltonstall Papers*, vol. 1, pp. 118–19.
[13] David Cressy, *Literacy and the Social Order: Reading and Writing in Tudor and Stuart England* (Cambridge, 1980); Kenneth A. Lockridge, *Literacy in Colonial New England* (New York, 1974).

Figure 9.   John Winthrop, *c.* 1629. Courtesy, American Antiquarian Society.

shopkeeper, regularly wrote letters on behalf of his illiterate neighbours. In 1663, for example, 'John Hasleden . . . told me that he loved
a wench in Ireland, and so the day after I writ a love letter for him
into Ireland.' The Irish woman would probably have to find someone
to decode Hasleden's letter and set down her reply.[14]

This ephemeral correspondence between people on the margins of
literacy sometimes comes to our attention in cases before the Mas-

---

[14] Hale (ed.), *Note-Book Kept by Thomas Lechford*, p. 189; A.A.S. MSS. 'Account book of
Dr. John Barton, 1662–1676'; William L. Sachse (ed.), *The Diary of Roger Lowe* (London, 1938), p. 43.

Figure 10.   John Winthrop, Jr., 1606–75. Courtesy of The Harvard University Portrait Collections.

sachusetts courts. Two episodes from Essex County are especially instructive. Samuel Leach of Salem acted as scrivener *circa* 1670 when his illiterate neighbour, Robert Pike, wanted to communicate with his estranged wife in England. Leach testified that he 'had written several letters home to England for Pike to his wife and children, and had read several answers'. On the other side of the Atlantic, at Ottery St. Mary, Devon, Philip Searles, a clothier, performed a similar task, reading to the illiterate Grace Pike the letters from her illiterate emigrant husband. Searles deposed that Mrs. Pike 'hath in this few late

years brought several letters to this deponent which came from her
husband Robert Pike out of New England, and hath requested and
desired this deponent to read them for her'. The letters concerned
arrangements for Grace Pike to join her husband in Massachusetts,
and her reasons for refusing to leave England.[15]

The ability even of illiterates to communicate across the ocean is
further illustrated by the efforts of Francis Chapple, a Marblehead
fisherman, to persuade his betrothed, Mary Litten, to marry him.
Since he did not know how to write, Chapple engaged his neighbour,
James Mander, to pen at least three letters on his behalf, and he also
sent Mary tokens of his love with friends who were returning to
England.[16] If an illiterate New England fisherman could conduct a
proxy correspondence with his distant illiterate sweetheart, any other
colonial settler could do likewise. Those in the coastal settlements
probably had some advantage in this regard through their contacts
with fishermen and mariners.

Correspondents who had lost the use of writing through old age
or infirmity could employ an amanuensis, just as illiterate correspondents could engage a scribe. Samuel Sewall's English cousin Sarah
took over the writing of his aunt Dorothy Rider's transatlantic correspondence in the 1680s because of her weakening hand. Thomas
Bailey wrote a letter to Increase Mather on behalf of his brother John
in 1682, 'I not being well and he writing better'. Job Lane of Malden,
Massachusetts, engaged a scrivener to write to his cousin in Yorkshire
in 1695, apologizing that 'by reason that I am lame in my right hand
and have almost lost the use thereof, you may only expect my mark
to your letters and bills for the future'.[17]

People who rarely wrote letters sometimes turned for help to those
they knew to be in frequent contact across the ocean. Their messages
sometimes travelled enfolded with others, or as a postscript. The
Winthrop letters are scattered with messages and communications of
this sort, added to or embedded in other correspondence. Sir William
Spring sent a letter in 1637 to his emigrant cousin at Watertown,
Massachusetts, enclosed in a letter to John Winthrop. Spring had
earlier inquired of another kinsman, Brampton Gurdon, how best to
send messages to Massachusetts. Herbert Pelham wrote to John

---

[15] *Essex Courts*, vol. 5, pp. 65–7.
[16] Essex Insitute, Essex County Court Papers, Litten v. Homan, 1686. I am indebted
to Daniel Vickers for this reference.
[17] [Sewall], 'Letter book of Samuel Sewall', M.H.S. *Collections*, ser. 6, vol. 1 (1886), p.
41; 'Mather papers', p. 488; W. H. Whitmore (ed.), 'Lane family papers', *N.E.H.G.R.*,
11 (1857), p. 110.

Winthrop in April 1637 enclosing 'a letter from your old friend who sent it to me in the winter and should have sent it to you by the first [ship] but slipped the opportunity, not being sure of a trusty messenger'.[18]

The Mather family performed a similar service in the next generation. John Bishop wrote to Increase Mather in 1677 that 'in your letter I received one enclosed from Mr. Hooke in England, my ancient choice friend, to who I would make return, and have herein sent it to you, supposing you to have intercourse with him, and so know how to send to him, as I do not'. Writing from Stamford, Connecticut, Bishop also sent Mather 'a letter to my own and only sister in England, which I would might reach her'.[19] Bishop was probably capable of sending his letters direct, without Mather's assistance, but found advantage in correspondence with the powerful Boston clergyman.

Writing a letter took time and trouble, but the effort could be satisfying and the result worthwhile. The basic requirements, besides literacy or literate assistance, included paper (an expensive import in early New England), pen and ink (which anyone who knew the formula could make), a writing surface, adequate light, and peace and quiet (none of which could be taken for granted). Powder to dry the ink and wax to make a seal would be useful additions.[20]

As a pioneer colonist, Thomas Dudley had to overcome the inconvenience of difficult conditions. He laboured to set down his impressions of New England in 1631, 'having yet no table, nor other room to write in than by the fireside upon my knee, in this sharp winter; to which my family must have need to resort, though they break good manners, and make me so many times forget what I would say, and what I would not'.[21] The rigours of the frontier are mentioned again by a letter-writer in Boston in December 1645 who complained that

---

[18] *Winthrop Papers*, vol. 3, pp. 364, 393.

[19] 'Mather Papers', p. 301. The international correspondence of the Mather family is described in Francis J. Bremer, 'Increase Mather's friends: the transatlantic Congregational network of the seventeenth century', A.A.S. *Proceedings*, 94 (1984), pp. 59–96.

[20] John Winthrop included a recipe for ink in a letter to his son in 1647; *Winthrop Papers*, vol. 5, p. 162; after his death in 1649, Winthrop's inventory included thirteen quires of paper, *ibid.*, p. 336. In 1663 John Hall sent his mother in Massachusetts 'a ream of horn paper, costing six shillings, and sixpence worth of sealing wax'; in 1671 he sent her three quire of paper at ninepence and three quire at fourpence; A.A.S. MSS., 'Letters of John Hall', 21 April 1663, 15 March 1671.

[21] 'Dudley's letter to the Countess of Lincoln', in *Chronicles*, pp. 303, 305.

'the times be so exceeding cold that ink and pen freeze extremely'. Stoves were lacking, and 'the weather causeth me to huddle up things rudely'.[22] On the other hand, there would be few ships leaving at that time of year, and therefore few occasions to send letters before the spring. Material conditions soon improved, but the colonies long remained primitive compared to the comforts and sophistication of London. John Hull wrote from Boston to advise a London merchant in 1671, 'Your pens are useless here, table books not being used here and most men carrying inkhorns in their pocket.'[23]

Letters usually took the form of a single sheet of paper, folded twice to provide space for the address to be written on the outside. A wax seal secured the folds. Although each of the surviving letters is different, a standard format seems to have been observed. First came a greeting, then perhaps a general expression of sentiment or religious exhortation, this to be followed by the heart of the matter – business news, cash reckonings, or requests – then some brief comments on the state of affairs, with perhaps some national or local news, and finally a paragraph of family affairs, presentation of duty and respects, with remembrances to friends and kinsmen.

Taking advantage of shipping delays, writers commonly left a large margin to one side or a space at the foot of their paper for postscripts containing fresh news or late instructions. Henry Jacie, writing to John Winthrop, Jr., in 1637, began afresh a letter written two or three months earlier and 'not yet sent away'. John Hull commenced one letter on 12 December 1671, finished it on 31 January, but then had another couple of weeks in which to augment it. The reason was that 'Mr. Greenough was ready to sail [on 9 February] but since it [the weather] came in very sharp and hath stopped him hitherto'. The ship, with its basket of letters, did not leave Boston until 19 February.[24] Sometimes the occasion of a parting traveller or an opportune ship actually prompted the writing of a letter. Thus John Hall in December 1669, 'Hearing yesterday that Mark King in a ketch was to sail forthwith to New England, I could not forebear putting pen to paper.' At other times a letter languished for want of shipping. Writing to his brother in Boston in 1676, Nathaniel Mather sighed, 'I know not when this will be gone from London. I send it as an adventure, not knowing whether any vessel be going thence.'[25]

Correspondence was generally slow and erratic. Passages from west

[22] 'Newsletter describing English settlements in New England'.
[23] 'Letter book of John Hull', p. 46.
[24] *Winthrop Papers*, vol. 3, p. 483; 'Letter book of John Hull', pp. 49–50.
[25] 'Letters of John Hall', 1 December 1669; 'Mather Papers', pp. 9, 44.

to east were faster ('downhill' as the sailors put it), so in principle news could travel more quickly from Massachusetts to old England. But in practice all hinged on the chance of shipping and the vagaries of the winds. During the summer months there were usually frequent sailings, but in winter the ports might be deserted. Often, for safety's sake, a writer made duplicates of letters and dispatched them on different ships, by different routes, at different times. Writing from Salem to a minister in London, John Higginson recommended sending letters 'after the manner of merchants, to send three letters in three several ships'. Writing from Somerset in 1639, John Wollcott informed his brother in Connecticut, 'I have writ unto you at this time three letters because if one miscarry the other may come to your hands.' George Wyllys, Jr., similarly duplicated letters from Bristol to his father in Connecticut, saying in 1641, 'I shall write in effect the same things to you again lest my former letters should miscarry.'[26] There was no telling which copy would arrive first or whether any would go astray.

Delay was more likely than actual loss. Hannah Dugard grieved in 1648 that 'many of your letters sent to us have miscarried, to our sorrow, and so we heard ours did to you last year', but this was unusual.[27] Duplication, patience and persistence made it possible to sustain an Anglo-American correspondence.

John Endecott's first letter from New England, written on 13 September 1628, reached London on 13 February 1629, fifteen weeks later. The company secretary acknowledged the receipt when he wrote back to Endecott on 16 February, and mentioned it again in his letters of 17 April and 21 April. These last letters went by ship from the Isle of Wight on 4 May and 11 May, and additional copies were included in a further packet of letters sent on 28 May 1629.[28]

Edward Trelawny's letter from Boston, dated 10 October 1635, reached his brother in Plymouth (England) the following 15 January. A letter John Winthrop wrote from Boston on 29 June 1636 reached his friend Robert Reyce in Suffolk on 3 November. A letter from another New England correspondent, dated 19 October 1636, reached Reyce on 8 January following. Reyce's reply, written 1 March 1637, was in John Winthrop's hands in Massachusetts the following 22 June.[29]

---

[26] *Saltonstall Papers*, vol. 1, p. 214; [Wollcott], 'Letter of John Wollcott', *N.E.H.G.R.*, 2 (1848), p. 373; 'Wyllys papers', pp. 14, 106.
[27] 'Wyllys papers', p. 106.
[28] *Chronicles*, pp. 131, 141, 172.
[29] Emerson (ed.), *Letters from New England*, p. 178; *Winthrop Papers*, vol. 3, pp. 346, 363.

A few more examples will indicate the varying turnaround time for this long-distance correspondence. John Wiswall's letter, written from Dorchester, Massachusetts, on 27 September 1638, reached its destination in Lancashire four months later on 22 January. Henry Dunster, Sr., writing from Lancashire in 1641, recounted the receipt of letters from his son Henry Dunster, at Cambridge, Massachusetts.

I have received four letters from you since you arrived in New England, the first dated the 17th of August by Robert Haworth of Bolton, the second dated the 21st of August, both of which came to my hands in seven weeks after you sent them . . . the third was dated the 29th of October which I received on Christmas Eve with a letter of Richard's [Henry's brother] enclosed in the same, the last one dated the 12th of October which I received of one Millns that hath been with you in New England who lodged with me about mid January.[30]

One of the Wyllys letters, sent from Connecticut on 29 May 1644, reached its addressee in England on the following 23 September. Job Lane's letter from Malden, Massachusetts, dated 4 October 1653, reached Jeremy Gould in London the following May. A letter from George Curwen, Salem merchant, took from December 1657 to March 1658 to reach London. It took from 4 November 1663 until the following October for a letter from John Winthrop, Jr., in New England to reach his kinswoman Priscilla Reade in London.[31] Several of Increase Mather's letters to his brother Nathaniel in the 1670s took six months or more to go from Boston to Dublin, although half that time could be taken moving the mail from England to Ireland. Letters arrived late and out of sequence, Nathaniel Mather remarking in 1679, 'I had one of a later date sooner.' Inadequate addresses and stays of shipping caused delays, and some letters did not arrive at all.[32]

Although two months was usually time enough to make an ocean passage, mail entrusted to the carrier system often took several weeks or months longer. It is no wonder that correspondents often stinted their news, saying that a better account could be obtained from arriving passengers. Passengers might also relate by word of mouth

[30] H.M.C., *Fourteenth Report* (London, 1894), pt. 4, p. 56; 'Dunster papers', M.H.S. *Collections*, ser. 4, vol. 2 (1854), p. 191.
[31] 'Wyllys Papers', p. 66; 'Lane family papers', p. 103; Essex Institute, Curwen Papers, vol. 1, p. 31; M.H.S. *Collections*, ser. 5, vol. 1 (1871), p. 101.
[32] 'Mather papers', pp. 10, 18, 22, 353. For the transmission of news in the later Stuart period see Ian K. Steele, 'Time, communications and society: the English Atlantic, 1702', *Journal of American Studies*, 8 (1974), pp. 7–9, and 'Moat theories and the English Atlantic, 1675 to 1740', in Canadian Historical Association, *Historical Papers. Communications Historiques*, (1978), pp. 18–33.

matters too delicate or too controversial to trust to paper. John Hall was reluctant to write words that might create dissension in his family. He recalled the warning of 'a very wise and godly minister' that 'letters being matters of record are very unfit to contain controversies which should be forgotten and obviated as soon as raised'. Samuel Baker apologized for not writing to Increase Mather, 'because I judged it prudence to keep silence'.[33]

Some letters went down with their ships, and others were destroyed or intercepted. Sometimes the mail arrived water-damaged and virtually illegible. Precious letters to England were ruined in 1632 when the *Lyon* foundered in the Chesapeake on its way home. Seven crewmen and five passengers were drowned, but thankfully, Winthrop recorded, 'most of the letters were saved'. One of these eventually reached Devon, but it was 'so washed and the writing scoured out that the greatest part of it was so white and clean with the salt water, as I suppose, where the lines had been, as if it had not been written upon'.[34] Other letters went astray when homebound ships were wrecked or ravaged by pirates. Letter bags on board ship were equipped with weights, so they could be thrown overboard to sink to avoid capture by enemies. Mail from Boston was consigned to the waves in 1666 when a ship fell in with Dutch privateers.[35]

Pirates were not the only danger. Letters were subject to interference, censorship and confiscation at any stage in their passage. Sensitive papers were susceptible to interception by the colonial leaders or their enemies. John Winthrop's letters aboard the *Gift* in 1630 were 'broken open by the purser and master aboard the ship and read'. Other sensitive correspondence, including 'the letters of some indiscreet persons amongst us who had written against the church government in England', fell into the hands of the Bay Colony's enemies when the courier, Christopher Levett, died on the journey home.[36] A well-wisher warned Winthrop in 1637 about incautious remarks in letters sent to England, 'If they should come to the eyes or ears of any one of many thousands of your adversaries, it would afford them

[33] *Winthrop Papers*, vol. 3, p. 281; 'Letters of John Hall', 13 March 1677; 'Mather papers', p. 513.
[34] *Saltonstall Papers*, vol. 1, p. 121; *Winthrop's Journal*, vol. 1, p. 100; *Winthrop Papers*, vol. 3, p. 109; M.H.S. *Collections*, ser. 5, vol. 8 (1882), p. 130.
[35] Robert C. Black III, *The Younger John Winthrop* (New York, 1966), p. 317; *Boston News-Letter*, 4 December 1704.
[36] *Winthrop Papers*, vol. 2, pp. 317, 325; *Winthrop's Journal*, vol. 1, p. 99; James Phinney Baxter, *Christopher Levett, of York, the Pioneer Colonist in Casco Bay* (Portland, Maine, 1893), p. 75.

matter enough to attempt your undoing.' For this reason some of the Winthrop letters of the 1630s were protected by cipher or code.[37] The regicide William Goffe, hiding in New England after the Restoration, warned his wife in London, 'Be careful what you write, for all the letters we receive come from the post house,' where they were presumably subject to scrutiny.[38]

Colonial leaders themselves were responsible for breaking open packets of letters. Agitated by the leakage of unfavourable news and the export of downright lies, officers of Plymouth Plantation opened John Lydford's letters to England in 1624. These were hostile reports that included 'slanders and false accusations' against the colony. The officials 'took copies' of some of these offending writings, 'but some of the most material they sent true copies of them, and kept the originals, lest he should deny them'. Massachusetts officials similarly intercepted a letter of grievances from John Pratt and forced him to recant.[39]

Letters were often relayed through several stages, through various carriers and mail drops, before reaching their final destination. Letters to correspondents in England could be addressed to such places as 'the sign of the Sun and Key in Red Cross Street' or 'with Mr. Kett, merchant in Gravel Lane in Houndsditch, London'. Writing from Norfolk in 1672, Samuel Petto advised Increase Mather, 'If you please to order letters to be left for me at Mr. Ponders, bookseller at the Peacock in Chancery Lane . . . he can send them to me at any time.' In the other direction, English correspondents sent letters to Job Lane 'at Malden in New England, to be left . . . at Mrs. Mary Ardell's at her house in the Town Dock, over against Mr. Thomas Clark, brazier, in Boston'.[40]

Mail arriving in New England from the merchantmen in Boston harbour could sometimes be supplemented by news and letters from the Newfoundland fishing fleet. The fishing ships usually set out earlier in the season than the emigrant vessels, and thereby provided an advance on communications from England. Couriers brought the news and letters down from northern New England. In April 1633 a

[37] *Winthrop Papers*, vol. 3, pp. 397, 94–5, 109, 164, 190.
[38] Thomas Hutchinson, *The Hutchinson Papers: A Collection of Original Papers Relative to the History of . . . Massachusetts* (1769; reprinted, Boston, 1865), vol. 2, pp. 161, 163, 184, 193; 'Mather papers', pp. 125, 156.
[39] Bradford, *History of Plymouth Plantation*, vol. 1, p. 383; M.H.S. *Collections*, ser. 2, vol. 7 (1818), pp. 126–9.
[40] 'Mather papers', pp. 325, 347; M.H.S. MSS. 'Miscellaneous, bound', 18 September 1672; 'Lane family papers', p. 110.

Figure 11. 'Massachusetts Bay, 1677'. Detail from William Hubbard, *The Present State of New England* (London, 1677). By permission of The Huntington Library, San Marino, California (RB 13805).

fishing vessel brought Richard Foxwell and a packet of letters to Piscataqua; William Hilton delivered them to John Winthrop, Jr., at Agawam (Ipswich) for further transmission to Boston. Letters reached Boston in 1642 by 'a ship newly arrived at the Isle of Shoals', but this precious link with the outside world was almost severed when the overland courier with 'all the letters from England' nearly drowned while crossing a river. Providentially, John Winthrop recorded, 'God preserved him'.[41]

Not surprisingly, some letters went astray, prompting calls for an organized postal service.[42] Taking a step in this direction, 'for preventing the miscarriage of letters', the General Court of Massachusetts ordered in 1639 that 'Richard Fairbanks's house in Boston is the place appointed for all letters which are brought from beyond the seas, or are to be sent thither'. Fairbanks was 'to take care that they be delivered or sent according to their directions', and was to be recompensed one penny for each letter.[43]

Mail delivery to New England had become unruly again by the 1670s, when 'letters are thrown upon the Exchange, that who will may take them up'. In order to safeguard incoming correspondence, especially merchants' letters, the Massachusetts council in 1677 appointed John Hayward to act as postmaster. Hayward could charge one penny for handling each single letter and twopence for every packet of two or more. Continuing this appointment in 1680, the council ordered that 'all masters of ships or other vessels do, upon their arrival, send their letters that come in the bag to the said post office, except as they shall particularly take care to deliver with their own hands'. In 1693 the colony established the General Letter Office in Boston, for incoming and outbound letters and packets.[44]

Many correspondents still preferred to make their own arrangements, through travellers, couriers or ships' captains. This was often more reliable than the system of letter baskets and official posts. Migrants and returners carried letters for friends and neighbours. John Winthrop, Jr., was a magnet for mail, and whenever he crossed the Atlantic he was burdened with messages and correspondence. John Davenport, minister at New Haven, entrusted a packet of letters to Mrs. Bressey when she returned to England in 1647.[45] Peter Gardner of Roxbury, Massachusetts, made two return voyages to England in the 1650s, each time delivering letters to Robert Smith in London. Philip Searles, a Devon clothier, carried letters from his friends in

---

[41] *Winthrop Papers*, vol. 3, p. 119; *Winthrop's Journal*, vol. 2, p. 55.

[42] *Calendar of State Papers, Colonial Series, 1574–1660* (London, 1860), p. 275.

[43] *Mass. Recs.*, vol. 1, p. 281. See also Mary E. Woolley, 'Early history of the colonial post office', *Publications of the Rhode Island Historical Society*, n.s., 1 (1894), pp. 270–91; and Wesley E. Rich, *The History of the United States Post Office to the Year 1829* (Cambridge, Mass., 1924).

[44] *Mass. Recs.*, vol. 5, pp. 147–8, 273; M.H.S. *Collections*, ser. 3, vol. 7 (1838), pp. 48–63, esp. pp. 50–4.

[45] Isabel MacBeath Calder (ed.), *Letters of John Davenport* (New Haven, Conn., 1937), pp. 82–3.

Massachusetts to neighbours in Devonshire. Edward Peggey delivered a letter from Henry Jackman to his wife in England, and brought back a reply to the errant husband in Massachusetts. Samuel Eps conveyed William Stoughton's letters from Boston to London in 1684.[46]

Prolific correspondents sent their letters in bundles. A typical packet from Samuel Sewall in Boston to his cousin Edward Hull in London included letters to 'Dr. Annesly, Madame Usher, uncle Dummer, cousin Andrews, three letters and two papers of Mr. Hawkins, Miss Key's letter, cousin Quincy two, Mr. Taylor's, cousin Storke about Richard Cornish's letter of attorney'.[47] While Sewall was in England in 1689 it was quite natural for him to collect letters and tokens to take with him on his return to New England. In a moment of leisure, two weeks out from Plymouth on 24 October 1689, Sewall recorded in his diary, 'sorted my letters, giving what belonged to Captain Clark inside his bag'. On his arrival in Boston he would begin the task of distribution, while providing his immediate circle with firsthand observations about the state of affairs in old England.[48]

John Hall's letters from England to New England vividly illustrate the vitality and versatility of transatlantic correspondence. John Hall, who was born in Massachusetts, moved to England in 1662. Between 1663 and 1685 he kept up a stream of letters to his mother and stepfather at Ipswich, Massachusetts, informing them of his health, fortune, dealings and feelings as he made his way in Charles II's England. His mother, Rebecca Symonds (née Swayne, alias Byley, Hall and Worcester through a succession of husbands), who had not seen England since the 1630s, was able to follow the affairs of her English kinsmen from the remoteness of northern Massachusetts, sending her own news in reply. Rebecca's various marriages had carried her into the cream of New England society, and her son John was well placed among the New England community in England. Ties of kinship and letters of introduction gave him entry to minor gentle circles in Essex and Wiltshire and to London businessmen.

---

[46] Massachusetts Archives, vol. 15A, p. 12; *Essex Courts*, vol. 5, p. 66, vol. 6, p. 173; British Library, Stowe 746, f. 89.

[47] [Sewall], 'Letter book of Samuel Sewall', M.H.S. *Collections*, ser. 6, vol. 1 (1886), p. 98.

[48] [Sewall], *The Diary of Samuel Sewall 1674–1729*, ed. M. Halsey Thomas (New York, 1973), vol. 1, pp. 199, 242.

John Hall was a dutiful and ambitious young man, pleased with the responsibility of handling his American family's English affairs. His first letter, written to his stepfather Samuel Symonds in March 1663, dealt with powers of attorney, backlogs of rents, lawsuits, and legacies, the kind of family business that was often the focus of correspondence between gentlemen and their stewards. His subsequent letters to his mother, while still concerned with rents, accounts and shipments, display more of a personal and emotional content. As he wrote to his mother in 1666, 'The only way by which at a distance I can discourse with you is by letters.'[49]

John Hall's letters describe the development of his faith and the ebb and flow of his health. His mother, three thousand miles distant, could thereby brood over the condition of her son's body and soul. In 1665 he alarmed her with news of his smallpox, and comforted her with news of his recovery; in 1666 he told her about the plague.[50] These letters from a loved one brought an immediacy and poignancy to information that might otherwise be impersonal and remote. The handwriting itself permitted a vicarious kind of contact.

Almost all of Hall's letters contained religious meditations, running from a sentence or two to an entire page. Although the family was scattered, Hall assured his mother they would all meet in heaven, 'Where I believe Christ Jesus hath provided mansions for us.' Meanwhile, they would communicate on paper. Writing at length in 1666, Hall noted, 'My end is to show myself a dutiful child to my mother, in my taking delight to converse with you.' After receiving four welcome letters from New England in 1668, he observed, 'Conference with near and beloved relations is exceeding pleasant.'[51]

John Hall usually accompanied his letters with material tokens – a silver ink box and pencil, a scarf for his sister, haberdashers' notions, and other luxurious trinkets his family had requested. He liked to surprise his mother with fashionable items that would make a stir in rural New England, and his letters include remarks about what was à la mode in London. In 1664, for example, he sent her a tortoiseshell fan, a 'flower satin mantle lined with sarsenet', and 'a pair of pastes, as they call them, to wear in the sleeves of your gown, as the fashion is here for some'.[52] These were affectionate gifts from son to mother, as well as minor introductions of London fashion to the remotest part of the British world.

[49] A.A.S. MSS. 'Letters of John Hall', 11 March 1663, 21 May 1666.
[50] *Ibid.*, 17 March 1665, 21 May 1666.
[51] *Ibid.*, 22 March 1665, 21 May 1666, 18 May 1668.
[52] *Ibid.*, 21 April 1663, 17 March 1665, 22 March 1665.

For what it shows about the cultural lag between London and New England, and for the epistolary manner of this urbane and dutiful son, it is worth quoting one letter of 1675 at length.

You sent for a fashionable lawn whisk. But so it is that there is none such now worn, either by gentle or simple, young or old. Instead whereof I have bought a shape and ruffles, which is now the wear of the gravest as well as the young ones; such as go not with naked necks wear a black whisk over it, therefore I have not only bought a plain one that you sent for but also a lace one such as are most in fashion. Secondly, you sent for a damson coloured Spanish leather for women's shoes. But there is no Spanish leather of that colour, and Turkey leather is coloured so on the grain side only, both which are out of use for women's shoes. Therefore I bought a skin of the leather that is all the mode for women's shoes, all that I fear it is too thick. But my cousin Samuel Eps told me that such thin ones as here are generally used would by rain or snow in New England be presently rendered of no service, and therefore persuaded me to send this which is stronger than ordinary....

As to the feathered fan, I could also have found in my heart to have let it alone because none but very grave persons (and of those very few) use it; that now is grown almost as obsolete as ruffs, and more rarely to be seen than a yellow hood. But the thing being civil and not dear, remembering that in the years '64 and '68 if I mistake not you had such fans sent, I got one made a purpose for you.[53]

Hall also sent paper and sealing wax, so that his mother would have no excuse not to write back. Unfortunately, her side of the correspondence has not survived.

The distant family became present in the imagination through these lively overseas letters. In 1668 Hall described a visit to his grandmother, 'with her daughter and her daughter's daughter, and her daughter's daughter's daughter, all well and merry together, even four generations one under another, a sight rarely to be seen; she desired me to remember her love to you'.[54] The family expanded with Hall's own wedding in 1669 to 'a suitable match' in Islington. Naturally, he sent his mother and sister 'a pair of wedding gloves', to include them in the occasion. With the same letter he enclosed 'my grandmother's funeral ring', a book that 'my aunt Joan said you had a great fancy for', and news of a public and private nature.[55] These tokens, sent with letters across the Atlantic, served as reminders of the family cycle of life and death. Rebecca Symonds remained emotionally involved with the English side of her family, and stayed abreast of their doings through correspondence, despite the enormous distance that separated her from them.

[53] *Ibid.*, 5 May 1675.
[54] *Ibid.*, 31 August 1668.
[55] *Ibid.*, 5 August 1669.

By 1675 John Hall had become a father, and he wrote to his mother to introduce the new granddaughter. Although Rebecca Symonds would never see the child, she could imagine her through John Hall's letter, 'expressing herself in her gobbering, ay-e, ay-e; da-dad'. Rendered phonetically, this was baby talk to bring tears to an old woman's eyes. Ten years later Hall had his daughter sit for a portrait and dispatched the picture with a letter to the grandmother in New England.[56]

Altogether, thirty-eight of John Hall's letters survive in the care of the American Antiquarian Society. Together with the transatlantic business letters of the merchant community, the fraternal letters of Puritans and dissenters, the political letters of New England's governors, and the occasional correspondence of other colonists, they are illustrative of the desire to stay in touch. Though less well known than the great printed collections, the Hall letters vividly illustrate the power of the pen and the linkage it facilitated between the colony and the homeland.[57] If New England was isolated and uncomfortable, as some critics charged, then letters across the Atlantic helped alleviate the condition.

Printed books and newsletters also kept colonists in touch with their English roots. On the eve of colonization in 1629 Robert Reyce had tried to dissuade John Winthrop from moving to New England, arguing, 'How hard will it be for one brought up among books and learned men to live in a barbarous place where is no learning and less civility!'[58] But contrary to their fears and expectations, book lovers who moved to New England were no more cut off from the literary culture and printed polemics of seventeenth-century England than they were from transatlantic business dealings or news of their loved ones back home. Their friends and former associates worked hard to supply the migrants with suitable reading. Robert Reyce, for example,

---

[56] *Ibid.*, 5 May 1675, 1 July 1685. The painting has not been traced. Rebecca Symonds remembered her English granddaughter in her will, proved 1695, sending money and 'a gold ring that was my mother's'; William Sumner Appleton, *Ancestry of Priscilla Baker Who Lived 1674–1731* (Cambridge, Mass., 1870), p. 135.

[57] See, in addition to the letters cited in this chapter, F. J. Powicke (ed.), 'Some unpublished correspondence of the Rev. Richard Baxter and the Rev. John Eliot', *Bulletin of the John Rylands Library*, 15 (1931), pp. 138–76, 442–6; [Shepard], 'Thomas Shepard to Hugh Peter, 27 December 1645', *American Historical Review*, 4 (1898–9), pp. 105–6; (Randolph), 'Letters and narrative of Edward Randolph', M.H.S. *Proceedings*, 18 (1880–1), pp. 254–60.

[58] *Winthrop Papers*, vol. 2, p. 106.

sent Winthrop 'a box of books' in 1636.[59] So long as there were agents to buy them and ships to carry them, books could reach Massachusetts within a few months of their publication in London. The colonists were disadvantaged through distance, but they were not all that worse off, in this regard, than their contemporaries in Cornwall, Cumberland or other remote parts of Britain.

The Massachusetts Bay Company had sent over the makings of an enviable library in 1629, and other books travelled among migrants' personal possessions. John Humphrey supplied Isaac Johnson and John Winthrop in 1630 with 'those new books that are lately come out' in London, including William Ames, *De Conscientia*, Richard Sibbes, *Bruised Reed*, and Jeremy Dike, *The Mischief and Miserie of Scandals*. Edward Howes, too, was a diligent provider of books and book catalogues to his colonial friends. Thomas Shepard asked Hugh Peter for books from England in 1645, and at one time it seemed that Archbishop Laud's confiscated library might find its way to New England.[60] The correspondence of the learned elite frequently turned to the topic of books, and merchants included books among their consignments of English items for New England. The London bookseller Richard Chiswell sent barrels of books to Increase Mather, along with reviews of which books were currently well esteemed.[61] This piecemeal importation was never enough for readers like Mather, whose appetite for print was unusually voracious, but it helped keep New Englanders abreast of English opinion. Throughout the colonial period literate New Englanders could turn to imported books as well as to the increasingly sophisticated output of their developing local press.

Books were to be lent and circulated as well as kept for private enjoyment. Their circulation was especially brisk among the community of divines. Daniel Maud, for example, borrowed books from John Cotton. Joseph Eliot wrote hungrily for Increase Mather to lend him books, 'out of a pity to a famished man'. Eliot was especially keen in 1678 to see 'such treatises historical or philosophical as you have by you, especially that concerning the designs of the French government in England'.[62] Dozens of worthy books also changed hand through wills.[63]

---

[59] *Winthrop Papers*, vol. 3, p. 346.
[60] *Mass. Recs.*, vol. 1, pp. 37f–h; *Winthrop Papers*, vol. 2, p. 330; *Winthrop Papers*, vol. 3, pp. 76, 77, 96, 131, 158–9; 'Shepard to Peter', *American Historical Review*, 4 (1898–9), pp. 105–6.
[61] 'Mather papers', pp. 575–7.
[62] *Suffolk County Wills: Abstracts of the Earliest Wills upon Record in the County of Suffolk, Massachusetts* (Baltimore, 1984), p. 44; 'Mather Papers', p. 376.
[63] *Suffolk County Wills*, pp. 4, 7, 30, 31, 43–4, 45, 62–3, 67, etc.

Books brought comfort, communication, wisdom and culture to New England. Some of them also brought trouble, at least to individual readers. The literary life could be gruelling, even leading to despair. Ann Hopkins, wife of the governor at Hartford, in 1645 fell into 'a sad infirmity, the loss of her understanding and reason', which was brought on 'by occasion of her giving herself wholly to reading and writing, and had written many books'.[64] Some books were unwelcome in Massachusetts, especially those critical of the government or the established religion. When the Quakers Mary Fisher and Anne Austin arrived in Boston harbour in 1656 they had 'about one hundred books taken from their trunks and chests and burned by the common hangman'.[65]

New Englanders who returned to England often headed for the booksellers around St. Paul's. Increase Mather browsed the London bookstalls during his visit to England in 1688 and packed up loads of books to take back to New England. Samuel Sewall similarly collected books in England in 1689, feasting on the abundance of the London market. Friends pressed books upon him as gifts for their American relations. In August he noted, 'Madame Usher sends a small book to Mr. Moody by me.' Sewall purchased maps of London, England, Scotland and Ireland, a Greek *Testament*, Leusden's *Hebrew Bible*, Sheppard's *Abridgement of the Laws*, Pole's *Annotations* and *Synopsis*, among others. His westbound luggage included one barrel and two punchions of books, some of which he gave away on his return to New England. John Hall similarly sent books from London, including some as gifts to his nephew Robert Hale.[66]

Almanacs and diurnals, 'gazettes and other prints', accompanied personal correspondence from England to New England throughout the seventeenth century.[67] A discussion of the English political news that reached the colonies through these means is reserved for the following chapter.

[64] *Winthrop's Journal*, vol. 2, p. 225.
[65] Caroline Hazard, *The Narragansett Friends Meeting in the XVIII Century* (Cambridge, Mass., 1899), pp. 10–11.
[66] A.A.S. MSS. 'Mather family papers', box 3, folders 4, 5;*Diary of Samuel Sewall*, vol. 1, pp. 231–5; 'Letter book of Samuel Sewall', p. 93; A.A.S. MSS. 'Letters of John Hall', 28 September 1682, 12 September 1683.
[67] 'Dunster papers', pp. 191, 195; 'Letter book of John Hull', p. 67.

10

'Dangerous and unsettled times': English news in New England

The surviving letters between American colonists and their friends and kin in England are evidence of the bonds of interest and affection that linked Boston, London and their hinterlands in a transatlantic community of information. Many of these letters also cast valuable sidelights on the unfolding political events in the home country. News, rumour and opinion circulated in old England, and some of it, especially pertaining to the 'godly' party, found its way to the American colonies. Not all the news was accurate, and not all the writers' apprehensions came true, but the correspondence effectively captures the mood and reflects the fears and fortunes of New England's friends in seventeenth-century England. Athough the reporting is selective, piecemeal and partisan, it has an immediacy and a personality that is often lacking from more conventional accounts. This chapter examines the flow to New England of information about English public affairs. It provides a fresh gloss on a familiar story.

The literate elite in colonial New England waited as eagerly for intelligence about church and state in England as they did for family news from the homeland. Whether out of sympathy for friends and kinsmen left behind or out of concern to understand God's plan, the colonists gathered and shared whatever information came to them from across the ocean. New Englanders were especially attentive to events in England during the critical middle decades of the seventeenth century, although news of Charles II's and James II's reigns was also of great interest.

The collapse of Charles I's religious policies was a matter of major significance to migrants who had left England for religious purposes. News of the political crisis of 1640–2, and of the civil war fighting and its aftermath, evoked sadness or jubilation in New England, according to the turn of events and the interpretation that could be put on them. Some colonists decided that the time was ripe to return to

235

their homeland to take part in the great reformation. Others thanked God for their distance from the English trauma, and reinterpreted their 'city on a hill' as a peaceable haven.

The receipt of English news in New England can be divided into three phases, conforming to the state of affairs in the homeland. Before 1640, through most of the period of the great migration, English affairs were seen as troubled but not desperate. Notwithstanding the activities of some bishops, and the haphazard persecution of outspoken Puritans, the news from England was largely without pattern, being simply the reportage of incidents, good and bad. Puritan correspondents told of suspensions and harassments, but they did not normally see them as catastrophic. Only the millennialists were seeking signs of the impending final days. With frequent sailings in the 1630s, news travelled easily, even if there was not much of significance to report.

From 1640 to 1660 the news from England was urgent, important and bewildering. The homeland was in crisis, with invasions, wars, revolution and revolutions within the revolution. Many New Englanders watched with fascination and horror as old England tore itself apart. Yet at this very time when news from the homeland was most anxiously awaited, the means to transport it was reduced to a trickle. Stays of shipping, dislocations of trade, and the virtual end of the New England emigrant trade made passages to New England infrequent and unpredictable compared to the active traffic of the 1630s. English correspondents had either to seize the opportunity of an imminent departure to send their news or find an alternative means to dispatch it. During this period of relative isolation the Newfoundland fishing fleet became the best source of news, though the information it brought was never sufficiently timely, accurate or complete.[1]

After the Restoration, and for the remainder of the seventeenth century, shipping increased, giving New Englanders access to a greater range of English news. The news itself, however, was uninspiring. The heroic urgency of the revolutionary decades had evaporated, and the colonists were treated instead to the squalid bickerings of later Stuart politics. In any case, most New Englanders of the later seventeenth century were American born, and for them the political news from old England was more likely to seem remote and uninteresting. Nostalgics, Anglophiles, merchants and politicians continued to take note of public occurrences in London, but with few exceptions the news was without moment.

[1] *Winthrop's Journal*, vol. 2, pp. 32, 69, 91, 183.

In ordinary circumstances a lag of two months separated the passing of events in England from reading about them in New England. Shipping, however, was seasonal. Merchants and mariners favoured springtime departures from England, and few ships set out to Massachusetts between September and March. News of winter events, then, would normally take several months longer to reach New England. English letter-writers sometimes apologized for the paucity of their news, and advised that better information might be obtained from arriving travellers. Oral reports were always a welcome supplement to written news, and the news-hungry leaders of New England gleaned what information they could from arriving passengers. Sensitive news and commentary, in particular, were more likely to come by word of mouth than to be written on paper. Newcomers were subjected to an intensive debriefing as the colonists pumped them for news.

George Wyllys felt excused from providing more details of the crisis in 1640, when he wrote to his father in New England, since 'you will have divers with you that came out of England and can relate you every particular'. William Bisbey advised a kinswoman in Connecticut in 1646, 'You will hear by passengers how matters go with us here, better than I can relate.' Stephen Winthrop, a New Englander serving in Cromwell's army, shrugged off a letter to his brother in 1648 with the remark, 'For news I must refer you to the passengers.'[2]

News from England reached the Winthrop party within a few months of their landing in Massachusetts in 1630. John Winthrop had letters from his son on board the *Thomas and William*, which set out just a few weeks after the *Arbella*, along with news from John Humphrey about English and Continental religious affairs. In 1632 the *Lyon* brought news of 'the prosperous success of the king of Sweden', while the *Mary and Jane* in 1633 carried less happy intelligence about political manoeuvres in London against the Massachusetts charter.[3]

Most of the news in the letters of the 1630s was of a private nature, concerned with shipments and payments, families and friends. News of political and religious developments in England was scant. Nor was much said about the war in Europe. Intimations of future difficulties, however, appear briefly in a letter from John Winthrop, Jr.'s friend

[2] 'The Wyllys papers ... 1590–1796', *Collections of the Connecticut Historical Society*, 21 (1924), pp. 11, 88; *Winthrop Papers*, vol. 5, p. 206.
[3] *Winthrop Papers*, vol. 2, pp. 309, 336; *Winthrop's Journal*, vol. 1, pp. 92, 101.

Francis Kirby, who advised in August 1633 that 'for domestic news it is bad. The Bishop of Canterbury died the last sabbath day and his place, as I hear, the king hath bestowed upon the Bishop of London'.[4] The new Laudian regime was frustrating, but it did not portend the collapse of the church or the kingdom. A colonist would have to be extraordinarily perspicacious to anticipate the breakdown into civil war. Three years later Lucy Downing could still claim with confidence that 'God doth now as graciously and gloriously hold forth Christ, and the word of reconciliation to us now here, as hath been known in England'. The religious situation in 1636 was certainly not so grim as to justify deep alarm for old England.[5]

Religious tension was mounting, however, not least in Winthrop's home territory, the diocese of Norwich. Robert Reyce wrote to Massachusetts in September 1636 about the episcopal campaign for uniformity, conducted locally by Mathew Wren. Despite the rise of altars and the profanation of the sabbath, the godly party appeared to be in good spirits.[6] Reyce wrote John Winthrop a long letter in March 1637, describing the condition of religion and reviewing affronts to the godly. By and large, in Reyce's reporting, the saints appear to have been holding their own, enjoying 'the just judgement of God' against their enemies. Reyce sent Winthrop copies of Wren's visitation articles and William Prynne's antiepiscopal *Newes from Ipswich*, so that the leaders of New England could see what their friends at home had to endure.[7]

James Downing, John Winthrop's nephew, took a more pessimistic view of the situation. By March 1637 he was already planning to move to New England, and recent events had hardened his determination to leave. 'The times are so bad that they grow worse and worse for the bishop[s] do grow so in favour with the king ... the king gives them much power and they do make use of it unto [the] great dishonour of God ... there is no sign of reformation at all.'[8] While this was the justification of the self-imposed exile, not uncommon in New England, it did not represent the mainstream of opinion even among Winthrop's informants. Most correspondents of the later 1630s either ignored the religious crisis in England or treated it as one more burden to be borne.

[4] *Winthrop Papers*, vol. 3, p. 136.
[5] *Ibid.*, p. 276.
[6] *Ibid.*, pp. 298–306.
[7] *Ibid.*, pp. 355–63, 371–6.
[8] *Ibid.*, p. 376.

Robert Stansby, deprived of his rectory at Westhorpe, Suffolk (in Wren's diocese of Norwich), sent John Winthrop a brief account of other suspended ministers, but he saw no great cause for alarm. 'My wife and I have our health and have a cheerful heart, I praise God, and notwithstanding our loss.'[9] Brampton Gurdon remarked in a letter to New England of April 1637, 'Our time-pleasing clergy grow exceeding bold, they have wind and tide with them, and little or no grace to stay their rage,' but he took delight in relating the scandals that attached to some of them.[10] Henry Jacie wrote to John Winthrop, Jr., a detailed account of the trial and sufferings of Burton, Bastwick and Prynne. But instead of bewailing the fate of these persecuted Puritans he interpreted their stand as a triumph, and concluded that 'the prelates...have lost greatly by it'.[11] On the basis of this correspondence the Winthrops and their friends in New England might reasonably have concluded that though times were tough in England, as indeed they were in America, God's cause there was not entirely in ruins.

It was not until 1640 that the pattern changed. Until that time the information reaching New England was marked by an overall cheerfulness, no matter how grim the news. After 1640 the communications are marked by a tone of sadness, growing into despondency, as correspondents concluded that old England was in serious trouble and that the world was turning for the worse. The precipitant was the Scottish war.

John Wollcott of Bishop's Lydiard, Somerset, anticipated this new mood in a letter to his 'loving brother' at Windsor, Connecticut, on 15 April 1639. 'You wrote to understand of the course of our country; it was never by my time so dangerous as now it is.'[12] This letter probably reached New England in July. Further news of the Scottish crisis reached Governor Winthrop in Boston in August by way of ships lately come in to Newfoundland. According to these reports, the English and Scottish armies 'skirmished three times but to little purpose, some men being hurt on either side and neither much prevailing. The king hath recovered his Scottish crown and sceptre. The people have great hopes of peace, both parts inclining that way'.[13] Nehemiah Bourne wrote to John Winthrop from Exeter on 14 November 1639

---

[9] *Ibid.*, pp. 380–1.
[10] *Ibid.*, pp. 386–7.
[11] *Ibid.*, pp. 484–8.
[12] (Wollcott), 'Letter of John Wollcott', *N.E.H.G.R.*, 2 (1848), p. 373.
[13] *Winthrop Papers*, vol. 4, p. 138.

that 'the war is ceased and forces withdrawn, but what the issue will be we know not, but it's much feared it will break out fresh again'.[14] These were still remote events, comparable to the tussles of the Thirty Years War, which did not yet appear to jeopardize either England or New England. There was no sign at this time of a drift to civil war or of God's harsh judgement on the kingdom.

John Harrison, Jr., wrote from London on 18 February 1640 with news that the crisis seemed to be over. Peace had been made and a parliament was impending. The most dramatic news came from the Continent, where Prague had fallen and Spanish troops were on the move. The English political system appeared to be functioning as usual.[15] Francis Kirby also reported hopes of reconciliation. On 22 February he wrote from London, 'We have now great hope of a parliament, and we heartily desire your prayers unto God to direct the heart of his majesty and the house of parliament with one unanimous consent to aim at glory of God and safety of this kingdom.' However, the horizon was still clouded, since 'the difference between his majesty and the Scots is not yet appeased'.[16]

Business as usual was also Edward Payne's message from London, dated 26 February 1640. His letter was full of plans for shipping and financial transactions, with barely a hint of the political storm. Payne's sole sentence on the subject said, 'I would fain see what this parliament will effect.'[17] Writing the same day, however, another Puritan merchant took a more pessimistic view. John Tinker informed John Winthrop that many people, including some prospective migrants, had 'hopes of some reformation in England by the intended parliament', but 'wise and judicious men' saw only 'troublesome times approaching both within and without the kingdom'. Although the Scottish commissioners had reached some 'reconcilement' with the king, relations were still strained and 'they resolve they will never have more bishops'. Tinker then changed the subject, remarking, 'I shall not trouble your worship further with any discourse of news, there being so little certainty in anything we hear.'[18]

Mathew Cradock wrote to John Winthrop on 27 February about preparations for the parliament. 'On Tuesday next the burgesses of London are to be chosen, being the 4 March. God in his mercy direct them and the whole kingdom in their choice, that this parliament may

[14] *Ibid.*, pp. 154–5.
[15] *Ibid.*, pp. 194–5.
[16] *Ibid.*, p. 201.
[17] *Ibid.*, p. 204.
[18] *Ibid.*, p. 205.

produce good to the realm, approaching evils being much to be feared.' Cradock himself would be elected.[19]

Thomas Gostlin, a kinsman and former neighbour of the Winthrops in Suffolk, took a similarly circumspect view of the approaching parliament. 'I pray God prosper it and cause some good effect by it,' he wrote on 2 March 1640, 'Otherwise I see nothing but all will be nought, the Lord can do what it pleaseth him.'[20] Writing from London a few days later on election day, 4 March, Nehemiah Bourne expressed the pessimism and confusion that became common among many of Winthrop's correspondents.

It is deplorable to see what we are forced to behold . . . Concerning the Scots, here is great preparation for war . . . many wise men stand not knowing what to judge of things, and at present I think mens' hearts are shaken more than ever, notwithstanding the parliament . . . the times that are approaching threaten heavy and sad things.[21]

Colonists in receipt of such communications shared the agitation and disquiet of members of the political nation in England as the first parliament in eleven years prepared for its perilous course. Though physically detached from England and separated by three thousand miles of ocean, the leading men of Connecticut and Massachusetts had not forfeited their membership in the articulate and politicized 'county community'. John Winthrop was a Suffolk Puritan as well as governor of Massachusetts. Given the quality of their correspondence, some families in New England were probably better informed about the English political situation than many people closer to the scene.[22]

The anxieties of the spring of 1640 are further indicated in a letter from Lawrence Wright to his colonial kinsman, written on 26 March. 'Our king upon his own charge provides for war thirty thousand foot and seven or eight thousand horse. We say against the Scots, but we know not; a few months will discover.'[23] Writing from Bristol on 8 April 1640, George Wyllys reported to Connecticut, 'The times are so ill and things so unsettled in the commonwealth that I have not nor as yet cannot . . . sell any land except for an extreme under value. . . . The parliament which is to begin the 13th of April gives many hopes of better times and a thorough settlement of peace with the Scots.' However, the letter continued, 'the times are very dangerous

[19] *Ibid.*, p. 207.
[20] *Ibid.*, p. 212.
[21] *Ibid.*, p. 214.
[22] See Anthony Fletcher, 'National and local awareness in the county communities', in Howard Tomlinson (ed.), *Before the English Civil War* (London, 1983), pp. 165, 173.
[23] *Winthrop Papers*, vol. 4, p. 220.

and unsettled here. This very day went a press out for land soldiers, which as report goes and all fear are speedily intended against Scotland.'[24]

John Venn shared similar fears in a letter to New England written in early April: 'God hath called a parliament appointed to begin the 13th of this instant, how long it will continue we are not worthy to know, nor what it will bring forth; we are full of fears . . . Some project is in agitation which time must discover, good from them we cannot expect.'[25]

Parliament met on 13 April. Winthrop learned the details from John Harrison, Jr., who sent him a detailed manuscript newsletter two days later. Harrison described the drama of the king's speech, when Charles 'drew forth from his pocket a letter sent by the Scotch lords to the French king for aid to invade England'. Armies were being raised in England and Ireland, and preparations were in hand to fight the Scots.[26]

The New England correspondents reported mixed reactions to the dissolution of the Short Parliament on 5 May. Benjamin Gostlin exclaimed to Winthrop in a letter of 8 May, 'The Lord be merciful unto us and turn the king's heart or else to this land in my foolish judgement is nothing to be expected but confusion . . . it grieve[s] my heart to think of the misery that is approaching.'[27] William Bisbey commented in the same vein in a letter written to Connecticut on 14 May 1640: 'The Lord fit us for the worst times, that we may keep faith and good consciences, bad times we have cause to expect. Here was a parliament called but dissolved and nothing done, we are full of fears generally.'[28]

John Winthrop's old friend, Brampton Gurdon, however, took a more defiant view of the situation when he wrote to the Massachusetts governor on 13 May. 'We are here in very hard condition in regard our parliament is dissolved, but let me tell you it comforteth the hearts of the honest men of both housen that they yielded not to give a penny to help the king in his intended war against the Scots.'[29] Edward Payne also found satisfaction in the parliamentary stand, although he was troubled by its dangerous consequences. 'The lower house of parliament stood very strongly for the privilege of the subject and for re-establishing of religion,' he recounted in a letter of 28 May. 'The

[24] 'Wyllys papers', pp. 9–11.
[25] *Winthrop Papers*, vol. 4, p. 221.
[26] *Ibid.*, pp. 226–7.
[27] *Ibid.*, pp. 237–8.
[28] 'Wyllys papers', p. 27.
[29] *Winthrop Papers*, vol. 4, p. 243.

King is much displeased.' Now 'the times are very troublesome', aldermen had been arrested, rioting apprentices had menaced the Archbishop of Canterbury and had torn down some of the prisons. 'What will ensue I know not, the Lord in mercy look down upon us, and Sir, if ever there were need of prayers and tears for a poor kingdom, now is the time.'[30]

New Englanders greeted these developments with a mixture of alarm and enthusiasm. Some were moved to return to England, to take part in the unfolding of an historic drama, whereas others gave thanks for the peacefulness of their American refuge. According to one's eschatological schema, the crisis in England could be seen as a working out of God's purposes, as a judgement against his enemies, and even as the prelude to Armageddon.

In response to this grim and confusing news from England, Massachusetts observed 23 July 1640 as 'a day of public humiliation, appointed by the churches in behalf of our native country in time of feared dangers'. William Hooke preached a sermon, later published as *New Englands Teares, for Old Englands Feares*, expressing 'brotherly compassion' for the land of 'our nativity'. It was a moment to focus attention on old England, to count the blessings of New England, and to speculate about what might happen next.[31] Thomas Lechford, in Boston, wrote a few days later, 'I hear things are at an ill way in our native country'; and again in September, 'We hear of great disturbances' in England. Subsequent days of fast and humiliation 'for the hazardous estate of our native country' were held in Massachusetts in November 1641, June 1643, August 1645 and December 1646, each in response to sad news from England.[32] The transatlantic Puritan community joined together in seeking the Lord. The devout London artisan, Nehemiah Wallington, writing to a friend in New England, observed that 'the year 1640 was a praying year here in old England as I make no question it was with you in Newland'.[33]

News of the Scots invasion (August 1640) and the calling of a second parliament (in November) filtered piecemeal across the Atlantic. Fish-

[30] *Ibid.*, p. 248.
[31] William Hooke, *New Englands Teares, for Old Englands Feares* (London, 1641). *Cf.* his later sermon, *New-Englands Sence, of Old-Englands and Jrelands Sorrowes* (London, 1645).
[32] Edward E. Hale (ed.), *Note-Book Kept by Thomas Lechford* (Cambridge, Mass., 1885), pp. 274, 312; *Mass. Recs.*, vol. 1, p. 339; vol. 2, pp. 38, 123, 167; vol. 3, pp. 86, 233, 239, 287. See also James M. O'Toole, 'New England reactions to the English civil wars', *N.E.H.G.R.*, 129 (1975), pp. 3–17, 238–49.
[33] British Library, Sloan MS. 922, f. 105. For more on Wallington see Paul S. Seaver, *Wallington's World: A Puritan Artisan in Seventeenth-Century London* (Stanford, 1985).

ing ships brought news in December 'of the Scots entering England, and the calling of a parliament, and the hope of a thorough reformation'.[34] On balance this seemed like good news, but there was little cause to rejoice. John Winthrop learned the details from his diligent London correspondents, and the story was augmented in letters sent to other colonists.

An interesting sidelight on English local reactions to the crisis of 1640 is contained in George Wyllys's financial accounts for that year. Wyllys expended £3 9s. for 'three muskets bought to send to New England, but in respect of the dangerous times I kept and have them still by me, being firelocks'.[35] Wyllys was in the West Country, many miles from the conflict on the Scottish border, and the rest of his family was in Connecticut. How many other people were sufficiently fearful in 1640 to equip themselves with weapons?

News of Laud's impeachment (December 1640) reached the colonies before the end of January. Lucy Downing, at Salem, shared the news in an exuberant note to her nephew, John Winthrop, Jr., in Boston. 'We have put his grace of Canterbury fast in the Tower, and if our St. Peter keeps the keys his grace is like to cool his shins ere he gets in this cold weather; for we speak only of his confusion and unpardonable sins.'[36] The gloating was premature since Laud was not actually committed to the Tower until the following March, but the sentiment was characteristic. Thomas Shepard thought fit to ask for the archbishop's confiscated library for Harvard College.[37]

News from England was at a premium during 1641 and 1642. The limited shipping at this time could not keep pace with political developments. The situation was so fluid and its unfolding so fast that all the colonists could see was flux and danger. Thomas Gorges sent the latest down from Maine to Boston in February 1641.

A letter came to one of our river that the Lord Deputy of Ireland hath three bills preferred against him ... Mr. Burton, Mr. Prynne and Mr. Bastwick are called to the parliament to relate their causes there, and great hope there is

---

[34] *Winthrop's Journal*, vol. 2, p. 19. Anthony Fletcher, *The Outbreak of the English Civil War* (London, 1981), provides the best modern narrative of the events of 1640–2. For an overview of the period see Derek Hirst, *Authority and Conflict: England 1603–1658* (London, 1986). Neither author cites the New England correspondence reviewed in this chapter.

[35] 'Wyllys papers', p. 38.

[36] *Winthrop Papers*, vol. 4, p. 311. 'Our St. Peter' is, of course, their kinsman Hugh Peter.

[37] [Shepard], 'Thomas Shepard to Hugh Peter, 21 December 1945', *American Historical Review*, 4 (1898–9), p. 106.

that religion will be more countenanced than it hath been. As I receive more I will not fail to certify you.[38]

Henry Dunster wrote from Lancashire on 20 March 1641 to his son at Cambridge, Massachusetts, reviewing the events of the Scottish invasion and the calling of parliament. Henry Dunster, Jr., president of Harvard College, would spread these reports among his associates throughout New England.[39] Deane Tyndal, writing from Maplestead, Essex, summarized the latest news in a letter he sent to his brother-in-law in New England on 7 April 1641. 'The parliament is yet sitting and there is an act passed for to have a parliament every third year. Four subsidies are granted, and the Lieutenant of Ireland [Strafford] is now upon his trial, but nothing yet concluded on.' John Winthrop received this letter eight months later, on 6 December, by which time Strafford was dead, Ireland was in revolt, and the Commons had voted the Grand Remonstrance.[40]

George Wyllys wrote from Bristol on 6 May 1641 with further news of the proceedings in parliament. 'We have an overwhelming of our hopes, in that the king hath lately declared himself in the lords' house that the Earl of Strafford is no traitor and that he shall not die.'[41] A short while later the situation had turned yet again. Robert Child wrote from England: 'We have here very much good news, the Lord be praised. Every three years we shall have a parliament. The Deputy is condemned by both houses. The archbishop is in the Tower, and will certainly be punished severely ... Lord prelates, deans, prebends are fallen.' The protestant cause appeared ascendant at home and abroad.[42]

How the colonists in New England learned of the outbreak of civil war is unknown, since so few letters of that period survive. The news, when it came, must have been sad but not necessarily surprising. Some would interpret the war as a heavy providence, without being too concerned with causes. Nehemiah Wallington wrote in 1642 to his migrant friend James Cole, describing troubles both public and private; he asked for more of New England's prayers. Robert Child,

---

[38] *Winthrop Papers*, vol. 4, p. 322.
[39] 'The Dunster papers', M.H.S. *Collections*, ser. 4, vol. 2 (1854), pp. 192–3.
[40] *Winthrop Papers*, vol. 4, p. 329.
[41] 'Wyllys papers', p. 17.
[42] *Winthrop Papers*, vol. 4, p. 334.

writing from Gravesend, Kent, in June 1643, could say no more than, 'Times here are extremely distracted; God send a good success to our armies.'[43]

That the war was a dangerous and violent conflict, not simply the remote unfolding of events, was brought home in the offhand remarks of some correspondents. George Wyllys was too busy to write much news in 1643, but in an account that he sent to Connecticut that year he casually mentioned the loss and inconvenience caused by 'the Cavaliers when they plundered my house'.[44] John Trapp, writing from Warwickshire, assured a correspondent in New England of his welfare, but added, 'Since I wrote last to you I was taken prisoner, lost my horse, and had my house pillaged.'[45] Such hardships were but pricks in God's service, but the report of them must have been alarming to the settlers of New England. American settlers knew war with their Indian neighbours, but were spared from facing Rupert's troopers or the European forces of the Antichrist.

Hundreds of former New Englanders were in England at this time, in public service or in private life; some of them took pains to send printed newsbooks and manuscript newsletters, which helped to satisfy the news-hunger of their friends and kinsmen in America. Their correspondence extended across the Atlantic the well-established tradition whereby agents in the metropolis sent newsletters to gentlemen in the provinces. Through their efforts, too, an enviable selection of printed gazettes and mercuries circulated in New England. Readers passed them from hand to hand and made manuscript copies for wider audiences. Herbert Pelham sent 'the printed news' to Thomas Dudley at Boston, for further transmission. Brampton Gurdon dispatched a supply of 'corantos out of this country which will afford you more intelligence than I am able to write'.[46] Ralph Josselin, who had cousins and friends in the colonies, contributed to the flow of information by sending 'a letter into New England . . . containing the news foreign and domestic' in September 1648. This was followed by 'three sheets in my small hand, being a relation of affairs foreign and domestic'.[47]

Colonial consumers of English news eagerly exchanged information

[43] British Library, Sloan MS. 922, f. 105; *Winthrop Papers*, vol. 4, p. 395.
[44] 'Wyllys papers', p. 60.
[45] *Ibid.*, p. 62.
[46] *Winthrop Papers*, vol. 5, pp. 157, 351; also pp. 158, 198, 204, 206, 213, 216, 280, 311, 320.
[47] Alan Macfarlane (ed.), *The Diary of Ralph Josselin 1616–1683* (London, 1976), pp. 134, 196, 302.

and commentary among themselves. The civil war newspapers that reached New England found an avid following, especially among the governing elite for whom the outcome of the war was a matter of political as well as religious significance. The Winthrops, Pynchons, Winslows, Dudleys and Hayneses shared in a network of information stretching from northern Massachusetts to the western frontier, and from Plymouth Colony to southern Connecticut, with outliers in New-foundland, Virginia, Bermuda and the Caribbean. Newsbooks and corantos passed between Governor Haynes at Hartford, William Pynchon at Springfield, Thomas Dudley at Roxbury and John Winthrop in Boston.[48] Winthrop sent Edward Winslow a 'large and painful relation of the state of England'. John Haynes sent Winthrop 'the late and last news from our native country' in December 1643, with the comment that it 'seems very sad and calls for our deepest humiliation'.[49] William Pynchon had news of the Solemn League and Covenant (September 1643) by February 1644, and wrote to John Winthrop, 'It is the high way of God for their deliverance. I hope it is now the day of Antichrist's great overthrow at Armageddon. I greatly long to hear whether the Scots be yet come in to aid of the parliament. I hope you will have news by the fishing ships ere long.'[50] Whether millennialists or pragmatists, men in these circles experienced great anxiety for news from England; their anxiety was by the fitful communications of the 1640s.

Connecticut had news by a late-arriving vessel in February 1644 of 'a great battle betwixt the king's and parliament's forces, since that of Newbury, at Aylesbury in Buckinghamshire, wherein the parliamentary forces prevailed, pursuing their victory with very great slaughter'. The same source reported heroic victories by the Earl of Warwick, whose fleet was said to have taken a royalist town and set its prisoners free. John Haynes, who had by this point heard more than enough news that turned out to be false, commented, 'I leave the truth of the report to be judged of by you, only latest letters give some probable conjectures of the possibility thereof.'[51]

More news from the beleaguered island came in a letter from the Rev. John Trapp, chaplain to the parliamentary army at Stratford. Writing on 16 May 1644 to his wife's kinswoman in Connecticut, Trapp reported, 'The parliament, for this half year past, have had great success, and there are propositions for an honourable peace

---

[48] *Winthrop Papers*, vol. 4, p. 444;. vol. 5, pp. 157, 271.
[49] *Winthrop Papers*, vol. 4, pp. 455, 418.
[50] *Ibid.*, p. 444.
[51] *Ibid.*, p. 508.

made ready by them to be presented to his majesty, but they are such as it is conceived he will never yield to.' The situation was still fluid, nothing was resolved. As to the war itself, 'There are very great preparations on both sides, and no small expectation what this summer will bring forth. York is close besieged by the English and Scots, Newcastle was said to have been yielded up to the Scots, but that report was crossed again. Lincoln was lately taken by the parliament forces.'[52]

How should New Englanders respond to this violent and chaotic situation? Trapp counselled prayer, since human action was so impotent. 'All is embroiled, the Lord compose us, and put that end to our miseries that may most make for his own glory.' His news continued, showing the religious arena to be as confusing as the political and military. 'In the assembly of divines there hath been much stickling for independency, but presbytery carries it. The church swarms with antinomians, anabaptists, and sects of all sorts. God of his mercy settle us!'[53] These reports were especially disturbing to New England Puritans who had endured the Antinomian crisis in the 1630s and who were experiencing radical challenges to their local religious hegemony in the 1640s.[54]

The news was no happier when Emmanuel Downing's letter of February 1645 arrived, describing old England as 'a most miserable distracted state'. Robert Child sent a brief report to New England on 1 March 1645 on the indecisive movement of the war: 'The king's forces taken Weymouth, the parliament's Scarborough.'[55] But a year later the news was more promising. Stephen Winthrop, trading at Teneriffe, heard 'good news' from England that he was anxious to impart to his father at Boston: 'The parliament still prevaileth. The king hath been once more beaten. And Bristol is taken, with Basing House near Newark and Exeter straightly besieged. . . . Prince Rupert and Maurice have made their peace with parliament and are going for Holland . . . it is thought the war is at an end.'[56]

That the troubles were not over was suggested in another letter Stephen Winthrop wrote from London on 27 March 1646. 'There is other difference begin to arise out of the dust, the parliament and

[52] 'Wyllys papers', p. 61.
[53] *Ibid.*, p. 62.
[54] See Stephen Foster, 'New England and the challenge of heresy, 1630 to 1660: the Puritan crisis in transatlantic perspective', *William and Mary Quarterly*, ser. 3, vol. 38 (1981), pp. 624–60; and Philip F. Gura, *A Glimpse of Sion's Glory: Puritan Radicalism in New England, 1620–1660* (Middletown, Conn., 1984).
[55] *Winthrop Papers*, vol. 5, pp. 5, 12.
[56] *Ibid.*, pp. 62–3.

the Scots do not well accord ... The difference is like to be between the City and the parliament, though not upon the like grounds ... the king hath no forces left considerable but stands out demands great things.'[57]

John Trapp reported on 2 May 1646, 'Things have gone on very prosperously for this twelvemonth on the parliament side, the contrary part being brought to a low ebb, to the great admiration and encouragement of all good hearts.'[58] Prescient correspondents advised, however, that the parliamentary victory was not necessarily a cause for thanksgiving. Celebration would be premature. William Bisbey wrote on 11 May 1646 that 'the king is come in to the Scottish army, but here is great fear what the issue of our divisions amongst ourselves may be'. He wrote again on 21 August, 'The times are yet troublesome with us; the king will not join with the parliament, and Ireland is in a sad condition.'[59] George Wyllys reported to his stepmother on 12 June the news that

Banbury castle is taken, but is still kept a garrison. Oxford and Worcester and most of the king's garrisons are besieged. The king himself is among the Scots, and there are 4000 fresh Scots lately come into this kingdom, which gives occasion of suspecting and fearing a difference between the two nations. The Lord prevent it or else we shall be in a worse condition than ever.[60]

Giles Firmin advised John Winthrop in July 1646, 'It is not a clear day in England, all clouds are not scattered; sometimes we fear they will gather again.'[61] Stephen Winthrop, writing from Worcester on 23 August 1646, warned that 'this kingdom is yet much unsettled, although here be no enemy appearing; the king will not sign the propositions nor yield to the parliament, which causes many jealousies'. This news, confirmed from other sources, was abroad in New England by October. It was time for Massachusetts to plan another day of fast and humiliation on behalf of old England.[62]

Shipping was scarce and news was scanty over the winter of 1646–7, so New Englanders had to wait until late in the following spring to learn how the crisis had progressed. John Winthrop had heard rumours of the army going to Ireland, but commented on 14 May, 'We shall hear no certainty till a ship come from England.' Robert

---

[57] Ibid., p. 70.
[58] 'Wyllys papers', p. 81.
[59] Ibid., pp. 88, 96.
[60] Ibid., p. 95.
[61] Winthrop Papers, vol. 5, p. 88.
[62] Ibid., pp. 98, 114–15; Mass. Recs., vol. 2, p. 167. On the complicated events between the end of the first civil war and the execution of the king see David Underdown, Pride's Purge: Politics in the Puritan Revolution (Oxford, 1971).

Child, now back in Boston, observed the same day that 'news here is little and uncertain'.[63] The news that eventually arrived gave further cause for alarm. Herbert Pelham wrote from London on 5 May 1647 that

the House yesterday sat long, and are at present in as great a straight as they have been some years past. I think the wisest heads in the kingdom see more cause for serious humiliation in regard of those approaching new dangers than formerly: the army much ado to be quieted, the kingdom much discontented with the House, and they one with another.[64]

This letter probably reached New England in July. Writing from London on 29 July 1647, Stephen Winthrop, by this time an officer in the parliamentary army, gave his opinion that 'the kingdom is now upon a great turn. God is doing some great work . . . A committee of parliament and City are with the army upon treaty, but not fully concluded.'[65]

Stephen Winthrop's letter probably arrived in New England in October 1647, about the same time as a letter from Patrick Copeland relaying a strange mixture of English news and rumour via Bermuda. Copeland's news, which had reached Bermuda from correspondents in Barbados, was that the king was in parliament's custody at Holmby House, but that he refused to sign the Covenant or the Newcastle propositions (March 1647).

But since we hear by others that there are new broils a-brewing, and that my Lord Fairfax and his Lieutenant Cromwell have sided with the king, and removed him from Holmby House to York, which seems to us very strange news, that they that have managed the parliament's and the kingdom's wars should now turn against them and the kingdom. As for Ireland, we hear it is given as lost, and that the French have preparations against it.[66]

Traffic from England to New England was once again scarce the following winter, but news continued to reach Boston from Virginia. Thomas Harrison wrote to John Winthrop from the southern colony in January 1648 about the confused events of the previous summer, when the army marched on London.

The malignants that come hither from the City and the malcontents from the army, with deepest indignation relate, that what the parliament have a mind to enact and establish they first communicate it to Lord General Cromwell, he to the agitators (so are his pious assistants and associates termed), they to the officers, these to the soldiers, and these last approving, petition for it to the parliament, and then they vote and grant it. Their printed

[63] *Winthrop Papers*, vol. 5, p. 160.
[64] *Ibid.*, p. 157.
[65] *Ibid.*, p. 174.
[66] *Ibid.*, p. 183.

pamphlets with rage and madness exclaim this independent parliament, backed by an over-awing, over-ruling independent army, will ruin them all. ... The last news from a sure and eminent hand is this: the king will not yet assent to the propositions, but yet makes forth a desire to comport and comply with the proposals of the army.[67]

This was a shrewd appraisal of current circumstances in England.

Harrison's next letter, a few months later, contained an observation on the crisis that was common among American Puritans: 'The saints in these goings down of the sun had never more light to see why their father hath thus removed them, nor ever more strong engagements to be thankful for it.'[68] Some of them were inclined to turn inward, clinging even closer to their dream of a pure New England way.

The next shipping season brought enigmatic and disturbing news. Stephen Winthrop wrote to his father on 1 March 1648, 'This kingdom is in a very unsettled condition and it is wonder all falls not in pieces one day.' Henry Jacie wrote on 12 March, 'What great alterations have been in the army, parliament and kingdom [since the previous summer].'[69] New Englanders were inured to such developments by the reports of the previous eight years.

George Downing, another former colonist in parliament's service, favoured John Winthrop with a review of recent events in a long letter written 8 March 1648. Downing's analysis of the situation bears comparison to well-known remarks by Oliver Cromwell and others, and is worth quoting at length for its reflections on the purposes for which the war was fought.

For the state of things here, it hath been very various, not only in the time of the war but more since; we having since the sheathing of that sword sometimes enjoyed our lucid intervals, but then all hath quickly been o'erclouded, that no mortal eye could in the face of things see anything but ruin. The main ground, as to human causes, hath been the great divisions among us. For while the common enemy was unsubdued there was some kind of agreement, all knowing that if he prevailed, all without distinction should be swallowed up in the common fate. But when he began to be very low, then everyone bethinks himself, what have I fought for all this while, why have I so deeply engaged myself in this unnatural war? Saith one, I fought and engaged for the removing evil counsellors from the king, and the settling his person in his just rights. Saith another, I engaged for the establishment of presbytery and pulling down episcopacy. Saith another, I fought against the king, as conceiving him rather to act than to be acted of any evil counsellors whatsoever; another, I fought against oppression in general, so if any church

---

[67] *Ibid.*, pp. 197–8.
[68] *Ibid.*, p. 213.
[69] *Ibid.*, pp. 203, 204.

government tend to an oppression and enslaving the consciences of men, so far, saith he, I fought against it.[70]

Moving from civil war motives to the post-war stasis, Downing summarized the various calls for action.

One cries out, settle the church government, punish errors and blasphemies, according to the covenant; another, remember your often declarations for liberty for tender consciences; one, bring home the king according to the covenant; another, it can't stand with the preservation of the true religion and liberty, etc. And thus for want of a downright plain understanding of the foundation of this war, without all equivocation, we have been likely often to have been embroiled in a more bloody, and by our quarrellings to give occasion to any third party to devour all.

Finally, after relieving himself of these opinions, Downing commented on the latest news for circulation in New England. 'That which is feared is a war with Scotland. What the issue will be the Lord only knows, only he seems to be shaking the great ones of the earth.'[71]

The worst of these fears was confirmed by the course of events. Hannah Dugard wrote from Warwick to her cousin in Connecticut on 10 April 1648, 'God's hand was so heavy upon us inasmuch that we fear his wrath is breaking out again, and that his sword is furbishing afresh, for here is great fears and stirrings of another war.' Herbert Pelham wrote from Suffolk to his cousin in Massachusetts on 19 April, reporting news of apprentice riots in London and fears of 'a more general rising throughout the City'. Robert Child wrote from Gravesend on 13 May 1648 to his friend, John Winthrop, Jr., with grim news: 'The war likely to break forth as bad as ever ... the army is much divided, the people much displeased ... the Scots threaten the army of sectaries (as they call them), the Prince and Duke of York are very active beyond seas.'[72]

Thomas Peters wrote from Cornwall on 26 June 1648 about the king's attempted escape from the Isle of Wight and about the renewal of hostilities in Kent, East Anglia, Cornwall and Wales. John Winthrop, Jr., received this distressing intelligence in New England the following 9 November, among the last news to arrive from old England that year. The Winthrops already had the gist of the story by way of Newfoundland, but now they had details. John Winthrop told his son on 30 September 1648 that 'the news out of England is very sad, all the counties are for the king, save Yorkshire'. More news by

---

[70] *Ibid.*, pp. 206–7.
[71] *Ibid.*, pp. 207.
[72] 'Wyllys papers', p. 107; *Winthrop Papers*, vol. 5, pp. 216–18, 222.

way of Newfoundland a few weeks later described the progress of the fighting in this second civil war.[73]

The autumn and winter of 1648 was a dry time for news in New England, but a hot time for events in the homeland. The remoteness of the colonies was especially frustrating to those who felt affected by the outcome. William Pynchon complained from Springfield, on the western edge of Massachusetts, 'I much long to hear out of England.' Humphrey Atherton wrote from Dorchester, Massachusetts, at the end of October, 'We have no late news from old England.' The drought was assuaged when a ship came unexpectedly to Boston ('God was pleased to change his voyage and send him to heaven by the way') with thirteen newsbooks that rapidly went into circulation. More news filtered in from various directions in December. Roger Williams in Rhode Island knew by 3 December of Cromwell's victories in Scotland (at Preston, August 1648) and of a commission 'sent from parliament to try the king'.[74]

A ship that made a rare winter passage ('some ten weeks from England') brought John Winthrop the news in February that 'the army requires justice against the king'. Cromwell had control of Scotland. The ship's master, 'who is a member of a congregational church in Dartmouth, affirms that in their county there are 100,000 men ready upon an hour's warning to assist the army, whose headquarters are now at St. Albans'. Another ship arriving in March confirmed this news but added little to it.[75]

By this time, of course, the king was dead, but the transatlantic time-lag prevented New Englanders hearing this twist to the story until the following spring. Stephen Winthrop, never the most diligent correspondent, wrote from London on 16 March 1649 with an account of Pride's purge (December) and its aftermath. The Rump 'voted the trial of the king, who is since beheaded, with Duke Hamilton, Lord Holland, Lord Capel, and more I believe will suffer yet; but I cannot enlarge to particular, passengers and books will inform best'. This letter, with printed accompaniments, was in New England by the following June, by which time the events were already widely known.[76] 'The king is beheaded! Oh dreadful judgement! The beginning of sorrows!' wailed John Brock of Dedham, Massachusetts.[77] Roger Wil-

---

[73] *Winthrop Papers*, vol. 5, pp. 233–4, 244–5, 261, 265–6.
[74] *Ibid.*, pp. 271, 274, 280, 287, 288.
[75] *Ibid.*, pp. 312, 322.
[76] *Ibid.*, pp. 320, 349.
[77] Clifford K. Shipton (ed.), 'The autobiographical memoranda of John Brock, 1636–1659', *A.A.S. Proceedings*, 53 (1943), p. 101.

liams in Rhode Island knew by 26 May 1649, by 'a Bristol ship come to the Isle of Shoals', that 'the king and many great lords and parliament men are beheaded. London was shut up on the day of execution, not a door to be opened'. Another ship arriving in June brought confirmation of the news 'but no other particulars'.[78]

England, sadly, was no more settled by the execution of the king than before. Stephen Winthrop, with the army in Suffolk, wrote on 16 July 1649 that Cromwell was setting out to subdue Ireland, while further war with Scotland appeared imminent. 'For matters in this nation, or state as it is called, they stand subject to daily mutations; people are full of dissatisfactions, yet there is a present quiet throughout the nation.' George Wyllys wrote from Warwick on 24 July 1649, in the same gloomy tone that he adopted a decade before, 'Things here are very unsettled.'[79]

'The present sad and deplorable condition of our dear native country' continued to trouble leading New Englanders throughout the period of the Interregnum. Massachussetts sponsored a series of days of fast and humiliation.[80] From Ipswich to New Haven and inland as far as Springfield there were those who hung on every word from the home country, gleaning, collating and disseminating the news. Recipients digested it, and filtered and funnelled it to their colleagues and kinsmen. John Winthrop, Jr., occupied a nodal point in this network, busying himself with an extensive regional as well as international correspondence. John Pynchon of Springfield, who shared kinsmen and correspondents with Winthrop, apologized in May 1654, 'I have no letters from England nor books of news; had I, I should readily impart them to you.'[81] Theophilus Eaton shared his newsbooks with John Winthrop, Jr., in February 1655, at a time when the most recent English intelligence dated from the previous September. 'We have received letters from England, with some printed weekly informations', he reported.[82]

In March 1655 John Davenport informed Winthrop, 'I have received some letters from England in Trumball's vessel, whereby I perceive that things are there in a doubtful state ... I send you by this bearer such books of intelligence as were sent me ... The smallpox hath been the death of many in England, and the spotted fever.'

[78] *Winthrop Papers*, vol. 5, p. 348.
[79] *Ibid.*, p. 356; 'Wyllys papers', p. 117.
[80] *Mass. Recs.*, vol. 3, pp. 233, 239, 287; vol. 4, p. 417.
[81] Carl Bridenbaugh (ed.), *The Pynchon Papers*, vol. 1. *Letters of John Pynchon, 1654–1700* (Boston, 1982), p. 5.
[82] M.H.S. *Collections*, ser. 4, vol. 7 (1865), p. 472.

Davenport later wrote to Winthrop, thanking him 'for the intelligence I received in your letters and for the two weekly intelligences which brother Myles brought me', which he now returned.[83] News continued to arrive erratically throughout the 1650s, but the reports were usually bewildering or depressing.

Samuel Mather wrote to a New England friend in 1651 describing England as 'a pleasant land, but deeply afflicted under many corrupt opinions'. Samuel Symonds, in Massachusetts, apologized to John Winthrop, Jr., in September 1652: 'I have little news at this time to acquaint you with, because it is a long time since any ship came from England.' John Haynes could not wait to spread the word in Connecticut in July 1653 when three ships arrived with 'news from England of astonishing nature'. Oliver Cromwell had expelled the Rump of the Long Parliament in April and had seized power.[84] Reticent as ever, Cromwellian soldier Stephen Winthrop could not bring himself to comment on these public events when he wrote to his elder brother in New England in August 1653, 'For news what should I write you? Every passenger will be able to tell you the latest.'[85]

The arrival in Boston harbour of three ships from London in June 1657 was a noteworthy occurrence that supplied the colony with fresh news as well as with valuable stocks of clothing.[86] In 1658 the news, as ever, was troubling. William Hooke, the New England preacher who was now engaged as a domestic chaplain to Oliver Cromwell, reported to John Winthrop, Jr., 'The state here hangs still upon uncertain points, and is balanced only by the hand of the Almighty.'[87] The Almighty would soon show His hand, although it would take many months for the reverberations to reach America. John Hull, the Boston mint master, read of the death of Oliver Cromwell, 'a man of excellent worth', on 25 February 1659. Cromwell had died the previous 3 September, so the news was almost half a year old by the time it reached Massachusetts.[88] The slow passage of such important intelligence was partly due to the winter season, but it also reflects the relative isolation of New England 'in these ends of the earth'. Details were slight, but Massachusetts felt moved to declare 15 June 1659

---

[83] Isabel MacBeath Calder (ed.), *Letters of John Davenport* (New Haven, Conn., 1937), p. 101; M.H.S. *Collections*, ser. 3, vol. 10 (1849), p. 36.

[84] M.H.S. MSS. 'Miscellaneous, bound', 26 March 1651; M.H.S. *Collections*, ser. 4, vol. 7 (1865), pp. 128, 463.

[85] M.H.S. *Collections*, ser. 5, vol. 8 (1882), p. 214.

[86] (Hull), 'The diaries of John Hull', A.A.S. *Transactions*, 3 (1857), p. 180.

[87] M.H.S. *Collections*, ser. 4, vol. 7 (1865), p. 588.

[88] 'Diaries of John Hull', p. 186.

another day of humiliation to mark 'the present unsettled estate and condition of our brethren in our native country'.[89]

〰〰〰〰〰

Rumours about the Restoration first reached New England by way of the Virginia tobacco ships. Other news arrived through the New-foundland fishermen. In December 1660 and again in the following January John Pynchon asked John Winthrop, Jr., 'if you have any news' from England. Winthrop sent what he had to Springfield. Pynchon thanked him, saying, 'there were many particulars in it which I knew not before.'[90]

The appropriately-named *Charles* arrived from London in July 1661 carrying eighty passengers and indisputable news of the Stuart Restoration. Charles II was proclaimed king in Massachusetts on 8 August 1661, fifteen months after his proclamation in London. Yet rumour abounded, and some New Englanders believed that the Restoration was but a temporary development. In 1662, according to Samuel Maverick, 'Strange reports are raised and blown about concerning the divisions of England' and prophecies persisted of further alterations to the English regime.[91]

In June 1662 Davenport reported from New Haven, 'By the way of Virginia I hear (but they say its treason to say so) that things are as bad as in Queen Mary's day.' This was obviously a wild exaggeration, since there were no human bonfires in Restoration London, but the Act of Uniformity and the beginnings of the Clarendon Code did not augur well for Nonconformists. Nor were the renewed Navigation Laws much loved by New England merchants.[92]

One long letter, containing a scurrilous and highly partisan account of the 'sad effects' of the Act of Uniformity, never reached its American destination. William Hooke wrote on 2 March 1663 to John Davenport with news of the ejected ministers, rumours of a 'new plot', comments on religion in England, Scotland and Ireland, and a synopsis of religious and political affairs in London. The searchers found this letter in 'a bundle of news books' and promptly confiscated it. Unless Hooke sent a duplicate by some other route his readers in New England might not learn that 'popery and popish worship is

[89] *Mass. Recs.*, vol. 4, pp. 382, 367; *Letters of John Davenport*, p. 169.
[90] *Pynchon Papers*, pp. 34–7.
[91] 'Diaries of John Hull', p. 203; *Mass. Recs.*, vol. 4, part 2, p. 30; 'The Clarendon papers', *Collections of the New York Historical Society* (1870), pp. 46, 48.
[92] Calder (ed.), *Letters of John Davenport*, p. 197; *Mass. Recs.*, vol. 5, p. 200.

openly set up at Somerset House', or that 'there is a toleration talked of, and expected by many'.[93]

Merchants, ministers and members of the New England elite continued to import English news during the second half of the seventeenth century, especially following developments that might affect the spiritual, political and commercial health of the colonies. English news spread along the coastline and into the hinterland, joining the various news networks of Virginia, New York, Connecticut and Massachusetts into a colonial community of information.[94]

Increasing commercial traffic in the 1660s brought a quickening of the flow of information to New England. Dozens of ships arrived from England in 1663, 'laden with goods and passengers' and bearing corantos and gazettes. Thirty ships lay in Boston harbour at one time. Seven ships from England arrived in a space of four days in the spring of 1664.[95] After the dearth of shipping during the 1640s and 1650s this allowed a wealth of communication. But the news was still sometimes interrupted by stays of shipping and by the exigencies of foreign wars. In August 1665 Samuel Wyllys complained, 'There is no news of any ship lately arrived from England, which makes a famine of certain news from Europe at present.' John Pynchon told Winthrop in April 1669, 'We are longing for news; if you have any it will be acceptable to hear it.' Again in September 1676, New Englanders complained, with Samuel Nowell, 'We have but little of news material stirring amongst us, there being no ship arrived lately from England.'[96]

News addicts bore such silences with frustration. Some were glad to share any report or gazette that would assuage their sense of isolation, as Thomas Shepard put it, 'in these outskirts of the earth'. Shepard borrowed John Winthrop, Jr.'s copy of the Royal Society Transactions in 1669 and circulated it in Massachusetts. John Pynchon of Springfield and Joseph Eliot of Guildford, Connecticut, sought English gazettes from Winthrop, 'the better [to] sympathise with the

---

[93] A. G. Mathews, 'A censored letter. William Hooke in England to John Davenport in New England, 1663', *Transactions of the Congregational Historical Society*, 9 (1924–6), pp. 262–83.

[94] M.H.S. *Collections*, ser. 3, vol. 10 (1849), pp. 51–2; *Pynchon Papers*, pp. 75, 78, 81, 84, 85. For an analysis of one of the most vigorous networks see Francis J. Bremer, 'Increase Mather's friends: the transatlantic Congregational network of the seventeenth century', A.A.S. *Proceedings*, 94 (1984), pp. 59–96.

[95] 'Diaries of John Hull', p. 209.

[96] *Letters of John Davenport*, p. 198; A.A.S. MSS., 'Letters of John Hall', 13 July 1667; M.H.S. *Collections*, ser. 3, vol. 10 (1849), p. 57; *Pynchon Papers*, p. 84; 'Mather papers', M.H.S. *Collections*, ser. 4, vol. 8 (1868), p. 572.

European stories of the sad effect of these wars'. Eliot also implored
Increase Mather for overseas news 'when it comes to hand'.[97] In this
regard they were like expatriate intellectuals of any age who hunger
for news of the mother country and of the wider world.

News of the great plague in London, at its peak in the summer of
1665, reached New England in the autumn. In November, Massachusetts held 'a solemn fast in reference to the sickness in England'.
Colonists held their breath, gave extra scrutiny to passengers from
overseas, and counted their blessings. The Symonds family at Ipswich,
Massachusetts had a belated firsthand account from John Hall in
London.[98] News of the Great Fire of London (September 1666)
reached New England in fragments. A ship from Barbados brought
the first account to New London on 6 January. Charles Hill cautiously
relayed it to John Winthrop, Jr.: 'Not knowing whether your honour
have account of the same, thought good to advise the lamentable loss
that was reported from England.' Another vessel arrived on 4 February, by way of Nevis and Jamaica, with 'dreadful tidings...of the
burning of the city of London'. John Hull's diary entry for 6 March
1667 tells how the story arrived in Boston: 'Came in Captain Martin
from England. Brought news of the burning of London in 2nd September last.' John Davenport was still digesting news about the Great
Fire in March 1667, six months after the event.[99]

Co-religionists in England continued to send a sad stream of tidings
to New England. Increase Mather for one was 'much troubled at the
abiding afflictions of Saints in England'. In 1669 John Hall wrote to
his family at Ipswich, Massachusetts, 'At Sarum a busy bishop and a
ranting recorder have troubled and imprisoned several good people
for private meetings at worship.' Hall's stepfather, Samuel Symonds,
would see that this news gained appropriate circulation. Early in 1672
Robert Atkyn wrote bitterly from England to a friend in Boston, 'We
here are full of looseness and prophaness, debauchery and what not,
crying sins abounding and little restraint, the mouths of good men
restrained.'[100] From a Puritan perspective, the 1670s was a decade for
lamentation on both sides of the ocean. This was the period of the

[97] M.H.S. *Collections*, ser. 3, vol. 10 (1849), p. 71; *Pynchon Papers*, p. 78; M.H.S. *Collections*, ser. 5, vol. 1 (1871), pp. 430–1; 'Mather papers', p. 375.
[98] Record Commissioners of the City of Boston, *Sixth Report*, 'Roxbury land and court
records' (Boston, 1881), p. 208; 'Letters of John Hall', 21 May 1666.
[99] *Winthrop Papers*, vol. 5, p. 66; 'Roxbury land and court records', p. 205; 'Diaries of
John Hull', p. 228; *Letters of John Davenport*, p. 267.
[100] A.A.S. MSS. 'Increase Mather's diary', 12 July 1666; 'Letters of John Hall', 5 August
1669; M.H.S. *Collections*, ser. 4, vol. 2 (1854) p. 224; Robert E. Moody (ed.), *The
Saltonstall Papers, 1607–1815* (Boston, 1972), p. 161.

fiercest and the most forlorn 'declension' sermons in New England. News reached Increase Mather in 1675 of 'the cruel useage of the bishops' in England, to which he attributed the death of a friend. Another friend, William Payne, wrote to Mather from London in February 1678 with a sheaf of personal, ecclesiastical and political information, including news of the intended reburial of Charles I.[101]

Naturally, rumours of the Popish Plot reached New England, just as they ran their course back home. Joseph Dudley reported to Fitz-John Winthrop in December 1678, 'Yesterday arrived two ships in eight weeks from London, confirming what we formerly heard: the danger of his majesty by the Duke's secretary, either by poison or poignard, procuring the disarming of all papists.' Nathaniel Mather wrote to his brother about the papists' 'deep and general design' and the ensuing trials, impeachments and executions.[102] Thomas Waterhouse, a former New Englander resettled in Essex, wrote breathlessly to Increase Mather in February 1679 that England lay 'in such a desperate trembling condition' as had not been seen in forty years. He gave details of the plot and of the English reaction. Nathaniel Mather told of the prorogation and dissolution of parliament, and other reports came in of the activities of the Duke of Monmouth and their suppression.[103]

John Richards, who served as the London agent for Massachusetts in the early 1680s, sent over digests and gazettes about the exploits of the Duke of York, the Quo Warranto proceedings, religious affairs, fires, riots and even the weather in England. Richards wrote long letters to Increase Mather, from which the Mather clan could distribute news through its various networks. Anyone who wanted could soon find out about a blazing star seen above London, the seizure of the Duke of Monmouth, or the sorrows of the English dissenters. Additional correspondence supplied accounts of an earthquake in Northampton, and the continuing harassment of England's godly ministers.[104]

Information was a kind of wealth, but one that could easily be shared. The younger John Cotton knew this when he insinuated to his cousin Cotton Mather in 1681, 'News from old England would be a kindness.' The Mathers were based at Boston, the hub of New England communications, whereas Cotton was down at Plymouth,

[101] 'Increase Mather's diary', 8 May 1675; 'Mather papers', pp. 15–17; Boston Public Library MS. Am. 1502/v2/34.
[102] M.H.S. *Collections*, ser. 6, vol. 3 (1889), p. 460; 'Mather papers', pp. 16–21.
[103] 'Mather papers', pp. 590–1, 16–21; M.H.S. *Collections*, ser. 6, vol. 3 (1889), pp. 460ff.
[104] 'Mather papers', pp. 494–501; Boston Public Library MS. Am. 1502/v5/37.

which had become something of a backwater.[105] Writing from New London in the same year, Simon Bradstreet asked Increase Mather, 'Pray let me understand by the bearer what news you have from England by private letters, etc. Perhaps some ships will be arrived before his return.' And in another note flattering Mather for his importance in the communications network, Bradstreet wrote, 'We have no news here but what comes from you.'[106] This was not strictly true, since New Englanders could count on a variety of potential sources for overseas information, but there was a gradient of information from Boston to the more outlying settlements. Colonists connected to the merchant and maritime community could construct a reasonable facsimile of English affairs, although the details were often late, one-sided and enigmatic. What would they make of this snippet, sent from London to the Boston merchant John Usher in 1683: 'No news but of men constantly failing, and troubles on dissenters'?[107]

Although by this time most colonists were less urgently concerned with developments in England than they had been a generation earlier, kinsmen and associates across the Atlantic continued to send political, religious, commercial and private news. The London merchant Daniel Allin shipped printed newsbooks to his cousin John Hull in Boston, Hull acknowledging in August 1672, 'I most kindly thank you for your intelligence constantly sent by gazettes and other prints.' Again in December Hull thanked Allin for 'your loving letters with the printed intelligence'. And in the following May he once more acknowledged a delivery of letters and gazettes from London. Daniel Allin kept up a stream of newsbooks, enabling the Boston mint master to share 'what news I had now from England' with his associates in Massachusetts.[108] Increase Mather, Wait Winthrop and Samuel Sewall performed a similar duty, collecting and distributing the printed news from England. Wait Winthrop spoke with the crews of ships coming in to Boston and passed along what he learned to his father in Connecticut. The most significant newsbooks were copied for wider circulation.[109]

So significant was the news of the death of Charles II in February

---

[105] 'Mather papers', p. 252.
[106] *Ibid.*, pp. 478, 479.
[107] M.H.S. MSS. 'Miscellaneous, bound', Charles Lidget to John Usher, 7 March 1683.
[108] A.A.S. MSS. 'Letter book of John Hull', pp. 27, 67, 93–4, 127.
[109] 'Increase Mather's diary', 8 August, 21 September, 11, 15 and 24 October 1666, 11 and 16 October 1676; [Sewall], 'Letter book of Samuel Sewall', M.H.S. *Collections*, ser. 6, vol. 1 (1886), pp. 38, 42; M.H.S. *Collections*, ser. 5, vol. 1 (1871), pp. 325, 288, 391, 393, 396, 397, 421, 423, 442, 456, 468.

1685 that the *London Gazette* that contained details was actually reprinted in Boston. Massachusetts had the news by 14 April and proclaimed the new king on 20 April. Cotton Mather was raised from his bed early in September 1685 by news of 'the calamities and confusions of the English nation'. Rumour was abroad of Monmouth's Rebellion, but the news of the royal victory at Sedgemoor on 6 July did not reach New England until 22 September. Affairs in England remained, as John Richards acknowledged, 'very perplexed'.[110] It was hard to judge whether the accession of James II was a providence or a malignancy. The new regime put a Catholic on the throne, but also promised toleration for protestant dissenters. Some of Increase Mather's English correspondents of this time had mixed feelings about whether they would rather be in New England.[111]

The dramatic events of November and December 1688, in which William of Orange landed in Devon and James II fled his kingdom, occurred at the wrong time of year for speedy reports to reach New England. The news filtered up from Virginia during February and March 1689, to be followed in April by a report of 'the Prince of Orange's declarations' and 'his happy proceedings in England', which the Boston printers immediately reproduced. Popular credence of these reports brought down the authoritarian regime of Edmund Andros, even before reliable news came in of the proclamation of William and Mary.[112]

News continued to arrive from England in the final decade of the seventeenth century, tardy, shredded and incomplete, yet enough to sustain a picture of political and religious life in the homeland. Those who cared had the opportunity to be almost as well informed about public affairs as their contemporaries in England.[113] The *London Gazette* circulated in Boston, as it did in other provincial British cities. From 1704 on, the *Boston News-Letter* provided a weekly printed diet of overseas news. Much of this was already half a year cold, and would already be known in political and shipping circles. The average lag between an occurrence in England and its report in the *Boston News-*

---

[110] *London Gazette*, 5–9 February 1684–5; 'Broadsides, ballads, etc. printed in Massachusetts 1639–1800', M.H.S. *Collections*, 75 (1922), no. 107; (Mather), 'Diary of Cotton Mather, 1681–1708', M.H.S. *Collections*, ser. 7, vol. 7 (1911), p. 93; 'Mather papers', p. 494.

[111] 'Mather papers', pp. 657–9.

[112] Ian K. Steele, 'Communicating an English revolution to the colonies', *Journal of British Studies*, 24 (1985), pp. 346–53.

[113] M.H.S. *Collections*, ser. 5, vol. 8 (1882), p. 325; M.H.S., 'Diary of John Marshall, 1689–1711' (microfilm).

Letter in its first year of publication was twenty-two weeks.[114] The late arrival of news from England even became a joke in some quarters. In December 1700, Nathaniel Saltonstall informed his friend Rowland Cotton, 'Captain Foster's ship is come lateley from England and, they say, brings news that Queen Mary is certainly dead.' Indeed, Queen Mary had died in 1694, and the colonists had known it for half a decade.[115]

---

[114] My calculation based on *The Boston News-Letter*, nos. 1–34. See also Boston's short-lived *Publick Occurrences both Foreign and Domestick* of 1690.
[115] 'Saltonstall papers', p. 266.

11

'The part of a kinsman': separation, reunion and the wider circle of kin

Migration naturally meant separation. Many travellers completely lost contact with the rest of their family when they moved to New England, just as migrants within England often drifted out of reach of their circle of kin. But emigration did not necessarily cut the migrants off from their homeland or their English relations. As previous chapters have shown, a web of kinship and an active flow of communication extended across the ocean in both directions. The potentiality of contact was ever present. Although the English and New English branches of migrant families could not offer each other all the comfort and support they wished, affectionate memory and continuing utility often kept them rooted in each other's minds. English and American lives interlocked from time to time despite emigration, as family members shared greetings and dealings by correspondence. Indeed, the fact of emigration may actually have heightened a sense of membership in some extended families. Having an uncle in London or a cousin in Connecticut gave one an interest in the affairs of those distant places, and also presented a store of opportunities for the long-distance exchange of favours.

Family papers, letters, diaries, journals, depositions and other documents show people on both sides of the Atlantic keeping up with their overseas kinsfolk, despite the obvious difficulties. Expressions of love and duty, relayed and transmitted among a widening family circle, provided an emotional lifeline to the distant side of the world. On both sides of the Atlantic people eagerly scavenged family news from travellers and casual acquaintances. They took pains to learn which of their kinsmen were alive or dead, who was marrying and who had been born. Each scrap of news contributed to a larger mosaic of family information. The evidence does not lend itself to quantification, so we cannot measure the volume or velocity of these extended family contacts. It seems clear, however, that the surviving material represents just a fraction of the interaction between the colonies and the homeland.

Often the communications were sporadic to the point of attenuation. Some people did not know whether their overseas relations were alive or dead. Many family links lay dormant, like desert flowers awaiting rain. But the means of communication were adequate for families to revive them if the need should arise. This chapter is concerned with the range and vitality of these transatlantic family connections.

The prospect of isolation, like the peril of the Atlantic crossing, often loomed larger in anticipation than in practice. When migrants to America left the dockside in England they quite naturally feared that they might never see their loved ones again. Mothers cried at the departure of their children; brothers and sisters said final farewells. Kinsmen and friends who had grown accustomed to each other's presence anticipated an end to their mutual familiarity and support. Although one in six or more of the migrants eventually went home, very few of those embarking could have anticipated the likelihood of return. Most people saw moving to America as an irrevocable step, a one-way passage to the distant side of the globe. Even those Puritans who dreamed of one day returning to a godly renewed England understood they were committing themselves to an exile of distance and separation that might last forever, or at least until they were reunited in heaven.

William Bradford's group left Leyden amidst 'sighs and sobs and prayers'. Theirs was a 'sad and mournful parting' that was renewed and intensified when the Pilgrims finally sailed from Plymouth. Members of the Winthrop fleet similarly poured out their hearts in scenes of 'bowel-breaking affections' as they took 'their last farewell of their native country, kindred, friends and acquaintances'. Emigration, in Edward Johnson's bulbous prose, signalled separation from 'all kindred of blood that binds the bowells of affection in a true lovers' knot'. Tearful embraces sealed the belief that this was indeed 'their last farewell'.[1] A keening echo followed the travellers across the Atlantic that might haunt them and their stay-at-home kinsmen for the rest of their lives.

Deane Tyndal told his kinsman John Winthrop, 'I cannot but lament

[1] William Bradford, *History of Plymouth Plantation 1620–1647* (Boston, 1912), vol. 1, p. 125; *Wonder-Working Providence*, pp. 51–4. See also Joshua Scottowe, *Massachusetts, or the First Planters of New-England* (Boston, 1696), p. 38.

when I think of your journey, for though the bond of love continues, yet the distance of place will not let us be so useful and comfortable one to another.' The extended family was severed, perhaps never to be reknit. Priscilla Fones, Winthrop's kinswoman through marriage, reacted with 'much grief' to the 'heavy news' of his parting.[2] When he embarked on the *Arbella* in 1630 Winthrop also left his wife behind with several of their children. It was a sombre moment, and Winthrop wrote, 'It goeth very near my heart to leave thee.' Margaret Winthrop planned to follow, but neither husband nor wife could tell what circumstances might keep them apart or what accident or illness might strike the other down. Synchronized prayer was the best they could endeavour until their eventual reunion on earth or in heaven. Each Monday and Friday at five they promised to meet in spiritual company, though separated by an ocean.[3]

Hundreds of wives in similar circumstances embraced their pioneer husbands with a sense that they might never see each other again. Edward Johnson left his wife and children in 1630 when he joined the first wave of the great migration. John Gallop ached to be reunited with his wife, whom he had left behind in England. Richard Crane left a wife and five children in England to go as a servant to Massachusetts, and he longed to be with them again.[4]

Elizabeth Whitehead recalled a mother's anguish in seeing her two sons leave for New England after their father died. 'The parting from them was a great grief unto me which brought me near unto death.' One traveller, prompted perhaps by the name of his port of embarkation, Gravesend, joked grimly that departure was like attending one's own funeral, when lamenting relations crowded aboard the *Susannah and Thomas* to say their farewells.[5]

Going to America, however, was not like going beyond the grave. Although the ocean imposed a formidable barrier, it was not the river of Lethe, and the separation it enjoined was never as permanent or complete as many people feared. Resourceful families kept in touch, achieved reunions and renewed associations that had been inter-

[2] *Winthrop Papers*, vol. 2, pp. 162–3, 153–4.
[3] *Ibid.*, pp. 225, 226.
[4] *Wonder-Working Providence*, p. 6. *Winthrop Papers*, vol. 3, p. 87; vol. 4, pp. 105–6, 238–9.
[5] Registry Department of the City of Boston (eds.), *Aspinwall Notarial Records, from 1644 to 1651* (Boston, 1903), p. 101; John Dunton, *The Life and Errors of John Dunton* (London, 1818), p. 81; John Dunton, *Letters Written From New England, A.D. 1686*, ed., W. H. Whitmore (Boston, 1867), p. 10. For a necessary caution see Chester Noyes Greenough, 'John Dunton's Letters From New England', *Publications of the Colonial Society of Massachusetts*, 14 (1911–13), pp. 222, 256.

rupted by distance or years. Most wives who saw their husbands sail away managed to join them within a short while. Community pressure or their own desire usually brought them together. John and Margaret Winthrop were reunited in 1631 when the *Lyon* brought wives and children to the colony. 'The like joy and manifestation of love had never been seen in New England.' John Eliot was joined by his betrothed a year after he settled in New England. Edward Johnson went back to collect his wife and seven children. John Wilson returned to England specifically to fetch his wife, but he was unable to persuade her to go with him to New England.[6]

The colonial authorities, like their English counterparts, disapproved of divided conjugal families. Such separations constituted disorderly behaviour, threatening social stability and patriarchal authority, as well as tempting the single partners to 'lewdness and filthiness'. Massachusetts ordered that 'men and women living within this jurisdiction whose wives or husbands are in England' should 'repair to their said relations by the first opportunity of shipping'.[7] In New Haven,

whereas some persons, men or women, do live or may come to settle within this colony, whose wives or husbands are in England or elsewhere, by means whereof they are exposed to great temptations, and some of them live under suspicion of uncleaness, if they do not fall into lewd and sinful courses; it is therefore ordered, that all such persons living within this jurisdiction shall, by the first opportunity, repair to their said relations.[8]

To forestall such problems the colony sometimes barred from settlement newcomers who were known to have left their wives behind. In 1682, for example, Boston denied admission to 'Thomas Blackford, driller, that hath a wife in England, and by information a vicious conversation', and to Charles Salter, carpenter, who likewise 'hath a wife in England'.[9]

Some couples used migration as a substitute for divorce, but few remained separated without the local courts attempting to engineer their reunion. John Leech of Salem, who was presented before the Essex County Court in 1649 for living apart from his wife, answered

---

[6] *Winthrop's Journal*, vol. 1, p. 70; *Wonder-Working Providence*, p. 6; Record Commissioners of the City of Boston, *Sixth Report* (Boston, 1881), p. 76. John Dunton, too, soon returned to his loving wife; Dunton, *Life*, p. 138.

[7] *The Book of the General Lawes and Libertyes Concerning the Inhabitants of the Massachusets* (Cambridge, Mass., 1648; facsimile, San Marino, Calif., 1975), p. 37. *Cf.* Henry Conset, *The Practice of the Spiritual or Ecclesiastical Courts* (London, 1685), pp. 253–6, on 'restitution of the conjugal yoke'.

[8] *New-Haven's Settling in New England* (1656; reprinted, Hartford, Conn., 1858), p. 58.

[9] Record Commissioners of the City of Boston, *Tenth Report* (Boston, 1886), p. 59. See also *Seventh Report* (Boston, 1881), 'Boston town records', p. 68.

that 'he often sent and wrote to her, but she was unwilling to come, and he was not able to live in old England'. Although the Atlantic lay between them they still maintained some kind of contact. John Leech, like the illiterate Robert Pike of Marblehead, continued to press for a reunion.[10]

Occasionally a wife came to New England without her husband, or remained in the colony after he went home. In 1649, for example, 'Mary Oliver, having been ordered to go to her husband in England in the next ship, was further enjoined to go by the next opportunity on penalty of twenty pounds.' (Thomas Oliver, calender of Norwich, his wife Mary, with two children and two servants had crossed over in 1637 aboard the *Mary Anne* of Yarmouth. Mary fell foul of the Massachusetts authorities in 1638 and again in 1646 for siding with Roger Williams. Thomas went back to England about 1648, but returned to the colony, and to his wife, a few years later.)[11]

The courts had no jurisdiction over wider ranges of kinship, but colonists of all kinds voluntarily acknowledged and cultivated their English links. Kinship linked people in East Anglia, Lancashire and in all the centres of emigration, to cousins or other relations in New England and the rest of the new American world. It was often the women of the family who sought or sustained contact, and their letters and messages make moving reading. Most of the contact was between former members of nuclear families – between siblings, parents and children – but uncles and aunts, nephews, nieces and all sorts of cousins also came into view.

The widow Elizabeth Whitehead, left alone in London after her children emigrated to New England, hungered for morsels of news from the colonies and attached herself to returning travellers in the hope of word from her boys. By keeping her ears open in the maritime community she spun emotional ties to a world she had never seen, but which mattered dearly to her heart. When one visitor from New England in 1647 'could tell me nothing concerning my children', she resorted to more purposeful means of communication and sought reassurance in a letter (probably dictated) to her brother-in-law who lived in Boston.[12]

Wine-cooper Robert Smith was more fortunate, though no more systematic, in collecting news of his distant kin. He emigrated to Massachusetts in the late 1630s with his two sisters, Mary and Anne. 'Not

[10] *Essex Courts*, vol. 1, pp. 159, 173; vol. 5, pp. 65–7.
[11] Savage, *Genealogical Dictionary*, vol. 3, p. 311.
[12] *Aspinwall Notarial Records*, pp. 101–2.

long after his arrival', Robert had a change of heart, as did an un-
heralded number of other participants in the great migration, and
went back home to London. His sisters soon married in Massachusetts
and raised families in New England. For years no contact existed
between brother and sisters, and Robert heard nothing of his new
American nieces and nephews. In 1648, however, a Massachusetts
yeoman named Peter Gardner visited England and found Robert
Smith keeping the Golden Lion tavern in London's Fetter Lane. New
England reminiscences flowed with the wine as Peter gave the landlord
news of his sister Mary. Two years later Peter Gardner again came
to London, carrying messages and tokens between the siblings. The
visitor from New England later recalled that Robert Smith 'did much
desire his company and discourse with him about his said sister and
did rejoice to hear of his said sister's, her husband and children's
health'. Once they regained contact, even by proxy, the divided
branches of the family could plan mutual support for each other in
the future. Robert went so far as to suggest that Mary send him one
of her American-born children to adopt as his heir.[13]

The leading gentry of New England quite naturally kept up with
their counterparts in England, whereas among the clergy and merchants a community of theological or economic interest generated
bulky files of letters. Family matters occupy a substantial part of this
widely-distributed archive, since many of the political, clerical and
commercial elite preferred to do business with their kin. John Hull
of Boston, for example, kept up a wide-flung business correspondence
that involved his cousins Edward Hull, Daniel Allin and Daniel Quincy
in London, his uncle Thomas Parris, and other kin in England
including his cousins Sarah and Caroline Parris, a cousin Judith, and
a cousin Thomas Bucknam. Samuel Sewall exchanged letters with
English relations including his uncle Stephen Dummer, cousins Nathaniel and Thomas Dummer, aunt Dorothy Rider, cousin Sarah,
cousin Quincy, and 'loving cousins' John Stork and Edward Hull.
Increase Mather corresponded with an even wider battery of kin,
including cousins and cousins of cousins in the north of England.[14]

Striking examples of long-distance dealing between distant relations

---

[13] Massachusetts Archives, vol. 15A, pp. 11–12.
[14] A.A.S. MSS., 'Letter book of John Hull'; (Sewall), 'Letter book of Samuel Sewall',
M.H.S. *Collections*, ser. 6, vol. 1 (1886); 'Mather papers', M.H.S. *Collections*, ser. 4,
vol. 8 (1868). See also Francis J. Bremer, 'Increase Mather's friends: the transatlantic
Congregational network of the seventeenth century', A.A.S. *Proceedings*, 94 (1984),
pp. 59–96; and Bernard Bailyn, *The New England Merchants in the Seventeenth Century*
(1955; reprinted, Cambridge, Mass., 1979), pp. 82, 87–91.

appear in seventeenth-century transatlantic letters. They illustrate the practical and symbolic importance of kinship, and reveal some of the elusive expectations associated with family extension. John Hall's letters are not the only ones to show the importance of family ties. Relations, even distant relations, found themselves entwined in knots of family obligation. Fragments of correspondence show people invoking or acknowledging a range of duties associated with cousinage, affinity or kinship by marriage or blood.

Correspondents hung on every word from their families overseas, however stale the news by the time it arrived. Inevitably, the lag in communication sometimes meant that people wrote to friends or kinsmen who were already dead. When Brampton Gurdon wrote to John Winthrop on 6 June 1649, 'I am very glad to hear of your health,' he was not to know that the governor had already succumbed to a final illness on 26 March. Learning in 1680 that his English uncle, aunt and grandmother had died, William Gilbert of Boston wrote home urgently to his grandfather for 'a more particular account of our friends who are living and who are dead'. Kinsmen could share in long-distance family mourning through the exchange of rings and other tokens.[15]

Cultivating one's family could bring potent but intangible rewards, involving affection, memory and membership. In addition to satisfying the drives of nostalgia and curiosity, these extended family associations proved advantageous in many practical ways. They could stimulate a chain of connections and mediations leading to favour, preferment and profit. Uncles and cousins, and other relations of various ages, experience and station, acted as agents and secured entry to valuable social networks extending beyond the family circle. It would be easier to pry loose a legacy, collect overdue rents, secure appointments or introductions and otherwise make one's way in the world with an interested family network on hand.

Affinal kin acquired through marriage were embraced in the network almost as readily as consanguinal kin, tied by blood. Christopher Jeaffreson, trading in the Caribbean, assured his brother-in-law in England, 'I think myself extremely happy in so faithful a friend, so loving a brother, and esteem him no less dear to me than if consanguinity had made the same knot that affinity tied.'[16] Marriage not

---

[15] *Winthrop Papers*, vol. 5, p. 351; *Essex Courts*, vol. 9, p. 478. After John Hull's death in Boston, in 1683 his executor sent mourning rings to cousins in England 'in remembrance of your loving kinsman'; 'Letter book of John Hull', p. 566.
[16] John Cordy Jeaffreson (ed.), *A Young Squire of the Seventeenth Century* (London, 1878), p. 281.

only gave each of the contracting partners new affinal kin but also gave all of their relations an added interest in the expanded family network. Second and subsequent marriages complicated the picture and increased the possibilities of interaction among kin. Kin acquisition was cumulative, for relations associated with one marriage did not cease to claim kinship after the death of the linking spouse.

William Bisbey of Warwickshire, for example, was related to George Wyllys in Connecticut because his brother Alexander Bisbey had been the first husband to Wyllys's second wife. William Bisbey addressed his colonial kinsman in 1640 as 'loving brother', and went on to pay his respects to 'all our cousins'. George Wyllys reciprocated, and in 1641 put his son George Wyllys, Jr., in touch with English relations including 'cousin' John Waker, yeoman of Snitterfield, whose wife was the late Alexander Bisbey's sister. The younger George Wyllys, home in England on his family's business, could thereby deal with a 'cousin' who was brother-in-law to his father's wife's first husband, and trustingly engage him as surety in the sale of his American family's land.[17]

John Winthrop, whose genealogy and correspondence have been studied to the point of exhaustion, was married four times and thereby became connected to several East Anglian and London families. His own children's marriages (and betrothal in the case of Forth Winthrop, who died in 1630) connected the Winthrops, and those of their affinity, to still more families in England and New England. These affinal connections could also be transmitted to subsequent generations, to be utilized by anyone who was able to recall them. The Winthrops exchanged letters with Priscilla Paynter, whose second husband (of three) was Thomas Fones, whose first wife was John Winthrop's sister Anne. Ursula Sherman, Priscilla's daughter by her first marriage, was betrothed to Forth Winthrop at the time of his death, and she too wrote to John Winthrop, Jr., signing herself 'your ever loving sister'.[18]

John Winthrop's English kinsmen were not loath to contact him if they thought it to their advantage. Laying claims on kinsmen was a variant of the familiar patronage scramble. In 1637, for example, Philip Forth addressed Winthrop as 'worthy cousin' and signed himself 'your obliged servant and kinsman'. In a postscript he added, 'I

[17] 'The Wyllys papers', *Collections of the Connecticut Historical Society*, 21 (1924), pp. 11, 14.
[18] For the ramifications of the Winthrop dynasty see R. C. Winthrop, *Life and Letters of John Winthrop* (Boston, 1869); Richard S. Dunn, *Puritans and Yankees: the Winthrop Dynasty of New England 1630–1717* (Princeton, N.J., 1962); and *Winthrop Papers*, vol. 3, pp. 9, 39–40, 189–90, 395–6.

salute your beloved wife, my good cousin your son, and all the rest of my kindred and friends with you to whom I pray and wish all happiness.' Philip Forth was a cousin to Winthrop's first wife, who had died in 1615.[19] Another 'loving cousin' letter reached John Winthrop from Joan Winthrop, the widow of the governor's cousin Adam. George Jenney wrote from London in 1640 to his 'brother' John Winthrop, with salutations to the governor's children. Jenney could claim this intimacy by virtue of his marriage to Mary Clopton, sister to Thomasine Clopton, who was Winthrop's second wife until her death in 1616. Other letters came the same year from Winthrop's brother-in-law Thomas Gostlin (married to his sister Jane), his nephew Benjamin Gostlin (son of Thomas), and his nephew Samuel Fones (son of Winthrop's sister Anne).[20]

As kinsmen, whether close or distant, these correspondents thought themselves entitled to more favourable attention. Philip Forth pressed a recommendation for one of his kinsmen. Joan Winthrop wanted relief from her poverty. George Jenney requested 'a courtesy of you for a special friend of mine'.[21] We do not know Winthrop's response, but at least he did not discard their letters. Their greetings and petitions brought these English relations to mind, not only to the addressee but to the rest of his family in New England.

Another relation, Ann Hoskins, directed a moving letter to John Winthrop, Jr., in 1638, in which she invoked the power of kinship. As daughter of John Winthrop, Jr.'s great-uncle John, by his second wife, Ann Hoskins asserted her family connection to the Winthrops of New England and addressed her kinsman as 'dear cousin'. Like Elizabeth Whitehead, Ann Hoskins had lost contact with her emigrant son. Nonetheless her lines of communication were not entirely severed, and she lived in hope of receiving news. 'I pray if my son be living let him write me a letter.' What distinguished this mother's plea from other attempts to renew contact with a missing migrant was Ann's boldness in approaching one of the most prominent men in the colonies. Kinship provided the key. She pressed John Winthrop, Jr., further, in the most revealing manner. 'I hope you have done *the part of a kinsman* for him as you promised.'[22] 'The part of a kinsman' included advice and support, and perhaps financial assistance and career encouragement. If young Hoskins survived, he might prosper

[19] *Winthrop Papers*, vol. 3, pp. 394–5.
[20] *Winthrop Papers*, vol. 4, pp. 18, 196–7, 199, 211, 216.
[21] *Ibid.*, p. 197.
[22] *Ibid.*, pp. 7–8, emphasis added. John Winthrop, Jr., may have visited his 'cousin' Ann Hoskins in Ireland on his way back to England in 1634.

with Winthrop kinsmen behind him. At the very least he might respond to avuncular pressure to write home to his mother.

A generation later in 1668 another Englishwoman sought help from a distant but distinguished American kinsman. Mary Elwald, wife of an impoverished London scrivener, felt emboldened by her straitened circumstances to apply for 'encouragement' from Richard Bellingham, then governor of Massachusetts. She had a slender kin connection with her correspondent across the ocean, and this she recited in order to engage his interest. Mary Elwald's connection to Bellingham rested on being 'one of Mr. William Goodrick's daughters'. She felt confident addressing the governor as 'dear uncle' and signing herself 'your loving and dutiful niece'. As a kinswoman she wished to tell Bellingham 'how precious the very remembrance of you was throughout all our family'. She assumed the right 'to speak out my mind in regard of my near relation to you', and so to ask for favours. She and her husband needed support, preferably in the form of an invitation to New England. 'If my husband or myself could have any encouragement we would, God willing, come by the return of the ship.'[23]

Like the Winthrop family, the Mather clan kept up a far-flung correspondence linking brothers and cousins, uncles and nephews, and religious well-wishers and associates throughout New England and the British Isles. Increase Mather recorded in his diary at Boston in 1675, 'I heard that Mr. John Thomson (my brother Nathaniel and he married two sisters), who was my special acquaintance when I was in England, was dead in Bristol.' The Mather network in New England quickly spread this news of a kinsman's death to all concerned. Next day Increase Mather 'went to Mr. Rawson's to read his daughter's letter' and learned of his brother Nathaniel's serious illness in Ireland. Nathaniel Mather recovered to send to Boston a steady stream of correspondence, thick with news of blood relations, other kinsmen, neighbours, friends, and brothers-in-Christ. Sensitive to his role in a caring family network, Nathaniel usually closed his letters with expressions of 'mine and my dear wife's love to yourself, our sisters and cousins'.[24] Cousinage was acknowledged, embraced and pursued.

People on the fringes of this network sometimes used their Mather connections to find out how their own close families fared. In 1683

---

[23] Massachusetts Archives, vol. 57, p. 52. This was, apparently, Mary Elwald's second letter to her American uncle. In response to an earlier appeal, Samuel Bellingham, the governor's son, had visited the Elwalds in London 'and had an extraordinary kindness for us'.

[24] A.A.S. MSS. 'Increase Mather's diary', 8 May 1675; 'Mather papers', pp. 14, 18, 40.

Nathaniel Mather wrote to his brother, 'A poor woman came to me bringing the enclosed (a message), and earnestly desiring I would send it to New England and get an answer whether her brother, Abraham Bell, a shoemaker, be living or heard of in Boston. If you know or can hear of such a one, I pray send word.' In the same letter Nathaniel renewed an earlier request for transatlantic information. 'I wrote formerly to enquire if any of the Palmers be living in or about Salem. A good friend of mine, and an elder of the church, their relation, desires to hear from them.'[25] The Bells and the Palmers may have been dead or indifferent, and at best they had been poor correspondents, but their kinsfolk at home still cared for them, and the Mathers willingly accepted the role of intermediaries to furnish contact.

Friends and neighbours, kinsmen, and kinsmen of kinsmen, sometimes approached the Mathers to smooth the way for emigration to New England, in the same way as people had earlier enquired of the Winthrops. In 1684, for example, Samuel Penhallow presented himself to Increase Mather in Boston with a testimonial written by Increase's brother Nathaniel. Nathaniel Mather explained, 'A good friend and near relative of mine, one Mr. Richard Lob, merchant in London, who married my sister Thomson, desires me to write in behalf of this gentleman, the bearer, his kinsman Mr. Penhallow of Falmouth in Cornwall, who designs to spend a year or two in New England.' A useful string in a complex family network was revealed and pulled, and Samuel Penhallow, who eventually settled at Portsmouth, New Hampshire, made his way to America through the kinsman of a kinsman of a kinsman.[26]

Daniel Hemingway, a mercer and draper in Lancashire, made his pitch to Increase Mather direct. As a kinsman to the Mathers, albeit remote, Hemingway expected more than the usual courtesy extended to English Nonconformists when he inquired about emigration in 1686. Establishing kinship took a full third of Hemingway's letter, for the relationship was neither close nor clear.

These lines are to acquaint you how nearly my wife is related to you, viz: her grandmother on the mother side was Abigail Holt, and sister unto your mother, and by marriage changed her name to Isherwood, and by that husband had two daughters, whereof Ann the elder married John Holme of Bolton, and had by him three sons and one daughter, which daughter, through providence, is my wife.

---

[25] 'Mather papers', p. 51.
[26] *Ibid.*, p. 59; Savage, *Genealogical Dictionary*, vol. 3, pp. 388–9.

If that were not enough, Hemingway went on to trace a second level of kin connection, explaining that his wife 'was the widow of one Samuel Mather when I married her, and by him had six daughters'. This Samuel Mather came from Winwick, the same Lancashire parish as Increase Mather's emigrant father, and was presumed to be some kind of relation. No doubt pleased with his reconstruction of kin connections, Hemingway concluded, 'This account may serve to satisfy you of the relation betwixt my wife and you, which is truth. *And now cousin*, I desire you to read these few proposals.' Three times more Hemingway addressed Increase Mather as 'cousin' and ended his letter with 'prayers from your loving kinsman, though unknown'. He evidently calculated that a letter from within the family would have more effect than one from a simple co-religionist, although his 'proposals' were unexceptional queries about church discipline, the climate, and business opportunities in New England. Increase Mather favoured his new-found cousin with a reply, but by the time this letter reached Lancashire in 1687 the religious situation had changed and Hemingway had no further interest in emigration.[27]

'The part of a kinsman' is one of the great unexplored areas of early modern social history. These letters throw some light on the question of who could invoke it, over what range of family connectedness, in what circumstances and to what effect. Probing the limits of the system, they make it clear that the claims of kinship could extend much wider than the inner circle of uncles and siblings, the penumbra of the nuclear family, and that on occasion they stretched to relations who were distant in genealogy as well as distant in miles. Ann Hoskins, Mary Elwald and Daniel Hemingway each touched one of the most responsive social and cultural chords of their times. By deploying the appropriate vocabulary and by invoking clearly-understood principles they transformed a mere genealogical connection into a relationship of effective kinship.[28]

Family members were expected to assist each other, to offer solidarity, comfort and contacts. A kinsman was supposed to respond to an unremarkable and even an unknown relation, simply because they were kin. At least among the merchants and gentry, and perhaps

[27] 'Mather papers', pp. 657–9, emphasis added.
[28] The workings of the English kinship system are discussed in David Cressy, 'Kinship and kin interaction in early modern England', *Past and Present*, 113 (1986), pp. 38–69.

descending the social scale, family ties signified mutual interest and reciprocal obligation. Duties and opportunities both came about in consequence of marriage or blood.

Petitioners like Mary Elwald and Daniel Hemingway might be expected to idealize family solidarity in the hope of benefiting from its exercise. Their letters asserting connection and requesting assistance mix hyperbole and obsequiousness, and sometimes read as if they thought it necessary to remind their correspondents of their duties, like referring to an ancient code of rules. But Bellingham and Mather each favoured their English relations with a reply, and may have gone further in performing their kinship duties. Other sources show the kinship system at work, as people responded to pleas and opened their arms to members of their extended kindred. There were limits, of course, but also remarkable reserves of goodwill.

Sir William Spring, of Pakenham, Suffolk, approached these limits when he assisted his cousin John Spring, who settled at Watertown, Massachusetts, in 1634. Sir William paid his cousin an allowance, and used his influence with John Winthrop (calling himself 'your unfained loving friend and faithfully affected brother') to keep his kinsman out of financial difficulties. Early in 1637 he apologized to Winthrop for 'the still important and large requests of my kinsman', explaining that 'other poor kindred I have too too many that daily call for help and must have it'. Like his friend Winthrop, Sir William Spring was accustomed to dealing with requests from less fortunate relations. However, he was about to reduce his charity. Brampton Gurdon, another cousin of Sir William Spring, told John Winthrop in April 1637 that Sir William 'desired me to desire you from him to stay your hand in yielding so much to his kinsman as heretofore. I find his desire is to cut his yearly maintenance, alleging what he have done for him and other like charges'.[29] The exasperated Sir William had done enough, but the only reason he had done anything at all was because John Spring was his cousin.

Robert Keayne, the Boston merchant, was especially sensitive to family obligations and wished the world to know he had carried his share. Recalling the kinsmanlike services he had performed for his brother-in-law John Mansfield, Keayne wrote,

I have done very much for him in England divers times, in releasing him out of prisons, in paying his debts for him, in furnishing him with a stock to set up his trade when he had spent all his own, in taking up many quarrelsome businesses which he in his distempered fits had plunged into of dangerous

[29] *Winthrop Papers*, vol. 3, pp. 363–5, 388.

consequence; yet I compounded them for him and, at his sister my wife's entreaty, with some other friends of hers I sent him over into New England when his life was in hazard. I paid his passage and some of his debts for him in England, and lent him money to furnish himself with clothes and other necessaries for the voyage. For many years I found him diet and clothes gratis.

Mansfield had settled in Massachusetts in 1635, a pain to all around him. Keayne's support of this troublesome relation went beyond the call of duty, and his account is in the form of an apologia, but it was not out of line with contemporary expectations.[30]

Keayne acknowledged the claims of kin again in 1654 when he wrote to John Winthrop, Jr., recommending his new nephew John Morse, 'who I suppose you know, and is *become* my kinsman by marrying my own sister's daughter; and so I have the more interest in him, at least by my counsel and advice'.[31] A more explicit statement of affinal duty would be hard to find. Keayne had kinship thrust upon him, and was more than ready for the part. In John Morse he found a much more attractive addition to the family than Mansfield, and Keayne may even have expected some reciprocal advantage from the relationship. But the essential link between them, and the foundation of Keayne's generosity, was neither neighbourliness, religion nor business dealings, but kinship.

Another revealing example of the language of kinship and the shouldering of its obligations occurs in the testimonial Charles Morton wrote in 1689 for 'the bearer, my cousin Nathaniel Randall. . . . He is of my blood (for his grandfather and my father were brothers) and *therefore* I can do no less than use my small interest in his behalf. . . . He is a stranger in a strange land, and has no kindred or friends to look to in this part of the world but my silly self and a poor orphan brother at Boston'. No close relationship bound Morton and Randall together. Apparently they had never even met before migrating (separately) to the colonies. Morton was a Nonconformist minister in his sixties who became vice-president of Harvard; Randall was a young man searching for opportunities, 'being now out of his time with his master'. Both, however, were recent newcomers to New England and recognized how important family connections and introductions could be in establishing a career. Morton's willingness to promote Randall in New England rested not on any praiseworthy qualities the young

---

[30] Record Commissioners of the City of Boston, *Tenth Report* (Boston, 1886), 'The last will and testament of me, Robert Keayne', p. 25.
[31] M.H.S. *Collections*, ser. 5, vol. 1 (1871), p. 378, emphasis added.

man might possess, but simply because 'he is of my blood'.[32] Whoever inspected this testimonial was evidently supposed to share its author's sentiments about familial expectations.

~~~~~~

A tangle of marriages and remarriages involving several lines and generations linked some of the leading families of seventeenth-century New England with their kinsmen overseas. This web of kinship spanned the Atlantic, with strands leading from rural East Anglia to northern New England, from southern Connecticut to London and the West Country, and with outliers in the Low Countries, Virginia and the islands. Family connections extended across the Anglo-American world in a dense and cross-hatched web. Attempts to display these links in an orderly genealogical chart end up with a thicket of connections and cross-connections that represent an active and extended kinship structure, further extended by being stretched overseas.

Surviving letters and papers reveal some of these family associations at work. Their power and complexity can be suggested in a simplified but still somewhat convoluted review of transatlantic ties among the Winthrop, Symonds, Reade and Lake families, which further involved Halls, Epses, Peters, Harlakendens and others. The following case-study reveals a well-placed cluster of Anglo-American families servicing and expanding their network, reciprocating favours and demonstrating solidarity through most of the seventeenth century. Some of these people, notably the Symondses and Harlakendens, represented traditional armigerous families of the kind that were chronically obsessed with lines and lineage. Most, however, sprang from second-tier East Anglian county families who were transformed into primary elites by migration to New England. Among them too were members of the minor gentry and prosperous traders and farmers, representing the top 20 per cent of colonial society. Humbler migrants lacked the resources, and perhaps also the motivation, to sustain such extensive transoceanic kinship links, although they too enjoyed social and emotional involvement with their family across the water when the occasion permitted.

John Winthrop, Jr., and Samuel Symonds became kinsmen to each other in the 1630s when they married two daughters of Edmund

---

[32] *Ibid.*, p. 436, emphasis added.

Reade, an Essex gentlemen who had died a decade before the great migration. Each acknowledged Edmund Reade as 'our father' and took to heart the Anglo-American interests and obligations that followed from their expanded relationship.[33]

John Winthrop, Jr., took Elizabeth Reade as his second wife in 1635. The marriage cemented the rest of the Reades and Winthrops in a bond of service and affection that continued for the rest of the seventeenth century. Winthrop's business dealings with Elizabeth's brother Thomas Reade were transformed into fraternal relationships by their becoming kinsmen. Before the marriage Reade addressed Winthrop as 'dear sir'; afterwards he called him 'honoured brother'. As business associates they had dealt cautiously with each other in the Rotterdam and Atlantic trade; as kinsmen they enjoyed a new level of trust and mutual interest, with a welter of relations and loved ones in common. Both the tone and the subject of their correspondence changed when Winthrop and Reade became 'brothers'.[34]

Samuel Symonds joined this fraternity when he married Elizabeth Reade's sister Martha in 1638. Symonds already had ten children by his first marriage to Dorothy Harlakenden, and he retained close ties to the influential Harlakenden family in Essex. This new marriage expanded his panoply of kin without necessarily shrinking his array of existing ties. When he married Martha, Symonds allied himself to the Reades, and simultaneously became an affinal kinsman to the Winthrops.[35] Martha Symonds (née Reade) had formerly been married to Daniel Eps, a gentleman of Kent, so Symonds and his battery of relations became connected to the Eps family as well. Martha moved to New England after Daniel Eps died in 1637, and soon married Samuel Symonds, who came from her home county of Essex. Martha's son, Daniel Eps, Jr., who became Samuel Symonds's stepson, bound the families further together when in 1644 he married his stepsister Elizabeth Symonds, Samuel Symonds's eldest daughter by his Harlakenden marriage.[36]

---

[33] M.H.S. *Collections*, ser. 4, vol. 7 (1865), p. 135. For the Winthrop-Reade connection see Robert C. Black III, *The Younger John Winthrop* (New York, 1966), pp. 80, 83, and Dunn, *Puritans and Yankees*, p. 66.

[34] M.H.S. *Collections*, ser. 4, vol. 7 (1865), pp. 113–16; *Winthrop Papers*, vol. 3, pp. 194, 206–7, 233–4.

[35] M.H.S. *Collections*, se. 4, vol. 7 (1865), p. 102; Savage, *Genealogical Dictionary*, vol. 4, p. 246; Abraham Hammatt, *The Hammatt Papers: The Early Inhabitants of Ipswich, Massachusetts 1633–1700* (Ipswich, Mass., 1899), pp. 355–60; William Sumner Appleton, *Ancestry of Priscilla Baker Who Lived 1674–1731* (Cambridge, Mass., 1870), pp. 24, 62, 103–9; For the Harlakenden family see *N.E.H.G.R*, 120 (1966), pp. 246–7.

[36] Savage, *Genealogical Dictionary*, vol. 2, p. 125. For the Eps family see *N.E.H.G.R.*, 71 (1917), pp. 91–2.

The Reade family connection also made the preacher Hugh Peter a kinsman of the Symondses and Winthrops. After old Edmund Reade died in 1623, his widow (née Cooke) married Hugh Peter. Peter therefore assumed the mantle of stepfather to Reade's six children, and ultimately gained kin connections with whomever those children married. Samuel Reade, eldest of the Reade children, wrote in 1636 to his 'loving brother' John Winthrop, Jr., mentioning letters recently received from 'my father' Hugh Peter.[37] Besides acknowledging Hugh Peter's position in an active Anglo-American family circle, this fragment illustrates the common adoption of intimate family terms like 'father' and 'brother' for relations acquired by marriage.

Hugh Peter discharged some of his kinship responsibilities when he wrote to the senior John Winthrop in 1641 suggesting a further marriage within the extended family.

I have a near cousin, with him a Justice of Peace's daughter with him very hopeful, and as handsome as any in the country, two hundred pounds for present and hopes to have one hundred more. I wish your sons, any, would take her and it. I am now seeking out a husband for her but wish yours far better every way. She is lately by her friends, my kindred, commended to my care. I am sometimes thinking of Thomas Reade though I have my fears.[38]

Later that year, when Hugh Peter and John Winthrop, Jr., journeyed back to England on the same ship, they shared more than seasickness and a common professional interest in the fate of God's people. One was technically step-father-in-law to the other, and each could call the other's kinsmen 'cousins'.[39]

The middle of the seventeenth century found brothers and sisters of the Reade, Symonds, Winthrop and Harlakenden families scattered throughout New England and the British Isles. Three Reade sisters, now Elizabeth Winthrop, Martha Symonds and Margaret Lake, had settled in New England. Their brother Thomas Reade had lived with them at Salem for a few years in the 1630s before returning to England. The other brothers, Samuel and William Reade, never crossed the ocean. Samuel Symonds and his immediate family established themselves at Ipswich, Massachusetts, while other Symondses stayed close to Great Yeldham in Essex. Symonds's kinsmen, the Harlakendens of Essex, had cousins and other relations in New England, as well as an important clan in East Anglia. Two siblings, Roger and Mabel Harlakenden, migrated to Massachusetts in 1635, and made

---

[37] *Winthrop Papers*, vol. 3, pp. 233–4, 206–7.
[38] *Winthrop Papers*, vol. 4, p. 316.
[39] *Ibid.*, p. 342; Dunn, *Puritans and Yankees*, p. 70.

productive marriages. Each could claim kin with dozens of settlers in the colonies and with scores of relations back home.

A large segment of the Winthrop family had relocated in America, but John Winthrop, Jr., made a habit of returning to England, and always found cousins and kinsmen waiting for him in London and East Anglia. Lucy Downing, John Jr.'s aunt, who had herself spent five years in New England, organized homecomings and spread New England news among a growing circle of kin.[40] Deane Tyndal's fear of 1629, that the distance of place would prevent emigrants and their English loved ones being 'useful and comfortable one to another', proved largely ungrounded, at least for this particular group of families. Despite their dispersal, they continued to follow the vital events in each other's lives and to support each other, by proxy or face to face, whenever possible.

Samuel Symonds and John Winthrop, Jr., continued as close friends. They exchanged letters between Massachusetts and Connecticut, and used their extensive connections to aid relations and to promote family affairs on both sides of the Atlantic. Each received frequent communications from England and passed them to the other for distribution to the rest of the family. Their English letters included reports of births and deaths, illnesses and achievements, so that even news of kinsmen who did not engage in correspondence reached distant quarters of the world.[41]

In 1654 Symonds sent a note to his 'brother' John Winthrop, Jr., asking him to 'tell my Sister Lake that the former news concerning her husband to be dead was untrue; they now write it was mistaken, and that he is living'. Hugh Peter wrote from England to confirm this intelligence that 'John Lake is alive and lusty'.[42] This was not altogether welcome news. John Lake had abandoned his wife Margaret Lake (née Reade), sister-in-law to both Winthrop and Symonds and stepdaughter to Hugh Peter, and left her in the miserable condition of not knowing whether her husband was alive or dead. Margaret's family possessed especially active lines of communication, but they were no match for John Lake's determination to disappear. The

[40] The reconstruction of this dense kinship network is based on relevant sections of Savage, *Genealogical Dictionary*; *N.E.H.G.R.*, *passim*; Henry F. Waters, *Genealogical Gleanings in England* (Boston, 1901); Hammatt, *Early Inhabitants of Ipswich, Massachusetts*; Appleton, *Ancestry of Priscilla Baker*; *The Probate Records of Essex County*, 3 vols. (Salem, 1916–20); *Winthrop Papers*; and various M.H.S. *Collections*.

[41] Symonds placed his son, significantly named Harlakenden Symonds, in charge of John Winthrop, Jr., for education at New London, Black, *The Younger John Winthrop*, p. 172; M.H.S. *Collections*, ser. 4, vol. 7 (1865), pp. 114–36.

[42] M.H.S. *Collections*, ser. 4, vol. 7 (1865), pp. 128, 130, 204.

Reades at home in England did their best for Margaret and her children, but the results were unsatisfactory. She then turned to her kinsfolk in New England for relief. Margaret Lake first settled at Ipswich, Massachusetts, under the eye of the Symondses, but by 1654 she was living at Pequot, Connecticut, close to her sister Elizabeth, more or less a Winthrop family dependent.[43] The fact that these extended families were not co-residential did not lessen their emotional and supportive power.

The intelligence that John Lake had turned up alive in England frustrated any plans that Margaret might have had to remarry. It also reminded the family that they had been cheated of an old inheritance. Edmund Reade had named Margaret's children John and Anna Lake as legatees, awarding them each fifty pounds in his will of 1623. More than a quarter of a century had passed, but they had never seen the money. Pressed by their 'sister' Lake, Samuel Symonds and John Winthrop, Jr., undertook to recover the bequest. They discussed the problem of the Reade inheritance in several letters of the 1650s and 1660s and canvassed their kinsmen back home.[44]

The Winthrop-Symonds-Reade nexus stayed active throughout the period of the Commonwealth and Restoration. When Fitz-John Winthrop, John Jr.'s son, went to England in 1658 at the age of nineteen, his father instructed him to make the most of the family network in the Old World, cultivating 'such of your uncles and aunts as are yet living, and other kindred and friends whether in England or Scotland'. The young colonial had access to a useful extended family. Dutifully he presented himself to his expectant English kin. Fitz-John remembered a few of his aunts and uncles, like the Downings who had spent some years in New England, but other relations were complete strangers. His father specifically instructed him to search out 'a kinsman of ours, Captain Gostlin'. In case Fitz-John Winthrop had forgotten that he had a cousin Gostlin, John Jr. explained, 'His father lived at Groton in Suffolk where your grandfather Winthrop and we lived. His mother was your grandfather Winthrop's own sister. I should be glad to hear of them all.'[45] Thomas Gostlin

---

[43] For the Lake family see *N.E.H.G.R.*, 84 (1930), pp. 304–16; Black, *The Younger John Winthrop*, 138.

[44] Appleton, *Ancestry of Priscilla Baker*, pp. 119–24; M.H.S. *Proceedings* (1862–3), pp. 254–8; M.H.S. *Collections*, ser. 4, vol. 7 (1865), pp. 114, 135.

[45] M.H.S. *Collections*, ser. 5, vol. 8 (1882), pp. 51, 52. Thomas Gostlin had written to Governor John Winthrop in 1640, tendering respect to 'cousin John and his wife ... cousin Dudley and his wife ... also to Stephen, Adam, Dean, Samuel and all the rest of our cousins and friends. ... Commend me also to my cousin Feke and tell her she still have an aunt in old England'; *Winthrop Papers*, vol. 4, pp. 212–3. John

and his son Benjamin had kept up a periodic correspondence with their Winthrop kinsmen in the 1630s and 1640s. Almost a generation later John Winthrop, Jr., used the opportunity of his son's visit to England to renew communication with a family extension in East Anglia, placing in his son's way whatever advantages might accrue from this renewal of the connection.

Fitz-John arrived in England, a land he had never seen, bearing a sheaf of letters and introductions. His English relations embraced him with warmth and generosity, befitting a returning kinsman. Immediately he spun in a swirl of family goodwill. He carried letters from his uncle Samuel Symonds to the Symonds kindred in Essex. His uncle Stephen Winthrop took care of him in London, opening the door to a military career. His great aunt Lucy Downing confided, 'Your uncle Colonel Reade . . . will be very glad to see you and to use his best endeavours for your preferment.'[46] The family greased the wheels of patronage, diligently engaging in nepotism. A message from Thomas Reade told Fitz-John that he 'should be very welcome to him, and he should be studious for his improvement, as far as in his power'. Emmanuel Downing would 'not be wanting to the same purpose' and 'was very mindful of him, if in his power to suit him with employment'. Hugh Peter offered to look after his young kinsman's interests 'upon a better account', with concern for his spiritual welfare as well as advantageous placement.[47]

Kinsmen in England tendered their services to their American visitor almost sight unseen. Although Fitz-John Winthrop came highly recommended, it was his lineage rather than his personality that interested the Reades, the Downings and the rest. A common ground in religion and politics offered additional satisfaction, but what really counted was affinity and blood.

John Winthrop, Jr., himself returned to this circle of support and affection when he came over to England in 1661 as agent for Connecticut. He brought with him his younger son Wait, so for a while there were three American Winthrops in London. Although burdened with official business, John Winthrop, Jr., continued to serve as an intermediary for members of his extended family. The former Reade sisters all had messages for their English cousins, and Samuel

Winthrop, Jr., had some dealings with his English cousin Benjamin Gostlin a few years later at the time of the Connecticut charter negotiations; Black, *The Younger John Winthrop*, pp. 216, 219–20.

[46] M.H.S. *Collections*, ser. 5, vol. 1 (1871), pp. 44–7.

[47] *Ibid.* See also Dunn, *Puritans and Yankees*, pp. 195–8.

Symonds sent further greetings to his Harlakenden kindred in Essex.[48]

Samuel Symonds never returned to England, but his relations back home were often on his mind. He told John Winthrop, Jr.,

I have still one brother living. He hath a good estate; he is a batchelor. When I was in England he loved me well. I know not now how I am in his mind, but brother if you did make a journey to see him, and, as occasion may be taken, to speak of me as you shall see good, I shall add this courtesy to your former high deservings. The rest of my cousins are, I take it, well provided for. I am loath to be as one utterly forgotten by one so related, if God see meet. But I confess it is a tender string, and he hath need of wisdom that can finger it well. He dwelleth at the Poole in Much Yeldham, near Castle Hedingham in Essex, about six miles from Earls Colne, where my kindred of the Harlakendens live, which if also you please to visit, kindly commending me to them all and every one of them, it will be very grateful.

This renewal of contact evidently paid off, for when Richard Fitz Symonds wrote his will in 1663 he left money to his brother and nephews in Massachusetts.[49]

Symonds urged Winthrop while he was in England to find and copy 'our father Mr. Edmund Reade's will'. Margaret Lake herself sent a follow-up letter to her 'brother', imploring him 'to be as helpful as you can' in the matter of the will. Winthrop and Symonds both expended energy on the project, not simply to placate an ill-used relation, but because such kinsmanlike activity was expected, and family honour was involved. In pursuing this almost-forgotten legacy they acted as exemplary advocates for the family at large, employing their legal and political resources on the family behalf. If money was due then it should be paid, as a matter of principle, but Margaret Lake may have found more gratification in seeing her powerful kinsmen exercise themselves in this matter than in any immediate hopes of financial recovery.[50]

By this time Margaret Lake had heard that her runaway husband was truly dead. She asked her 'brother' Winthrop to perform the 'courtesy' of finding out 'how he ended his days, as also ... whether there was anything left me or no'. She also wanted Winthrop to send news of 'my cousin Thomas Cooke' and other distant kin: 'I would desire you enquire whether my sister Breadcale, who dwells in Lee in Essex, be living. You may hear of her, if living, at Irongate where

[48] M.H.S. *Collections*, ser. 4, vol. 7 (1865), p. 136.
[49] *Ibid.*, pp. 135–6; Appleton, *Ancestry of Priscilla Baker*, pp. 46–50, 70.
[50] M.H.S. *Collections*, ser. 4, vol. 7 (1865), p. 135; ser. 5, vol. 1 (1871), p. 99.

boats come weekly from Lee.'[51] Poor Margaret Lake, living out her twilight years in Connecticut, and forever grieving over lost inheritances and a missing husband, still had a vivid picture in her mind of the barges and bustle of Essex and London. Facilitating contact with her sisters and cousins was the least that John Winthrop, Jr., could do to gratify an ageing relation. Thomas Cooke was Margaret's cousin on her mother's side, of Essex yeoman stock; 'sister Breadcale' meant Elizabeth Breadcake (née Lake), Margaret's sister-in-law, whose husband Thomas had spent some time at Salem. We do not know whether Winthrop succeeded in finding Thomas Cooke, but sadly the directions for locating Elizabeth Breadcake were unusable since she had already been dead for a decade.[52] Margaret Lake's relations represented the outer edge of the Winthrop-Reade orbit, where contact was weak and intermittent, but even these distant kin could occasionally be drawn into the circle.

Several of Samuel Symonds's sons and stepsons visited England in the 1660s and 1670s. They too were able to plunge straight into a seethe of relations. Whether they were born in England or America, and whether they visited England for business or pleasure, they applied themselves energetically to family affairs. As a calling card they brought family news, greetings from New England, and an introduction in terms of consanguinity, marriage or descent.

John Hall, Samuel Symonds's stepson by his third wife, crossed over to London to disentangle a contested legacy and decided, as he put it, 'to tarry longer in the land of my fathers sepulchres'. He not only wrote regularly (and intimately) to his mother in Massachusetts but also relayed family news to other kinsmen in New England, and transmitted their messages and greetings to relations in England. During the 1660s and 1670s, John Hall occupied an important position as an Anglo-American family intermediary, a nodal point in a widely-distributed kinship network. Like Fitz-John Winthrop, he arrived in London with a sheaf of introductions and messages. His Symonds stepfather proved especially helpful and pulled strings for the young colonial with his Symonds kinsmen in Essex.[53]

Besides his Symonds relations, Hall tapped into a complex extended family on his mother's side, since Rebecca, born Swayne, had been married to Henry Byley, John Hall, Sr., and William Worcester before marrying Samuel Symonds. Remnants and extensions of all these

[51] *Ibid.*, ser. 5, vol. 1 (1871), p. 99.
[52] *N.E.H.G.R.*, 84 (1930), pp. 304–16; Peter Wilson Coldham (ed.), *English Adventurers and Emigrants, 1609–1660* (Baltimore, 1984), p. 53.
[53] A.A.S. MSS. 'Letters of John Hall', 3 May 1664, 11 March 1663.

families were scattered on both sides of the Atlantic, and John Hall and his mother endeavoured to keep track of them. Over the next twenty years Hall had dealings with dozens of English and American kinsmen. His contacts included relations of his long-dead father, kinsmen by marriage through his mother's successive husbands, and the Symonds circle in East Anglia and Massachusetts. These people by far outnumbered the non-kin associates and friends mentioned in his letters. Writing home to his mother at Ipswich in New England, John Hall sent news of 'my uncle Swayne', 'aunt Joan', stepbrothers Henry Byley and Samuel Symonds, Jr., 'my cousin John Rolfe', 'my cousin Banks Kenton', and more. In 1663 he transmitted messages for Samuel Symonds, 'whose kinsman in Essex desires to hear from him'. He saw 'Mr. Symonds of Essex' again in 1666, 'who desired to be recommended to my father'. Hall's visitors from New England included his stepbrother Harlakenden Symonds and his cousin Samuel Eps, and his circle widened to include their relations. By his will of 1691 John Hall left legacies to his mother in Massachusetts, his wife and daughter in Middlesex, and a string of relations including 'my cousin Robert Hale, my sister Rebecca Hale's son... my uncle Mr. Bennett Swayne and my aunt Swayne', aunts Rotherford and Oliver, and cousins Hale, Evans, Ackerod, Leadford, Soutton and Hall.[54]

Transatlantic kinship bonds were strongest in the generation of first settlement, and were revived by back-migration, but an inevitable attenuation set in during later years. Without occasional visits, face-to-face contact or at least the memory of personal interaction, the emotional intensity of these linkages began to fade. Correspondence between the Reades, Symonds and Winthrops, however, continued beyond the end of the seventeenth century, demonstrating that the connections could be maintained. After Colonel Thomas Reade died in 1662, John Winthrop, Jr., wrote from Hartford, Connecticut, to comfort the widow Priscilla Reade in London with an exchange of news about the welfare and whereabouts of various cousins, nephews and more distant kin in England and abroad. Among those Priscilla hoped would help her in her widowhood was 'cousin Eps', her Symonds relation who could link her to the Halls. Although part of her family lived in New England, 'far off, and can't do me that help you would', Priscilla Reade nonetheless considered them, as they considered her, perpetually available for comfort and support.[55]

---

[54] 'Letters of John Hall', 21 April 1663, 21 May 1666, and *passim*. For Hall's family see *N.E.H.G.R.*, 3 (1849), p. 55; 47 (1893), pp. 136–39, 245, 506–9; 52 (1898), 44–45, 50; Waters, *Genealogical Gleanings*, pp. 683, 687, 780–2.
[55] *M.H.S. Collections*, ser. 5, vol. 1 (1871), pp. 100–1.

When John Symonds of Great Yeldham, Essex, died in 1694 his widow Jane Symonds, niece by marriage to Samuel Symonds of Massachusetts, wrote to her kinsman Fitz-John Winthrop to report her husband's death. Sending love and respect to all her relations in New England, she desired 'in particular to be remembered to my cousin Harlakenden Symonds, who is the only one I know there, and to the rest pray give my service though unknown'. Although she had never seen New England she felt a sense of community with distant relations there, a feeling they reciprocated. Twenty-two years had passed since Harlakenden Symonds's visit to Essex, yet still it stirred memories among the elderly at Great Yeldham.[56]

Remnants of this kinship network still operated in 1699 when Adam Winthrop of Boston ventured into trade with England. Adam turned for help to his Connecticut cousin Fitz-John Winthrop, who had recently returned from representing the colony in the old country. Fitz-John in turn applied for assistance from his kinsman Samuel Reade in England. Samuel was the only surviving son of Fitz-John's old army commander Thomas Reade, and grandson to the patriarch Edmund Reade through whom so many of the leading colonists and stay-at-homes were related. Samuel Reade and Fitz-John Winthrop inherited the habit of correspondence that had begun with the previous generation. Writing from London in 1706, Samuel complained to his 'dear cousin' Fitz-John that more than six months had passed since last hearing from him. He closed his letter, 'With service to our relations, rest Sir, your affectionate kinsman and servant, Samuel Reade.'[57] Though conventional and formulaic, these phrases reinforced and summarized the extended family connections of the previous seventy years.

〜〜〜〜〜〜

The seventeenth-century kinship system, as illustrated by the examples in this chapter, was egocentric and bilateral, contextual and informal. Far from being narrow, shallow and restricted, as kinship in early-modern England is often depicted, the system was highly flexible, adaptive and wide-ranging.[58] Kin consciousness centred on the nuclear family and its immediate extensions, but more distant relations

---

[56] *Ibid.*, p. 111.
[57] M.H.S. *Collections*, ser. 5, vol. 8 (1882), p. 364; ser. 6, vol. 3 (1889), p. 328.
[58] This discussion is based on Cressy, 'Kinship and kin interaction'; Alan Macfarlane, *The Family Life of Ralph Josselin* (Cambridge, 1970), pp. 105–60; and Keith Wrightson, *English Society 1580–1680* (London, 1982), pp. 44–51.

could readily be drawn in. Depending on circumstances, even latent kin could become effective, and distant kin could come close. Such was the case when Mary Elwald and Daniel Hemingway contacted their relations in Massachusetts, or when John Hall returned to his aunts and cousins in England.

The family of solidarity extended much wider than the family of residence. Awareness of kinship by affinity and blood stretched much farther than the immediate family of siblings and surviving parents to embrace a range of relations, uncles and aunts, in-laws and cousins at various degrees of removal. Any one of them might be called upon to perform a favour. We find distant relations, virtual strangers who lived on opposite sides of the Atlantic, seeking assistance and offering mutual support on the sole ground of acknowledgement of kin. Not enough is known about kin interaction elsewhere to judge whether these families were unusual in this regard, but the evidence that survives shows their effective orbit of kin to have been broad in its compass and generous in its effect. Although the *frequency* of interaction among kin cannot be measured, and may have been slight, the *value* of such contacts was potentially enormous.

Family linkage served as a lubricant in a variety of social, political, and economic transactions, involving a host of tangible and intangible benefits and obligations. To the Winthrops and Reades, and to the other families connected with them, a dense and extended kindred was a store of wealth, to be drawn on as need arose. Members of these Anglo-American families drew on distant and latent kin, as well as on closer relations, whenever the circumstances suited them. Neither distance in miles nor distance in genealogical relationship posed disabling barriers.

In this egocentric system, each individual formed the hub of a distinctive kinship 'universe', surrounded by relations who might be acknowledged and utilized. We can depict the system graphically by showing in Figures 12 and 13 the kinship universe of selected individuals. To choose a Winthrop for this purpose would produce a crowded chart, and in any case could be challenged as unrepresentative since this much-studied family had exceptional resources at its disposal. Shown instead are the kinship universes of Margaret Lake and John Hall, minor players in the Anglo-American drama but each the interested central 'ego' of their particular family networks.

The evidence presented here clearly demonstrates how kinship ties linking England and New England could survive the wrench of emigration to persist throughout the seventeenth century. Newcomers to the colonies, no matter when they arrived, usually brought with

In New England | In England

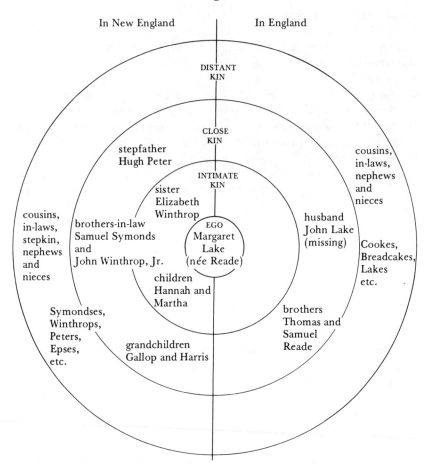

DISTANT
KIN

CLOSE
KIN

stepfather
Hugh Peter

cousins,
in-laws,
nephews
and
nieces

INTIMATE
KIN

sister
Elizabeth
Winthrop

cousins,
in-laws,
stepkin,
nephews
and
nieces

brothers-in-law
Samuel Symonds
and
John Winthrop, Jr.

EGO
Margaret
Lake
(née Reade)

husband
John Lake
(missing)

Cookes,
Breadcakes,
Lakes
etc.

children
Hannah and
Martha

Symondses,
Winthrops,
Peters,
Epses,
etc.

grandchildren
Gallop and Harris

brothers
Thomas and
Samuel
Reade

Figure 12.   Kinship universe of Margaret Lake, 1598–1672

them direct knowledge and experience of their extended family in
old England. They retained memories and family lore based on face-
to-face dealings with their English kin. Opportunities for family cohe-
sion were further reinforced if kinsfolk migrated together, or if other
relations came over to join them. Similarly, New Englanders returning
to old England reactivated family associations. Their correspondence
and other dealings joined brothers, brothers-in-law, parents, children,
husbands, wives, nephews, uncles, cousins, and other kinsmen in a
transatlantic community of care, support and information. Even if
the network was only infrequently activated, that did not detract from
its potential utility and enduring significance.

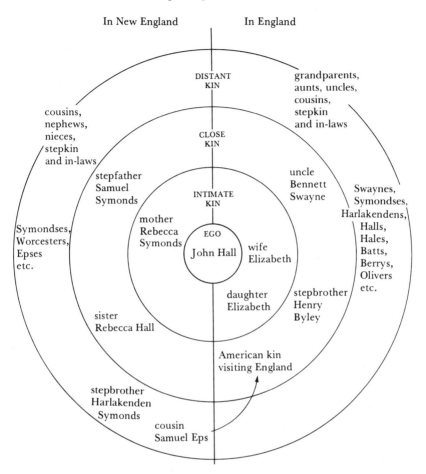

In New England   In England

DISTANT
KIN

grandparents,
aunts, uncles,
cousins,
stepkin
and in-laws

cousins,
nephews,
nieces,
stepkin
and in-laws

CLOSE
KIN

stepfather
Samuel
Symonds

uncle
Bennett
Swayne

INTIMATE
KIN

Swaynes,
Symondses,
Harlakendens,

mother
Rebecca
Symonds

EGO
John Hall

wife
Elizabeth

Halls,
Hales,
Batts,
Berrys,
Olivers
etc.

Symondses,
Worcesters,
Epses
etc.

daughter
Elizabeth

stepbrother
Henry
Byley

sister
Rebecca Hall

American kin
visiting England

stepbrother
Harlakenden
Symonds

cousin
Samuel Eps

Figure 13.   Kinship universe of John Hall, 1642–91

Colonists born and raised in New England, on the other hand, usually lacked the direct experience of English kinsmen on which the primary networks were based. The kinship universes of most New Englanders of the second generation were mostly American. Usually they married locally and built their kinship networks in the colonies. Unless they made visits to the homeland, or unless their English kinsmen moved to New England, they had to depend on information transmitted by parents, family stories, and the limited vicarious contact of correspondence. In these circumstances the family across the water could grow dim and attenuated.

Reminders of England probably became less frequent as settlement moved inland, away from the opportunity to glean news from seafarers and travellers, so colonists of the second and subsequent generations risked drifting apart from their English kinsmen. Unless replenished by new migrant streams or renewed through political, religious or mercantile correspondence, the family links of the early eighteenth century were likely to be more tenuous than those of the 1640s or 1670s.

Yet opportunities for long-distance kin contact continued to arise, and circumstances or necessity sometimes thrust them together again. Prompted by trade or travel, by news of an unexpected legacy, or by petitions from unknown relations, distant cousins of a younger generation could reactivate the transatlantic kinship network of their elders. The circle might adapt to strange configurations, yet remain unbroken.

When New Englanders of the second generation visited old England on business they not only called on their living relatives but also displayed a keen interest in their family origins. Some of them even developed an interest in English genealogy. John Hall visited his mother's home town in Wiltshire, and sought out half-remembered relations. John Hull of Boston took time in 1662 to examine the parish register at his wife's birthplace in Northamptonshire. (He may have been checking on her age or parentage.) The merchant Jonathan Curwen of Salem also travelled to Northamptonshire, where, he noted in his diary, 'I went to my grandmother Herbert.' Samuel Sewall similarly used the opportunity of his visit to England in 1689 to explore his roots and to learn about his family. Besides visiting living uncles and cousins, he saw his grandfather's name in a parish register and stood by his aunt Dorothy's grave.[59]

Less mobile New Englanders could use other means to satisfy their curiosity. John Leverett sent to old England in 1672 for a transcript of the Leverett family baptisms from the Boston parish register. Daniel Denison of Ipswich, Massachusetts, writing to his grandchildren in 1672, 'thought it meet to acquaint you with your predecessors and your descent from them'. He then related a family saga populated by a broad array of English and American ancestors, cousins and kins-

---

[59] A.A.S. MSS. 'Letters of John Hall'; [Hull], 'The diaries of John Hull', A.A.S. *Transactions*, 3 (1857), p. 152; A.A.S. MSS. 'Account book of John Corwin'; (Sewall), *The Diary of Samuel Sewall 1674–1729*, ed. M. Halsey Thomas (New York, 1973), pp. 196, 209.

men, who had stayed in touch through memory, visits and correspondence.[60]

Families like the Symondses and Halls, Winthrops and Reades, kept up a transatlantic correspondence, braced by occasional visits back and forth, which lasted for more than half a century. These contacts solidified an emotional attachment between kinsfolk in England and New England at a time when politics and economics seemed to pull the two societies apart. The letters of support or condolence, the mourning rings and other tokens that passed between them, kept the sense of kindred alive, even as ageing members of the network died. Sometimes they laboured with imperfect information, and acted on news that was wrong or out of date. Sometimes messages went astray, and loved ones drifted beyond the reach of available communications. Sometimes, indeed, they did not know whether their relations were alive or dead. Yet always the means existed to renew the links.

[60] Robert E. Moody (ed.), *The Saltonstall Papers, 1607–1815* (Boston, 1972), vol. 1, p. 162; (Denison), 'Autobiography of Major-General Daniel Denison', *N.E.H.G.R.*, 46 (1892), pp. 127–32. See also Harrison Tilghman, 'Letters between the English and American branches of the Tilghman family, 1697–1764', *Maryland Historical Magazine*, 33 (1938), pp. 152–3.

Epilogue

I have argued here that many of the people who went to New England did so on the basis of inadequate information and that their motives for migration were by no means clear-cut. Puritanism was obviously important, providing an inspiration, a vocabulary and a rationale, but it is by no means certain that the majority of New England's settlers were driven by religion. Most people's decisions involved random and personal factors as much as reasoned calculation, and even the celebrated Puritan leaders were often seeking resolution to the problem of thwarted prospects and unsuccessful lives. Many migrants regretted their move, and some of them went back home. English affairs, both public and private, continued to be important elements in the emotional life and in the business dealings of many seventeenth-century colonists. The most prominent New Englanders, and many lesser lights, cultivated and cherished their transatlantic family connections.

Some of these observations go against the grain of current American historiography. Early America, in this account, is much more fragile, its purpose more tentative, its identity less robust. The colonies appear pinched and provincial when viewed from the standpoint of Stuart England, but this is how many people in the seventeenth century, on both sides of the ocean, considered them. Massachusetts and its neighbours were fragments of English culture and society, but they were never utterly detached from their origins. During the first few generations of settlement the colonists looked homeward rather than towards an American future.

Seventeenth-century New England was an English province, and many of its features – a literate culture overlaying oral traditionalism, a market economy with an agrarian base, an individualistic and competitive social order in tension with commonweal communalism – had long been part of old England. These features were not the product of 'Anglicization', 'Americanization' or 'modernization', but existed from the beginning as part of the settlers' 'English ways' and 'cultural baggage'. Of course, the absence of feudalism and the demands of the frontier made a difference, but much of American 'exceptionalism' founders against comparative English history. Recent work by other historians on commerce, diplomacy, the family, evangelism, law, custom and the flow of information within the Atlantic community bolsters these conclusions, and may make some of them seem old hat.

New England began with a truncated social structure, in which the traditional aristocracy and the poor were missing. But social differentiation increased with time. The colonies soon had their gentle elite and their strolling poor, although never to the extremes of old England. English visitors found late seventeenth-century New England mean and backward, but they did not find it ineffably strange.

The Puritan religious leadership, with its control of the organs of government, was one feature of New England that contrasted strongly with the more heterogeneous and secular traditions in the old country. Only the 'godly rule' of the 1650s in England bears comparison to the interlock of pulpit and magistracy in Massachusetts. The Church of England was latitudinarian from its beginnings, despite the efforts of Whitgift and Laud, while the English Christian magistracy acted independently of the church. The sheer diversity of religious expression in England, especially after the revolution, makes New England appear narrow and austere. But studies of popular religion in the colonies may alter this impression. New England's 'declension' sermons indicate the insecurity rather than the hegemony of later-Stuart American Puritanism.

Many of the threads that bound England and New England together were wearing thin by the beginning of the eighteenth century. Although imperial and commercial links were strong, and may have been getting stronger, the personal ties between colonists and their contemporaries in metropolitan Britain gradually became attenuated. American provincial patriotism eventually supplanted wistfulness for old England. Localist sentiment narrowed the vision and shrank the world. The vast majority of the inhabitants of Massachusetts in 1700 had been born in America, and increasingly they referred to themselves, and not just to the defeated Indians, as 'Americans'.

Colonial New Englanders of the third and fourth generations still cared about their cousins, but they were more likely to find them as neighbours or in nearby towns than across the ocean. Local kinship links among the settlers and their descendants mattered more than their increasingly tenuous connections overseas. England became as remote in the mind of ordinary New Englanders as the colonies had nearly always been for people in Britain. Most New Englanders in the age of Cotton Mather were probably quite satisfied with this state of affairs. Not for them the homesickness or transatlantic yearnings of their elders and forebears. Colonists who had previously experienced London might complain about isolation on the 'outskirts of the earth', but for those who only knew America, their own piece of ground was the centre of the world.

≈≈≈≈≈≈≈

Many more questions present themselves than can be considered here. To the discussion of what people in England knew about New England we might add consideration of their respective knowledge and impressions of the other migrant destinations, Virginia, Maryland, Bermuda and the Caribbean. Similar questions could be asked about migrant readiness for Canada or Australia in the nineteenth century. The comparative focus might be sharpened by a study of regional perceptions within Great Britain. If Londoners and East Anglians were often ignorant of America, how much did they know, and what misconceptions did they have, of northern England, Ireland or Scotland? In what ways has geographical literacy changed since the beginnings of transoceanic migration and since the various revolutions in communication?

The information exchange between England and New England, especially the export of news about the English political emergency and civil wars, should be considered in its metropolitan as well as its colonial context. The Wyllys and Winthrop families in America were well informed because they were members of the English Puritan gentry, and leaders of the 'county community' in New England. Although no longer enfranchised in England, they remained members of the English 'political nation'. How did their information about the crisis in London compare with the information available to minor gentlemen in Cornwall or Cumberland? To what extent did their humbler neighbours share their interest in high politics and religion? How alert to these matters were the labourers and the smaller farmers of New England, and would their involvement have been very different if they had remained at home in Warwickshire or Suffolk? If they were Puritans, by conviction or convenience, how did they see themselves, their situation and their place in the world? How comparable were their networks of patronage and kinship to those of their contemporaries in England?

New England's involvement with the homeland could be compared to that of other settler societies in the seventeenth century and later. It is likely that the protestant planters of Ireland, the servants who went to the Chesapeake and the free migrants who later went to Australia and New Zealand also experienced ambivalent feelings about their place of settlement and their country of origin. How common were these back-directed sentiments, and were they a stimulus or a brake to colonial development? Nor should these questions be confined to the British diaspora, since similar stories might be found among the Germans, the French, the Scandinavians and the Spanish.

Finally, the question arises as to when and how the immigrants reconciled themselves to the American continent and to an American future. Involved in this question are matters of identity, localism, nationalism and relationships with the wider world, which have been under discussion for more than three hundred years.

Bibliography

1. Manuscript sources

AMERICAN ANTIQUARIAN SOCIETY (A.A.S.)

'Account book of Dr. John Barton, 1662–1676'
'Account book of John Corwin, 1655–1685'
'Boston papers, 1634–1893'
'Increase Mather's diary, 1659–1717'
'Letter book of John Hull, 1670–1685'
'Letters of John Hall, 1663–1685'
'Records of the Council for New England, 1622–23'

BEINECKE LIBRARY, YALE UNIVERSITY

Osborne Files, 'Newsletter describing English settlements in New England, etc.', 24 December 1645 (Robert Child to Samuel Hartlib?)

BODLEIAN LIBRARY

Tanner 68, 314

BOSTON PUBLIC LIBRARY

Am. 1502/1/12
Am. 1502/2/34–37
Am. 1502/5/11–12
'Boston town papers, 1637–1733'
MS. q.BOS.679.1, 'Strangers bonds, 1679–1700'

BRITISH LIBRARY

Add. 24516
Egerton 2526
Sloan 922
Stowe 746

Bibliography

DORSET RECORD OFFICE

B2/8/1, 'Dorchester borough records, court book'
B2/16/5, 'Dorchester Corporation minutes'
B2/28/1, 'A Catalogue of the bookes in the library of
    Dorchester, with the givers, taken in the yeare 1631'

ESSEX INSTITUTE

Curwen Papers
Philip English Papers
Essex County Court Papers, 1686

GUILDHALL LIBRARY

MS. 7936, 'Original correspondence of the New England Company 1657–
    1714'
MS. 7938, 'Papers relating to the proceedings of the Corporation for Prop-
    agating the Gospel in New England' (transcript of Bodleian Library, Raw-
    linson MS. C.934)

LANCASHIRE RECORD OFFICE

QSP/284/5

MARYLAND HISTORICAL SOCIETY

Ms. 1699, 'Edward Rhode's journal'

MASSACHUSETTS HISTORICAL SOCIETY (M.H.S.)

'Miscellaneous, bound'
'Diary of John Marshall, 1689–1711' (microfilm)

MASSACHUSETTS ARCHIVES

Vols. 8, 9, 15A, 39, 57, 60, 69, 100

NORFOLK RECORD OFFICE

Accn. 21.8.81, R152 C
Norwich Archdeaconry Wills
Ormesby St. Margaret parish register
PD 78/47; PD 90/1; PD 209/167

PUBLIC RECORD OFFICE (P.R.O.)

C2/Chas I/B86/3; C2/Chas I/B93/34   CO.1/9/101, 113
E.157/20
E.190/38, 43, 490, 604, 824, 875–6, 947–50

Bibliography

PC2/42–51
SP16/260/13–17
SP16/267/67
SP16/278/65
SP. Domestic and Foreign, Miscellaneous, no. 26
G., A. D. M., 'Ships, merchants and passengers to the American colonies 1618–1668', typescript (1982)

2. Printed primary sources

Acts of the Privy Council, Colonial Series, 1613–1680 (London, 1908).
An Advertisement Concerning the Province of East New Jersey in America, Published for the Information of Such as Are Desireous to Be Concerned Therein, or to Transport Themselves Thereto (Edinburgh, 1685).
Alexander, William, *An Encouragement to Colonies* (London, 1624).
Alexander, William, *The Mapp and Description of New-England* (London, 1630).
Archives of Maryland, 54 vols. (Baltimore, 1883–1937).
Backhouse, James (ed.), *The Life and Correspondence of William and Alice Ellis* (London, 1849).
[Barnard], 'Autobiography of the Rev. John Barnard', in M.H.S. *Collections*, ser. 3, vol. 5 (1836), pp. 177–243.
Baxter, James Phinney (ed.), *Documentary History of the State of Maine*, vol.3, *'The Trelawny Papers'* (Portland, Maine, 1884).
Bishop, George, *New England Judged, Not by Man but by the Lord: And the Summe Sealed up of New-Englands Persecutions* (London, 1661).
The Book of the General Lawes and Libertyes Concerning the Inhabitants of the Massachusetts (Cambridge, Mass., 1648; facsimile San Marino, California, 1975).
Boston News-Letter, nos. 1–34 (1704).
Bouton, Nathaniel (ed.), *Documents and Records Relating to the Province of New Hampshire*, vol. 1, *1623–1686* (Concord, N.H., 1867).
Bradford, William, *History of Plymouth Plantation 1620–1647*, 2 vols. (Boston, 1912).
Bradford, William, *Of Plymouth Plantation 1620–1647*, ed. Samuel Eliot Morison (New York, 1963).
Brereton, John, *A Briefe and True Relation of the Discouerie of the North Part of Virginia; Being a Most Pleasant, Fruitful and Commodious Soile* (London, 1602).
Bridenbaugh, Carl (ed.), *The Pynchon Papers*, vol. 1 *Letters of John Pynchon, 1654–1700* (Boston, 1982).
Brigham, Clarence S. (ed.), 'The records of the Council for New England', A.A.S. *Proceedings*, n.s., 22 (1912), pp. 237–47.
'Broadsides, ballads, etc. printed in Massachusetts 1639–1800', M.H.S. *Collections*, 75 (1922).
Calder, Isabel MacBeath (ed.), *Letters of John Davenport* (New Haven, Conn., 1937).
Calendar of State Papers, Colonial Series, 1574–1660 (London, 1860).
Calendar of State Papers, Domestic, 1630–40 (London, 1857–1902).
Child, John, *New-Englands Jonas Cast up at London* (London, 1647), ed. W. T. R. Marvin (Boston, 1869).
[Clap], 'Roger Clap's memoirs', in Alexander Young (ed.), *Chronicles of the*

Bibliography

First Planters of the Colony of Massachusetts Bay, from 1623 to 1636 (1846; reprinted, Williamstown, Mass., 1978), pp. 343–67.

'The Clarendon papers', *Collections of the New York Historical Society* (New York, 1870).

Clarke, John, *Ill Newes from New-England, or, a Narrative of New-Englands Persecution*, in M.H.S. *Collections*, ser. 4, vol. 2 (1854), pp. 3–64.

Clayton, John, 'A letter... to the Royal Society', in Peter Force (ed.), *Tracts and Other Papers Relating... to the Origin, Settlement, and Progress of the Colonies* (Washington, D.C., 1844), vol. 3, no. 12.

Coldham, Peter Wilson (ed.), *English Adventurers and Emigrants, 1609–1660* (Baltimore, 1984).

Coldham, Peter Wilson (ed.), *Lord Mayor's Court of London Depositions Relating to Americans 1641–1736* (Washington, D.C., 1980).

(Colt), 'The voyage of Sir Henry Colt', in V. T. Harlow (ed.), *Colonising Expeditions to the West Indies and Guiana, 1623–1667* (London, 1925), pp. 54–100.

Conset, Henry, *The Practice of the Spiritual or Ecclesiastical Courts* (London, 1685).

Cope, John, *A Religious Inquisition* (London, 1629).

Cotton, John, *God's Promise to His Plantation* (London, 1630).

Cotton, John, *The Way of Congregational Churches Cleared* (London, 1648).

D., C., *New-Englands Faction Discovered* (London, 1690).

Danckaerts, Jasper, *Diary of Our Second Trip from Holland to New Netherland, 1683* (Upper Saddle River, N.J., 1969).

Dane, John, 'A declaration of remarkabell provedenses in the corse of my lyfe', in *N.E.H.G.R.*, 8 (1854), pp. 149–56.

Danforth, Samuel, *A Brief Recognition of New Englands Errand into the Wilderness* (Cambridge, Mass., 1671).

Davies, James, 'Relation of a voyage unto New England... 1607', ed. B. F. De Costa and Charles Deane, M.H.S. *Proceedings*, 18 (1880), pp. 82–117.

The Day-Breaking if not the Sun-Rising of the Gospel with the Indians in New-England (London, 1647).

Deane, Charles (ed.), 'Records of the Council for New England', A.A.S. *Proceedings* (1867), pp. 51–131; A.A.S. *Proceedings*(1876), pp. 49–63.

[Denison], 'Autobiography of Major-General Daniel Denison', *N.E.H.G.R.*, 46 (1892), pp. 127–32.

[Dudley], 'Dudley's letter to the Countess of Lincoln', in Alexander Young (ed.), *Chronicles of the First Planters of the Colony of Massachusetts Bay, from 1623 to 1636* (1846; reprinted, Williamstown, Mass., 1978), pp. 301–41.

Dunster, Henry, and/or Thomas Weld, *New-Englands First Fruits* (1643; reprinted, New York, 1865).

'Dunster papers', M.H.S. *Collections*, ser. 4, vol. 2 (1854), pp. 190–98.

Dunton, John, *The Life and Errors of John Dunton* (London, 1818).

Dunton, John, *Letters Written from New England, A.D. 1686*, ed. W. H. Whitmore (Boston, 1867).

Eburne, Richard, *A Plain Pathway to Plantations (1624)*, ed. Louis B. Wright (Ithaca, N.Y., 1962).

Emerson, Everett (ed.), *Letters from New England: The Massachusetts Bay Colony, 1629–1638* (Amherst, Mass., 1976).

Evelin, Robert, *Directions for Adventurers* (London, 1641).

Firth, C. H. and R. S. Rait (eds.), *Acts and Ordinances of the Interregnum*, 3 vols. (London, 1911).

Fleming, Robert, *The Fulfilling of the Scriptures* (London, 1669).

Force, Peter (ed.), *Tracts and Other Papers Relating . . . to the Origin, Settlement, and Progress of the Colonies* (Washington, D.C., 1844).

Fox, George, *Journal* (London, 1694).

Gardyner, George, *A Description of the New World. Or, America Islands and Continent* (London, 1651).

'Good news from New-England: with an exact relation of the first planting of that countrey' (London, 1648), reprinted in M.H.S. *Collections*, ser. 4, vol. 1 (1852), pp. 195–218.

Gordon, Sir Robert, *Encouragements for Such as Shall Have Intention to Be Under-Takers in the New Plantation* (Edinburgh, 1625).

Gorges, Sir Ferdinando, *America Painted to the Life* (London, 1659).

Green, Mary Ann Everett (ed.), *Diary of John Rous . . . 1625 to 1642* (London, 1856).

Greene, Jack P. (ed.), *Great Britain and the American Colonies, 1606–1763* (Columbia, S.C., 1970).

Hakluyt, Richard, 'Discourse of western planting', in E. G. R. Taylor (ed.), *The Original Writings and Correspondence of the Two Richard Hakluyts* (London, 1935), vol. 2.

Hakluyt, Richard, *The Principall Navigations, Voiages and Discoueries of the English Nation* (London, 1589).

Hale, Edward E. (ed.), *Note-Book Kept by Thomas Lechford . . . 1638 to . . . 1641* (Cambridge, Mass., 1885).

Hall, Clayton C. (ed.), *Narratives of Early Maryland, 1633–1684* (New York, 1910).

Hall, David D. (ed.), *The Antinomian Controversy, 1636–1638* (Middletown, Conn., 1968).

[Hammond], 'Diary of Lawrence Hammond', M.H.S. *Proceedings*, ser. 2, vol. 7 (1891–2), pp. 144–72.

Harriot, Thomas, *A Briefe and True Report of the New Found Land of Virginia* (London, 1588).

Heimert, Alan, and Andrew Delbanco (eds.), *The Puritans in America: A Narrative Anthology* (Cambridge, Mass., 1985).

Higginson, Francis, 'New-Englands plantation', in M.H.S., *The Founding of Massachusetts* (Boston, 1930), pp. 81–97.

Higginson, Francis, 'A true relation of the last voyage to New England', in M.H.S., *The Founding of Massachusetts* (Boston, 1930), pp. 59–75.

H.M.C., *Twelfth Report*, pt. 1 (London, 1888).

H.M.C., *Thirteenth Report*, pt. 4 (Rye corp.) (London, 1892).

H.M.C., *Fourteenth Report*, pt. 4 (London, 1894).

H.M.C., *Report on the Manuscripts of the late R. R. Hastings* (London, 1947).

H.M.C., *Report on the Pepys Manuscripts Preserved at Magdalene College, Cambridge* (London, 1911).

H.M.C., *Report on the Records of the City of Exeter* (London, 1916).

Hoadly, Charles J. (ed.), *Records of the Colony and Plantation of New Haven, 1638–49* (Hartford, Conn., 1857).

Hooke, William, *New-Englands Sence, of Old-Englands and Jrelands Sorrowes* (London, 1645).

Bibliography

Hooke, William, *New Englands Teares, for Old Englands Feares* (London, 1641).
Hosmer, James Kendall (ed.), *Winthrop's Journal 'History of New England' 1630–1649*, 2 vols. (New York, 1908).
Hotten, John Camden (ed.), *The Original Lists of Persons of Quality . . . Who went from Great Britain to the American Plantations 1600–1700* (1874; reprinted, Baltimore, 1974).
Howgill, Francis, *The Popish Inquisition Newly Erected in New-England* (London, 1659).
[Hull], 'The diaries of John Hull', A.A.S. *Transactions*, 3 (1857), pp. 108–281.
Hutchinson, Thomas, *The History of the Colony and Province of Massachusetts-Bay*, ed. Lawrence Shaw Mayo (Cambridge, Mass., 1936).
Hutchinson, Thomas, *The Hutchinson Papers: A Collection of Original Papers Relative to the History of . . . Massachusetts*, 2 vols. (1769; reprinted, Boston, 1865).
Ingram, Bruce S. (ed.), *Three Sea Journals of Stuart Times* (London, 1936).
James, Sydney V., Jr. (ed.), *Three Visitors to Early Plymouth . . . John Pory, Emmanuel Altham and Isaak de Rasieres* (Plymouth, Mass., 1963).
James, Thomas, *The Strange and Dangerous Voyage of Captaine Thomas Iames* (London, 1633).
Jameson, J. Franklin (ed.), *Johnson's Wonder-Working Providence* (New York, 1910).
Janeway, James, *Mr. James Janeway's Legacy to His Friends: Containing Twenty-Seven Famous Instances of God's Providence in and about Sea Dangers and Deliverances* (London, 1675).
Jeaffreson, John Cordy (ed.), *A Young Squire of the Seventeenth Century* (London, 1878).
Jewson, Charles Boardman (ed.), 'Transcript of three registers of passengers from Great Yarmouth to Holland and New England 1637–1639', *Norfolk Record Society*, 25 (1954), pp. 6–30.
Joensen, Einar (ed.), *Tingbókin 1615–54* (Tórshavn, 1953).
Josselyn, John, *An Account of Two Voyages to New England* (Boston, 1865).
Josselyn, John, *New Englands Rareties Discovered* (London, 1672).
Larkin, James F. (ed.), *Stuart Royal Proclamations* vol. 2, *1625–1646* (Oxford, 1983).
Larkin, James F., and Paul L. Hughes (eds.), *Stuart Royal Proclamations* vol. 1, *1603–1625* (Oxford, 1973).
Latham, Robert, and William Mathews (eds.), *The Diary of Samuel Pepys*, vol. 5 (London, 1971).
Lechford, Thomas, *New-Englands Advice to Old England* (London, 1644).
Lechford, Thomas, *Plain Dealing, or News from New England*, ed. Darrett B. Rutman (New York, 1969).
Levett, Christopher, 'A voyage into New England begun in 1623 and ended in 1624', in James Phinney Baxter, *Christopher Levett, of York, the Pioneer Colonist in Casco Bay* (Portland, Maine, 1893).
The London Gazette, 11–14 November 1667; 5–9 February 1684–5.
Macfarlane, Alan (ed.), *The Diary of Ralph Josselin 1616–1683* (London, 1976).
McGiffert, Michael (ed.), *God's Plot: The Paradoxes of Puritan Piety, Being the Autobiography and Journal of Thomas Shepard* (Amherst, Mass., 1972).
Massachusetts Historical Society, *The Founding of Massachusetts* (Boston, 1930).
'Mather papers', M.H.S. *Collections*, ser. 4, vol. 8 (1868).

Bibliography

[Mather], 'Diary of Cotton Mather, 1681–1708', M.H.S. *Collections*, ser. 7, vol. 7 (1911).

Mather, Cotton, *Magnalia Christi Americana*, 2 vols. (Hartford, Conn., 1820).

Mather, Cotton, *The Sailours Companion and Counsellor* (Boston, 1709).

Mather, Cotton, *Things for a Distress'd People to Think Upon* (Boston, 1696).

[Mather], 'The autobiography of Increase Mather', ed. M. G. Hall, A.A.S. *Proceedings*, 71 (1961–2), pp. 271–360.

Mather, Increase, *A Brief Relation of the State of New England, from the Beginning of that Plantation to this Present Year, 1689* (London, 1689).

Mather, Increase, *The Life and Death of that Reverend Man of God, Mr. Richard Mather* (Cambridge, Mass., 1670).

[Mather], 'Richard Mather's journal', in Alexander Young (ed.), *Chronicles of the First Planters of the Colony of Massachusetts Bay, from 1623 to 1636* (1846; reprinted, Williamstown, Mass., 1978), pp. 447–81.

Mather, Richard, *A Farewell Exhortation to the Church and People of Dorchester* (Cambridge, Mass., 1657).

Mather, Richard, and William Tompson, *An Heart-Melting Exhortation Together with a Cordiall Consolation. Presented in a Letter from New England, to their Dear Countreymen of Lancashire* (London, 1650).

Mathews, A. G., 'A censored letter. William Hooke in England to John Davenport in New England, 1663', *Transactions of the Congregational Historical Society*, 9 (1924–6), pp. 262–83.

Maverick, Samuel, 'Briefe description of New England', M.H.S. *Proceedings*, ser. 2, vol. 1 (1884–5), pp. 231–49.

[Michel], 'Report of the journey of Francis Louis Michel', *Virginia Magazine of History and Biography*, 24 (1916), pp. 1–43, 113–41, 275–303.

Miller, Perry (ed.), *The American Puritans, Their Prose and Poetry* (New York, 1956).

Milton, John, *Paradise Lost* (London, 1674).

Moody, Robert E. (ed.), *The Saltonstall Papers, 1607–1815*. Vol. 1, *1607–1789* (Boston, 1972).

Morison, S. E. (ed.), *Records of the Suffolk County Court 1671–1680*, 2 vols. (Boston, 1933).

Morrell, William, *New-England, or a Briefe Enarration of the Ayre, Earth, Water, Fish and Fowles of that Country... in Latine and English Verse* (London, 1625).

Morton, Thomas, *The New English Canaan... or an Abstract of New England*, ed. Charles Francis Adams, Jr. (Boston, 1883).

New-Haven's Settling in New England (1656; reprinted, Hartford, Conn., 1858).

News from New-England, Being a True and Last Account of the Present Bloody Wars (London, 1676).

Noble, John (ed.), *Records of the Court of Assistants of the Colony of the Massachusetts Bay, 1630–1692*, 3 vols. (Boston, 1901–28).

Norton, Humphrey, *New-Englands Ensigne* (London, 1659).

Noyes, Nicholas, *New-Englands Duty and Interest, to be an Habitation of Justice, and Mountain of Holiness* (Boston, 1698).

Oakes, Urian, *New-England Pleaded With* (Cambridge, Mass., 1673).

Ogilby, John, *America: Being the Latest and Most Accurate Description of the New World* (London, 1671).

Oliver, F. E. (ed.), *The Diaries of Benjamin Lynde* (Boston, 1880).

Orr, Charles (ed.), *History of the Pequot War* (Cleveland, 1897).

Bibliography

Oxenbridge, John, *New-England Freemen Warned and Warmed* (Cambridge, Mass., 1673).

Pope, Robert G., *The Notebook of the Reverend John Fiske 1644–1675* (Salem, Mass., 1974).

Powell, William S., *John Pory, 1572–1636: The Life and Letters of a Man of Many Parts* (Chapel Hill, N.C., 1977).

Powicke, F. J. (ed.), 'Some unpublished correspondence of the Rev. Richard Baxter and the Rev. John Eliot', *Bulletin of the John Rylands Library*, 15 (1931), pp. 138–76, 442–6.

[Pratt], 'John Pratt's apology', M.H.S. *Collections*, ser. 2, vol. 7 (1818), pp. 126–9.

Prince, Thomas, *The People of New-England Put in Mind of the Righteous Acts of the Lord* (Boston, 1730).

The Probate Records of Essex County, Massachusetts, 3 vols. (Salem, Mass., 1916–20).

Proportion of Provisions Needfull for Such as Intend to Plant Themselves in New England, for One Whole Yeare (London, 1630).

Publick Occurrences both Foreign and Domestick (Boston, 1690).

Putnam, Eben (ed.), 'Two early passenger lists, 1635–1637', *N.E.H.G.R.*, 75 (1921), pp. 217–25.

Quinn, David Beers (ed.), *The Roanoke Voyages 1584–1590* (London, 1955).

[Randolph], 'Letters and narrative of Edward Randolph', M.H.S. *Proceedings*, 18 (1880–1), pp. 254–61.

Record Commissioners of the City of Boston, *Second Report*, 'Boston town records' (Boston, 1877).

Record Commissioners of the City of Boston, *Third Report*, 'Charlestown records' (Boston, 1878).

Record Commissioners of the City of Boston, *Fourth Report*, 'Dorchester town records' (Boston, 1880).

Record Commissioners of the City of Boston, *Sixth Report*, 'Roxbury land and church records' (Boston, 1881).

Record Commissioners of the City of Boston, *Seventh Report*, 'Boston records, 1660–1701' (Boston, 1881).

Record Commissioners of the City of Boston, *Tenth Report*, 'Miscellaneous papers' (Boston, 1886).

Records and Files of the Quarterly Courts of Essex County Massachusetts, 1636–1686, 9 vols. (Salem, Mass., 1911–75).

'Records of the Council for New England', A.A.S. *Proceedings* (1867).

'Records of the Particular Court of Connecticut 1639–1663', *Collections of the Connecticut Historical Society*, 22 (1928).

Registry Department of the City of Boston (ed.), *Aspinwall Notarial Records from 1644 to 1651* (Boston, 1903).

A Relation or Iournall of the Beginning and Proceedings of the English Plantation Setled at Plimoth in New England (London, 1622).

Ricard, Herbert F. (ed.), *Journal of John Bowne 1650–1694* (New Orleans, 1975).

Rosier, James, *A True Relation of the Most Prosperous Voyage Made This Present Yeere 1605 by Captaine George Waymouth* (London, 1605).

Rous, John, *New England a Degenerate Plant* (London, 1659).

Sachse, William L. (ed.), *The Diary of Roger Lowe* (London, 1938).

Bibliography

Savage, James (ed.), *The History of New England from 1630 to 1649, by John Winthrop*, 2 vols. (Boston, 1853).

Scott, W., and J. Bliss (eds.), *Works of... William Laud*, 7 vols. (Oxford, 1847–60).

Scottowe, Joshua, *Massachusetts, or the First Planters of New-England* (Boston, 1696).

Selement, George, and Bruce C. Woolley (eds.), *Thomas Shepard's Confessions* (Boston, 1981).

[Sewall], 'Letter book of Samuel Sewall', M.H.S. *Collections*, ser. 6, vol. 1 (1886).

[Sewall], *The Diary of Samuel Sewall 1674–1729*, ed. M. Halsey Thomas, 2 vols. (New York, 1973).

Shepard, Thomas, *The Clear Sunshine of the Gospel Breaking Forth upon the Indians in New-England* (London, 1648).

Shepard, Thomas, 'Election sermon in 1638', *N.E.H.G.R.*, 24 (1870), pp. 361–6.

Shepard, Thomas, *Wine for Gospel Wantons* (Cambridge, Mass., 1668).

[Shepard], 'Thomas Shepard to Hugh Peter, 27 December 1645', *American Historical Review*, 4 (1898–9), pp. 105–6.

Sherwood, George (ed.), *American Colonists in English Records*, 2 series (London, 1932–3).

Shipton, Clifford K. (ed.), 'The autobiographical memoranda of John Brock, 1636–1659', A.A.S. *Proceedings*, 53 (1943), pp. 96–105.

Shurtleff, Nathaniel B. (ed.), *Records of the Governor and Company of the Massachusetts Bay*, 5 vols. (Boston, 1853–4).

Smith, John, 'An accidence, or the path-way to experience, necessary for all young seamen', in Edward Arber and A. G. Bradley (eds.), *Travels and Works of Captain John Smith*, 2 vols. (Edinburgh, 1910), pp. 785–804.

Smith, John, 'Advertisements for the unexperienced planters', in Arber, *Smith*, pp. 917–66.

Smith, John, 'A description of New England', in Arber, *Smith*, pp. 175–231.

Smith, John, 'New-England's trials', in Arber, *Smith*, pp. 233–72.

Smith, John, 'The generall historie of Virginia, New England and the Summer Isles', in Arber, *Smith*, pp. 273–784.

Steele, Robert (ed.), *Tudor and Stuart Proclamations* (Oxford, 1910).

Steere, Richard, *A Monumental Memorial of Marine Mercy* (Boston, 1684).

Stock, Leo Francis (ed.), *Proceedings and Debates of the British Parliaments Respecting North America* vol. 1, *1542–1668* (Washington, D.C., 1924).

[Stoughton], 'A letter of Israel Stoughton, 1635', M.H.S. *Proceedings*, 58 (1924–5), pp. 446–58.

Stoughton, William, *New-Englands True Interest* (Cambridge, Mass., 1670).

Suffolk County Wills: Abstracts of the Earliest Wills upon Record in the County of Suffolk, Massachusetts (Baltimore, 1984).

Tappan, Robert N. (ed.), *Edward Randolph; Including His Letters and Official Papers... 1676–1703*, 3 vols. (Boston, 1898–9).

[Taylor], 'Diary of Edward Taylor', M.H.S. *Proceedings*, 18 (1880–1), pp. 5–18.

Tillam, Thomas, 'Upon the first sight of New England, June 29, 1638', A.A.S. *Proceedings*, 53 (1943), p. 331.

Trask, William B. (ed.), *Suffolk Deeds* (Boston, 1880–1906).

Bibliography

Underhill, John, 'Newes from America, or a new and experimentall discoverie of New England', in Charles Orr (ed.), *History of the Pequot War* (Cleveland, 1897).

Vaux, W. S. W. (ed.), *The World Encompassed by Sir Francis Drake* (London, 1854).

Vincent, Philip, 'A true relation of the late battell fought in New England between the English and the Pequet salvages', in Charles Orr (ed.), *History of the Pequot War* (Cleveland, 1897).

W., J., 'A letter from New-England in 1682', in George P. Winship (ed.), *Boston in 1682 and 1699* (Providence, R.I., 1905), pp. 71–84.

Ward, Ned, 'A trip to New-England', in George P. Winship (ed.), *Boston in 1682 and 1699* (Providence, R.I., 1905), pp. 29–70.

Waters, Henry F., *Genealogical Gleanings in England*, 2 vols. (Boston, 1901).

Weld, Thomas, *An Answer to W. R. His Narration of the Opinions and Practices of the Churches Lately Erected in New-England, Vindicating Those Churches from an Hundred Imputations Fathered on Them* (London, 1644).

Weld, Thomas, *A Short Story of the Rise, Reign and Ruin of the Antinomians, Familists, and Libertines, That Infected the Churches of New-England* (London, 1644).

Wheelwright, John, *Mercurius Americanus, Mr. Welds His Antitype, or, Massachusetts Great Apologie Examined* (London, 1645).

White, John, 'The planters plea' (London, 1630), in M.H.S., *The Founding of Massachusetts* (Boston, 1930), pp. 143–201.

Whitfield, Henry, *The Light Appearing More and More Towards the Perfect Day, or a Farther Discovery of the Present State of the Indians in New England* (London, 1651).

Whitmore, W. H., (ed.), 'Lane family papers', *N.E.H.G.R.*, 11 (1857), pp. 102–12, 231–41.

Wigglesworth, Michael, 'God's controversy with New England', M.H.S. *Proceedings*, 12 (1871), pp. 84–92.

Winship, George Parker (ed.), *Sailors' Narratives of Voyages along the New England Coast 1524–1624* (Boston, 1905).

Winslow, Edward, 'New-Englands Salamander', M.H.S. *Collections*, ser. 3, vol. 2 (1830), pp. 110–45.

[Winthrop], M.H.S., *The Winthrop Papers* vols. 2–5, *1623–49*, (Boston, 1931–47).

[Winthrop], 'The humble request of His Maiesties loyall subjects, the governour and the company late gone for New-England', in Alexander Young (ed.), *Chronicles of the First Planters of the Colony of Massachuestts Bay, from 1623 to 1636* (1846; reprinted, Williamstown, Mass., 1978), pp. 294–8.

Winthrop, John, 'A modell of Christian charity', in M.H.S., *Winthrop Papers*, vol. 2, pp. 282–95.

[Wollcott], 'Letter of John Wollcott', *N.E.H.G.R.*, 2 (1848), pp. 373–4.

Wood, William, *New England's Prospect*, ed. Alden T. Vaughan (Amherst, Mass., 1977).

'The Wyllys papers . . . 1590–1796', *Collections of the Connecticut Historical Society*, 21 (1924).

Young, Alexander (ed.), *Chronicles of the First Planters of the Colony of Massachusetts Bay, from 1623 to 1636* (1846; reprinted, Williamstown, Mass., 1978).

Bibliography

3. Secondary works

Adams, James Truslow, *The Founding of New England* (1921; reprinted, Boston, 1949).

Allen, David Grayson, *In English Ways: The Movement of Societies and the Transferal of English Local Law and Custom to Massachusetts Bay in the Seventeenth Century* (Chapel Hill, N.C., 1981).

Anderson, R. C. 'Lists of men-of-war 1650–1700, part 1, English ships, 1649–1702', *Society for Nautical Research Occasional Publications*, 5 (1935).

Anderson, Terry Lee, and Robert Paul Thomas, 'White population, labor force and extensive growth of the New England economy in the seventeenth century', *Journal of Economic History*, 33 (1973), pp. 634–61.

Anderson, Virginia DeJohn, 'Migrants and motives: religion and the settlement of New England, 1630–1640', *New England Quarterly*, 58 (1985), pp. 339–83.

Andrews, Charles M., *The Colonial Period of American History*, 4 vols. (New Haven, Conn., 1934–8).

Andrews, K. R., N. P. Canny and P. E. H. Hair (eds.), *The Westward Enterprise: English Activities in Ireland, the Atlantic, and America 1480–1650* (Liverpool, 1978).

Appleton, William Sumner, *Ancestry of Priscilla Baker Who Lived 1674–1731* (Cambridge, Mass., 1870).

Axtell, James, *The School upon a Hill: Education and Society in Colonial New England* (New Haven, Conn., 1974).

Aylmer, G. E., *The King's Servants: The Civil Service of Charles I* (London, 1961).

Bailyn, Bernard, *The New England Merchants in the Seventeenth Century* (1955; reprinted, Cambridge, Mass., 1979).

Baker, William A., *Colonial Vessels: Some Seventeenth-Century Sailing Craft* (Barre, Mass., 1962).

Banks, C. E., 'English sources of emigration to the New England colonies in the seventeenth century', M.H.S. *Proceedings*, 60 (1927), pp. 366–73.

Banks, Charles Edward, *The Planters of the Commonwealth* (1930; reprinted, Baltimore, 1975).

Banks, Charles Edward, *The Winthrop Fleet of 1630* (1930; reprinted, Baltimore, 1972).

Barbour, Violet, 'Marine risks and insurance in the seventeenth century', *Journal of Economics and Business History*, 1 (1928–9), pp. 561–96.

Baxter, James Phinney, *Christopher Levett, of York, the Pioneer Colonist in Casco Bay* (Portland, Maine, 1893).

Bercovitch, Sacvan, *The American Jeremiad* (Madison, Wisc., 1978).

Bercovitch, Sacvan, 'The historiography of Johnson's *Wonder-Working Providence*', *Essex Institute Historical Collections*, 104 (1968), pp. 138–61.

Bercovitch, Sacvan, *Puritan Origins of the American Self* (New Haven, Conn., 1975).

Black, Robert C. III, *The Younger John Winthrop* (New York, 1966).

Boorstin, Daniel J., *The Americans: The Colonial Experience* (New York, 1958).

Breen, T. H., and Stephen Foster, 'Moving to the New World: the character of early Massachusetts immigration', *William and Mary Quarterly*, ser. 3, vol. 30 (1973), pp. 189–222.

Bibliography

Bremer, Francis J., 'Increase Mather's friends: the transatlantic Congregational network of the seventeenth century', A.A.S. *Proceedings*, 94 (1984), pp. 59–96.

Bremer, Francis J., *The Puritan Experiment: New England Society from Bradford to Edwards* (New York, 1976).

Bridenbaugh, Carl, *Vexed and Troubled Englishmen 1590–1642*, rev. ed. (Oxford, 1976).

Burg, B. R., *Richard Mather* (Boston, 1982).

Caldwell, Patricia, *The Puritan Conversion Narrative: The Beginnings of American Expression* (Cambridge, 1983).

Canny, Nicholas, 'The permissive frontier: the problem of social control in English settlements in Ireland and Virginia 1550–1650', in K. R. Andrews, N. P. Canny and P. E. H. Hair (eds.), *The Westward Enterprise: English Activities in Ireland, the Atlantic, and America 1480–1650* (Liverpool, 1978), pp. 17–44.

Carr, Lois Green, and Russell R. Menard, 'Immigration and opportunity: the freedman in early colonial Maryland', in Thad W. Tate and David L. Ammerman (eds.), *The Chesapeake in the Seventeenth Century* (New York, 1979), pp. 206–42.

Carroll, Peter N., *Puritanism and the Wilderness: The Intellectual Significance of the New England Frontier, 1629–1700* (New York, 1969).

Cawley, Robert Ralston, *Unpathed Waters: Studies in the Influence of the Voyagers on Elizabethan Literature* (Princeton, N.J., 1940).

Cliffe, J. T., *The Yorkshire Gentry from the Reformation to the Civil War* (London, 1969).

Collinson, Patrick, 'A comment: concerning the name Puritan', *Journal of Ecclesiastical History*, 31 (1980), pp. 483–8.

Cressy, David, 'Books as totems in seventeenth-century England and New England', *Journal of Library History*, 21 (1986), pp. 92–106.

Cressy, David, 'Describing the social order of Elizabethan and Stuart England', *History and Literature*, 3 (1976), pp. 38–41.

Cressy, David, 'A drudgery of schoolmasters: the teaching profession in seventeenth-century England', in W.R. Prest (ed.), *The Professions in Early Modern England* (London, 1987).

Cressy, David, 'Kinship and kin interaction in early modern England', *Past and Present*, 113 (1986), pp. 38–69.

Cressy, David, *Literacy and the Social Order: Reading and Writing in Tudor and Stuart England* (Cambridge, 1980).

Cressy, David, 'Puritans at sea: the seventeenth-century voyage to New England', *Log of Mystic Seaport*, 36 (1984), pp. 87–94.

Cressy, David, 'The vast and furious ocean: the passage to Puritan New England', *New England Quarterly*, 57 (1984), pp. 511–32.

Cronon, William, *Changes in the Land: Indians, Colonists, and the Ecology of New England* (New York, 1983).

Crouse, Nellis M., 'Causes of the great migration 1630–1640', *New England Quarterly*, 5 (1932), pp. 3–36.

Davies, K. G., *The North Atlantic World in the Seventeenth Century* (Minneapolis, 1974).

Deane, Charles, 'Remarks on the small size of ships used in crossing the Atlantic, 1492–1626', M.H.S. *Proceedings*, 8 (1865), pp. 464–6.

Bibliography

Delbanco, Andrew, 'The Puritan errand re-viewed', *Journal of American Studies*, 18 (1984), pp. 343–60.

Duffy, John, 'The passage to the colonies', *Mississippi Valley Historical Review*, 38 (1951–2), pp. 21–38.

Dunn, Richard S., *Puritans and Yankees: The Winthrop Dynasty of New England 1630–1717* (Princeton, N.J., 1962).

Dunn, Richard S., 'Servants and slaves: the recruitment and employment of labor', in Jack P. Greene and J. R. Pole (eds.), *Colonial British America: Essays in the New History of the Early Modern Era* (Baltimore, 1984), pp. 157–94.

Dunn, Richard S., *Sugar and Slaves: the Rise of the Planter Class in the English West Indies, 1624–1713* (New York, 1973).

Elliott, Emory, *Power and the Pulpit in Puritan New England* (Princeton, N.J., 1975).

Emerson, Everett, *Puritanism in America 1620–1750* (Boston, 1977).

Fairbanks, Jonathan L., and Robert F. Trent (eds.), *New England Begins: The Seventeenth Century*, 3 vols. (Boston, 1982).

Fletcher, Anthony, 'National and local awareness in the county communities', in Howard Tomlinson (ed.), *Before the English Civil War* (London, 1983), pp. 151–74.

Fletcher, Anthony, *The Outbreak of the English Civil War* (London, 1981).

Foster, Stephen, 'English Puritanism and the progress of New England institutions, 1630–1660', in David D. Hall, John M. Murrin and Thad W. Tate (eds.), *Saints and Revolutionaries: Essays on Early American History* (New York, 1984), pp. 3–37.

Foster, Stephen, 'New England and the challenge of heresy, 1630 to 1660: the Puritan crisis in transatlantic perspective', *William and Mary Quarterly*, ser. 3, vol. 38 (1981), pp. 624–60.

Frost, Isaac, 'Home-sickness and immigrant psychoses', *Journal of Mental Science*, 84 (1938), pp. 801–47.

Galenson, David, *White Servitude in Colonial America: An Economic Analysis* (Cambridge, 1981).

Gemery, Henry A., 'Emigration from the British Isles to the New World, 1630–1700: inferences from colonial populations', *Research in Economic History*, 5 (1980), pp. 179–231.

Gemery, Henry A., 'European emigration to North America, 1700–1820: numbers and semi-numbers', *Perspectives in American History*, n.s., 1 (1984), pp. 283–342.

Gmelch, George, 'Return migration', *Annual Review of Anthropology*, 9 (1980), pp. 135–59.

Gottfried, Marion H., 'The first depression in Massachusetts', *New England Quarterly*, 9 (1936), pp. 655–78.

Greene, Jack P., and J. R. Pole (eds.), *Colonial British America: Essays in the New History of the Early Modern Era* (Baltimore, 1984).

Greenough, Chester Noyes, 'John Dunton's letters from New England', *Publications of the Colonial Society of Massachusetts*, 14 (1911–13), pp. 222–56.

Gura, Philip F., *A Glimpse of Sion's Glory: Puritan Radicalism in New England, 1620–1660* (Middletown, Conn., 1984).

Gutman, Herbert G., 'Afro-American kinship before and after emancipation in North America', in Hans Medick and David Warren Sabean (eds.), *Interest and Emotion: Essays in the Study of Family and Kinship* (Cambridge, 1984), pp. 241–65.

Hall, David D., *The Faithful Shepherd: A History of the New England Ministry in the Seventeenth Century* (1972; reprinted, New York, 1974).

Hall, David D., John M. Murrin and Thad W. Tate (eds.), *Saints and Revolutionaries: Essays on Early American History* (New York, 1984).

Hall, David D., and David Grayson Allen (eds.), *Seventeenth-Century New England* (Boston, 1984).

Hambrick-Stowe, Charles, *The Practice of Piety: The Puritan Devotional Discipline in Seventeenth-Century New England* (Chapel Hill, N.C., 1982).

Hammatt, Abraham, *The Hammatt Papers: The Early Inhabitants of Ipswich, Massachusetts, 1633–1700* (Ipswich, Mass., 1899).

Handlin, Lilian, 'Dissent in a small community', *New England Quarterly*, 58 (1985), pp. 193–220.

Hazard, Caroline, *The Narragansett Friends Meeting in the XVIII Century* (Cambridge, Mass., 1899).

Hirst, Derek, *Authority and Conflict: England 1603–1658* (London, 1986).

Horton, John T., 'Two bishops and the Holy Brood: a fresh look at a familiar fact', *New England Quarterly*, 40 (1967), pp. 339–46.

Howell, Roger, *Puritans and Radicals in North England* (Lanham, Md., 1984).

Hunt, William, *The Puritan Moment: The Coming of Revolution in an English County* (Cambridge, Mass., 1983).

Janis, I. L., 'Group identification under conditions of extreme danger', in Dorwin Cartwright and Alvin Zander (eds.), *Group Dynamics: Research and Theory*, 3rd ed. (New York, 1968), pp. 80–90.

Jennings, Francis, *The Invasion of America: Indians, Colonialism, and the Cant of Conquest* (New York, 1976).

Johnson, Richard R., *Adjustment to Empire: the New England Colonies, 1675–1715* (New Brunswick, N.J., 1981).

Jones, Howard Mumford, 'The colonial impulse: an analysis of the "promotion" literature of colonization', *Proceedings of the American Philosophical Society*, 90 (1946), pp. 131–61.

Kiesler, Charles A., *The Psychology of Commitment: Experiments Linking Behavior to Belief* (New York, 1971).

Kittredge, George Lyman, 'Robert Child the Remonstrant', *Publications of the Colonial Society of Massachusetts*, 21 (1920), pp. 1–146.

Kupperman, Karen Ordahl, 'Climate and mastery of the wilderness in seventeenth-century New England', in David D. Hall and David Grayson Allen (eds.), *Seventeenth-Century New England* (Boston, 1984), pp. 3–37.

Kupperman, Karen Ordahl, *Settling with the Indians: The Meeting of English and Indian Cultures in America, 1580–1640* (New York, 1980).

Kussmaul, Ann, *Servants in Husbandry in Early Modern England* (Cambridge, 1981).

Lamb, George, *Series of Plans of Boston... 1630, 1635, 1640, 1645* (Boston, 1905).

Langdon, George D., Jr., *Pilgrim Colony: A History of New Plymouth 1620–1691* (New Haven, Conn., 1966).

Laslett, Peter, *The World We Have Lost, Further Explored* (London, 1983).

LeGuin, Charles A., 'Sea life in seventeenth-century England', *American Neptune*, 27 (1967), pp. 111–34.

Bibliography

Lockridge, Kenneth A., *Literacy in Colonial New England* (New York, 1974).

Lockridge, Kenneth A., *A New England Town: The First Hundred Years*, exp. ed. (New York, 1985).

Love, William DeLoss, *The Fast and Thanksgiving Days of New England* (Boston, 1895).

McCusker, John J., and Russell R. Menard, *The Economy of British America, 1607–1789* (Chapel Hill, N.C., 1985).

McElroy, John William, 'Seafaring in seventeenth-century New England', *New England Quarterly*, 8 (1935), pp. 331–64.

MacFarlane, Alan, *The Family Life of Ralph Josselin* (Cambridge, 1970).

McGiffert, Michael (ed.), *Puritanism and the American Experience* (Reading, Mass., 1969).

Mason, George Carrington, 'An Atlantic crossing in the seventeenth century', *American Neptune*, 11 (1951), pp. 35–41.

Menard, Russell R., 'From servant to freeholder: status mobility and property accumulation in seventeenth-century Maryland', *William and Mary Quarterly*, ser. 3, vol. 30 (1973), pp. 37–64.

Middlekauff, Robert, *The Mathers: Three Generations of Puritan Intellectuals* (New York, 1971).

Miller, Perry, *Errand into the Wilderness* (1956; reprinted, New York, 1964).

Morgan, Edmund S., 'The historians of early New England', in Ray Allen Billington (ed.), *The Reinterpretation of American History* (San Marino, Calif., 1966), pp. 41–63.

Morgan, Edmund S., 'The labor problem at Jamestown, 1607–1618', *American Historical Review*, 76 (1971), pp. 595–611.

Morison, Samuel Eliot, *Builders of the Bay Colony*, rev. ed. (Boston, 1964).

Morison, Samuel Eliot, *The Oxford History of the American People* (New York, 1965).

Murdock, Kenneth B., *Increase Mather, the Foremost American Puritan* (Cambridge, Mass., 1926).

O'Toole, James M., 'New England reactions to the English civil wars', *N.E.H.G.R.*, 129 (1975), pp. 3–17, 238–49.

Orpen, Patrick K., 'Schoolmastering as a profession in the seventeenth century: the career patterns of the grammar schoolmaster', *History of Education*, 6 (1977), pp. 183–94.

Potter, J., 'The growth of population in America, 1700–1860', in D. V. Glass and D. E. C. Eversley (eds.), *Population in History* (Chicago, 1965), pp. 631–88.

Powell, Sumner Chilton, *Puritan Village: The Formation of a New England Town* (Middletown, Conn., 1963).

Quinn, David Beers, *England and the Discovery of America, 1481–1620* (New York, 1974).

Quinn, David Beers, *Set Fair for Roanoke: Voyages and Colonies, 1584–1606* (Chapel Hill, N.C., 1985).

Quintrell, B. W., 'Lancashire ills, the king's will and the troubling of Bishop Bridgeman', *Transactions of the Historic Society of Lancashire and Cheshire*, 132 (1983), pp. 67–102.

Redstone, Vincent B., 'Notes on New England voyages', *N.E.H.G.R.*, 104 (1950), pp. 15–21.

Bibliography

Rich, Wesley E., *The History of the United States Post Office to the Year 1829* (Cambridge, Mass., 1924).

Richardson, R. C., 'Puritanism and the ecclesiastical authorities: the case of the diocese of Chester', in Brian Manning (ed.), *Politics, Religion and the English Civil War* (London, 1973), pp. 3–33.

Robbins, William G., 'The Massachusetts Bay Company: an analysis of motives', *The Historian*, 32 (1969), pp. 83–98.

Robinson, Philip S., *The Plantation of Ulster: British Settlement in an Irish Landscape, 1600–1670* (Dublin, 1984).

Ronda, James P., 'Generations of faith: the Christian Indians of Martha's Vineyard', *William and Mary Quarterly*, ser. 3, vol. 38 (1981), pp. 369–94.

Ronda, James P., ' "We are well as we are": an Indian critique of seventeenth-century Christian missions', *William and Mary Quarterly*, ser. 3, vol. 34 (1977), pp. 66–82.

Rose-Troup, Frances, *The Massachusetts Bay Company and Its Predecessors* (New York, 1930).

Rutman, Darrett B., *John Winthrop's Decision for America: 1629* (Philadelphia, 1975).

Rutman, Darrett B., *Winthrop's Boston: A Portrait of a Puritan Town, 1630–1649* (1965; reprinted, New York, 1972).

Rutyna, Richard A., 'Richard Coy of Essex County, 1625–1675: a biographical sketch', *Essex Institute Historical Collections*, 104 (1968), pp. 75–9.

Sachse, William L., 'The migration of New Englanders to England, 1640–1660', *American Historical Review*, 53 (1948), pp. 251–78.

Salerno, Anthony, 'The character of emigration from Wiltshire to the American colonies, 1630–1660', Ph.D. thesis, University of Virginia, 1977.

Salerno, Anthony, 'The social background of seventeenth-century emigration to America', *Journal of British Studies*, 19 (1979), pp. 31–52.

Salisbury, Neal, *Manitou and Providence: Indians, Europeans, and the Making of New England, 1500–1643* (New York, 1982).

Savage, James, *A Genealogical Dictionary of the First Settlers of New England*, 4 vols. (Boston, 1853–4).

Scobey, David M., 'Revising the errand: New England's ways and the Puritan sense of the past', *William and Mary Quarterly*, ser. 3, vol. 41 (1984), pp. 3–31.

Seaver, Paul S., *Wallington's World: A Puritan Artisan in Seventeenth-Century London* (Stanford, 1985).

Sharpe, Kevin, 'Archbishop Laud and the University of Oxford', in Hugh Lloyd-Jones, Valerie Pearl and Blair Worden (eds.), *History and Imagination* (New York, 1981), pp. 146–64.

Sharpe, Kevin, 'The Personal Rule of Charles I', in Howard Tomlinson (ed.), *Before the English Civil War* (London, 1983), pp. 53–78.

Shipps, Kenneth W., 'The Puritan emigration to New England: a new source on motivation', *N.E.H.G.R.*, 135 (1981), pp. 83–97.

Shipton, Clifford K., 'Immigration to New England, 1680–1740', *Journal of Political Economy* 44 (1936), pp. 225–39.

Shuffelton, Frank, *Thomas Hooker 1586–1647* (Princeton, N.J., 1977).

Sibley, John Langdon, *Biographical Sketches of Graduates of Harvard University* vol. 1, *1642–1658* (Cambridge, Mass., 1973).

Bibliography

Simmons, R. C., *The American Colonies: From Settlement to Independence* (New York, 1976).

Smith, Abbot Emerson, *Colonists in Bondage: White Servitude and Convict Labor in America 1607–1776* (New York, 1971).

Smith, Daniel Scott, 'Child-naming practices, kinship ties, and change in family attitudes in Hingham, Massachusetts, 1641 to 1880', *Journal of Social History*, 18 (1985), pp. 541–66.

Smith, Daniel Scott, 'The demographic history of colonial New England', *Journal of Economic History*, 32 (1972), pp. 165–83.

Souden, David, 'English indentured servants and the transatlantic colonial economy', in Shula Marks and Peter Richardson (eds.), *International Labour Migration: Historical Perspectives* (London, 1984), pp. 19–33.

Souden, David, ' "Rogues, whores and vagabonds": indentured servant emigrants to North America', *Social History*, 3 (1978), pp. 23–41.

Spufford, Margaret, 'First steps in literacy: the reading and writing experiences of the humblest seventeenth-century spiritual autobiographers', *Social History*, 4 (1979), pp. 407–35.

Spufford, Margaret, 'Puritanism and social control?' in Anthony Fletcher and John Stevenson (eds.), *Order and Disorder in Early Modern England* (Cambridge, 1985), pp. 41–57.

Stearns, Raymond P., *The Strenuous Puritan: Hugh Peter 1598–1660* (Urbana, Ill., 1954).

Stearns, Raymond P., 'The Weld-Peter mission to England', *Publications of the Colonial Society of Massachusetts*, 32 (1934), pp. 188–246.

Steele, Ian K., 'Communicating an English revolution to the colonies', *Journal of British Studies*, 24 (1985), pp. 346–53.

Steele, Ian K., 'Moat theories and the English Atlantic, 1675 to 1740', Canadian Historical Association, *Historical Papers. Communications Historiques*, (1978), pp. 18–33.

Steele, Ian K., 'Time, communications and society: the English Atlantic, 1702', *Journal of American Studies*, 8 (1974), pp. 1–21.

Stein, Roger B., 'Seascape and the American imagination: the Puritan seventeenth century', *Early American Literature*, 7 (1972), pp. 17–37.

Stone, Albert E., 'Sea and the self: travel as experience and metaphor in early American autobiography', *Genre*, 7 (1974), pp. 279–306.

Stout, Harry S., 'The morphology of remigration: New England university men and their return to England, 1640–1660', *Journal of American Studies*, 10 (1976), pp. 151–72.

Stout, Harry S., 'University men in New England 1620–1660: a demographic study', *Journal of Interdisciplinary History*, 4 (1974), pp. 375–400.

Taylor, Philip, *The Distant Magnet: European Emigration to the U.S.A.* (New York, 1971).

Thomas, Keith, *Religion and the Decline of Magic* (New York, 1971).

Tilghman, Harrison, 'Letters between the English and American branches of the Tilghman family, 1697–1764', *Maryland Historical Magazine*, 33 (1938), pp. 148–75.

Tindall, George Brown, *America: A Narrative History* (New York, 1984).

Turner, Victor W., *Dramas, Fields and Metaphors: Symbolic Action in Human Society* (Ithaca, N.Y., 1974).

Bibliography

Turner, Victor W., *The Ritual Process: Structure and Anti-Structure* (Chicago, 1969).

Tyack, N. C. P., 'English exports to New England, 1632–1640: some records in the Port Books', *N.E.H.G.R.*, 135 (1981), pp. 213–38.

Tyack, N. C. P., 'The humbler Puritans of East Anglia and the New England movement: evidence from the court records of the 1630s', *N.E.H.G.R.*, 138 (1984), pp. 79–106.

Tyack, N. C. P., 'Migration from East Anglia to New England before 1660', Ph.D. thesis, University of London, 1951.

Underdown, David, *Pride's Purge: Politics in the Puritan Revolution* (Oxford, 1971).

Underdown, David, *Revel, Riot and Rebellion: Popular Politics and Culture in England 1603–1660* (Oxford, 1985).

Venn, John and J. A., *Alumni Cantabrigienses*, pt. 1, 4 vols. (Cambridge, 1922–7).

Vickers, Daniel, 'Work and life on the fishing periphery of Essex County, Massachusetts, 1630–1675', in David D. Hall and David Grayson Allen (eds.), *Seventeenth-Century New England* (Boston, 1984), pp. 83–117.

Wall, Robert E., Jr., *Massachusetts Bay: The Crucial Decade, 1640–1650* (New Haven, Conn., 1972).

Walter, John, and Keith Wrightson, 'Dearth and the social order in early modern England', *Past and Present*, 71 (1976), pp. 22–44.

Walzer, Michael, *The Revolution of the Saints* (Cambridge, Mass., 1965).

Waterhouse, Richard, 'Reluctant emigrants: the English background of the first generation of the New England Puritan clergy', *Historical Magazine of the Protestant Episcopal Church*, 44 (1975), pp. 473–88.

Waters, John J., 'Hingham, Massachusetts, 1631–1661: an East Anglian oligarchy in the New World', *Journal of Social History*, 1 (1967), pp. 351–70.

Winthrop, R. C., *Life and Letters of John Winthrop* (Boston, 1869).

Woolley, Mary E., 'Early history of the colonial post office', *Publications of the Rhode Island Historical Society*, n.s., 1 (1894), pp. 270–91.

Wrightson, Keith, *English Society 1580–1680* (London, 1982).

Wrigley, E. A., and R. S. Schofield, *The Population History of England, 1541–1871* (Cambridge, Mass., 1981).

Ye Antient Wrecke: Loss of the Sparrow-Hawk in 1626 (Boston, 1865).

Zakai, Avihu, 'Exile and kingdom: reformation, separation, and the millennial quest in the formation of Massachusetts and its relationship with England, 1628–1660', Ph.D. thesis, Johns Hopkins University, Baltimore, Md., 1983.

Ziff, Larzer, *The Career of John Cotton: Puritanism and the American Experience* (Princeton, N.J., 1962).

Zuckerman, Michael, 'Pilgrims in the wilderness: community, modernity, and the maypole at Merry Mount', *New England Quarterly*, 50 (1977), pp. 255–77.

Zwingmann, Charles, 'The nostalgic phenomenon and its exploitation', in Charles Zwingmann and Maria Pfister-Ammende (eds.), *Uprooting and After* (New York, 1973), pp. 19–29.

313

Bibliography

The following works appeared after this study was completed.

Anderson, Robert Charles, David Grayson Allen, and Virginia DeJohn Anderson, 'Communications: On the English migration to early New England', *New England Quarterly*, 59 (1986), pp. 406–24.

Aylmer, G. E., 'Collective mentalities in mid seventeenth-century England: the Puritan outlook', *Transactions of the Royal Historical Society*, ser. 5, vol. 36 (1986), pp. 1–25.

Bailyn, Bernard, *The Peopling of British North America: An Introduction* (New York, 1986).

Barbour, Philip L. (ed.), *The Complete Works of Captain John Smith, 1580–1631* (Chapel Hill, N.C., 1986).

Delbanco, Andrew, 'Looking homeward, going home: the lure of England for the founders of New England', *New England Quarterly*, 59 (1986), pp. 358–86.

Tucker, Bruce, 'The reinvention of New England, 1691–1770', *New England Quarterly*, 59 (1986), pp. 315–40.

Tyack, Nicholas, *Anti-Calvinists: the Rise of English Arminianism c.1590–1640* (Oxford, 1987).

Index

Index

Index

Index

Index

Index

Index

Wiswall, John 224
witches 165–6
Wokingham (Berks.) 186
Wollcott, Henry 58
Wollcott, John 58, 147, 223, 239
Wood, William 17, 18, 44, 112, 118, 124, 148, 203
Woodyeates, James 48
Worcester (Worcs.) 249
Worcester, Rebecca, *see* Symonds, Rebecca
Worcester, William 182, 284
Wouster, Peter 125

Wren, Mathew 89, 90, 141, 238
Wright, Lawrence 241
Wright, Robert 99
Wyllys, George 58–9, 188, 270
Wyllys, George, Jr. 58–9, 180, 203, 223, 237, 243, 245, 246, 249, 254, 270
Wyllys, Mary 214
Wyllys, Samuel 257
Wyllys family 58, 180, 241

Yarmouth (Norfolk) 65, 197
Young, Christopher 197
Youngs, John 66